WHO WROTE THE NEW TESTAMENT?

WHO WROTE THE NEW TESTAMENT?

The Making of the Christian Myth

BURTON L. MACK

HarperSanFrancisco

An Imprint of HarperCollins*Publishers*

WHO WROTE THE NEW TESTAMENT? *The Making of the Christian
Myth*. Copyright © 1995 by Burton L. Mack. All rights reserved.
Printed in the United States of America. No part of this book may
be used or reproduced in any manner whatsoever without written
permission except in the case of brief quotations embodied in critical
articles and reviews. For information address HarperCollins
Publishers, 10 East 53rd Street, New York, NY 10022.

HarperCollins®, 📖®, and HarperSanFrancisco™ are trademarks of
HarperCollins Publishers Inc.

FIRST EDITION

Library of Congress Cataloging-in-Publication Data
Mack, Burton L.
Who wrote the new testament? : the making of the Christian myth /
Burton L. Mack.
Includes bibliographic references and index.
ISBN 0–06–065517–8 (cloth)
ISBN 0–06–065518–6 (pbk.)
1. Bible. N.T.—Criticism, interpretation, etc. 2. Bible. N.T.—
Controversial literature. 3. Bible N.T.—Canon. 4. Bible.
N.T.—Evidences, authority, etc. 5. Bible. N.T.—Authorship.
6. Christianity—Origin. I. Title.
BS2361.2.M13   1995   95–8937
225.6—dc20

95 96 97 98 99 ❖ RRD(H) 10 9 8 7 6 5 4 3 2

For Curt
Whose ancient texts are the Mission Mountains,
and whose other culture is the Nez Perce

CONTENTS

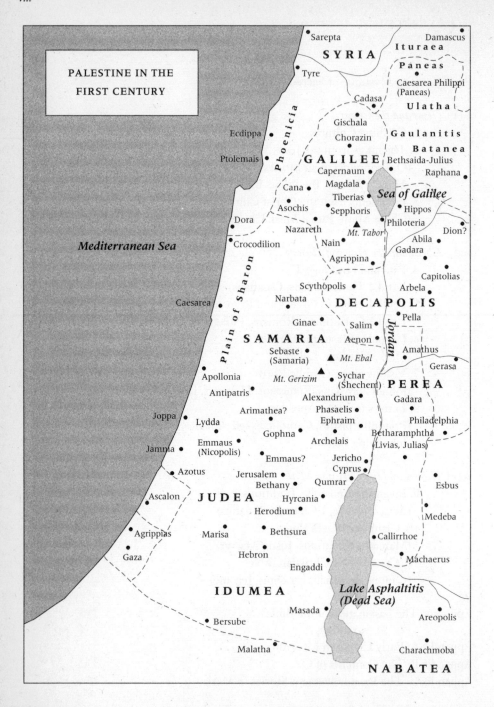

PALESTINE IN THE
FIRST CENTURY

Mediterranean Sea

SYRIA
Sarepta
Damascus
Ituraea
Tyre
Paneas
Caesarea Philippi
(Paneas)
Cadasa
Ulatha
Phoenicia
Ecdippa
Gischala
Gaulanitis
Ptolemais
Chorazin
Batanea
GALILEE
Bethsaida-Julius
Capernaum
Raphana
Cana
Magdala
Sea of Galilee
Tiberias
Asochis
Sepphoris
Hippos
Dora
Philoteria
Nazareth
Dion?
Crocodilion
Mt. Tabor
Abila
Nain
Gadara
Agrippina
Plain of Sharon
Scythopolis
Capitolias
Caesarea
Narbata
Arbela
DECAPOLIS
Ginae
Salim
Pella
Jordan
SAMARIA
Aenon
Amathus
Apollonia
Sebaste
(Samaria)
Mt. Ebal
Gerasa
Antipatris
Mt. Gerizim
Sychar
(Shechem)
PEREA
Joppa
Arimathea?
Phasaelis
Gadara
Lydda
Ephraim
Philadelphia
Gophna
Emmaus
(Nicopolis)
Archelais
Betharamphtha
(Livias, Julias)
Jamnia
Emmaus?
Jericho
Azotus
Jerusalem
Cyprus
Qumran
Esbus
Bethany
Ascalon
Hyrcania
JUDEA
Herodium
Medeba
Agrippias
Marisa
Bethsura
Callirrhoe
Gaza
Hebron
Machaerus
Engaddi
IDUMEA
Lake Asphaltitis
(Dead Sea)
Bersube
Masada
Areopolis
Malatha
Charachmoba
NABATEA

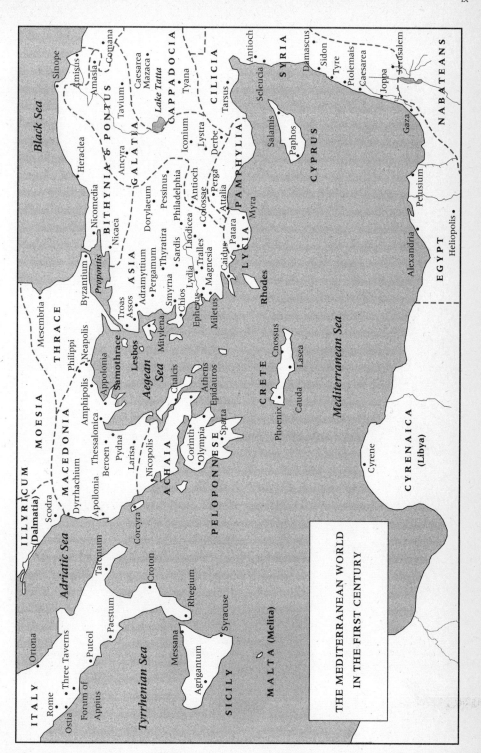

THE MEDITERRANEAN WORLD
IN THE FIRST CENTURY

THE MYSTIQUE OF SACRED SCRIPTURE

Fascination with sacred scriptures seldom surfaces for observation or remark. Their mystique is subtle, something that most persons in a culture would hardly recognize even if mentioned. I have been pondering that mystique, asking why the Bible has such a curious hold on our minds and imaginations. I have not been thinking about the obviously embarrassing public displays of foolish obsessions with the Bible in our time, listening for the hoofbeats of John's four horsemen of the apocalypse, for instance, or citing Paul to prove that gays are sinners in the eyes of God. Madness of that sort can pop up in times of social and cultural crisis no matter what the issue or the mythic authorities might be. I am thinking instead about all of the seemingly innocent ways in which the Bible is taken for granted as a special book, and about all of the ways in which it works its magic in our culture without ever being acknowledged, consulted, or read.

The range of procedures for consulting the Bible is astounding. Students tell me that their grandmothers used to seek "a word for the day" by letting their Bibles flop open to a "verse for the day." Ministers, priests, rabbis, preachers, and teachers by the thousands pore over these texts in quest of some lesson or message fit for their classes or congregations. Groups are now forming outside the formal boundaries of institutional religion to study the Bible in the hope of discovering some fundamental truth felt to have been lost in our recent past. Think of the intellectual labor invested in the academic study of the Bible, the production of scholarly studies and guides for interpreting the Bible, and the huge flow of literature that constantly pours forth from church houses and commercial publishers of books on the Bible. One might well wonder at all this activity swirling around a single book.

This constant consultation of the Bible is partially explained by the important role assigned to the Bible in our religious institutions. Readings from the Bible are essential to liturgies, lessons from the Bible are basic for teachings and doctrines, and references to the Bible are felt to be necessary in the construction of theologies by those charged with the intellectual life of religious traditions. The remarkable thing about this kind of appeal to the Bible, however, is that it does not seem to matter whether all of the theologies and teachings so derived agree. And it does not matter that, for a particular teaching or view, the "biblical" basis may consist of only a small set of sentences taken out of context and pressed into a dogma. This is true even at the highest levels of serious theological discourse. A study by David Kelsey (1975) has shown that, as one moves from one theological system to another among the Christian traditions in America, the selection of biblical texts said to be basic for the system also changes. It is as if everyone knows that the voices recorded in the Bible are many and diverse but that everyone continues to treat the Bible as if it spoke with a single voice. And even though the Bible is treated as a book with a single message, everyone understands that it must be studied as if the message were hidden or un- clear. It is treated as if it were a collection of divine oracles that have to be decoded in order to arrive at the truth they contain. Is it not odd that one needs to consult the Bible, study the Bible, comb through the Bible, or pierce the surface of its enigmatic language in order to discern the hidden truth that gives it the authority it has for our religions? Is it not odd that we have not taken note of this curious preoccupation with the relentless "study" of the Bible in our society and that we do not ask what it is about the Bible and our religions that lies behind such fascination?

The Bible also works its magic in our culture outside the bounds of religious in- stitutions, although the ways in which it influences our collective sense of values and patterns of thinking as Americans are not readily recognized or discussed openly among us. Most of us do know, however, that biblical imagery and themes pervade the history of Western literature, theater, art, and architecture. We also know that the Bible was always involved in the conquest of other lands. During the "age of dis- covery," for instance, Columbus studied the Bible in order to plan his voyages, and he read the parable of the feast in Luke 14:16–24 as a commission to circle the globe and "compel" the heathen to convert as Luke 14:23 enjoins (J. Z. Smith 1986). Should not such examples of the Bible's influence in the history of our expansive civ- ilizations bring a little frown of embarrassment to our faces?

We also have a vague notion of the importance attached to the Bible in early American history. It was the one book everyone had in hand, and it shaped the way we viewed the land, treated Native Americans, and constructed our institutions, in- cluding schools, universities, and the curricula of higher education. Many Ameri- cans have been quite intentional about treating the Bible as a charter for our nation. Thomas Jefferson, for example, thought it important to match the level of enlight- enment we had reached in American democratic institutions with a Bible purged of its myths and miracles. Thus the "Jefferson Bible" contained only the pristine teachings of Jesus. As for the unpurged Bible, segregation in the South was long jus- tified by quoting the curse on Ham's posterity in Genesis 9:20–27 on the one hand, and arguing for the right to demand obedience from a slave by citing Paul on the other. When the lure of "developing" the "vacant" lands to the West in the late nineteenth century reached its peak, volumes of utopian poetry were written by leading American authors, such as Walt Whitman, rife with biblical themes about our manifest destiny as the people of God, called to create a paradise in the midst of an erstwhile wilderness. And the clichés we have used to announce our presence to the world have all been taken from biblical imagery: "righteous nation," "city set on a hill," and "light to the nations." What do you suppose we would have said about ourselves if we had not had the Bible?

In our own time, it is the frequent mention of the "Judeo-Christian tradition" that reveals how naively and automatically the Bible plays its role in public discourse. The term *Judeo-Christian* means that we stand in the "biblical tradition," and the biblical tradition is regarded as the source for the values that make our society respectable and legitimate. No one finds it strange to hear senators quoting from the Bible or objects when presidents-elect place their hands upon it while taking the oath of office. It is as if we take our place in history by unreflected reference to the Bible. A vague recollection of the biblical story seems to be in everyone's mind, a story that begins at the creation of the world with Adam and Eve in the garden, that courses through the Bible and then through the history of Western civilization to flow into the fulfillment of its promise in America with a culmination in the future of consequence for all the peoples of the world. Those who have studied American popular culture tell us that the Bible has profoundly influenced the way we tell our stories, look for meanings, quest for transformations, imagine our futures, and hope for apocalyptic solutions to our problems. If the Bible is that important to our culture, is it not strange that we have not questioned the reasons why?

I have also been impressed with the authority we grant the Bible when discussing issues of social consequence. The list of issues currently under discussion includes the place of creationism in public schools, the role of women in our society, social attitudes toward various sexual orientations, Jewish-Christian relations, theories of white supremacy, patriarchal institutions, the use of natural resources, the definition of family values, understanding violence, how best to relate to other cultures, and what responsibility we have for maintaining human rights around the world. Most of these issues could be discussed without referring to the biblical heritage, but the Bible is always lurking in the background, and positions have been taken on all of them that ultimately appeal to the Bible as the final word. When that happens, thinking and reasonable discussion stop. We do not know how to proceed after the Bible has been invoked. We are all complicit in letting an appeal to the Bible count as an argument.

One of the reasons for our silence when confronted with a proof text from the Bible is that we simply do not know what to make of the Bible and its contents. Thus we do not know what to say in response to those who use the Bible as an authority for their views. Despite the enormous investment in biblical studies in our society, there is actually very little public knowledge about the Bible. One cannot assume that anyone knows why the individual books of the Bible were first written, how they were understood by those who first read them, when and why they were brought together in a single volume, what the historical significance of that moment was, how the Christian church has reinterpreted all of them many times in the course of Western cultural history, and what the lasting effect of that layered text has been. It is the strange authority granted to the Bible in our society, an acquiescence that pertains whether one is a Christian or not, together with the poverty of our knowledge and public discussions of the Bible, that is the stimulus for this book. Here we are with the Bible on our hands and we do not know how we got it, how it works, or what to make of it in public forum.

So I decided to write this book. I am a biblical scholar and historian of religion who has been engaged in the academic study of religion and culture for thirty years. A wealth of information is available in these fields of study that can help us understand how the Bible came to be, and how and why the Bible continues to affect our culture. This knowledge is vast, detailed, and scholarly, but it is not arcane. We know much about the history, literature, religion, and cultures of the ancient Near East and about the Greco-Roman world where the clash of cultures took place that gave birth to both Judaism and Christianity. We have detailed knowledge of the original languages and contents of each book of the Bible, and for most of them it is possible to describe the circumstances that occasioned the writing. We are also able to say why a new piece of literature was written, how each writing drew upon other texts, ideas, and myths, and how the creative edge in a new literary composition was achieved by its author. As for understanding the ways in which the ancients thought about God, practiced religion, constructed their societies, and valued human relationships, we are not at a loss. There are exceptionally rich resources in the fields of classical studies that shed much light upon the history of Israel, early Judaism, and Christianity. And as for theory, the history of religions draws upon an even wider cluster of academic disciplines, including ethnography, cultural anthropology, comparative religions, and the sociology of religion. It seems a shame that no-nonsense knowledge of this kind is seldom called upon when discussing the Bible in either parochial or public forums. Perhaps a no-nonsense book about the making of the Christian Bible will help.

As everyone knows, the Christian Bible is not the same as the Hebrew Bible, and even among the main traditions of Christianity, the books included in the various Bibles do not agree. A major difference is found between the Protestant Bible, which excludes a number of books from the Old Testament, the so-called Apocrypha, and the Roman Catholic and Orthodox Bibles, which include these and, in response to the Protestants, call them deuterocanonical (a "second" canonical corpus). The story of the formation of the Christian Bible cannot be told without explaining the differences among Protestant, Catholic, and Hebrew Bibles, or without reference to the Jewish scriptures that Christians came to call the Old Testament, for the way each of these collections of scriptures took shape affected the other collections and left lasting marks upon the cultures that produced them. It is, however, the New Testament part of the Bible that makes it a Christian Bible, and it is the

Christian Bible that has influenced our culture. We shall see that the New Testament was linked to the Jewish scriptures of the Old Testament in just a certain way, and that it is this link which gives the Christian Bible its peculiar logic and force. This linkage is what we eventually need to understand in order to have some public discussion about the Bible's continuing attraction in our own time. But in order to understand that link and its logic, we need to see why the New Testament writings were written in the first place and how they eventually became the New Testament of the Christian church.

As I toyed with the idea of writing such a book about the New Testament, I found myself confronted with a sort of catch–22. The catch is that for most people the New Testament is taken as proof for the conventional picture of Christian origins, and the conventional picture is taken as proof for the way in which the New Testament was written. The conventional picture comes to focus on a very small set of persons and events as storied in the gospels. It is the story of Jesus' appearance in the world as the son of God. A divine aura surrounds this special time that sets it apart from all the rest of human history. Most people suspend their disbelief and let the story stand as the miraculous moment that started the Christian religion. All that followed, including the transformation of the disciples into apostles, the birthday of the first church in Jerusalem, the conversion of Paul, and the writing of the New Testament gospels and letters by the apostles, is thought to be a response to those first incomparable events. Thus the unfolding history is imagined on the model of dominoes falling in place when triggered by an original impulse. This creates a circular, interlocking pattern of authentication in which the New Testament is both the result of and the documentation for the conventional view of Christian beginnings.

For this reason the New Testament is commonly viewed and treated as a charter document that came into being much like the Constitution of the United States. According to this view, the authors of the New Testament were all present at the historic beginnings of the new religion and collectively wrote their gospels and letters for the purpose of founding the Christian church that Jesus came to inaugurate. Unfortunately for this view, that is not the way it happened. Scholars locate the various writings of the New Testament at different times and places over a period of one hundred years, from the letters of Paul in the 50s of the first century, through the writing of the gospels of Mark and Matthew in the 70s and 80s, the gospels of John and Luke around the turn of the second century, and on to the acts, letters, and other writings during the first half of the second century, some as late as 140 to 150 C.E. (appendix A). This fact alone introduces another history of Christian beginnings that is not acknowledged by or reflected in the writings of the New Testament.

To make matters worse for the conventional view, these writings stem from different groups with their own histories, views, attitudes, and mix of peoples. In some cases it is possible to trace the connections between two different writings. An example would be the way in which the gospel attributed to Matthew was dependent upon the gospel attributed to Mark. But even in cases such as these a careful reading of two related writings always produces a long list of their differences. No two writings agree upon what we might have thought were fundamental convictions shared by all early Christians. Each writing has a different view of Jesus, for instance, a particular attitude toward Judaism, its own conception of the kingdom of God, a peculiar notion of salvation, and so on. This means that the impression created by the New Testament of a singular collection of apostolic documents, all of which bear "witness" to a single set of inaugural events, is misleading.

We now know that there were many different responses to the teachings of Jesus. Groups formed around them, but then went different ways depending upon their mix of peoples, social histories, and discussions about the teachings of Jesus and how they were to be interpreted and applied. Some were of the type we call Jesus movements. Others became congregations of the Christ whose death was imagined as a martyrdom to justify a mixture of Jews and gentiles as equally acceptable in a new configuration of the people of God (or "Israel"). Still others developed into enclaves for the cultivation of spiritual enlightenment or the knowledge (*gnosis*) Jesus had taught. Each of these branches of the Jesus movements, including many permutations of each type, imagined Jesus differently. They did so in order to account for what they had become as patterns of practice, thinking, and congregating settled into place. And they all competed with one another in their claims to be the true followers of Jesus. Many of these groups had their own gospels (R. Cameron 1982), and some produced rather large libraries that are still available to us from the second, third, and fourth centuries. As for the New Testament, it turns out to be a very small selection of texts from a large body of literature produced by various communities during the first one hundred years. These New Testament texts were collected in the interest of a particular form of Christian congregation that emerged only by degrees through the second to fourth centuries. Toward the end of the book I will begin referring to this type of Christianity as "centrist," meaning thereby that it positioned itself against gnostic forms of Christianity on the one hand, and radical forms of Pauline and spiritist communities on the other. It was centrist Christianity that became the religion of empire under Constantine, collected together the texts we now know as the New Testament, and joined them to the Jewish scriptures to form the Christian Bible. When these writings were first written there was no centrist tradition, and none of them fully agreed with the others with respect to their views of Jesus, God, the state of the world, or the reason for the Jesus movements.

It is also the case that, with the exception of seven letters by Paul and the Revelation to an otherwise unknown John, the writings selected for inclusion in the New Testament were not written by those whose names are attached to them. Many modern Christians find this fact difficult to comprehend, if not downright unnerving. The problem seems to be that, if so, someone must have been lying. A better way to understand this phenomenon is to realize (1) that most literature of the early Christian period was written anonymously, (2) that the concept of an apostolic age was a second-century creation, and (3) that the later attribution of this literature to names associated with apostles can be explained in ways that show it was not considered dishonest. One helpful observation is that anonymous authorship of writings intended for use in social institutions such as schools, temples, and royal bureaucracies was standard practice in the scribal traditions of the ancient Near East. Another is that, in the early period of collecting lore, interpreting teachings, and trying out new ideas fit for the novel groupings spawned by the Jesus movements, many minds, voices, and hands were in on the drafting of written materials. No one thought to take credit for writing down community property even though authorial creativity is everywhere in evidence. Even the earliest collections of teachings and stories about Jesus, such as the Sayings Gospel Q, the Gospel of Thomas, and the little sets of anecdotes and miracle stories from the pre-Markan tradition bear the marks of literacy and creativity, though none was signed by an author.

As for the later attribution of anonymous literature to known figures of the past, that also was a standard practice during the Greco-Roman period. In the schools of rhetoric, for example, teachers had their students write speeches and letters appropriate for such figures to see if the student had fully understood the importance of a historical figure. It was what a recognized figure stood for that was deemed important, not his personal profile. Scholars agree, in any case, that for these and other reasons, most of the writings in the New Testament were either written anonymously and later assigned to a person of the past or written later as a pseudonym for some person thought to have been important for the earliest period. Striking examples of the latter are the two letters said to have been written by Peter, both of which are clearly second-century creations.

Thus, over the course of the second and third centuries, centrist Christians were able to create the impression of a singular, monolinear history of the Christian church. They did so by carefully selecting, collecting, and arranging anonymous and pseudonymous writings assigned to figures at the beginning of the Christian time. As they imagined it, this history was foretold by the prophets of the Old Testament, inaugurated by Jesus and his sacrifice for the sins of the world, established by the apostles in their missions, and confirmed by the bishops in their loyalty to the teachings of that illustrious tradition. And because all the New Testament writings were now regarded as written by apostles and their associates, the differences among their views of Christian beginnings were effectively erased. In the centrist Christian imagination, the four gospels merged into an amalgam of the one gospel story, and the letters of Paul and the other apostles were read as "witnesses" to these dramatic events that inaugurated the Christian time. This means that the impression modern readers have of the New Testament as a charter document for Christianity, a kind of constitution written in concert by a college or congress of apostles, is thoroughly understandable. That is exactly what the centrist Christians of the fourth century intended. The problem is that this charter was created for the fourth-century church by means of literary fictions. It is neither an authentic account of Christian beginnings nor an accurate rehearsal of the history of the empire church. Historians of religion would call it myth.

If we want to understand the reasons for the emergence of Christianity in all its forms, what the fundamental attraction was, why people invested themselves in it even to the point of taking on new personal and social identities, why some came to believe in the mythic claims at the core of the centrist creed and thus the New Testament, and why that kind of Christianity won out over others to influence fifteen hundred years of Western culture, we will have to pop open the catch–22. We need to dismantle the New Testament as a singular collection and locate each writing in its own time and place. We need to reconstruct the history of the many groups that formed in the wake of Jesus and ask about their ideas, activities, and motivations. We need, in brief, to set the conventional picture of Christian origins aside and redescribe the times by using all the information available to us from whatever source we can find. Only by doing so will we be able to gain a fresh perspective on the writings of the New Testament and ask about the rhymes and reasons that gave birth to their mythologies.

It will not be easy to set the conventional picture aside. That is because the texts that need to be reassessed are so intricately entangled with that picture. Consider the fact that the very names for these texts belong to the myth of Christian origins and that we have no other names for them. I will have to refer to "Mark," for instance, as the author of the Gospel of Mark, and to "Matthew" when referring to the author of the Gospel of Matthew, even though both are pseudonyms that support the conventional myth. Scholars grow accustomed to this problem and solve it by learning to imagine an unknown editor behind the apostolic fictions. This "editor" then becomes a figure representing the very complex processes of literary production in school and community traditions where many hands are known to have contributed to a composition. No critical scholar thinks about a historical Matthew when referring to the Gospel of Matthew or when using the name *Matthew* as a shorthand designation for either the author or the text of this gospel. But for many people the mere mention of the name *Matthew* immediately conjures up the conventional picture of Jesus and his disciples according to the gospel story. I will therefore have to ask the reader to understand my predicament as we proceed. I will have to use the conventional names for these New Testament texts, but I hope not to be misunderstood. I will not be referring to the familiar figures of the traditional picture of Christian origins.

This picture of Christian origins will not be easy to set aside for another reason as well. It is not just that the traditional picture is supported by the composition of the New Testament, and that the New Testament has been the only set of texts available for imagining and "documenting" that picture. The fact is that Christians have an investment in that picture and that investment takes the form of believing that it is true. This has resulted in a conviction or desire to accept the gospels as histories, accounts of what literally must have happened in order to inaugurate the

Christian faith. Unfortunately, biblical scholars are not immune to this desire, and the history of New Testament studies is dotted by the failed attempts of conservative Christians to counter critical scholarship and argue for the gospels as memoirs of the disciples who were with Jesus when it all happened. An example of conservative scholarship that argues for the historical accuracy of the gospels can illustrate this point.

In the library of Magdalen College in Oxford are three papyrus fragments from the twenty-sixth chapter of the Gospel of Matthew. They contain partial lines of text from ten scattered verses (Matt. 26:7–8, 10, 14–15, 22–23, 31, 32–33). Since their acquisition in Egypt in 1901 and facsimile publication in 1953, these fragments have been known to scholars and recognized as coming from a second-century C.E. codex (leaves bound together to make a book, in distinction from a scroll). There are four main reasons for this dating: (1) The fragments are of papyrus, thus from a time earlier than the shift to parchment which took place around the beginning of the third century C.E.; (2) The fragments are not from a scroll but from a codex, a shift in practice that took place during the second century; (3) The fragments are similar to other examples of papyrus fragments of New Testament texts from the second and third centuries; and (4) A second-century date fits the pattern of what we otherwise know about the writing, copying, and dissemination of early Christian writings during the second to fourth centuries.

In a recent article, however, Carsten Thiede, a German papyrologist, has proposed that the Magdalen fragments may be dated to the mid-first century (1995). His theory is based on the observation that these fragments were written in uncial script (upright, block letters), a practice that was generally abandoned during the course of the first century. In order to make his case, Thiede has argued: (1) that the script is similar to some Greek texts from Pompey and Herculaneum that have been dated to the first century; (2) that a Greek fragment found among the Dead Sea Scrolls was from the Gospel of Mark, showing that there must have been a deposit of Christian writings with the Essenes before the destruction of the temple; and (3) that, if early Christians were so oriented to texts and so concerned about preserving their written gospels, they must have started using codices about that time. The conclusion Thiede wants to draw from this argumentation is that the Gospel of Matthew must have been written mid-first century by a disciple who had known Jesus and was still alive to record that history as it actually happened. What is more, since the fragments use an abbreviation for the proper name, Jesus, as well as for his designation as lord, Thiede thinks that his disciples must have recognized that the historical Jesus was in fact divine.

Critical scholars will not be impressed. The fragments are easily explained as second-century texts; uncials could still have been used as late as 85 C.E., the traditional scholarly date for Matthew; Thiede's Dead Sea Scrolls scenario is preposterous; his theory about the Markan fragment among the Dead Sea Scrolls has been discredited; and the mass of detailed scholarship on the origins and history of early

Christian movements and their writings has simply been swept aside in the eager pursuit of a chimera. From a critical scholar's point of view, Thiede's proposal is an example of just how desperate the Christian imagination can become in the quest to argue for the literal facticity of the Christian gospels.

Others, however, including the media, may think the "discovery" sensational. It does not seem to matter that the "hard external evidence," as an article in *Time* called it (Ostling 1995), amounts to the vague redating of three questionable fragments buttressed by flimsy argumentation. Apparently, a fragment in the hand is worth a hundred years of learning packed away in the dusty books of scholars. It is as if the gospels *must* be "historical," to agree with Christian persuasion, and thus any artifact will do. When asked what that means, however, what it is about the gospels that must be historical in order for Christianity to be true, the usual response from the average Christian is first a slight hesitation, as if that question had not occurred to the innocent believer, and then the answer is given, "Why, all of it, of course." And that is where the conversation and thinking usually stops. All of it? Are we to think that all of it is historical: portents, miracles, resurrections, cosmic journeys, apocalyptic visions, angels, a crucified god, divine "breakthroughs," and metaphysical transformations? Are we to make an exception for that chapter of human history, a record of events held to be true even though fantastic according to normal criteria for making judgments? Are we to feel confident about the accuracy of the gospel's account on the basis of three second-century fragments that a scholar has tried to redate? The *Time* article was captioned: "An expert claims hard evidence that Matthew's Gospel was written while eyewitnesses to Christ were alive." That is certainly sensational enough to get the media juices flowing. And it may sound good to many Christians to think that a gauntlet has been thrown to all those liberal scholars who say it did not happen the way the gospels say it did. But the average, literate, non-specialist reader will be stymied. What indeed is one to do with the hoopla of the Matthew fragments? How can one tell which "expert" to heed? On what basis can anyone make a considered judgment? One can't. The non-specialist needs more information. A larger picture of Greco-Roman times, early Christian movements, and the history of early Christian literature is absolutely necessary in order to reevaluate any specific bit of "evidence" that may catch someone's attention. This book is my attempt to paint that larger picture.

The plan for the book is to take the New Testament apart for a thorough examination of each individual writing, parceling them out to their own specific junctures of social and cultural history, and tracing the subsequent fate of each through the period of the Bible's formation. Each writing will be given a separate discussion, including basic information about its date, authorship, literary form, relation to other texts, and the social circumstance for its composition. Information of this kind is readily available in a large number of textbooks known as Introductions to the New Testament. Since I draw upon this scholarship mainly to set the stage for asking another set of questions, I shall not belabor the details. For the reader who wants to see detailed summaries of this traditional scholarship on introductory matters, I recommend the books by Duling and Perrin (1994) and Koester (1982). I assume this scholarship before going on to describe the importance of a text in the larger context of Christian beginnings in the world of late antiquity.

This larger sweep of Christian beginnings will become a kind of outline that needs to be colored in. An introductory chapter about the clash of cultures during the Greco-Roman period will set the stage. We shall see that the breakdown of traditional societies during the Hellenistic period had far deeper consequences for personal and social well-being than is usually thought. After that, and against that background, we can place each of our texts at a particular moment in the history of early Christian groups and see how each was responding to its times. We can do that by noting the way in which a group had formed and the role it saw itself playing in the larger scheme of things. The scholarly terms for these activities, one behavioral, the other intellectual, are *social formation* and *mythmaking*. Social formation and mythmaking are group activities that go together, each stimulating the other in a kind of dynamic feedback system. Both speed up when new groups form in times of social disintegration and cultural change. Both are important indicators of the personal and intellectual energies invested in experimental movements. Just as in our time of social change and multicultural encounters, so during the Greco-Roman period, the merger of peoples and the disintegration of traditional societies sparked new patterns of association and called forth new ways of thinking. Social conflict, curiosity about other cultures, and experimentation with human relationships unleashed remarkable intellectual efforts to reconceive the human enterprise. Early Christians were not unaffected. They were actively engaged in just such experimentation. That is, in fact, exactly what the Jesus movements were all about. If we do not come to see that, we shall never be able to understand the messages or mythologies of the New Testament writings.

A novel notion called the kingdom of God generated the excitement and influenced the formation of many different Jesus groups. We shall have to ask why this notion was so attractive and why this kingdom movement spread, without assuming that the attraction was rooted in a common conviction about Jesus as a personal savior or that conversions were generated by the apocalyptic preaching of a Paul. Instead, we shall have to credit the personal and intellectual investments of many, many people in a new religious movement. We shall see that the notion of the kingdom of God called for reimagining society and that it contained both a critical (countercultural) and a constructive (or utopian) edge. And we shall see that entertaining such an idea unleashed enormous energy, triggering social experiments that were daring and igniting the most fantastic images of a desired transformation of the world. Social formation and mythmaking must therefore be given a prominent place in our redescription of early Christian history. In every early Christian community from which we still have any evidence, social formation and mythmaking fit together like hand and glove.

The excitement created by talk of the kingdom of God may be difficult for some modern readers to grasp. That is because the Christian religion is often thought to be solely about personal salvation, not the vision of a sane society. And we live in a time when "personal religious experience" and "private belief systems" draw upon our culture's radical individualism to define the essence of any religion. That is bound to frustrate our attempt to understand the importance and power of social concepts and mythologies in antiquity. However, we shall confront such concepts at every turn in our investigation. That is because Christians actually saw themselves as a social construct. They were, they said, a congregation, a household, a family, a people, a nation, a temple, a city of God, or a kingdom. All of the terms used for the status of the individual Christian were taken from social models: brother, sister, saint, helper. And as for the language of "justification," "salvation," or "redemption," it invariably meant the process of transferring one's social location from the constraints of an ethnic or national identity to the "freedom" and "acceptance" experienced within the new congregation. Even the so-called "christological titles" (Christ, Lord, Son of God) were social roles taken from social concepts and mythologies. They were not attributed to Jesus in order to imagine his personal divinity, as if becoming a god would have been a very important thing to have happened to a person. They were, instead, ways of imagining how important he had become as the "king" of the "kingdom" to which his followers now belonged. His followers did not congregate in order to enhance their chances of gaining eternal life for themselves as solitary persons. They had been captivated by a heady, experimental drive to rethink power and purity and alter the way the authorities of their time had put the world together. They did that by creating a social space where it was okay to misbehave. As the offensive practice of one early Jesus group illustrates, they "ate with tax collectors and sinners" without even washing their hands (Mark 2:15–17; 7:1–14). That is more than making a statement. That is actual social formation.

I shall therefore lift up profiles of groups and communities, paint portraits of authors where information or clues exist, and try to keep track of the people behind our texts as they come into view over the first several generations. They were a colorful lot for the most part, outspoken and more than a bit boisterous at times. A touch of humor and a strong streak of contentiousness show that they were real people honestly involved in a serious reorientation of social and cultural alignments. The issues that surfaced for debate and the decisions that were thought to make a difference swirled around matters of primary significance for life together as social creatures—ethnicity, family relations, traditional values, ethics and etiquettes, rights and roles of leadership, and the bases of authority, ranking, and honor. To take but one example of a social code that caused contention, the Pharisaic laws of purity were so important in some early social groups that they occasioned vociferous debate, realignments of traditional loyalties, and the redrawing of group boundaries. Families were split apart and the structure of village authorities was rearranged by taking sides on the definition of purity. Why? Because social relations were in the process of being reconsidered and realigned in light of the novel social vision they called the kingdom of God.

As everyone knows, however, these early Christians did more than argue about power and purity or test the conventional codes of behavior by violating table etiquette. They also entertained some very extraordinary ideas, especially in regard to Jesus, his transformation into a divine cosmic being, and his status as lord of all history and creation. And the claims these Christians made about knowing the mind of God, his ways with the world, and the apocalyptic ending to all human history when the kingdom of God would finally be "revealed" were nothing short of fantastic. If we cannot say how these early Christians came to such ideas, and for what reasons, we shall not be able to escape the catch–22 even though we may catch sight of their many social formations. It would still be possible to think that the events imagined in their mythology had really overwhelmed them. That is the way the conventional myth of Christian origins paints the picture: first the miraculous and incomparable events surrounding the appearance of Jesus as the son of God, then the preaching of this gospel and the formation of the church. If we want to change that sequence we shall have to explain the emergence of these mythic ideas some other way. That other way will be to pay attention to mythmaking in the process of social experimentation.

That early Christians engaged in mythmaking may be difficult for modern Christians to accept. The usual connotations of the term *myth* are almost entirely negative. And when it is used to describe the content of the New Testament gospels there is invariably a hue and cry. That is because, in distinction from most mythologies that begin with a "once upon a time," the Christian myth is set in historical time and place. It seems therefore to demand the belief that the events of the gospel story really happened. And that means that the story cannot be "myth." It may help some to note (1) that mythmaking is a normal and necessary social activity, (2) that early Christian mythmaking was due more to borrowing and rearranging myths taken for granted in the cultures of context than to firsthand speculation, and (3) that the myths they came up with made eminent sense, not only for their times and circumstances, but also for the social experiments in which they were invested. That, at least, will be my challenge. That is what I want to show by writing this book. But how do myths make sense? And what kind of sense does the Christian myth make?

Every culture has a set of stories that account for the world in which a people find themselves. These stories usually tell of the creation of the world, the appearance of the first people, ancestral heroes and their achievements, and the glorious beginnings of society as a people experience it. Terrain, village patterns, shrines, temples, cities, and kingdoms are often set in place or planned at the beginning of time. Scholars understand these myths as the distillation of human-interest stories first told in the course of routine patterns of living together, then rehearsed for many generations. Telling stories about one another is what we do. It belongs to the life and work of maintaining human relations and constructing societies. Telling stories is how we do our catching up, checking one another out on views and attitudes, and gathering information to justify judgments we need to make about something we call character. It does not take long before there are too many stories to recall and retell. Even in a brief family history, sorting takes place naturally over time, and only the most vivid stories are ever rehearsed. Some, however, are told again and again. These become stories that several generations might share. As the size of a social unit expands, the number of shared stories shrinks. These stories invariably become dense icons, packed with features characteristic for the people as a whole. As the past generations fade from memory, these stories are allowed to slip into a "once upon a time" where a honing of ancestral symbols takes place.

In cultures where there is interest, capacity, and circumstance to remember more than three or four generations, where writing is invented and records kept, it is customary to develop a "historical" imagination as a kind of linear basket to hold the stories of importance for the collective memory of a people. Now only the most compact and generalized icons collect "at the beginning," the point in the past beyond which the human imagination cannot reach. The others may be sprinkled here and there through the "history," but sequence is not always important, and many of the stories in the basket may not be connected to one another in any particular way. Rhyme and reason may be superimposed, however, in the interest of borrowing some of the luster of the past for the present shape of the society. When that happens, we can begin to speak of an epic. Epic is a rehearsal of the past that puts the present in its light. Setting the present in the light of an illustrious past makes it honorable, legitimate, right, and reasonable. The present institution is then worth celebrating. Naturally, both the past and the present may be highly romanticized or idealized, for epic is myth in the genre of history. The stories of Gilgamesh in ancient Sumerian and Akkadian civilizations were epic. For the Greeks, Homer was epic. Pindar's poetry of illustrious family lines was epic on a small scale. The local histories of shrines, temples, and peoples in the eastern Mediterranean during the Hellenistic period were epic on a medium-sized scale. And the history of Israel, which, from the very beginning of the world aimed at the establishment of a temple-state in Jerusalem, was epic for the Jews.

When the second temple was destroyed in 70 C.E., the Jews had a problem on their hands. Not only their ancient history, contained in the five books of Moses, but an immense body of literature from the Hellenistic period documented their intellectual investment in the temple-state as the proper goal of human history from the foundation of the world. Christians also had a problem. They had no right to claim the history of Israel as their own. But early Jewish Christians had wanted to think of themselves as the people of God, heirs of the promises to Israel, or even the new Israel for a new day. It was natural to do so in order to feel right about the new Jesus movements. And so, before the destruction of the temple, early Jesus people and Christians had already started to point to this or that feature of the history of Israel in order to claim some link with the illustrious traditions of Israel. As we shall see, all of the early myths about Jesus were attempts to paint him and his followers in acceptable colors from the Israel epic. But these attempts were fanciful, ad hoc, and incapable of competing with the obvious logic of the Jewish epic. The Jewish epic was a history that aimed at the establishment of a temple-state in Jerusalem, not a Christian congregation. When the temple's end came, however, and the epic's logic was in total disarray, Christians had their chance to revise it in their favor. It was then that revising the Israel epic became a major focus for early Christian myth-making. Examples will be found in the New Testament gospels, all of which set their stories of Jesus at the end of the story of Israel. This happened during the late first century, the period during which the mythology of Jesus as the son of God swept through many Christian communities. And then, from the middle of the second century on, the fur really started to fly. Both Jews and Christians wanted to read the history of Israel in their favor, and each needed the Jewish scriptures as documentation for social formations that did not match the temple-state at the end of Israel's story. Two myths were devised then, and they are still playing havoc with what otherwise might be a reasonable conversation between Christians and Jews about the texts we sometimes call the Hebrew Bible, sometimes the Old Testament.

We will have to keep track of these groups and this literature as best we can for about three hundred years or we will not be able to catch the important shifts in group life and thought that had to happen before the collection known as the New Testament came into existence and the idea of a Bible finally was possible. All these shifts need to be described if we want to understand the logic that resulted in the Bible. Just as with each separate writing, so the Bible itself came together at a certain juncture of social and cultural history. The reasons for the selection and arrangement of writings in the Bible cannot be found in any of the individual books read separately. The reasons have to be taken from the Christian authors of the second to the fourth centuries. Only at the end of this period, when we finally catch sight of the Bible as we know it, will we see that it demands a particular way of reading the history of Israel, puts a special spin on the appearance of the Christ, and grants uncommon authority to the apostles and their missions. By then it will be clear to us that the book was important because it gave the church the credentials it needed for its role in Constantine's empire. We may then call it the myth of origin for the Christian religion. It will be the Christian myth in the form of the biblical epic that granted the Christian church its charter. It will be that epic that determines the Bible's hold upon our American mind. The Bible's mystique is oddly misnamed by calling it the "Word of God." We must come to see that, or we shall never be able to talk about the Bible in public forum when discussing our cultural history and its present state of affairs. What kind of a charter, do you suppose, is given to our culture if the Bible turns out to be our epic, our myth of God's designs upon both our past and our promise?

At the end of the book, I shall return to the questions with which we began about the reasons the Bible continues to fascinate us. I will offer a number of suggestions that draw upon what we will have learned about the Bible's composition. I will mention the Bible's function as an epic charter for America, explain why that is not the way we like to have it described, and pursue two features of its composition that will help us understand why, despite our uneasiness with the notions of biblical epic and cultural influence, it continues to have a kind of mystical power. One feature results in a peculiar enchantment attached to its epic function. The other is an invitation to treat the Bible as if it were a crystal ball or an equation capable of getting to the heart of any human matter. Each of these enchantments is firmly embedded in the structure of the Bible's narrative arrangements, the one by design, the other by accident, and each is attached to a set of linguistic levers that automatically triggers wondrous mental gymnastics whenever the Bible is read. These mental gymnastics are truly amazing feats of the human mind, and we shall take a moment at the end of the book to marvel at the lengths to which our imaginative capacities let us leap and tumble in the Bible's big tent. Then, however, we will have to wonder aloud about the continuing value of the Bible's guidance as we chart our global futures. And the final question will be whether, given our moment in a postmodern world, we can continue our acrobatics on the Bible's high wire without losing our balance.

And so the story begins. I am pleased that you've joined me in the venture.

PART 1

Jesus and the Christ

1

CLASHING CULTURES

Cultures clashed in Greco-Roman times, and the Eastern Mediterranean filled to bursting with a heady and volatile mix of peoples, powers, and ideas. Confusing for most, exhilarating for some, the energies unleashed by these uncertain times peaked during the first century C.E. and resulted in extravagant social experimentation and imaginative intellectual projections. The reason for the outpouring of intellectual energy, and for the struggle to find new ways to group, was that the cultural traditions flowing into the mixing bowl were no longer supported by the social institutions that had produced and sustained them. People were on their own to manage as best they could with only the memory of provincial values to guide them in a helter-skelter cosmopolitan age. Most rose to the challenge, and the inventiveness of some proposals for dealing with multicultural forces and surviving the machinations of the blind goddess called Fate (*tyche*) was nothing short of genius. We need to understand both the malaise and the creativity of these times, for it was just at this juncture that Judaism and Christianity emerged. As we shall see, the attractiveness of early Christianity is best explained as one of the more creative and practical social experiments in response to the loss of cultural moorings that all peoples experienced during this time.

Three model societies were in everyone's mind during the Greco-Roman age (second century B.C.E. to second century C.E.): the ancient Near Eastern temple-state, the Greek city-state (*polis*), and the Roman republic. Eventually, they all came tumbling down in the aftermath of Alexander the Great's campaigns. We are accustomed to thinking of Alexander as the enlightened ruler who introduced the peoples of the ancient Near East to the glories of Greek culture and so created the Hellenistic age, where we locate the foundation for Western civilization. We do not usually consider the negative effects of his campaigns which brought to an end the last of the illustrious empires of the ancient Near East, especially those of the Persians and the Egyptians, and tarnished the classical Greek ideal of the *polis* by using its model for imperialistic purposes. These effects must be in mind as we proceed. After

Alexander, the memories of both the temple-state and the *polis* were still alive. They were the models proper to civilization. But the societies organized on those models were gone forever. In their place were warring kingdoms, with the Romans waiting in the wings.

The temple-state was a model of civilization that had been honed to perfection by three thousand years of fine tuning. Historian of religion Jonathan Z. Smith (1987) has helped us see that the model consisted of two systems of social stratification governed by the notions of power and purity. A king occupied the apex of a system of power that filtered down through a hierarchy of control in which all members of the society had their places. He had the authority to organize labor, tell people what to do, and get things done. The king was sovereign, and his power determined that he be regarded as the locus of what we now call the sacred with its capacity both to attract and terrify. Purity, on the other hand, was the notion that governed a classification of things and people concerned with the order, stability, and harmonious hum of society. Society was understood as an organic unit of human activity and social well-being. Priests presided over a system of temple sacrifice designed to set right things that had gone wrong or gotten out of place. At the apex of this system in which everyone and everything had a proper place, the high priest represented sanctity or holiness. Holiness was the pristine splendor that evoked awe. The two systems of power and purity were merged in such a way that everyone knew his or her place in relation to both authority (power) and propriety (purity). The two systems also worked as binary opposites. The king was highest in power, lowest in purity (by virtue of his function as warrior and "executioner"), while the high priest was highest in purity, lowest in power.

The importance of Smith's work is enormous, not only for explaining the social logic invested in the Jerusalem temple of Greco-Roman times, but also for understanding how precious and profound life could be in a society working on this model. The temple-state was not a church or "worshiping community" as traditionally imagined by Christians with only their Old Testaments to guide them. The temple-state organized labor, administered justice, and distributed goods by means of bureaucracies centered in the temple buildings and palace compound. The temple announced national pride, served as monument to the achievements of the past, put people in touch with the world of the gods, provided daily pageantry, dispensed prescriptions for the healing of all ills, and called for civic processions, feasts, and festivals on the grandest scales possible. As civic center, the temple also supported priests, artists, artisans, granary experts, couriers, accountants, scribes, teachers, and intellectuals. For the people, this social arrangement resulted in a tightly knit, patriarchal system of religion and politics that placed great value on stable families, public honor, social propriety, and personal loyalty to the king and the cult of the temple deity who ruled over the land. The book of Psalms in the Hebrew Bible and the Wisdom of Ben Sira in the Apocrypha of the Christian Bible contain fine examples of the pride and piety possible in a temple-state. The temple-state had been the basic form of vigorous and complex civilizations in the ancient Near East since the third or fourth millennium B.C.E.

The temple-state also produced a particular kind of law. With an all-powerful king on the one hand, and priests in charge of righting wrongs on the other, laws were needed to strike a balance between the two systems of governance. An intellectual class of scribes filled the niche between power and purity and mediated between the interests of the king and the temple priests. They had to do this cautiously, without calling attention to themselves or taking any credit for their ideas and achievements. Thus we have no name for the influence they exercised similar to the "power" of the king or the "purity" of the high priest. And they did not sign the works they authored. But it is obvious that the codes of law developed in the course of ancient Near Eastern civilizations, as well as the myths and ritual texts for the temple liturgies, were created by scribes as a professional class of intellectuals. No king in his right mind would have legislated the famous code of Hammurabi, for instance, for it severely limited the king's power to do as he pleased. Nevertheless, the scribes who achieved this legislation gave full credit to the king for being so enlightened, as the prologue to Hammurabi's code shows. The prologue harks back to the creation of the world when the gods gave Hammurabi the task of causing "justice to prevail in the land." Hammurabi himself is cast as the speaker who, after reporting on his divine commission, provides almost one hundred lines of self-praise in the pattern of "I, Hammurabi, the one who designed the temple, . . . who made his kingdom great, . . . who plumbed the depths of wisdom." At the end of the prologue, just before the code begins, his words are, "When Marduk commissioned me to guide the people aright, to direct the land, I established law and justice in the language of the land, thereby promoting the welfare of the people. At that time [I decreed]. . . ." (Pritchard 1955, 163–80). Reading this prologue and turning to the code that follows, however, we see a marvelous stroking of the king's ego on the one hand, and the record of a great advance in legal theory on the other, both authored by anonymous intellectuals during the seventeenth century B.C.E.

It was the same for the myths that portrayed the will of the gods, for the rules that determined how purity was defined, and for working out the logic of which sacrifices took care of which transgressions. The detailing of the rules governing purity was not a particularly religious act, and priests would not have deduced them automatically from the temple sacrifices. Priests were a professional intellectual class concerned with the well-being of society as a whole. Persons and things were "clean" when they were in their usual place doing their ordinary, healthy thing in the regular pattern of activity customary for the society; "unclean" when out of place, broken, and in need of mending. Persons became unclean when "contaminated" by illness or when untoward circumstances prevailed, such as handling a corpse for burial, or when acting in such a way that social relationships were violated. Professional intellectuals codified the sacrificial system of the temple and merged it with a kind of household guide for healthy living. Purity codes were the way these ancient civilizations defined social well-being, diagnosed social and personal ills, and prescribed remedies for healing all manner of social and physical disorders. The book of Leviticus in the Hebrew Bible contains illustrations of both kinds of law, civil and cultic. Leviticus can also serve as an illustration of the mythic strategy, widespread in the ancient Near East, for the scribes to attribute their legal legislation to the will of the gods of the royal temple cult. Only so could the fundamental dynamics of the social structure retain its creative tension between the two systems of difference represented by the king and the high priest.

When the Jews returned from exile in Babylon in the late sixth century B.C.E., they wanted to rebuild Jerusalem on the ancient model of the temple-state, holding in mind as a golden age the kingdoms of their own David and Solomon. But they were confronted with a very serious problem. They were allowed to rebuild the temple but were still governed by foreign powers and thus could not install a king. Since kings belonged to the model, and being ruled by a foreign king had always meant contamination, Jews were challenged to exercise a bit of ingenuity. They did it. They cheated a bit on the model by denying that the presence of foreign kings was all that critical, and by daring to think of their own high priest as the "sovereign" of the temple-state. This stratagem worked quite well during the fifth and fourth centuries under Persian hegemony and during the third century as well under the Ptolemies, the successors of Alexander's conquests in Egypt. Then, however, around 200 B.C.E., the armies of the Seleucids took over, the heirs of Alexander's dominions centered in Antioch. The Seleucids were more aggressive in their programs of Hellenization and political control. Jews tensed. Internal conflict divided the people on the question of allowing the Seleucids to turn Jerusalem into a Hellenistic city. Guerrilla warfare erupted under the Maccabees, a family of seven brothers from the Judean countryside who called for national independence under the banner of the "traditions of the fathers." The Maccabees (from "hammer," a nickname originally given to one of the seven brothers) eventually succeeded in taking control of Judea and then assumed the roles, not only of high priest, but of king as well. This was a very presumptuous move without precedence, and it startled and angered other leading Jews.

The Maccabean dynasty, also called Hasmonean after their family name, lasted only eighty years, from 142 to 63 B.C.E. The Maccabees spent the first forty years annexing their neighbors' lands of Idumea, Samaria, Transjordan, and Galilee. Alas. The lands were already occupied, and the people living in these lands did not regard their annexation as a great homecoming. So the Maccabees spent the next forty years trying to convince their converts in these adjacent lands and their fellow Jews at home that they had the right to rule them. It did not work. The Hasmoneans were no match for the ideological conflicts that increased dissension within or the cultural forces of Hellenism that continued to penetrate from without. The Samaritans, for example, remained surly. A strong reaction against the Hasmonean control of the temple among some priestly families in Jerusalem resulted in the withdrawal of these priests to a barren shelf above the Dead Sea and their establishment of a commune at Qumran. And a party called the Pharisees (probably from the Hebrew word meaning separatists) developed schools of ethics, piety, and politics based on the law of Moses to counter Hasmonean accommodation to Hellenistic practices. The Pharisees were harsh critics of the Hasmonean establishment and, together with the priests at Qumran, they wore the Hasmoneans down. When second-generation Hasmoneans could not resolve an internecine struggle for power in 63 B.C.E., one of the two brothers involved appealed to Rome for help, and the Roman general Pompey solved the problem by turning Palestine into a Roman province. From that time on it was Rome who appointed the high priests and kings in Palestine. The Herodians who ruled in Palestine during the time of Jesus were Roman puppets from Idumea and could not lay claim to Jewish traditions and loyalties.

With Pompey's intervention in 63 B.C.E., the Jewish experiment we call the second-temple kingdom was over. The Romans kept the temple system alive for another one hundred years, however, for it did provide the basic structure for economic and political control in Palestine. But in the end the fragmentation of Jewish society took its toll, and the Romans, responding to warring factions of new guerrilla movements in Judea, marched on Jerusalem and destroyed the temple in the Roman-Jewish war of 66–73 C.E. That event was final. It marked the failure of the last attempt any people had made in the wake of Alexander to continue to organize society on the model of the ancient Near Eastern temple-state. By dint, and against all odds, the Jews had kept the model alive. But the tides of cultural change had finally overwhelmed them. Their achievement was not to put the model into practice, but to etch it so deeply into the collective memory that its image would continue to haunt and trouble the Jewish imagination from that time until the present. Christians also would not be able to put the image of the temple at Jerusalem out of their minds.

The story of the Greek city-state is different. The *polis* was a creation of the Greek spirit of independence and free thinking on the one hand, and the practical need for aristocratic clan leaders to band together on the other. In the course of the eighth and seventh centuries B.C.E., the patriarchal heads of large, landed family estates formed councils, defined citizenship, and voted on officers to administer cooperation in matters of common interest such as commerce, the games, and the defense of their territories. The city arose as the place where these country barons met and had their townhouses, supporting a pattern of moving back and forth between the center of civic activity and the country estates where their households and production were located. Thus the notion of democracy was born (from *krateo*, to rule, and *demos*, meaning a "district" in the countryside, and ultimately, the "people" of the country). It was a notion firmly lodged in a particular, aristocratic, social construction of the city-state. And from among the many cities in Greece that practiced crude forms of democracy, it was Athens, with its assemblies, speeches, debates, binding votes, and legislation, that rose to prominence and defined the model.

Athens was not the city where all the institutions and intellectual achievements characterizing Greek culture originated. Homer and the early philosophic traditions had their home in Ionia, the games at Olympus, and the art of rhetoric in the Greek colony at Syracuse. But Athens was the place where all of these cultural manifestations flowered and took their place as part of the ideal city. Schools of various kinds were developed for instruction in primary education, art, philosophy, and the professions (such as rhetoric and medicine). The Athenian assembly took the form of a deliberative body whose judgments were recognized as the legislation of law (*nomos*). A calendar of feasts and festivals turned archaic, local rituals into civic affairs. Pomp and an exceptionally high spirit of competition attended the theater and the games. When in the fourth century B.C.E. Plato and Aristotle set the philosophic agenda for scientific thinking, including theorizing about politics, law, and the city-state, they did so with the culture of Athens in mind.

In the turmoil created by Alexander's campaigns, Greek thought and culture took the eastern Mediterranean by storm. The Greek city-state was the major symbol and vehicle for the spread of Hellenizing institutions. Hellenistic cities by the dozens popped up from Antioch to Alexandria, founded by the Ptolemies and the Seleucids as the primary means for consolidating and maintaining their control of the Alexandrian legacy in the east. By the classicist James Kinneavy's count (1987, 67) thirty-five Hellenistic cities had been established in Palestine before the Roman-Jewish war brought all of that activity to an end. With these cities came Greek learning and the institutions that sustained it: theaters, schools, *gymnasia* (athletic fields), games, processions, and the *agora*, or marketplace, styled as a forum for public debate and display. The slogans that undergirded both the city and the culture it represented were freedom, citizenship, and autonomy. It was this package that promised to replace the ancient temple-state with something far superior. It did not take long for the peoples of the east to read the signs of the times, learn some Greek, and see how far they might go in exploring Greek ways of looking at the world.

Alas and alack. Athens was not an article for export. Then as now, democracy was not easily transplanted in other lands. Problems soon surfaced that threatened the tight combination of the Hellenistic city and the culture it symbolized. One was that the *polis* was now being used as an implement of conquest by foreigners. The Ptolemies and the Seleucids developed the strategy of founding a new *polis* close to an old indigenous city at the center of a district's commerce and governance in order to supplant the native city. Another problem was that the foreigners were not really Greeks, but Macedonians and others whom Alexander had collected along the way as those most loyal to his military campaigns. That gave a distinctly militaristic cast to the whole enterprise. A third was that citizenship, or full participation in a city's governance, was reserved for colonists, denying franchise to the people of the territory who now had to trek to the new city and kowtow in order to carry on mundane business. And a fourth was that these cities ruled their districts at the pleasure of the "great kings" in Alexandria and Antioch. Since kings and foreign franchise did not fit the rhetoric of the democratic model, the Hellenistic city actually debased the *polis* ideal.

Instead of enhancing the grand traditions of classical Greece, the Hellenistic city generated ideological confusion and cultural conflict. What happened was that Greek culture lost its connection with the Greek city-state. Greek philosophy, learning, and ways of thinking could now be used to criticize the colonial civilization created by the Greek city. The *polis* and the ancient Near Eastern temple-state had collided, and neither was able to work effectively. Only the cultures they once symbolized, and the patterns of thought that belonged to them, were left to converge as best they could in the new Hellenistic age. This period of social and cultural history was not an age of Greek enlightenment for the benighted peoples of the east, as has frequently been imagined in modern times. It was a period of strenuous cross-cultural encounters. New ways of living together in a suddenly expanded universe of many different peoples had to be explored without guidance from the centers of power.

As for the Roman republic with its patrician and senatorial traditions, it outfoxed itself when, in the course of the second and first centuries B.C.E., its military influence rapidly spread throughout the Mediterranean world. Power shifted to field commanders who first formed the famous triumvirates and then fought for the office of *princeps*, or emperor, to rule over the lands Rome had accidentally inherited from the failed successors of Alexander. Like dominoes falling in line, beginning with Magnesia in Lydia (taken from Antiochus III in 190 B.C.E.), then Pydna in Macedonia (168 B.C.E.), Corinth and Carthage (146 B.C.E.), Pergamum (133 B.C.E.), and on to Palestine and Egypt, the lands of the eastern Mediterranean became Roman provinces in a very short period of time. The old aristocracy at Rome with its senate and republican traditions could not control the new distribution of power required to govern such a vast empire.

The Romans were rather good at keeping order throughout the Mediterranean world, building roads, quelling civil disturbances, and ridding the lands and seas of pirates and bandits (hence the so-called *pax romana*). They were also good at public works. What they added to the cities where their legions took up residence were aqueducts, civic buildings, and baths. They did not demand ideological loyalty of their provinces, only cooperation with their Roman governors and the payment of taxes (hence *procurator,* meaning both governor and procurer). And they developed a practical approach to legislation that made it possible for them to mediate in matters where ethnic and cultural strife threatened social harmony. But law and order is one thing, building public works another, and creating a common culture still another. None of their subject peoples was fascinated with Roman history, religion, and culture. Roman law and order were cold. Some said ruthless, but that overlooks the limited interest Rome took in the peoples they governed. The Romans were more efficient than ruthless. They had no desire to create either fear or loyalty on the part of their subjects. Thus the city on the Tiber was respected, but it was not loved. The dramas and intrigues of Rome's leading families were considered gross and offensive. And even though a provincial people might be thankful to the Roman legions for clearing their territories of bandits and highwaymen, no one appreciated their obviously superior and repressive military presence. The Romans did not inspire loyalty, and the empire they created did not have a cultural soul. Law and order are never enough to keep a people dancing.

What were the people to do, living in such a mixed-up world? Many found themselves transplanted throughout the large empire of cities, peoples, and different cultures that resulted from the wars of the Greco-Roman age. Warring was constant from the death of Alexander in 323 B.C.E. to the annexation of Egypt as a Roman province in 30 B.C.E. However, these wars were localized and spotty, leaving vast areas of the empire to govern themselves as best they could as long as they caused no trouble and paid their taxes. So being transplanted by force of a foreign power was not the only way dispersion occurred. Many people moved of their own accord to seek a better livelihood in one of the Hellenistic cities that had sprung up, armies and ethnic tensions notwithstanding. And those still living in their own lands were not deprived of the mixing of peoples taking place. Foreign presence and military power, contact with other peoples, and the need to deal with cultural conventions that differed from their own were all too obvious for that. Thus the mix of peoples, cultures, and political powers was the single most obvious and challenging feature of the times.

Not only were peoples of all ethnic extractions living together in cities without a common culture, the histories of incessant warring and rapid political changeovers settled into convoluted layers of bitter memories and hatreds. How to live in a multicultural world that lacked adequate guidelines for such cross-cultural transactions was the challenge. Some were now calling the Mediterranean basin "the inhabited world" (*oikoumene*, from *oikeo*, to inhabit, colonize, administer), but to inhabit such a world without losing one's sense of identity, the kind of identity one had by belonging to a people, now required skills that one's own traditional culture could not provide. Even the Hellenes were now under the rule of the Romans, living in diaspora ghettos, and struggling with ethnic conflicts in the very cities they had built as colonies, such as Alexandria and Antioch. So what were people to do?

At the surface level, people responded in all of the ways one might expect. Most understood that the situation and its terms were a *fait accompli*, learned enough Greek (the *lingua franca*) to get by, created monikers to stereotype people who were different from their own kind, engaged in ethnic joking, held their heads high, and got on with the business of making a living. Some even found the diversity invigorating and took it as an opportunity for esoteric adventures or entrepreneurial activity that traded on the breakdown of traditional institutions. Business boomed, and a new class of parvenus arose that changed forever the old patterns of wealth and property characteristic of aristocratic empires and their landed estates. But the breakup of established social units and the erosion of conventional territorial and cultural boundaries created some raw edges as well. Social tensions rooted in culturally conditioned values, taboos, and attitudes toward the other are not easily overcome.

And so, beneath the surface, serious cultural conflict swirled around such issues as homosexuality (a moral problem for Jews, for instance, but not for the Greeks); prostitution (accepted by the Greeks as a fact of city life but regarded by the Jews as threatening family values); the laws that governed marriage, divorce, and the treatment of slaves; the cultural and cultic significance of foods and family meals; the public role of women; proper attire; and attendance at the baths, athletic events, banquets, civic feasts ("sacrifices"), and festivals. Differences in codes of purity, propriety, ranking, honor, and shame created friction for people of diverse cultural and ethnic backgrounds. Lifestyles, gestures, and behavioral characteristics otherwise taken for granted among one's own people were now on display as features that marked an ethnic minority. Ethnicity was the common coin for stereotyping. On the street, the first thing someone wanted to learn about a stranger was where he or she was from and of what ethnic extraction. The trick was to find out who the other was—Cyprian? Syrian? Egyptian? Greek?—before having to tell on oneself. It was shrewd to do so and safer that way. No wonder people tended to seek out their own kind in foreign cities and form ghettolike communities where familiar signs of recognition prevailed. In Alexandria, for example, Jews, Greeks, Egyptians, and others tended to live in districts of the city known as their quarters.

How to keep one's culture alive was the question. The artifacts of erstwhile societies were in fragments, and any conscious attempt to reconstruct a "little Syria" or a "little Egypt" in one's own quarter of a foreign city had to work with the transportable bits and pieces that remained. One would have to take a few of these pieces, cluster them as signs that the group's traditions were not dead, and create a center for people to meet in mutual recognition of their common cultural heritage. Movable artifacts included books, rituals, calendars, statues, symbolic attire, and adornment. Social conventions that could be kept alive in distant lands included special foods, the structure of family life, kinship arrangements, patterns of hospitality, and traditional ways of resolving conflict internal to the group. But without the support of one's own land and its institutions, innovation was called for. Innovation was on display everywhere during this period.

Shrines popped up in memory of or in devotion to traditional gods or heroes. Upright stone markers, called *stelae*, could be inscribed with the virtues of a homeland god or goddess to announce at a crossroads in some foreign land the presence of an ethnic people. Enclaves were also possible, where real retreat and the intentional cultivation of a lost culture could be pursued. Such, for instance, were the monasticlike *therapeutae* (caretakers, or those attending to the cultivation of the religious traditions) described by first-century Jewish philosopher Philo of Alexandria. Schools, libraries, oracles, and healing cults also spread throughout the Mediterranean basin from origins specific to particular lands and localities. Professional entrepreneurs of

divination, dream interpretation, and magic capitalized on the demise of ancient religious institutions where functions such as these had formerly been integrated into
and controlled by the regular round of cultic activity integral to a society (Brown
1971; J. Z. Smith 1993, 172–89).

It was also during this period that the famous mystery cults spread, complete
with myths, rituals, priests, and priestesses (Burkert 1987). These cults are best understood as replications away from home of religious institutions that were once located in a particular land and people. The "mysteries" of Isis, Osiris, Serapis, Attis,
Adonis, Mithra, the "Great Mother," and the Syrian Goddess are examples of diaspora cults that represented archaic religions and cultures rooted in other times and
lands. The mysteries of Demeter, on the other hand, resisted transplantation but
were still available as a kind of pilgrimage goal for Greeks throughout the empire.
Lovely stories are still available to us of dreams in which a homeland god or goddess
requests a devotee in a foreign land to build a shrine or a little temple there so as not
to be forgotten. And once the processions began everyone would have to take note
of the people and the gods from another land that now resided in their midst. We
have accounts of the priests of Isis processing through a town in lands far from
home. They would go down to the sea on the yearly *navigium Isidis*, the festival of
Isis, protectress of ships at sea, and everyone would have to acknowledge the power
and presence of the Egyptian goddess.

Of even greater importance for the early history of Judaism and Christianity was
another way to create a small social unit within a larger urban environment. Variously called fellowships (*koinoniai*), festive companies (*thiasoi*), or clubs (*collegia*), associations sprang up wherever people got together regularly around a common
interest. Interests ranged from ethnic fellowship and craft guilds, through societies
that aimed at the preservation of cultural traditions and the care of religious shrines,
to funeral associations and mystery cults. The basic pattern of association was the
same. Members would meet approximately once a month, share a common meal in
the midafternoon (the usual time for the "evening" meal), invoke the patron mascot
or deity, acknowledge the club symbols, conduct business, and spend the rest of the
early evening socializing. Associations elected officers, charged dues, and took steps
to protect their interests.

Associations often substituted for societies that had been destroyed. Signs and
symbols of the homeland culture could be displayed. A little taste of home away
from home could be cultivated in the cuisine. With the doors shut, conversation
could turn to matters unfit for the public arena. And building a network of associations from city to city was a distinct possibility. Guests and friends from afar could
be received and entertained at the meetings of the association and at the homes of
members of an association. Networks provided hospitality for members who traveled to other cities and created the sense of belonging to a people who had spread
throughout the empire. In the case of Jewish associations, at first called "houses of
prayer" and later "synagogues" (from the Greek *synagoge*, gathering), buildings were
actually constructed to serve as educational, religious, and social centers. There is

even some evidence for a banking system centered at the temple in Jerusalem and supported by synagogues throughout the empire.

Associations allowed for patterns of social intercourse that did not readily mesh with the social conventions of the society at large. Such was the case with the social role of women, for whom the association provided a semipublic arena beyond the confines of their traditional place in the home. There is evidence of women serving as members, patrons, and leaders of various kinds of associations. Thus the association should be seen as a very creative and important moment in the history of Western civilization. Its novelty was that a way had been found to sustain subcultural, or minority groups within a large, diversified society and to experiment with new ways to construct social units. The Romans were not always comfortable with the existence of associations. And they did, on occasion, take steps to control or even outlaw them. But there was little they could do to contain the energies that people invested in this social experiment. The combination of concepts was just too attractive: free association, membership, self-governance, the cultivation of shared interests, having a name and a place, rules, symbols, signs of recognition, and so on. To think that a traditional culture could be kept alive by a small, intentional social unit in the diaspora was a very attractive idea. As we shall see, the Christians also, though experimenting with a cross-cultural rearrangement of antique artifacts and not the preservation of a single cultural heritage, found the association a ready-made vehicle for their own assemblies (*ekklesiai*).

But for many intellectuals, trying to preserve a cultural heritage in miniature was not an adequate response to the Greco-Roman age. They wanted to see the world as a whole. They wanted to see the many cultures fitting into some large design. The world had always been viewed as a whole. Every people of antiquity had imagined themselves at the center of a vast universe that had been created just for them, with a special place for them to construct their kind of society. Their intellectuals had reflected deeply on the matter and worked out all the ways in which their temple-state or city-state was a fitting reflection of the universe. With the Greeks, the world was a *cosmos*, an arrangement of basic elements held together by a kind of glue and adorned with loveliness (*cosmos* means adornment or beautiful arrangement), like a splendid garment. For the Jews, the world was a chorus of living creatures, carefully planned in the wisdom of God and rejoicing daily, as did the sun, moon, and stars, to take their place once again in making the earth a fit habitation for humankind. God would ask, "Stars, where are you?" and they would answer, "Here we are." With the Egyptians, the sun's rotation around the world created a precisely balanced undulation of the forces of life and death. The gods had set things up that way just for the purpose of fostering life in the Nile valley. According to one theology, the rays of the sun came down to caress the earth on either side of the Nile and so nurtured its coming to life.

And the gods! Every universe was home to the gods, personified abstractions of those forces imagined to have put the world together as the "house" for human habitation. No person, no generation, can ever take credit for constructing such a complex arrangement of negotiated agreements as a human society. And besides, a society is always already there when any given person comes along and finds it pulsing. Myth is the way we humans have of saying that the world was already there. And since the gods were imagined as agents, connections could be made to bring the rhyme and reason of the universe into contact with the social world in which people lived. In the ancient Near East, kingship dropped from heaven to validate the city of the king. In second-temple times, the wisdom of God's creation sought for a resting place among humans and found it in the temple at Jerusalem (Sirach 24). And in Egypt, the *ba*s (essences) of all the gods came down daily to dwell in their statues in the temples throughout the land. We think that the people of antiquity imagined the universe on the model of the society they had constructed. They, however, thought that their society had been planned or built at the beginning of the world on the model of the universe they inhabited. And that thought was critical. It made them right, legitimate, centered, and at home in the world. It was the correspondence of the "little world" (*microcosm*) to the universe (*macrocosm*) that mattered. In Egypt, when in a temple, one looked up and saw the starry heavens painted on the ceiling, a reminder of the big house that the little house resembled in miniature. And as for the Greeks, once the notion of society as a *polis* had been conceptualized, the *cosmos* itself was imagined as a great world city. During the Greco-Roman age the people of the "inhabited world" (*oikoumene*) were referred to by Greek philosophers as citizens of the world city (*cosmopolitans*).

But what was the shape of that world city now in the wake of Alexander and the Romans? And what should be the shape of the new multicultural society below? That was the question. None of the older models, either of the universe or of the city-states and temple-states they had supported, was good enough to encompass the new world in view. And the older models differed too much from one another to answer the question merely by being squeezed into one. The only thing they all had in common was a pattern of thought that viewed the world as a hierarchy of concentric circles with the universe all encompassing, society in the middle ring, and the individual in the center, surrounded by both the city and the cosmos. Thus the Greeks frequently thought in terms of a correlation between *cosmos, polis,* and *anthropos* (human being). The Jews thought in terms of creation, the temple-state in Jerusalem, and the Jewish people centered there. With both the *polis* and the temple-state crossed out of the equation, the middle term was missing, and the individual was now left standing in the midst of a large and confused universe to negotiate with the gods and the uncertain forces of human destiny as best one could. And suddenly, standing there looking directly at the universe, with only the fragmented memories of sane city-states to guide one's meditation and all the old worldviews blinking for attention on the cosmic screen, there were just too many gods and heroes, pictures of priests and kings, ideal cities and perfect laws, powers and creation myths to comprehend. All were bright lights floating free in the heady mix of images available for contemplating the structure of a new world order. But how to rearrange them? How to find the key that would make it possible to see the world as a whole again, account for the human diversity and cosmic expanse that had come into view, and understand all the powers that had been unleashed as capable of working together for human well-being? Some despaired of integrating religion and society, culture and the present political system, or even of imagining the world as a divinely ordered home for human habitation.

Every intellectual tradition pouring into the Greco-Roman world focused its energies on this question. Egyptian priests, Jewish sages, Syrian scribes, Greek philosophers, Hellenistic teachers, Roman historians, and many others turned their attention to the problem of reimagining the world as a place fit for human habitation. Some tried to match the gods of one cultural tradition with the gods of another, thinking that the differences might not be so great after all. Thus the Greek god Hermes and the Egyptian god Thoth were thought to be the same deity since both were "messengers" in their respective pantheons. Other scholars set to work reducing the myths of the gods to rational accounts of the natural order by means of allegory, thinking that beneath all of the fantastic stories, there must be a reasonable view of the world. Thus Hermes-Thoth was allegorized by the first-century Stoic philosopher Cornutus as the poetic expression of the scientific concept of the *logos*, the "logic" at the heart of the universe. Plato's myth of the creation of the world by a divine craftsman (*demiurgos*) who followed the plans in the mind of the highest god was very popular. Plutarch used it to allegorize the myths of Isis and Osiris as stories that encoded profound understanding about the structure of the cosmos. Jews used Plato's myth to imagine how the world could have gotten so out of shape when it was God's wisdom that had planned it. It was the *demiurgos* who did it, or perhaps it was the material that was faulty, or maybe humans had just been too dense or contrary to see the perfect pattern behind it all. Surely the failures of human societies cannot have ruined God's perfect plan for the world. The world created by wisdom must indeed exist. Perhaps it exists as a spiritual realm known only to those who could "see through" the corruption of the physical world by means of divine inspiration. A fine example of this kind of thought is available in the Wisdom of Solomon and in the works of Philo of Alexandria. And so attempt after attempt was made to salvage the fragments of bygone myths and worldviews in the hope that their secrets might reveal some reason to think that the universe was still a good place, a divine creation with human well-being in mind.

Slowly, however, it dawned on people that the universe might not be all that friendly. The only thing about the universe that seemed to be ordered was the movement of the stars. And that movement was like clockwork, unfeeling and predetermined. But it was calculable. Astrology flourished. There was also much talk about *tyche*, the goddess of fate, and *fortuna*, the goddess of fortune. Unfortunately, both of these divine powers were fickle. And there was great interest in dreams and magic; dreams because they might at least give you a chance to know ahead of time what would befall, and magic because it gave you a slight chance to be in control of something in an otherwise capricious world. So with the elision of the city from the ancient equation of *cosmos*, *polis*, and *anthropos*, the world itself was no longer comprehensible, and human existence was threatened with insignificance.

The human spirit is amazingly creative and resilient. Not to be overwhelmed by the unfeeling forces of fate in the universe, and the fact that the Romans were firmly in control of their soulless empire, many intellectuals refused to give up on the quest for a social model fit for the times. The quest took two quite different directions. Some turned to the schools of Greek philosophy in order to get started, while others turned to the national epics to re-search the wisdom of the past. Those working in the traditions of the schools of Greek philosophy seemed to know that they would have to do theory in a vacuum. They could not draw upon any feature of the present state of affairs as if it were an essential ingredient for imagining an ideal world. So what the philosophers came up with, as they pursued what we could call a social-political anthropology, was very speculative mythology. It was not the rationalization or justification of any contemporary social formation, or a glorification of some presently grand human accomplishment such as the *pax romana*. It was an exercise in theory, exploring the ways in which certain forces fundamental to social life might possibly be understood to relate to one another. Three factors immediately came to the surface, and the attempt to understand them exercised the best minds in all of the school traditions struggling to revise their conceptual grasp of the world: (1) how to define law, (2) how to understand political power, and (3) how to describe personal virtue. These are the very questions that confront us as well in our global, multicultural situation at the end of the twentieth century.

A concept of law was fundamental to the Greek design of the *polis*, the Jewish charter for the temple-state, and the Roman system of courts and governance. In the case of the Greeks, law was the term that linked the city to the cosmos on the one hand, and to its citizens on the other. The term was *nomos*, meaning "convention," the result of traditional agreements, especially those that had been reached by debate and legislation in the council of the city-state. *Nomos* was the standard for judging legality and rightness. To be right in a legal sense was good, but it did not make one virtuous. In the case of the Jews, on the other hand, law was divine instruction and command. It was not the result of human legislation. To live according to the law of Moses was not only right, it made one righteous. As for the Romans, law was a very practical matter, flowing from the will of the emperor and the senate as decree, but judged constantly by its effectiveness in maintaining peace and order. If a decree made matters worse, it was a simple matter to change it.

Thus the philosophical discussions about the law came to focus on a fundamental problem of definition. The question was whether one might imagine a law that was written into the structure of the universe. Legislation, the ultimate foundation for *nomos*, was no longer thought of as a mark of democratic advance. It was now thought of as merely human wisdom at best or as a convenience for self-serving kings and tyrants at worst. The alternative to *nomos* had always been the will of the gods, but now that there were so many gods in the picture, the notion of the will of the gods had also become very fuzzy. If it were possible to imagine something like a "law of nature," that would really do it. It would not be legislation. It would not be based on a parochial claim to special revelation from the gods, such as in oracles or the Jewish myth of the law given to Moses. Law would be rooted ultimately in the divine creation of the ordered universe. And so the terms of this debate throughout the Greco-Roman period were the famous contrasting pair: nature (*physis*) and law (*nomos*). In Alexandria, for instance, a line of Jewish thinkers from Aristobulus in the early second century B.C.E. to Philo in the first century C.E. expended immense effort in allegorizing the laws of Moses as coded expressions of "natural law." The effort was worth it. It countered the charge that Jewish myth and laws were silly, and it gave Jewish laws the kind of philosophical muscle that everyone was eager to claim for his or her own traditions.

But what about power in the hands of a king whose word also counted as law? It was not easy to imagine how the divine law, written into the structure of the universe, could make any difference in the real world. This problem was serious, and the only recourse available to the philosophic tradition was, first, to distinguish between a good king and a bad king, and then to connect the good king to the law of nature. Thus the terms of this debate were the famous contrasting pair: kings and tyrants. "Tyrant" meant autocratic, self-serving, and bad, while "king" became an abstract ideal for the perfect ruler. Intellectuals squirmed. No one really wanted a king. Kings certainly did not fit well with the city-state ideal or the notion of natural law. But kings were all there were. Kings and commanders. You couldn't seem to get rid of them. So why not try to imagine one that would be acceptable? Scribes researched the traditions. Allegorists looked for mythic models. Philosophers made lists of fitting attributes. And descriptions of the ideal king began to fill the libraries of the intellectual community. Finally, all seemed to agree, the perfect king would be the one who lived completely in accordance with the divine law of nature. He would be the very embodiment of the law (*nomos empsychos*). His laws would be more like instruction than decrees. And his power to influence conformity with the law would be more a matter of setting an example than of executing justice (Goodenough 1928). Some king! An example of just such a picture can be found in chapter 17 of the Psalms of Solomon.

As you can see, fantasy and the Greek penchant for abstract definition took over at this point. But no one was fooled. No one thought that it was actually possible to have a king like that. These intellectuals were still living in the real world, fully aware of how that world actually worked and how one had to work it. So what was the point of all this intellectual labor? It was a serious attempt to tackle fundamental issues of human well-being and go as far as one could in conceptualizing a sane and equitable society. The image of the ideal king could be used to chide and criticize the tyrants. That was something. And knowing that the actual state of affairs was not conducive to the collective well-being of society as a whole also had its value. It allowed for a savvy critique of the status quo. And it forced the question of whether it was possible for anyone to live with integrity in the Greco-Roman world with its confusions about laws and the fact of illegitimate uses of power.

This question resulted in a purely personal, individualistic approach to the question of virtue. Philosophers and teachers in the schools of popular ethical philosophy, Stoics especially, but Cynics as well, gave up on the idea that building abstract models of perfect societies might change the world for the better. They instead turned all their attention to the plight of the lone individual. Personal virtue was all that mattered, they said. And anyone could be virtuous by living in accordance with (the laws of) nature. Virtue was, after all, the highest and noblest human pursuit. Why not accept the fact that the individual was all alone in the universe without the support of a social world that guaranteed well-being? Wasn't it possible for a person to know what needed to be known about the structure of the universe and do what needed to be done in order to live "according to nature" (*physis*) and so achieve honorable character? The world was filled with popular philosophers, teachers, books, and self-help guides for living with integrity even under the untoward circumstances of the Greco-Roman age.

The Stoic recommendation was particularly popular. The idea was that a person could learn or discern what was "naturally" right and live "according to nature" if one only would. The goal was to be unaffected by the crowd, untouched by the accidents of life that otherwise would be felt as pain, and unmoved by the power that tyrants and others might have over you. The Stoics were fully aware that this would require a heroic effort, and might even get you in trouble with the powers that be. But therein lay the reward of a chance to manifest true nobility. And then a funny thing happened. The Stoics learned how to use the social model of the ideal king as an icon for personal meditation. The only true king was a sage, they said, and as for the mark of the sage, it was knowing and living in accordance with nature. If one did that, they said, one would truly be a citizen of the great world city. One would become a cosmopolitan, a sovereign example of virtue at its highest imaginable level of human achievement. This philosophy was a radically individualistic response to the breakdown of cultures in the Greco-Roman age, and it spread like wildfire. The Stoics had succeeded in reducing the entire system of *cosmos, polis,* and *anthropos* to the status of a psychological metaphor.

For other thinkers, especially those with cultural roots in the eastern Mediterranean provinces, radical individualism was hardly an answer. Ancient Near Eastern cultures had developed a strong sense of the importance of belonging to a people. Theirs was a social anthropology that placed high value on family, kinship, genealogy, tradition, purity, social justice, cultic law, and religious piety. These values were very deeply ingrained in the collective unconscious, and they determined the way in which people thought about the world. In response to the troubled times, for these people, only a social vision would do. And it would not be enough to construct an ideal kingdom simply on the foundation of systematic thought and logic. It would have to honor the achievements of the past, reflect the promise of the past, account for the present malaise, and project an imaginable future for all the people who were now crowding into the picture. The ideal kingdom would have to offer a social alternative to the social confusion of the Greco-Roman age.

This social approach to cultural critique led to passionate interest in the grand epic traditions that every people brought with them to the Greco-Roman mix. The Greeks had their combination of Homer, Hesiod, and age-old tales about the gods and heroes. The Syrians had their chronicles; the Samaritans their books from Moses; the Egyptians their dramatic cycles of Isis and Osiris; the Romans their records of Romulus and Remus; and the Jews their history from the foundation of the world. Every aristocratic family, local shrine, and city with any pretense at all also had its genealogy and history intact even though its power and glory were threatened or gone. What was left from the past was illustrious epic, but of course all epics were now tarnished. Some intellectuals thought, nonetheless, that the epics were still of value. Epics contained information that a study of the *cosmos* could not provide. Epics brought the gods into the story. Epics might go all the way back to the creation of the world where the connections were first made between the cosmic order and the origin of civilization. Epics were the reservoir of the wisdom of the past. They revealed the characteristics of a people, explained their attitudes toward neighboring peoples, recorded failures and achievements, and marked the moments when certain features of a social order were established. Epics were instructive. Epics accounted for a people as a people. They must hold the clues to what went wrong. They might provide some hints about how to set things right again. They could at least be used to mourn the loss of ancient glories and view the Romans with disdain.

Two epics attracted the most attention, and competition between them was fierce. Homer had the edge because the dominant culture was Greek. But the story of Israel also created a great deal of interest even outside Jewish circles. That is because Jewish culture drew upon its epic tradition in order to undergird a set of ideas and values that, although threatened by the Greco-Roman age, were still found attractive. The concepts of a righteous god, a divine law, a creation designed to enhance both wonder and morality, a vision of society based on social justice, and rituals for the observance and celebration of sane, rational, family-centered life could all be gathered from their epic. It was a story of the people that stretched from the creation of the world to the construction of the temple-state in Jerusalem. It was a reasonable contrast to the stories of fickle gods and arrogant heroes with which the Greeks had to make do. And Moses, the author of the five books called *torah* (instruction), was clearly a match for Homer. Some said Moses was earlier than Homer, that he had lived somewhere near the very beginning of human history, and that whatever Homer knew, he must have learned from Moses. But the more important advantage was that the "law of Moses" was not just law, even though everyone had learned to translate *torah* with *nomos*, but real epic. Creation, the origin of the species, and culture bringers, along with violence, folly, the rainbow's promise, patriarchal legends, eternal covenants, and the destiny of a people all took shape before laws in the narrower sense ever entered the picture. It was something to think about. And many did.

Scholars with social questions in mind became obsessed with the books of Moses as the second-temple history ran its course. Some retold the story at length in the interest of saying how grand the history of Israel had been and how respectable the Jewish people were (Josephus, Jubilees). Others highlighted aspects of the story that gave the present shape of society its epic constitution, leaving out the parts that did not fit (Sirach 44–50; Mack 1985). And others still read Moses and the prophets to lift up a forgotten ideal, use it to criticize the status quo, and say what had to happen in order to set things right (Qumran). In every case, the strategy was the same: revising the epic in light of present circumstances from a particular point of view to support a critical judgment about the present state of affairs. Historians of religion would say that these Jewish scholars followed a typical pattern of mythmaking.

This pattern works in the following way. The current state of affairs is not living up to the promise of the past. The recent past comes under critique. The stories of the more distant past are rehearsed to make sure of the promise. The aim is to see the promise more clearly, more precisely, and test the reasons for having thought that it was true. This brings focus to bear upon a certain moment, epoch, or feature of the history that can serve as a key to its fundamental logic and promise. Reseen, and lifted from its ancient history as an ideal model, the figure can then be used as an image of what the people and their culture were, are in essence, or should be. The image can then be used as a contrast to the present situation in order to render a critique, provide a model for rebuilding, or project a hopeful future. In our time, this pattern of thinking can be recognized in the frequent reference to the Judeo-Christian tradition, the American dream, or the Constitution of the United States. In second-temple times, the epic of Israel was a rich reservoir of ideal types, and all of them were used at one time or another in the process of mythmaking. Adam, Abraham, the covenants, Moses, the exodus, the law, the temple charter in Leviticus, the entrance into the land, David, Solomon, the building of the temple, the kingdoms, the prophets, and so forth could all be cast as icons of Israel's sociology and used for comparison and contrast with the contemporary situation.

The Jews did not need to learn a new set of tricks to use their epic this way. Jews had been revising their epic history since the time of David and Solomon. Reimagining the past was their way of mythmaking. The past provided standards for contemporary social critique. It could also lend authority to proposals for shaping society anew. Biblical scholars count four major revisions of the epic before the deportation of Jews in 587 B.C.E. brought to an end the kingdoms of Israel and Judah. These revisions are traditionally known as *J* for the Yahwist, *E* for the Elohist, *D* for the Deuteronomist, and *P* for the Priestly school. In each case, these revisions markedly changed the constitution of Israel by rewriting the epic. In the case of P, for instance, the book of Leviticus was added to Moses' instructions and the stories of sacrificial covenant were added to the legends of the patriarchs in order to locate the legal foundations for the temple-state at the beginning of the epic. After the exile no one dared to actually rewrite the story in this way, for the five books of Moses were now in many hands in many lands, "published," as it were, so that changing the text itself was not the thing to do. But other ways were found to rehearse the story from a revisionist perspective. The author of Chronicles rewrote the history in a separate account, adding some things and leaving out some things to make it read another way. Ben Sira summarized the epic in a poem that gave him the opportunity to recast it radically. At Qumran and in the synagogues of Alexandria, two different methods of writing commentaries on the Jewish scriptures were devised. Everyone was involved in retelling the story of Israel.

The problem with this approach as a response to the Roman era was that an ethnic bias belonged to every national epic. How could reading a provincial epic ever produce enlightenment fit for a multicultural scene? Jewish intellectuals were painfully aware of this problem, especially in the diaspora where the cultural mix was a fact of daily life and the Jews were on display with their meetings, associations, and schools. It was there that scholars with a philosophic bent tackled the problem of Jews and "the nations" (*ethne*, later translated by the old Latin, *gentilis*, "foreign," from which we get the English "gentiles."). A great deal of speculation centered on the figure of Adam, the first human being. It is important to realize that, in early Jewish thought, a personified abstraction could be storied as an individual without losing its generic or social significance. Thus "Adam" meant humankind, and "Israel" meant the people of Israel, even though each could also be pictured and storied as a particular person. One of the two stories in Genesis about the origins of the human race said that humankind had been created in the image of God. That was certainly cause for reflection, and scholars in the wisdom tradition, from Ben Sira, through the author of the Wisdom of Solomon, to Philo, lingered long over that text. The story of Noah, also, was a good place to reflect on the standing of the nations in the eyes of the God of Israel. The rainbow's promise was not the private property of the Jews. And even Abraham, the figure with whom the story of Israel actually began, was curiously blessed and chosen by God to receive the promises long before the divine instructions were given to Moses. What about the way God treated Abraham as a sign that the gentiles must be welcomed into the family of God? It may seem strange to us that, given the availability of very sophisticated anthropologies and psychologies in the Greek philosophical traditions, Jewish thinkers would prefer to work out their classifications of human beings by worrying these old stories into making a point or two about where the gentiles stood in the larger scheme of things divine. But to see the point about the gentiles there in one's own epic, that is what made the point telling.

This approach did not break out of the ethnic bias inherent in the Jewish epic, but it did allow Jewish intellectuals to recognize their multicultural world and deal with it without having to give up on their own grand traditions. And it did force the issue of exclusivity. Philo's allegorical commentaries on the five books of Moses document a major effort in the Alexandrian synagogue to interpret the laws of Moses so that gentiles could understand them, appreciate them, and keep them. We now know that non-Jews found diaspora synagogues to be a very attractive subcultural association, and that gentiles did gather around to study the scriptures, rehearse the epic, honor the one God, celebrate the feasts and festivals, and learn to keep the Jews' laws with their high ethical standards. Naturally there were debates galore about whether the gentiles would have to go all the way in order to belong to the association of Israel. That would have meant being circumcised, keeping whatever form of kosher was in practice, and perhaps paying a temple tax. Some Jews said yes, they should go all the way. Others said no, it did not matter. But either way, the result of the Jewish preoccupation with their scriptures was that Homer and the Greek philosophical tradition were not the only resources available for doing social critique or for thinking about better and less better ways to live together in the Greco-Roman age.

Galilee happened to be a perfect place to experiment with social critique and try out new ideas about a better way to live. Its people were wide awake, worldly wise, and protective of their way of life. They had survived the foreign rule, at one time or another, of all the powers in the ancient Near East without, apparently, taking sides. There is no record of Galileans fighting under their own banner, trying to rid their land of unwanted foreign kings. They had no capital city to defend and no king to rule them. They granted token allegiance to each new foreign king and then looked for ways to protect themselves from the king's long arm. They could do that because they enjoyed a bit of distance from the cultural and political forces that swirled around them. That was because Galilee was not open to or easily annexed by either the kingdoms to the north or to the south. It formed a little inland district of its own, bounded by mountains to the north, west, and south, and the Lake of Genneseret (or Sea of Galilee) to the east. Their way of life was worth protecting. They lived among rocky hills and gentle valleys, dotted with small villages and abundantly watered by springs and rains. They were self-sufficient, producing a healthy economy of fish, wine, grains, olives, and fruits, as well as crafts. There were mineral hot springs at Tiberias and Gadara. These, and the tropical climate around the Sea of Galilee, made the area attractive as a health resort. And with major roadways open to the main north-south highways, one along the seacoast and another across the highlands of the Transjordan to the east, Galilee had constant contact with the rest of the world.

It is important to remember that Galilee was ruled by the kings of Jerusalem only twice in the preceding one thousand years, and then for only brief periods of time. David did add Galilee to his kingdom, it is true, and the old stories tell about the tribes of Naphthali, Asher, Issachar, Zebulun, and Dan settling there. However, these stories also say that the tribes of Israel were not able to drive out the indigenous inhabitants. And as for belonging to the kingdoms of David and Solomon, an arrangement that lasted less than eighty years (1000 to 922 B.C.E.), Solomon gave twenty Galilean cities back to Hiram, king of Tyre, in exchange for building materials. Then, what was left of Galilee was part of the old northern kingdom of Israel centered at Shechem (Samaria), not Jerusalem. After that kingdom came to an end in 722 B.C.E., Galilee was ruled by Damascus, Assyria, Neo-Babylonia, Persia, the Ptolemies, and the Seleucids before it was again overrun by kings in Jerusalem (the Hasmoneans) in 104 B.C.E. There is nothing to suggest that the Galileans were happy about this annexation. The people who lived in Galilee were Galileans, not Syrians, not Samaritans, not Jews. It was, as the later rabbis would say, the "district of the gentiles."

During the Hellenistic period, Galilee was introduced to Greek language, philosophy, art, and culture through the founding of cities on the Greek model in strategic locations up and down the Jordan river valley (Caesarea Philippi, Philoteria, Scythopolis), on the eastern side of the Sea of Galilee (Bethsaida, Hippos, Gadara), along the seacoast to the west (Ptolemais, Dora, Caesarea), and eventually within Galilee itself (Sepphoris, Tiberius, Agrippina). With them came Greek learning, Greek schools with their *gymnasia*, theaters, forums, and political institutions. During the time of Jesus there were twelve Greek cities within a twenty-five-mile radius of his hometown, Nazareth.

Jesus grew up in Galilee and apparently had some education. He was certainly bright enough, judging from the movements that remembered him as their founder. But as we are now coming to see, it is all but impossible to say anything more about him as a person, much less write a biography about his life. The "memories" of him differ, and they are so obviously mythic that the best we can do is to draw a conclusion or two from the earliest strata of the teachings attributed to him. These teachings belonged to the movements that started in his name. We have to infer what kind of a teacher he was from the teachings that developed in these movements. He must have been something of an intellectual, for the teachings of the movements stemming from him are highly charged with penetrating insights and ideas. He also must have been capable of suggesting ways to live with purpose in the midst of complex social circumstances. But he was not a constructive, systematic thinker of the kind who formulate philosophies or theologies. He did not create a social program for others to follow or a religion that invited others to see him as a god. He simply saw things more clearly than most, made sense when he talked about life in his world, and must have attracted others to join him in looking at the world a certain way. What we have as evidence for this is the way his followers learned to talk about living in the world. They said that Jesus had talked that way too.

The tenor of that talk can be seen in the teachings of Jesus his followers preserved. These teachings are really a collection of pithy aphorisms that strike to the heart of ethical issues, not the usual proverbs, maxims, or principles that one would expect from the founder-teacher of a school tradition. But a close analysis of these aphorisms reveals the interweaving of two themes that mark the genius of the movement. One is a playful, edgy challenge to take up a countercultural lifestyle. This challenge was made in all seriousness, but it was marked by humor, and one can still sense the enjoyment these Jesus people took in watching the conventional world do double takes at the very thoughts they expressed and the behavior they enjoined. The closest analogy for this kind of invitation to live against the stream is found in Cynic discourse of the time. It does appear that Jesus was attracted to this popular ethical philosophy as a way for individuals to keep their integrity in the midst of a compromising world. The other theme is an interest in a social concept called the "kingdom of God." This concept was not worked out with any clarity, but the ways it was used show that something of a social vision appeared in the teachings of Jesus. The kingdom of God referred to an ideal society imagined as an alternative to the way in which the world was working under the Romans. But it also referred to an alternative way of life that anyone could take at any time. In this sense the kingdom of God could be realized simply by daring to live differently from the normal conventions. The kingdom of God in the teachings of Jesus was not an apocalyptic or heavenly projection of an otherworldly desire. It was driven by a desire to think that there must be a better way to live together than the present state of affairs. And it called for a change of behavior in the present on the part of individuals invested in the vision. Thus the teachings of Jesus can be described as the creative combination of these two themes, or a challenge to the individual to explore an alternative social notion.

If so, Jesus' genius was to let the sparks fly between two different cultural sensibilities, the Greek and the Semitic. The Greek tradition of philosophy had been forced to focus on the question of individual virtue as a last-ditch stand for human dignity and integrity in a world without a *polis*, one that was no longer structured as a sane society. The Cynic-like challenge in the teachings of Jesus picked up on this bottom line from the grand traditions of Greek philosophy. The ancient Near Eastern legacy said that individualism would not do. People were only people when they lived together. A person had to belong to a working society in which ethical values addressed the well-being of the collective. A social anthropology determined that some social vision give guidance to a critique of the Roman world and suggest a better way to live together. By bringing the two cultural traditions together and making contact between them, the pitch for a change in personal lifestyle and the vague but potentially powerful symbol of an alternative society, the electrodes short-circuited, and Jesus started a movement. Everything essential was present in the package: social critique, alternative social vision, divine sovereignty, and personal virtue. And yet, nothing was present except general ideas. Nothing was spelled out. Everything was left to more talking, thinking, and experimentation with the new ideas.

And that is exactly what happened. Kingdom talk started with the teachings of Jesus and then attracted more and more people. We can't be sure of all the ways little groups formed, or how the kingdom movement spread from place to place.

What we do know is that, by the time writings from the Jesus people began to appear, talk about the kingdom had resulted in the formation of wondrously different kinds of association. One line can be traced from the earliest Jesus movement, through Matthew's gospel, to later communities that understood themselves as Jewish Christians. These people emphasized lifestyle and found a way to bring the behavior of the Jesus movement into line with more traditional Jewish codes of ethics. This approach produced communities that lasted for centuries, such as the Ebionites and Nazareans. But they were not the ones that gave birth to the Christianity of the Bible. Another line takes off from the Sayings Gospel Q, runs through the Gospel of Thomas where Jesus' teachings were understood to bring enlightenment about one's true self, and ends up in gnostic circles. These people cultivated the invitation to personal virtue and thought of the kingdom of God as an otherworldly dimension of spiritual existence where true human being had its origin and end. This approach may have been the most attractive form of Christianity during the second to fourth centuries. But it was finally squelched by the institutional form of Christian tradition that called itself the church. The church's trajectory had worked its way through northern Syria and Asia Minor where the Christ cult formed to justify the inclusion of both gentiles and Jews in the kingdom of God. It was this trajectory that converged on Rome, developed the notion of the universal church (from *catholicus*, meaning "general"), and created the Bible as its charter.

And so a new religion emerged. As we prepare to enter into the provincial world of its first manifestations in Galilee, trying to keep up with its rapid spread throughout the eastern Mediterranean, eventually to see it become the religion of the Roman Empire, a word of caution may be in order. The ways these Christians addressed the issues of their time will often appear to be silly, sometimes absurd, frequently extravagant, and only once in a while breathtaking. We will need some good shoes with very sharp spikes to keep from falling off the logs as we jump from text to text in this period of rapid social and cultural change. The present chapter was written to help us keep our balance as we proceed. Every feature of the Greco-Roman age mentioned here will return for reconsideration in the early history of Christianity: law, kings and tyrants, kingdoms, associations, meals, myths, rituals, cosmologies, cosmogonies, the gods, the mystery cults, noble deaths, redeemers, oracles, epic history, and ethics. That Christianity emerged just when it did, that it drew now upon some Jewish roots, now upon Greek ideas, and that it eventually found itself infatuated with the thought of Roman power, are all crucial for the story about to be told. Only by keeping the larger world in view will it be possible to see that these early Christians were not gullible, eccentric, or mad, given to ecstasies, visions, and religious experiences of personal transformation. Though their claims were often wild and extravagant, we need to see that they were actually engaging their troubled times. Early Christianity was a creative, if daring, response to the multicultural challenge of the Greco-Roman age.

2

TEACHINGS FROM THE JESUS MOVEMENTS

Jesus movements started in Galilee during the 30s and 40s of the first century C.E. Loosely knit groups of people gathered around a novel combination of three ideas that had been in the air since the breakdown of traditional cultures characteristic of the Greco-Roman age. The combination of these ideas generated a great deal of excitement. One was the vague notion of a perfect society conceptualized as a kingdom. This was a notion that many groups had used to imagine a better way to live than suffering under the Romans. The Jesus people latched onto this idea and acted as if the kingdom they imagined was a real possibility despite the Romans. They called it the kingdom of God.

A second idea was that any individual, no matter of what extraction, status, or innate capacity, was fit for this kingdom and could act accordingly if only one would. The idea of personal responsibility for virtue, or actually living in accordance with one's view of the world, had been thoroughly discussed by popular philosophers of all persuasions during the Hellenistic period. The Jesus people said, in effect, "Come on, you can do it, you can live as if you belonged to the kingdom of God," and "If you do, the kingdom of God will surely take place in this very world."

The third idea was a result of the combination of the first two. It was the novel notion that a mixture of people was exactly what the kingdom of God should look like. What a heady social concept that must have been, cutting across social and cultural boundaries, putting together a radically individualistic appeal with a thoroughly social aim, and insisting that the gap between an unbelievable ideal and its social incarnation could actually be bridged! No wonder these people attracted attention.

Imagine yourself going to market in the next larger village and overhearing two or three persons talking about these ideas. You smile, think they are engaging in adolescent craziness, and move on to the next stall. But a line or two may have caught your attention, and on the next market day you cannot resist looking to see if they are there again. They are not, and you ask a man selling pots if he remembers

43

them, knows anything. He does remember but knows nothing. You ask around. Two or three others had listened in and knew the village where one of the young persons lived. So little by little you are drawn into an informal network of unlikely acquaintances, some of whom become rather regular contacts, until finally you find yourself meeting once in a while with a small group of friends who have gotten quite serious about the novel set of ideas.

At first the talk has to be about the ideas themselves, how everyone in the group understands them, and what anyone in the group may have heard that others in other groups said. You find yourself startled to see how many different thoughts and views there are. You thought you knew what a kingdom was and what the word *god* meant. You say that "kingdom" has to mean kingdom, does it not, and "god," God, doesn't it? The others look at you, smile, ask whose god you have in mind, tease you about being Jewish, then get serious and listen while you spell out what you think these big words mean. And so it goes until, having reached a few agreements among yourselves on what the kingdom of God must look like, your group starts to wonder what is wrong with the world that it works another way. Now social and cultural critique become the order of the day, until finally you catch one another's eyes across the room and someone says, "Well, why don't we, at least, treat each other as if we belonged to the kingdom?"

And so the Jesus movements began. Each group or small network of groups worked out the details as they went along. We can see at once that different cultural backgrounds and personal histories would determine the way in which a given group came to its own understanding of the kingdom of God. For the first forty years we are able to identify at least seven different streams within the Jesus movement, though there may have been many more. We are fortunate to know anything, because this was a very experimental period when rapidly expanding groups were radically changing their views. At first no one thought to record any of this history, and besides, there was little to report except lore, hearsay, and ad hoc conversations. That we have any written materials from this period at all is a combination of sheer historical accident on the one hand, and laborious scholarly investigation on the other. The historical accident is that some of the first attempts to write things down and share ideas were saved, embellished, and eventually reworked by later writers whose writings happened to be included in the New Testament. If that had not happened, most of the memories and records of the early period would have been lost forever, for neither the early movements nor the later church were interested in keeping these early memory traditions alive.

From this early period we can identify five different groups of Jesus people from whom we have some documentary evidence, plus a "family of Jesus" group for which there are only a handful of clues, and the congregations of the Christ to which we shall turn in the next chapter. I will refer to the five groups within the Jesus movement as (1) the Community of Q who produced the Sayings Gospel Q, (2) the Jesus School that produced the pre-Markan pronouncement stories, (3) the

True Disciples who produced the Gospel of Thomas, (4) the Congregation of Israel who composed the pre-Markan sets of miracle stories, and (5) the Jerusalem Pillars about whom we have only an early report from Paul in his letter to the Galatians.

Each of these groups differs from the others in important ways, but they do share some characteristics. One common feature has already been noted, namely their investment in the idea of the kingdom of God and the fact that they all were engaged in some kind of group formation. Another feature that may have been shared, though it is more difficult to document in every group, is the practice of meeting together for meals. And, of course, all of them considered Jesus the founder of their movement. But after that, each group developed differently, and the different views and practices that developed are evidence for the fact that Jesus did not provide a program for starting a new religion. If he did, his followers did not understand what it was. The many views they came up with, both about what the kingdom should be and about what Jesus must have been, tell against a clear and common conception of the kingdom. We are thus faced with the fact that many people were involved in thinking about the kingdom and drawing conclusions about what their group should be like. The road from Jesus to the Christian religion that finally emerged in the fourth century, with its myth of Jesus as the son of God solidly in place, is a very long and twisty path. Christianity was not born of an immaculate conception. It was the product of myriad moments of intellectual labor and negotiated social agreements by the people investing in the experiment.

This discovery has been difficult for many Christians to accept. That is because the traditional picture of Christian beginnings starts with a Jesus who knows in advance what is required of him and his disciples in order to establish the Christian religion. The way Luke tells the story in his two-volume history of Christian origins, for instance, is that after his death but before his ascension Jesus announced the establishment of the First Christian Church of Jerusalem by means of the outpouring of God's Spirit on the next day of Pentecost (Acts 1–2). We now know that Luke wrote his gospel and the Acts of the Apostles in the early second century, seventy-five or more years after the time of Jesus, and that he had his reasons for wanting to imagine things that way. We shall explore those reasons later. For now, the point to be made is that there is not a trace of evidence in any of the early Jesus materials to support such a view. No early Jesus group thought of Jesus as the Christ or of itself as a Christian church. We will have to account for such ideas when we encounter them for the first time in later texts from more developed communities. In the present chapter, our task will be to give the Jesus movement its due, describing each of the groups we know about separately, and treating them as understandable, human efforts to respond to the challenging idea of the kingdom of God in the midst of the Greco-Roman world.

But what, then, about the historical Jesus? Should not a book about Christian origins and the New Testament start with a chapter on the historical Jesus? The answer is no. It is neither possible nor necessary to say very much about the historical

Jesus. The first followers of Jesus were not interested in preserving accurate memories of the historical person. Jesus was important to them as the founder-teacher of a school of thought. As the various systems of thought began to take shape in the several branches of the Jesus movement, the "voice" and "image" of Jesus changed to match the shifts in the content of his "teachings." This should not be thought of as the dishonest manipulation of the facts. It agrees with what we know in general about movements organized around the teaching of a founder-teacher. We might call to mind the modern movements based on the teaching of nonviolence as a way to effect social and political change. If asked whose teaching that is, anyone would say it was Gandhi's, or Martin Luther King's, leaders of movements who taught nonviolence. As long as the movements are still alive and growing, even long after the deaths of their founders, no one would dare take credit for the "teaching," despite one's intellectual investment in the burgeoning systems of new information and instruction about nonviolence that have developed in the meantime.

In the Hellenistic world the situation was even more clearly in the favor of the continual attribution of new teachings to a founder-teacher. That is because the standard practice in any school tradition was to enlarge and refine the school's teachings by reworking the collection of sayings attributed to the founder of the school. And since biographical data were only "recorded" in oral lore and snippets of anecdotal reminiscence, it was very easy to reshape the profile of an honored founder-teacher of the past to match newer collections of teachings attributed to him within a growing school tradition. Students learned how to do that in school because the matter of first importance was the teaching, not the historical teacher, and the matter of second importance was to imagine that the teacher had actually lived in accordance with his teaching. That correspondence between espousal and deed was the way the ancients judged the character of a person and marked an important figure of the past for honor. From our modern point of view, the images of Jesus we shall encounter may seem to be confused combinations of memory and imagination, and it may trouble us that they cannot be made to agree at the level of "historical" memory. What we need to realize is that the many portrayals of Jesus that explode in early Jesus and Christian literature are evidence for the rapid development of the movements stemming from him. Each group created Jesus, not in its own image exactly, but in the image appropriate for the founder of the school it had become or wanted to become.

Thus this book does not require a chapter on the historical Jesus. It will contribute to the modern scholars' quest for the historical Jesus in only one respect, and that will be to show that one social role for Jesus is more plausible than several others that have been suggested. That role is a kind of teacher, a conclusion that can be drawn from the nature of the earliest layers of his teachings as his followers remembered them. Knowing Jesus was a teacher is all we need to get started, for the story to be told is not about Jesus and the influence of his unique personality, life, and achievements. That would be to continue thinking mythically, as if reimagining the historical Jesus could put us in touch with the source of Christian faith and enlightenment a bit better than keeping the gospel picture of Jesus in mind. No. The story to be told is about the ways in which his followers honored him as the founder of their movements. It is about mythmaking and the investment his followers made in the social experiments that resulted from Jesus' teachings. The most one can say about the importance of the historical Jesus is that, in light of the discussion in chapter 1 concerning the intellectual challenge characteristic for the times, he can be ranked among the creative minds of the Greco-Roman age. But he would have been more the poet or the visionary, less the systematic thinker, for his teachings turned on insights and suggestions, as we shall see, not on strategies for promoting a long-range plan. His importance as a thinker and teacher can certainly be granted and even greatly enhanced once we allow the thought that Jesus was not a god incarnate but a real historical person.

This chapter is therefore devoted to the movements that regarded Jesus as their founder-teacher and from which we have some literary documentation. It is very important to realize that these movements developed as schools of thought, not as religious communities of the kind that gathered in celebration of the Christ myth. It is also important that the picture of Jesus portrayed in the New Testament gospels be set aside. That portrayal did not occur until Mark wrote his story of Jesus after the Roman-Jewish war. We shall be looking in on Jesus movements from an earlier period when memory and imagination worked only with sayings, teachings, and anecdotes to develop the voice and character of the founder of their schools.

THE SAYINGS GOSPEL Q

Q will put us in touch with the first followers of Jesus. It is the earliest written record we have from the Jesus movement, and it is a precious text indeed. That is because it documents the history of a single group of Jesus people for a period of about fifty years, from the time of Jesus in the 20s until after the Roman-Jewish war in the 70s. The remarkable thing about this group is that they developed into a tightly knit community and produced a grandly sweeping mythology merely by attributing more and more teachings to Jesus. They did not need to imagine Jesus in the role of a god or tell stories about his resurrection from the dead in order to honor him as a teacher. The earliest layer of the teachings of Jesus in Q are the least embellished of any of his sayings in any extant document. That means that Q puts us as close to the historical Jesus as we will ever be. Thus the importance of Q is enormous. It has enabled us to reconsider and revise the traditional picture of early Christian history by filling in the time from Jesus until just after the destruction of Jerusalem when the first narrative gospel, the Gospel of Mark, was written.

Q is from the German word *Quelle*, meaning "source." The text got that name when scholars discovered that both Matthew and Luke had used a collection of the sayings of Jesus as one of the "sources" for their gospels, the other being the Gospel of Mark. Scholars have known for over 150 years that something like Q must have existed, but they took it for granted until recently. After all, we already knew what the content of the document was, for the teachings from it were right there in the gospels of Matthew and Luke. And besides, since we did not have an independent manuscript of Q, that having been lost in the shuffle early in the second century, extremely detailed knowledge of both Matthew and Luke would be necessary should one want to reconstruct the original text they had in common. One would have to line up the sayings from Matthew and Luke in parallel columns and decide between them in cases where the wording differed slightly. What a surprise it was, then, when a few scholars got curious, started to reconstruct a unified text, and took a close look at Q as a piece of literature all its own, a piece of literature that had sustained a Jesus movement for half a century before Matthew and Luke ever thought to merge it with Mark's story of Jesus. Voilà. An entirely different world of Christian beginnings came into view. I have told that story in my book *The Lost Gospel* (1993), where the reader will find an English translation of the text of Q and a more detailed history of the Community of Q.

Since the text of Q will not be found printed separately in anyone's copy of the New Testament, I will have to refer to its contents in this book by citing chapter and verse in the Gospel of Luke. Luke is preferred over Matthew because, in the majority of cases, Luke did not alter the terminology and sequence of the sayings as much as Matthew did. I will therefore quote Luke as if I were citing Q (thus Q 11:1–4 = Luke 11:1–4). The disadvantage of this approach is that, without having the text of Q in hand, you may not find it easy to reimagine how these familiar sayings must have sounded coming from the mouth of another kind of Jesus, one that was not on his way to Jerusalem to die according to the plot of Mark's story. The Greek text in parallel columns is available in John Kloppenborg's *Q Parallels* (1988). A critical edition of the unified Greek text is being produced by the International Q Project under the direction of James Robinson at Claremont.

Q brings the early Jesus people into focus, and it is a picture so different from that which anyone ever imagined as to be startling. Instead of people meeting to worship a risen Christ, as in the Pauline congregations, or worrying about what it meant to be a follower of a martyr, as in the Markan community, the people of Q were fully preoccupied with questions about the kingdom of God in the present and the behavior required if one took it seriously. The picture is busy. People are bumping into one another in the country villages, on the road, at one another's homes, and in the towns. There are mothers and neighbors, farmers and lawyers, tax collectors and Roman soldiers, all crowding into the picture. It is a picture of life in the public arena of first-century Galilee, life defined as the encounter with other human beings in their various social roles. The people of Q were taking it on the bounce, intrigued with what happened when one chose to deviate from the usual norms of behavior and live by the rule(s) of the kingdom of God.

Recent scholarship has found it possible to identify three layers of instructional material in Q. Each of these layers corresponds to a stage in the history of the Q community. That makes Q an especially precious document, for it allows us to trace the history of the early Jesus movement through periods of change in the way it talked about the kingdom and understood itself in relation to that idea. No other text or set of texts from the first century lets us fill in an entire history of an early "Christian" community-in-the-making in this way. Scholars now refer to these three layers as Q¹, Q², and Q³. The earliest layer, Q¹, consists largely of sayings about the wisdom of being a true follower of Jesus. Q², on the other hand, introduces prophetic and apocalyptic pronouncements of judgment upon those who refused to listen to the Jesus people. And Q³ registers a retreat from the fray of public encounter to entertain thoughts of patience and piety for the enlightened ones while they wait for their moment of glory in some future time at the end of human history. An outline of Q divided into its layers of tradition is given in appendix B.

The remarkable thing about Q¹ material is that it argues for a countercultural lifestyle by turning aphorisms into behavioral prescriptions. An outrageous retort, such as "Let the dead bury the dead," can be isolated at the core of a small cluster of sayings that turn it into a principle for behavior befitting the new kingdom. In this case, the behavior recommended is that of single-minded commitment to the kingdom (Q 9:57–62). These units of composition were not completely destroyed in the subsequent rearrangements and additions to the collection, thus giving modern scholars the chance to recognize the earlier material. The resulting themes of seven blocks of Q¹ material can be summed up as follows. The first rather large unit (Q 6:20–49) consists of Jesus' teaching on such things as those to whom the kingdom of God belongs ("the poor, the hungry, those who are crying"), how to treat others ("as you want people to treat you, do the same to them"), and making judgments about others ("don't judge and you won't be judged"). The second block of Q¹ material is about becoming a follower and working for the kingdom of God (Q 9:57–10:11). The third is about having confidence to ask for God's ("the Father's") care (Q 11:1–13). The fourth says that one should not be afraid to speak out (Q 12:2–7). The fifth explains that one should not worry about food and clothing and that the desire for personal possessions is foolish (Q 12:13–34). The sixth teaches that, like weed seeds and leaven, the kingdom will eventually take over (Q 13:18–21). And the seventh is about the cost of being a follower and the consequences of not taking the movement seriously (Q 14:11, 16–24, 26–27, 34–35). If we date this material about 50 C.E., toward the end of the first twenty years of the movement, we can see what the Jesus people had been doing. They had been deeply involved in defining exactly what it meant to belong to the school of Jesus. And they had spent a great deal of thought and intellectual effort in finding arguments for a certain set of attitudes and actions as definitive for the kingdom of God. Can we sharpen the profile of the lifestyle they were recommending?

If we make a list of the imperatives that lie close to the core of the smaller units of Q[1] material, we can begin to see that a program of some kind must have been in the minds of these early Jesus people. The list includes the following imperatives or rules of kingdom behavior:

Love your enemies. (Q 6:27)
If struck on one cheek, offer the other. (Q 6:29)
Give to everyone who begs. (Q 6:30)
Judge not and you won't be judged. (Q 6:37)
First remove the stick from your own eye. (Q 6:42)
Leave the dead to bury their dead. (Q 9:60)
Go out as lambs among wolves. (Q 10:3)
Carry no money, bag, or sandals. (Q 10:4)
Say, "The kingdom of God has come near to you." (Q 10:9)
Ask, and it will be given to you. (Q 11:9)
Don't worry about your living. (Q 12:22)
Make sure of God's rule over you. (Q 12:31)

A rather risky program seems to have been in effect. If we ask about the overarching rationale for such behavior, themes begin to surface that suggest a thoroughgoing critique of conventional culture. Riches, misuse of authority and power, hypocrisies and pretensions, social and economic inequities, injustices, and even the normal reasons for family loyalties are all under suspicion. The kingdom ideal is being set over against traditional mores by directing that the followers of Jesus should practice voluntary poverty, severance of family ties, renunciation of needs, fearlessness in speaking out, nonretaliation, and, in general, living as children of the God revealed in the natural order of the world who "makes his sun rise on the evil and on the good" (Matt. 5:45; cf. Q 6:35). Quite a program. Does it make any sense?

The answer is yes, indeed. The lifestyle of the Jesus people bears remarkable resemblance to the Greek tradition of popular philosophy characteristic of the Cynics. Cynics also promoted an outrageous lifestyle as a way of criticizing conventional mores, and the themes of the two groups, the Cynics and the Jesus people, are largely overlapping. The Cynics saw themselves as "spies" on the foolish ways of conventional behavior, "physicians" whose profession was to diagnose the ills of society, and "disciples" of a simple way of life "according to nature." You can read about this in Epictetus' Discourse III, chapter 22, "On the calling of a Cynic," and in Diogenes Laertius' Lives of Antisthenes, Diogenes of Sinope, and Crates. Cynics were well-known figures throughout the empire, and everyone seemed to understand them. They were gadflies whose social critique had a point, and who made it with strikingly humorous twists of memorable gestures and sayings. Popping pretensions and pointing up the foolishness of normal standards of honor and shame were exactly what everyone expected from the Cynics. And their willingness to become the butt of their own biting but humorous style of critique had been a part of the social scene for centuries. Cynics helped the common people gain a little perspective on the way their world was working, take potshots at those in power in their palaces, and keep their sense of balance and humanity with knowing nods and humor. So people would have had no trouble understanding what the Jesus people were saying.

The difference between the Jesus people and the Cynics was the seriousness with which the Jesus people took the new social vision of the kingdom of God. This reflects the influence of a Jewish concern for a real, working society as the necessary context for any individual well-being. It was this interest in exploring an alternative social vision that set the Jesus movement apart from a merely Cynic-like call for an authentic lifestyle only in the interest of individual virtue or integrity. One can still detect some Cynic-like humor in the aphoristic style of the core sayings: "Where your treasure, there your heart" (Q 12:34); "Can the blind lead the blind?" (Q 6:39); "Everyone who asks receives" (Q 11:10). Thus the earliest phase of the Jesus movement must have been characterized by a more playful spirit than that characterizing the Q¹ material as we now have it. But the process of forming groups and taking themselves seriously as groups set a serious, non-Cynic attitude. All of the blocks of Q¹ material reveal a studied attempt to spell out a clear set of codes for the Jesus movement as a social formation, codes that rotate around the need to know who truly belonged. The instructions in Q 10:1–11, for example, are for proper behavior when representing the Jesus movement in another town. These instructions show that a network of small house groups came into existence and could be counted upon to support the movement. Thus an early period of trying out a new kingdom idea by means of a Cynic-like lifestyle had evolved into a much more complicated enterprise. The focus was not just on a list of codes for defining a true disciple, but on setting standards for recognition and authentic relationships within the community of fellow followers of Jesus. The social formation of the Jesus people and the social vision of the kingdom of God had started to mirror each other.

The mood in Q² is drastically different. The process of social formation had taken its toll. Families had been torn apart, a Jewish code of strict behavior had been held up by others to chide or ostracize the Jesus people, certain towns had told them to bug off, and some erstwhile members had decided that the stress was too much. Loyalty was now the issue, and some Jesus people had to decide between the movement and their families. Those who stayed true despite the social tensions found some new reasons for saying yes to the Jesus movement, but most of these reasons were the flip side of rather extravagant arguments as to why their opponents were so wrong. "Shame on you Pharisees. You are like graves, outwardly beautiful, but full of pollution inside" (Q 11:42; cf. Matt. 23:27). "I am telling you, Sodom will have a lighter punishment on the day of judgment than that town" (Q 10:12).

Thus, instead of a playful, aphoristic style of social critique characteristic of the earliest period of social experimentation, or even the more serious tone of instruction that defined the later development at the Q¹ level, these Jesus people had taken up a decidedly judgmental stance toward the world. Threatening apocalyptic pronounce-ments of doom were being directed against those who refused the kingdom program. It was now a matter of who was right, we or they. And the time for the kingdom's full realization had been postponed until the *eschaton* (last thing, end of history). It is ob-vious that the God who clothed the lilies and provided for the daily bread of any who asked would have to get involved with human history and its conflicts if the Jesus people were to project a future for their kingdom. But that apocalyptic future meant, in effect, yet another time of testing, a final testing, even for the followers of Jesus. And so, to the already high cost of discipleship had been added the threat of a final failure. If one's loyalty ever slackened, one might not enter the kingdom at the final judgment: "I tell you, everyone who has will receive more, and from the one who does not have, even what he has will be taken away" (Q 19:26). That some were will-ing to pay that price can mean only that the Jesus movement had somehow contin-ued to be a very attractive alternative to the social ills of the time.

The social conflicts reflected in Q^2 probably took place during the 50s and 60s, although some of the sayings are best understood as language coined in the very shadow of the Roman-Jewish war. With this kind of language ringing in their ears, the scribes in the Jesus movement had to revise their handbook of instructions from Jesus. They retained the earlier blocks of wise ethical instruction that we now identify as Q^1, for these had become the standard teaching for the community. But they added prophetic and judgmental material to match the new mood. And they arranged the new handbook very carefully, weaving the judgmental material in and out of the earlier set of instructions to give the impression that the earlier material had originally been given with the final judgment in mind. This design is high-lighted in the outline of Q in appendix B. However, two conceptual problems had to be solved in order to make such a revision work. One was that the Jesus people were accustomed to thinking of Jesus as a wisdom teacher and now needed to imagine him as having also been an apocalyptic prophet. That required a big shift in characterization. The other was that, having experienced failure and having postponed the fulfillment of their vision until a final day of vindication, the com-munity was now in need of being very sure they were on the right track. That re-quired a much broader horizon of cosmos and history than this community had ever considered or needed.

Both of these conceptual problems were solved by imaginative revisions of their picture of Jesus and his place in the epic history of Israel. These revisions were ingenious. Their first move was to introduce the figure of John (the Bap-tizer) and let *him* step forth first as a prophet of judgment and preacher of repen-tance (Q 3:7–9). Their second move was to have John predict a certain "com-ing one" who would separate the wheat from the chaff on "his threshing floor," wherever and whenever that might be (Q 3:16–17). Then, these scribes let John and Jesus talk about each other to see what each knew about the other (Q 7:18–19,

22–28, 31–35). As these scribes imagined it, Jesus recognized John as the last of the prophets of Israel and thus the "one to come," and John predicted an even "greater" one to come, who, of course, was Jesus. Jesus was "greater," according to the scribes, because he was both a sage *and* a prophet. He was a sage by virtue of his Q^1 teachings. He was a prophet by virtue of the apocalyptic judgments that soon would be heard from his lips. The astonishing possibility given with this simple bit of imaginary history was that, as the child of wisdom, Jesus could know what God had wanted from the beginning of creation. And as an apocalyptic prophet, he could know what would happen at the end of time. Result: Jesus became the seer of history past and the prophet of history's end. His followers could now be sure they were right where they ought to be, linked up with God's great plan for Israel and ready to take their places when the final judgment occurred. That imaginative solution to their conceptual problems has to be judged as a stroke of ingenious mythmaking no matter what one thinks of the myth itself. As for the historical John (the Baptizer) and the relation of his movement to that of Jesus, scholars are still puzzling over several options. The important thing for our purposes is that John entered the picture of the Q community's imagination of Jesus at a second stage of mythmaking in order to reimagine Jesus' own role (Cameron 1990). With such a Jesus as one's teacher, how could the Community of Q go wrong? They already knew the standard God would use at the end of time to judge between them and the rest of the world.

The Q^3 additions were made some time after the Roman-Jewish war. They include the lament over Jerusalem (Q 13:34–35), the story of Jesus' temptation (Q 4:1–13), statements about the importance of the Mosaic law (Q 16:16–18), and a final promise to the faithful: "You who have followed me will sit on thrones, judging the twelve tribes of Israel" (Q 22:28–30). Q^3 was not a major revision of the handbook, but it did introduce a number of new ideas about the relationship of the Q people to the history of Israel, and it did upgrade the mythology of Jesus to the level of a divine being who could be imagined talking to God as his Father and debating with Satan as his tempter. The topic in both cases was Jesus' own "authority over all the world" (Q 4:6–7). It seems that the dust had settled from the Q^2 period and that the people of Q had toned down their sharp responses to those who were critical of them. Perhaps the war had taken care of erstwhile antagonists or changed the social landscape so drastically that the prewar stance of the movement now looked silly even to the Jesus people. In any case, the book of Q received a few additions that dulled the radical edge of the earlier material and made a kind of peace with more traditional ways of being the people of God while waiting for the kingdom. It was the book of Q at the Q^3 level that attracted the attention of other Jesus groups, was copied and read for another generation within the Jesus movements, and was eventually incorporated into the gospels of Matthew and Luke. Then it was lost to history until modern scholars reconstructed it.

THE PRONOUNCEMENT STORIES

The synoptic gospels include many little stories about Jesus that scholars call pronouncement stories. Jesus is depicted in a certain situation; someone questions what he is saying or doing; and Jesus gives a sharp response. In most cases, these stories are embellished in order to describe the situation, explain why the questions are raised, and name the opponents. But even if the story turns into a little dialogue or debate, Jesus always has the last word, and it is frequently the case that the longer story can be reduced to a single exchange of challenge and response. Here are some examples. I have numbered them for later reference with a *J* prefix for *Jesus:*

(J–1) When asked why he ate with tax collectors and sinners, Jesus replied, "Those who are well have no need of a physician." (Mark 2:17)

(J–2) When asked why his disciples did not fast, Jesus replied, "Can wedding guests fast while the bridegroom is with them?" (Mark 2:19)

(J–3) When asked why his disciples plucked grain on the sabbath, Jesus replied, "The sabbath was made for people, not people for the sabbath." (Mark 2:27)

(J–4) When asked why they ate with unclean hands, Jesus replied, "It is not what goes into a person, but what comes out that makes unclean." (Mark 7:15)

(J–5) When asked who was the greatest, Jesus replied, "Whoever wants to be first must be last." (Mark 9:35)

(J–6) When someone addressed him as "Good Teacher," Jesus replied, "Why do you call me good?" (Mark 10:18)

(J–7) When asked if the rich could enter the kingdom, Jesus replied, "It is easier for a camel to go through the eye of a needle." (Mark 10:25)

(J–8) When someone showed him a coin with Caesar's inscription and asked, "Is it lawful to pay taxes to Caesar or not?" Jesus replied, "Give to Caesar Caesar's things, and to God, God's." (Mark 12:17)

(J–9) When a woman from the crowd raised her voice and said to him, "Blessed is the womb that bore you and the breasts that you sucked!" Jesus replied, "Blessed rather are those who listen to what God says and do what he says." (Luke 11:27–28)

(J–10) When someone from the crowd said to him, "Teacher, tell my brother to divide the inheritance with me," Jesus replied, "Man, who made me a judge over you?" (Luke 12:13–14)

These stories are quite similar to large numbers of anecdotes told by the Greeks about the founders of the various schools of philosophy. The Greek penchant for crisp formulation and clever rejoinder is obvious, as is the delight in quick wit and biting humor. Called *chreiai* (useful), anecdotes such as these were used to imagine a teacher being put to the test, staying true to his teachings, and emerging unscathed from a difficult, challenging situation. Thus *chreiai* were "useful" for composing what the Greeks called a "life" (*bios*, from which we get "biography"). That is because, beneath the humor, there was another very serious function for these little stories. The *chreiai* were capable of creating the impression of a teacher's character (*ethos*), the way in which one lived in accord with one's teaching by virtue of one's wisdom and even in the most trying circumstances. The *chreiai* created what scholars call a rhetorical situation, replete with circumstance, speaker, speech, and audience. To capture a founder's rhetorical skill and character in a single stroke with humor was quite an achievement. It meant that good *chreiai* could be used to put a school tradition on display. One can see how the *chreia* was put to work as a major building block in the *Lives of Eminent Philosophers* by the early third-century writer Diogenes Laertius, where distinctions among the various school traditions were exactly the point of a comprehensive history.

Anecdotes of the kind told about Jesus were especially frequent among the Socratic, Cyrenaic, and Cynic traditions. Since that is so, it will be helpful to compare the stories just cited with a few typical Cynic anecdotes. A game of sorts seems to have been played with the Cynics by those courageous enough to confront them. Since Cynics lived in a kind of negative symbiosis with society, espousing indifference to its conventions, but actually being fully dependent upon it for their livelihood, almost any typical situation could be turned into a trap. The trick was to catch the Cynic in some inadvertent inconsistency by pointing out his lack of complete independence from society. The Cynic reveled in these encounters, taking them as opportunities to expose normal expectations as ridiculous. Thus the anecdote was a perfect medium for distilling the nature of such exchanges. In order to win, the Cynic had to put an altogether different construction upon things as if the challenger had not understood the situation. Strategies ranged from playful put-downs, through erudite observations and insights about human existence, and biting sarcasms, to devastating self-deprecations. But the retort was always phrased with a sense of humor in order to ease the blow. Here are some examples from Diogenes Laertius. I have numbered them for reference by using *C* for *Cynic*:

(C–1) When censured for keeping bad company, Antisthenes replied, "Well, physicians attend their patients without catching the fever." (DL 6:6)

(C–2) When someone said to Antisthenes, "Many praise you," he replied, "Why, what wrong have I done?" (DL 6:8)

(C–3) When someone wanted to study with him, Diogenes gave him a fish to carry and told him to follow after him. When for embarrassment the student soon threw it away and left, Diogenes laughed and said, "Our friendship was broken by a fish." (DL 6:36)

(C–4) "Most people," Diogenes said, "are so nearly mad that a finger makes all the difference. If you go about with your middle finger stretched out, people will think you mad, but if it is the little finger, they won't." (DL 6:35)

(C–5) When someone reproached him for frequenting unclean places, Diogenes replied that the sun also enters the privies without becoming defiled. (DL 6:63)

(C–6) When asked why he was begging from a statue, Diogenes replied, "To get practice in being refused." (DL 6:49)

(C–7) When asked by someone whether he should marry, Bion answered, "If your wife is ugly she will be your bane, if beautiful you will not keep her to yourself." (DL 4:48)

(C–8) Crates declared that ignominy and poverty were his native land, a country that fortune could never take captive. (DL 6:93)

(C–9) When one of his students said to him, "Demonax, let us go to the Asclepium and pray for my son," he replied, "You must think Asclepius very deaf that he cannot hear our prayers from where we are." (Lucian, *Demonax* 27)

The Greeks measured response by its humor and cleverness, and a certain logic was involved in getting off the hook unscathed. The French classicists Marcel Detienne and Jean-Pierre Vernant have used the term *metis*, or cunning intelligence, for the kind of crafty wisdom required (1978). Whereas *sophia* was the wisdom appropriate to conceptual systems and stable orders, *metis* was the savvy needed for contingent and threatening situations. *Metis* was the wisdom practiced by rhetors, doctors, navigators, and actors, as well as any who found themselves threatened by stronger forces or opponents. *Metis* was the skill required to size up the situation, bend to the impinging forces, feign entrapment, then suddenly shift positions in order to escape or, if lucky, turn the tables to come out on top. In the case of net fighting, for instance, the weaker would feign vulnerability, wait for the opponent's overreach, then grab his net and swing it back upon him. The Cynic anecdote is an excellent example of *metis* in the genre of riposte.

The logic worked as follows. A questioner put the Cynic on the spot (C–5): How can you frequent places that are socially unacceptable (more than likely a euphemism for houses of prostitution)? The first move was to identify the issue underlying the challenge. In this case it was the notion of being "contaminated" by visiting an "unclean" place, that is, a socially unacceptable place. The second move was to shift focus and find an example of "entering unclean places" in which contamination did not occur. The sun, for instance, "enters" privies without getting dirty. The clever discorrelation between the two instances of entrance into unclean places created the humor. Explicit instruction was not the object. The interlocutor might not go away to meditate on theories of things clean or unclean. But he may well have laughed and let the Cynic go his way, or even caught the point about the arbitrary nature of the category *unclean* when used for a specific social circumstance. As for the Cynic, having accepted the challenge and having managed a momentary confusion in the logic of the situation, he was able to escape entrapment.

The anecdotes attributed to Jesus operate by the same logic. In every case the Cynic swerve is characteristic of Jesus' rejoinder. The shifts in orders of discourse are easily identified. In J–1, the issue of contamination is scuttled by shifting the focus from meal codes to medical practice. It is similar to the anecdote about

Antisthenes in C–1. In J–2 the discrepancy pertains to times when fasting was appropriate and times when it was inappropriate. J–3 rides on the distinction between two sabbath rules, one a proscription and the other an allowance. In J–4 the incongruous is created by juxtaposing meal codes with a scatological observation. It is similar to Diogenes' response in C–5, which confuses social and natural contaminations. The put-downs in J–5 and J–6 ride on the critique of common social values having to do with class. The ambiguity of the terms is used to advantage in statements of contrast, much the same as in the response of Antisthenes when told he was being praised by many (C–2). In J–7 there are two twists. One is to shift from the question of ability to a consideration of difficulty, thus appearing to say yes, the rich might be able to enter the kingdom. But the other is to use an example of difficulty so ridiculous as to say no, there is not a chance. In J–8 the political (legal) and the religious (natural) orders are conjoined in a conundrum. As a conundrum, the answer is similar to Bion's response to the question about marriage in C–7. In J–9 two notions of blessedness are set in contrast but then confused by a shift in the orders of social relationship in view. And the Jesus anecdote in J–10 is quite like a large number of Cynic anecdotes in which students are sternly corrected for some misperception and thrown back upon their own resources for seeing things more clearly and for taking up the Cynic way. A milder form of the teacher's stance toward a would-be student is illustrated in C–3.

There are many Jesus *chreiai* in the Gospel of Mark. Because of the way in which these stories end, leaving Jesus' remark as the last word on the question, scholars call them pronouncement stories. Mark used pronouncement stories to great advantage in the construction of his gospel, partly because they were the appropriate building blocks for the "life" (*bios*) he wanted to write, partly because they turned on conflict, a conflict basic to the plot Mark wanted to develop, and partly because they were the kind of story that Mark's own community had learned to tell about Jesus. A full list of the pronouncement stories in Mark is given in appendix C. Of these, twelve stories feature issues that divided the Jesus people from the Pharisees. Most of these have been identified by scholars as pre-Markan, stories that were being told in Mark's community before Mark decided to use them for his life of Jesus. These are the stories that interest us, for they make a set and can be used as a window into a branch of the Jesus movement that had run up against the school tradition of the scribes and Pharisees. In good Greek fashion, the Jesus people of Mark's community imagined Jesus as the champion of their own school tradition, and they pitted Jesus against the Pharisees by telling *chreiai*. This means that they thought of themselves as disciples in the School of Jesus.

The pronouncement stories that feature Jesus in debate with the Pharisees all address questions that have to do with purity. As discussed briefly in chapter 1, the concept of purity was basic to the Jewish system of social and practical propriety. From a large system of legal, ethical, and sacrificial law that had been developed during the second-temple period, Pharisees had succeeded in isolating a small list of ritual practices they could perform at home. These would count, they said, as full observance of the Jewish law and tradition. The list included tithing (or offering one-tenth of one's agricultural production to the priests), giving to charity (alms), sabbath observance (including daily prayers and a fast day during the week), cleanliness (or washing after activities that made one unclean), and rules that governed the selection of foods, the preparation of foods, and the people with whom one ate (or "table fellowship"). These rules should not be thought of as laws, for the Pharisees had no official authority over any Jewish institution. They were signs of piety for a progressive sect engaged in redefining what it meant to be Jewish in the shadow of the temple's end. They were, however, extremely important rules for the recognition of any Jew who wanted to be "pure," that is to be recognized in the Jewish community as loyal to Jewish traditions.

If we make a list of the issues under debate in the pre-Markan pronouncement stories, the result is a remarkable correlation with Pharisaic concerns. Note the occurrence of questions regarding table fellowship ("Why does he eat with tax collectors and sinners?" Mark 2:17), fasting ("Why don't your disciples fast?" Mark 2:18), washing ("Why do your disciples eat with unwashed hands?" Mark 7:5), sabbath observance ("Why are they doing what is unlawful on the sabbath?" Mark 2:24), and alms ("Why wasn't the money given to the poor?" Mark 14:5). There are also a number of other issues that stand between the Jesus people and the Pharisees, such as questions about the legitimacy of divorce, the payment of taxes, the Mosaic law, the basis of authority, the signs of honor, and the cause of illness and "unclean spirits." So it seems as if this branch of the Jesus movement had to work out its self-definition in vigorous debate with Pharisaic standards. Why?

The most likely scenario is that some Jesus people had continued to think of themselves as Jewish even though they were fully in favor of the Jesus movement. One can imagine the spread of the Jesus movement into the regions of Tyre and Sidon where one of the pronouncement stories is set (Mark 7:24–30). This branch must have attracted Jews who continued to participate in the life of the synagogues there, or who belonged to families who did. Eventually, however, they became embroiled with family, friends, and synagogue leaders over the issue of standards by which loyalty could be measured. The problem was that the Jesus movement was a place for all kinds of people to meet and manifest the kingdom of God, and purity codes were not thought important or appropriate. At some point the difference between Pharisaic purity codes and the "uncleanness" of the Jesus people became a critical issue, and some people had to decide whether to go with the Jesus people or give up that association. Perhaps there was a conflict of loyalties to programs sponsored by the Jesus movement and some local synagogue. Perhaps family relationships were strained because of participation in the Jesus group. Perhaps the events of social and political history, such as the approach of the Roman-Jewish war, forced the taking of sides and one's Jewish loyalties were sorely strained. It was, in any event, the Pharisaic definition of Jewishness that set the issues. Real Pharisees need not always have been around. It was what they stood for and represented that was taken so seriously, both by the Jesus people and their antagonists.

In every story, the response of the Jesus people followed the same line of logic. They said in effect, "Yes, you who are challenging us are quite right. We do violate the codes of the scribes and Pharisees. But it cannot be helped. Being 'unclean' by their standards is just the point of our movement. Our table is open to 'sinners' because the kingdom of God has to include everyone. You can call us unclean if you like, but we think we are right even though we know that you must think we are wrong. We belong to the School of Jesus, and we do have some reasons to back up our case."

So Jesus came to be imagined as the founder-teacher of a movement that had worked out its self-definition in debate with Pharisaic teachings. This gives us a picture that is quite different from the Community of Q or, as we shall see, the Thomas people, the Congregation of Israel, and the Jerusalem Pillars. A particular Jesus group, innocently and heavily invested in thinking of itself as okay by both Jewish and Jesus standards, though open to non-Jews as a matter of course, experienced a social history that forced it to clarify its position in regard to Pharisaic rules. These people fell back on normal Hellenistic practice for a school tradition, namely to attribute all their reasons for thinking the way they did to their founder. But they did not have many reasons. They had not developed any theory or myth of Jesus' authority as a divine man, savior, or martyr for the new cause. And they had not developed an apocalyptic view of divine judgment upon their opponents at the end of history. What they did was to cast Jesus in the role of a lawyer, just like the stereotype of the scribes of the Pharisees, but then enhance his rhetorical skill in order to best the scribes at their own game.

Since part of the scribes' game was to appeal to the Hebrew scriptures as precedent law, these Jesus people also turned to the Hebrew scriptures to find some arguments for their champion. What they looked for were stories that could work both ways, as embarrassing contradictions for the scribal position as well as positive precedent for the Jesus people. An example would be the reference to what David did in Mark 2:23–28. When David and his companions were hungry, he did what was "not lawful," namely eating the bread from the altar in the temple, just as Jesus and his disciples were charged by the Pharisees for "picking grain" unlawfully on the sabbath. The argument was that just as David was justified in breaking the temple law, so Jesus should be thought of as justified in breaking the Pharisees' code. This kind of reasoning was apparently the best this group could come up with.

An exceptionally irregular feature occurred when these people decided to use Jesus anecdotes to register their debate with the scribes of the Pharisees. One learned in school how to turn a *chreia* into the story of a little debate between the protagonist and his challengers. One also learned how to "elaborate" the point of a *chreia* by providing a coherent set of arguments in its favor. In this case, the arguments were one's own, not those of the protagonist of the *chreia*. As the Jesus people developed *chreiai* into more elaborate argumentations, however, they chose not to take the credit for the arguments they had found. Instead, just as with the attribution of new teachings to the founder of a school, they let Jesus take the credit both for the *chreia* and for the arguments in its favor. And it so happened that the standard outline for the elaboration of a *chreia* ended with an authoritative pronouncement (Mack and Robbins 1989). This resulted in giving Jesus two prominent pronouncements in each elaborated *chreia*, with the last statement invariably making a pronouncement on the correctness of his own views. Thus, at the end of the *chreia* about plucking grain on the sabbath, Jesus says, "The sabbath was made for people, and not people for the sabbath. *So* the son of man is [circumlocution for "I am"] lord even of the sabbath" (Mark 2:27–28, emphasis added). Thus, whether inadvertently or on purpose, the Jesus School produced a self-referential authority for their founder-teacher. At first such a picture of Jesus seems fragile, if not foolish, and the logic of such argumentation weak. Should this self-referential style of Jesus' teachings be combined with other mythic roles for Jesus, however, an extremely impenetrable symbol of authority could result. We shall see one example of just such a development when we come to the Gospel of Mark. In the meantime, how should the Jesus School now take their place in the world, having cut themselves off from a prominent definition of Jewishness, one that apparently had been important enough for them to have taken the Pharisees' challenge very seriously? We cannot tell for sure, for we have only the Gospel of Mark as the next window into their thinking. Looking through that window, however, it does appear that the Jesus School suffered a period of deep disorientation and anger in the process of becoming an independent sect.

THE GOSPEL OF THOMAS

In 1945 a collection of Jesus' sayings came to light among the Coptic-Gnostic texts of the now famous Nag Hammadi library. The *incipit*, or title, reads: "These are the hidden sayings that the living Jesus spoke and Judas Thomas the Twin recorded." The signature at the end reads: "The gospel according to Thomas." Scholars were stunned. Here was a real manuscript very much like the hypothesized Q, proving that Jesus people had actually produced gospels consisting only of his teachings. Of course it was in Coptic, and some of the sayings sounded gnostic, so at first it was difficult to see where the Gospel of Thomas might fit into the picture of Christian origins. Subsequent research has demonstrated that the importance of this discovery for reconstructing the early Jesus movements is enormous. The Coptic text is available with an English translation in a recent publication by HarperCollins (Marvin Meyer 1992). A commentary in the *Hermeneia* series is promised by Ron Cameron. The Coptic manuscript is a translation from an original Greek text that scholars date during the last quarter of the first century.

Like the Sayings Gospel Q, the Gospel of Thomas consists only of the sayings of Jesus. In both cases there is a narrative scene at the beginning to set the stage for the

rest of the document. In Q the appearance of John (the Baptizer) is used to introduce Jesus as an exceptional combination of prophet and sage. The Gospel of
Thomas begins with thirteen sayings that introduce Jesus as the source of esoteric
knowledge and that set Thomas apart from the other disciples. At the end of this introductory section there is a touch of narrative in which Jesus takes Thomas aside
and "spoke three words to him." When Thomas returns to his friends, they ask him
what Jesus said to him, and he replies, "If I tell you one of the sayings he spoke to
me, you will pick up rocks and stone me, and fire will come from the rocks and con-
sume you" (GTh 13). Despite this narrative scene, however, a scene which is not set
in any recognizable time or place, there is no biographical interest in Jesus' life,
whether in Galilee or in reference to a crucifixion and resurrection in Jerusalem.
The Thomas people, like the Q people, were interested only in Jesus' teachings.
They thought of themselves as the True Disciples of Jesus.

A comparison with the book of Q is instructive. Both documents are about the
same length and both consist of the same kind of material: pithy aphorisms, instructions on behavior, analogies and parables to explain the kingdom of God, and statements that criticize those who are in the wrong. Of even greater significance is the
fact that approximately one-third of the sayings in the Gospel of Thomas have parallels in Q, and 60 percent of these are from the earliest layer of Q (Butts and Cameron
1987; Bradley McClean 1995; Kloppenborg 1990). Since scholars have not been able
to find any indication that the Gospel of Thomas copied these sayings either from Q
or from the synoptic gospels, it means that the Thomas tradition saved sayings from
an early period when the Jesus movements shared similar teaching material. A few of
those sayings having parallels in Q are even less obviously interpreted than in Q.
However, many of the sayings are not only different from any found in Q but enigmatic and purposefully riddlelike. The conclusion must be that, like Q, the Gospel of
Thomas documents a Jesus movement with its own distinctive history.

Unraveling that history is a bit more difficult than in the case of the Q people.
That is because scholars have not yet found a way to assign sayings in the Gospel of
Thomas to layers in the history of its transmission. The collection did not grow in a
way similar to that of Q, saving entire blocks of material that belonged to an earlier
stage of composition. However, it is possible to make some observations about several kinds of material that must reflect stages in the history of the Thomas people.

Starting with the last stage of collection, it is clear that a gnostic interpretation
was intended for the collection as a whole. The first saying is about all of the sayings: "Whoever discovers the interpretation of these sayings will not taste death"
(GTh 1). One can see that the point of Jesus' instruction at this last stage of the collection was understood as some kind of enlightenment with respect to a disciple's
own destiny. Reading through the collection with that in mind, one sees that the
disciple's enlightenment had to do with understanding one's true identity as a spiritual being. If the topic is the kingdom of God, the hidden interpretation is that "the
kingdom is inside you and it is outside you" (GTh 3), or that it is "spread out upon
the earth, and people do not see it" (GTh 113). If the question concerns the world,

the interpretation is that it is a "carcass" (GTh 56), a (mere) "body" (GTh 80), or a "field" that belongs to someone else (GTh 21). Jesus himself is not a "teacher" like other teachers. Instead, those who have arrived at the true interpretation of his teachings have become enlightened just as he is the enlightened one. They will no longer need him once they have come to see the light: "I am not your teacher. Because you have drunk, you have become intoxicated from the bubbling spring that I have tended" (GTh 13). "Whoever drinks from my mouth will become like me; I myself shall become that person, and the hidden things will be revealed to that person" (GTh 108). Thus Jesus is the symbol of enlightenment, the light itself: "I am the light that is over all things. I am all: From me all has come forth, and to me all has reached. Split a piece of wood; I am there. Lift up the stone, and you will find me there" (GTh 77). This means that the true disciple must "Look to the living one as long as you live, or you might die and then try to see the living one, and you will be unable to see" (GTh 59). But "looking to the living one" is the same as coming to know one's own true being, and "When you know yourselves, then you will be known, and you will understand that you are children of the living father" (GTh 3). A disciple who comes to see that he or she does not belong to the world but to the kingdom of God becomes a "passerby" with respect to the world (GTh 42) and a "single one" with respect to union with the divine. At the end of one's life there will be a return to the kingdom of light from which one originally came into the world (GTh 49–50).

To end with a gnostic interpretation of the teachings of Jesus means that the Thomas people took a turn at some point in their history that the people of Q did not take. Fortunately for our purposes, the circumstances that accompanied that turn can still be discerned in a subtheme that courses through the Gospel of Thomas from beginning to end. That theme features "the disciples" of Jesus and the questions they ask of him, something completely lacking in the book of Q. The reference to the disciples is frequently collective. But Peter, Matthew, James, Thomas, Salome, and Mary are mentioned by name. James and Thomas serve as guarantors of the tradition. Salome and Mary say the right things and represent the True Disciples. Peter, Matthew, and "the disciples" collectively represent some group or groups of Jesus people with whom the Thomas people disagree.

Throughout the text, these disciples ask the wrong questions and have to be corrected. Two themes occur repeatedly. One is that the disciples keep wanting to know about the future, when and where the kingdom will appear, and how they will know when it appears. It is obvious that some apocalyptic interpretation of Jesus' teachings was in view. Jesus treats their interest in the future as a gross misunderstanding of his teaching and goes on to explain that the kingdom is already present. The other theme has to do with ritual behavior. The disciples want to know whether and how they should fast, pray, give to charity, wash, diet, and whether circumcision is required. In every case Jesus treats their questions as silly and then goes on to turn the mention of the practice into a metaphor of enlightened self-understanding. So, for example, when the disciples ask Jesus, "Tell us how our end will be," Jesus responds by saying, "Blessed is the one who stands at the beginning: that one will know the end and will not taste death" (GTh 18).

This material is clearly polemical. The Thomas people knew that other Jesus groups had developed into apocalyptic communities on the one hand, and what might be called Jewish-Christian communities on the other. They were at pains to distinguish themselves from both these groups and did so by having Jesus himself counter the wrongheadedness of each. In order to do that, they developed two different rhetorical strategies. One was simply the put-down: No, you do not understand. "What you look for has come, but you do not know it" (GTh 51). This strategy meant that brand new sayings had to be crafted. The other approach was to take a treasured saying that seemed to say what the Thomas people did not want Jesus to say and interpret it away from its obvious meaning. An example is the apocalyptic saying, "Two will rest on a couch; one will die, one will live" (GTh 61). In Q, a similar saying is clearly intended in an apocalyptic sense: "I tell you, on that night there will be two in one bed; one will be taken and the other left" (Q 17:34). In the Gospel of Thomas, by contrast, this saying is reinterpreted by having Salome understand correctly that the reference was not to an event of separation at the *eschaton* (end of time), but to an event of enlightenment involving Jesus and herself, for Jesus had lain with her at her table and taught her the true meaning of "die" and "live" (GTh 61–62).

Thus we can be sure of at least three moments in the history of the Thomas people. They began as a Jesus movement that may have had much in common with the earliest phase of the Q movement. At some point they found themselves taking issue with two developments that others were entertaining, the cultivation of an apocalyptic mentality and a codification of ritual activities similar to Jewish practices. Having resisted both options, each of which was linked to a different view of what the community of Jesus people should be like, the Thomas people developed an ethos of detachment from the social world and cultivated the notion of an imaginary kingdom of light as the real world. This light-realm was thought to be a haven from the vicissitudes of a world seen as greedy, violent, and destructive. Many sayings in the Gospel of Thomas see the world as a place where one could be "gobbled up" or "eaten alive." By living "from" the light and "in" the light of true self-awareness, one could realize self-sufficiency and the sense of detachment that the gnostics called "repose." The goal was to remain "untouched" by the people, events, and concerns that motivated and controlled the social world.

But what about the turn that the Thomas people took away from the people of Q and other branches of the Jesus movement? Was it any sharper than the turn taken by the Q people when they made their shift toward an apocalyptic view of history? Probably not. Both movements had their roots in the same tensive combination of ideas that was characteristic of Jesus' teaching, a call to change lifestyles and to manifest the kingdom of God. The Q people were haunted by the social vision that came with the language of the kingdom of God; the Thomas people picked up on the radical individualism of the lifestyle challenge. Neither was able to keep the original tension in balance, but both developed in ways that were understandable as responses to the troubled times.

As for the social aspect of the kingdom of God, it appears that the Thomas people must have had a sense of community despite the radical reduction of all the kingdom symbols to metaphors of inward vision. The sayings are addressed to would-be disciples in the plural; there are instructions about how to view and treat one another as True Disciples; and there are a few hints that the group was interested in the symbolic significance of some rituals, such as baptism and table fellowship. So, although we cannot be sure of their practices, the Thomas people must have met together in order to cultivate their quest for personal transcendence.

It is extremely important to see that the Thomas people developed the mythology of a Jesus movement by investing the sayings of Jesus with private and esoteric significance. Although these teachings counted as teachings of Jesus, they were actually the teachings of the Thomas community, for the Thomas community developed as any Hellenistic school tradition would have, by continuing to attribute new ideas to the founder of the school. But since the Thomas people knew that other movements held other views about the teachings of Jesus, they would have seen things differently. They would have said, "These are the hidden sayings that the living Jesus spoke and Judas Thomas the Twin recorded."

Some scholars have been troubled by the term *living Jesus*, thinking that it must refer to the mythology of Jesus' resurrection from the dead. That would mean that the Thomas people were Christians who had turned the crucified savior into a gnostic redeemer. It is likely that the Thomas people were aware of Christian mythologies, and it is possible that their use of the term *living Jesus* was intended to bounce off such a mythology. But it is not the case that their view of Jesus as the embodiment of "light," "life," and "wisdom" was dependent upon a mythology of the resurrection. The wisdom of God, a female divinity with an elaborate mythology, could "exalt her sons" (Mack 1973). And the great figures of the history of Israel, such as Moses in the eyes of a Philo of Alexandria, could easily be imagined as having been transformed into the cosmic *logos*, or a "second god," without dying a sacrificial death. So Jesus became the symbol of incarnate light and life because that is what his teachings dispensed. There was no need for Jesus to perform miracles, prophesy the end of the world, die on the cross as a savior, or come again for the final judgment. His ubiquitous presence was already known everywhere his hidden teachings were correctly interpreted.

THE MIRACLE STORIES

Mark's story of Jesus is packed with preposterous stories of miracles that Jesus performs and of miraculous things that happen to Jesus. These stories create the impression of a divine power dramatically entering human history in the person of

Jesus. That of course was the author's purpose. As in the case of the pronouncement stories, however, Mark's use of miracle stories built upon an earlier collection that had a different rationale. That rationale can be seen in two sets of five miracle stories that originally had their home in a pre-Markan Jesus movement.

Most readers of the Gospel of Mark soon notice that there are two miracle stories about Jesus and the disciples crossing the sea, and two stories about Jesus feeding a crowd in the open. Why two? This question then triggers other questions about the miracles that take place around and about these major events (Mark 4:35–8:10). Why so many? In 1970, a study by Paul Achtemeier showed that Mark had used two sets of five miracle stories, each of which had originally been intended to stand on its own. This did not immediately tell us why Mark had used two sets instead of one, but it did suggest that there must have been some rhyme or reason for the set of five stories independently of the way Mark used them to help compose his gospel. That was because both sets followed the same pattern: first a sea-crossing miracle, then a combination of one exorcism and two healings, ending with an account of feeding a multitude. The two sets are the following:

STILLING THE STORM	WALKING ON THE SEA
(4:35–41)	(6:45–51)
THE GERASENE DEMONIAC	THE BLIND MAN AT BETHSAIDA
(5:1–20)	(8:22–26)
JAIRUS' DAUGHTER	THE SYROPHOENECIAN WOMAN
(5:21–23, 35–43)	(7:24B–30)
THE WOMAN WITH A HEMORRHAGE	THE DEAF-MUTE
(5:25–34)	(7:32–37)
FEEDING THE 5000	FEEDING THE 4000
(6:34–44, 53)	(8:1–10)

We must wait for the later discussion of Mark's gospel in order to ask why he needed two sets instead of just one. For now it is the significance of the pattern that we want to understand, for it gives us another window into yet another moment of mythmaking in the early Jesus movements. At first glance these stories look like reports of miracles, especially healings, typical for the Greco-Roman age. Hundreds have been collected for comparison, and the genre in general is exactly the same, whether for the miracles from the shrine at Epidauros, those reported of the Greek god of healing, Asclepius, or those told about Jesus (Kee 1983). But then some differences begin to be noted. Achtemeier and others have been able to show that, although the formal features of the individual stories correspond to the way in which miracle stories were told throughout the Greco-Roman empires, the content of the Jesus stories had a special twist. Themes and certain details seemed to be reminiscent of miracles associated with the epic of Israel. A miraculous sea crossing and a miraculous feeding of the people in the wilderness were standard items in the story of the exodus from Egypt, for instance, and features of the three miracles in the middle of the sets made one think of the miracles of Elijah and Elisha, prophets among the people during the confusion of political powers that followed the breakup of the kingdom of David and Solomon. A survey of the Jewish literature of the period showed that references to the miraculous sea crossing and the provision of manna in the wilderness were often used to recall the entire story of the exodus. And as for the haunting allusions to the miracles of Elijah and Elisha, there is some evidence of popular lore about Elijah returning to restore Israel in time of trouble. Perhaps, so the suspicion began to develop, some Jesus group wanted to portray Jesus as a founder figure who looked somewhat like Moses and a little like Elijah.

Once the pattern and its symbolism were seen, a third observation about the miracle sets gained in significance. It was that the problems facing the people in these stories were extreme. They were hopeless cases of illness, including demon possession and death. A closer look showed that the people represented very unlikely candidates for (re)entry into the society of Israel. According to the purity system of the time, these people were impossibly unclean, either with a problem beyond remedy or simply because they were outside the boundaries of the Jewish system of classification. They include a Gerasene, a Syrophoenecian, an official (most likely Roman), women, children, the blind, lame, deaf, and dumb. None of these would have been ostracized by Jewish attitudes of the time, but all of them were off the charts whenever the priests ranked the social roles of importance for a working society (Neyrey 1986). What if the people in the stories were pictured that way in order to make a point, just as Jesus was pictured in the roles of Moses and Elijah to make a point? What would the point have been?

The point turns out to be a wondrous myth of origin for a group of Jesus people. Jesus, the founder of the new movement, was like Moses, the leader of the children of Israel out of Egypt, and like Elijah, the prophet whose appearance would restore the children of Israel to their rightful role as the people of God. But that only underscored the fact that the congregation Jesus led and cared for looked peculiar. It was made up of socially marginal people who did not fit the picture of Israel as the Jewish people. To make such an incongruous mix of people look legitimate according to Jewish standards, one would certainly need a lot of "miracles" of some kind. Thus miracles were used as a theme to associate Jesus and the people he collected with Moses, Elijah, and the people of Israel. The miracle set did so by making dramatic the transformation of these unlikely people on the one hand, and then by framing that effect with allusions to the exodus story on the other. The result was a strong suggestion that the listener or reader might think of the new Jesus movement as if it were a Congregation of Israel.

As soon as this main point comes into focus, the contours of a Jesus movement also begin to emerge. It was a movement that had developed quite a strong self-consciousness about itself as a group. The people were ethnically mixed, gathered for meals, had leaders who cared for the association and its needs, perhaps had some way of distributing food among themselves, and may have been in the process of rit-ualizing and symbolizing their common meals. Here was a Jesus movement that took a look at its members, noticed the social formation taking place, delighted in its novelty, realized how strange they must appear to others, wondered how to imagine themselves in comparison with other peoples, found the comparison with "Israel" fascinating, and had a great time trying out various scenarios before settling on the set of miracles that cast Jesus in the roles of a Moses and an Elijah.

Notice that there is no polemic in these stories, as if other ways of being or be-longing to Israel are wrong, and no claim that the Jesus movement is the only right way to be Jewish. Notice that there is no reference to a conflict that Jesus must have had with the Jewish authorities, and no need to think that these people had been transformed by the message of a dramatic crucifixion and miraculous resurrection. It was a daring combination of thoughts that produced this set of stories, but a com-bination that can be imagined for a Jesus movement in northern Palestine in need of a myth of origin. Moses was the legendary prophet-king of special significance for the Samaritan epic, and the Elijah-Elisha cycle of stories was a tradition of the northern kingdom of Israel. Moses and Elijah were not the private property of the Jews. And once the idea of using miracle stories to recast the Jesus movement as a new congregation of Israel was in place, other sets of miracle stories could be made to highlight yet other features of the unlikely congregation of the wilderness way. Mark got the picture and used two sets to great advantage for his own storytelling purposes, as we shall see. And in the Johannine tradition yet another set of five mir-acle stories with the very same pattern was reinterpreted many, many times on the way to the writing of an altogether different kind of gospel. It may even be the case that, though we lose sight of this community with Mark's (mis)use of its myth, we can catch up with a later stage in its development when we come to the Gospel of John. We shall see.

THE PILLARS IN JERUSALEM

At some point during the first twenty years of the Jesus movements, a group formed in Jerusalem, presumably made up of Galileans. They left no written records or documents that we know of, but secondary reports can tell us some things about them. It is important to reconstruct what we can, simply because the picture most of us have in mind is highly mythologized and will frustrate our redescription of Christian origins unless we subject it to some analysis.

The earliest report we have is from Paul's letter to the Galatians, written in 55 C.E. In this letter he tells of two visits he made to the "pillars" in Jerusalem for the purpose of comparing his gospel with theirs. Unfortunately, Paul does not go on to give us an account of their "gospel," but he does mention the names of Cephas (Peter), James, and John, and he does indicate the main issue. The overriding question had to do with the acceptance of gentiles into the kingdom movement, and especially whether the pillars in Jerusalem would demand that a gentile be circumcised. It is important to see that this was a question Paul himself wanted to have answered. It reflects issues that he had encountered in the Christian congregations to which he had been converted and especially in those he had founded. So we cannot be sure that the Jerusalem group had ever thought about such a problem, much less would have shared Paul's concern or interest in such a question. From Paul's report of the meeting, however, it is significant that they agreed that gentiles need not be circumcised and that their only request of Paul was that he "remember the poor," most probably a reference to themselves and their impoverished constituency. That is not much to go on, but it does allow us to think that the Jerusalem group must have been a Jesus movement, not a Christian congregation of the Pauline type, a distinction to be discussed in the next chapter.

Three features of the Jerusalem group allow us to build a profile: (1) We have the names of its leaders, Cephas (Peter), James, and John; (2) Their location in Jerusalem and interest in residing there is taken for granted; (3) And there is the (apparent) acceptance of some distinctly Jewish ideas and practices, such as the purity codes governing table fellowship. The problem of making sense out of these three features is that no other early Jesus movement of which we have knowledge shared any of them. That Jesus had disciples (or students) is an idea integral to the Community of Q, the Congregation of Israel that produced the miracle story sets, and the Jesus School of the pronouncement stories. But none of these groups mentions Peter, James, and John, or any other disciple by name. The next mention we have of these named disciples, after reading about them in Paul's letter, is in Mark's gospel, written in the 70s, and Mark's story puts them in a bad light as students who did not understand their teacher. The same is true of the role played by Peter and "the disciples" in the Gospel of Thomas. These disciples were too dense to get the picture of the kingdom Jesus painted. We have to wait for Matthew's story, written in the 80s or 90s, to find the triumvirate rehabilitated as the perfect understudies of Jesus to whom the "keys to the kingdom" were given (Matt. 16:17–19). So we do not know very much about the real Peter, James, and John, the pillars at Jerusalem.

As for other groups thinking that Jesus had any interest in Jerusalem, there are only two sayings in the material we have from the Jesus movements that bear on the question, and both are merely sidelong glances on the destruction of the temple in 70 C.E. One is the lament in Q^3, "O Jerusalem. . . . How often would I have gathered your children together. . . . Behold your house is forsaken and desolate" (Q 13:34–35). The other is the saying of Jesus that "predicts" the temple's destruction, a most problematic saying in the Gospel of Thomas because, in its Markan form, it appears to be a Markan creation (GTh 71; Mark 14:58; Mack 1988, 294). That means that the motivation for the pillars to have taken up residence in Jerusalem has to be left to speculation, for there is no indication that other groups of Jesus people made a connection between Jesus, the Jesus movement, the kingdom of God, and the city of Jerusalem.

That leaves the matter of the pillars' adherence to Jewish purity codes. Where questions of ritual purity surface in all of the other Jesus movements, the answer is the same: the Jesus people do not keep these codes. There is, in fact, a tendency to take pride in rejecting such an approach to group respectability and self-definition. So what are we to make of the fact that the pillars were on the other side of the issue?

It is extremely difficult to understand what the Jerusalem group may have been thinking. There is nothing in the teachings of Jesus or in the early stories about him that would suggest a motivation for Jesus and his disciples going to Jerusalem in the first place, much less for Galileans to move there after Jesus was gone. Mark's story does not help, as we shall see, for three important reasons. One is that the plot he devised to get Jesus to Jerusalem could have been imagined only after the Roman-Jewish war. The second is that, if we were to accept Mark's story of Jesus' march to Jerusalem to confront the Jewish establishment, and he was killed as a great threat to the temple-state for something as innocuous as teaching and demonstrating in the temple courtyard, it is hard to imagine why his followers would not also have been threatened or killed when they took up residence to promote his program (M. Miller 1995). The third reason Mark's story doesn't help is that, according to Mark, Jesus and his disciples were bent on violating Jewish purity codes, not supporting them. So we need to come up with some other scenario that can make sense of the data we have from Paul.

Mark was tendentious and critical in his portrayal of the disciples. That means that the disciples he had in mind must have represented a position with which Mark strongly disagreed. Might it have been a difference of opinion with regard to purity codes? In the Gospel of Thomas, Peter and the disciples do represent interest in keeping the Jewish purity codes. And that agrees with Paul's characterization of Peter and the pillars in Jerusalem. If Paul and the Gospel of Thomas are right about Peter and purity, that would certainly fit as the position against which Mark was writing. Thus, though we have no way of knowing for sure, it seems that Peter and company simply drew a set of conclusions about the kingdom of God in the teachings of Jesus that differed from other Jesus groups.

We might note that the Jerusalem experiment was apparently short-lived. At the end of Mark's story, Peter and the disciples are told to go to Galilee, perhaps instead of staying in Jerusalem to form a Christian congregation there. Mark may have known that Peter and the Jerusalem group were no longer residing in Jerusalem. Later traditions tell of the "flight" of the Jerusalem group to Pella on the eve of the war (Eusebius, *Ecclesiastical History* 3,5,3), and Paul mentions that Peter later resided in Antioch (Gal. 2:11). As for James, it is said that he was martyred in the year 62 C.E., also during the buildup of hostilities that precipitated the outbreak of the Roman-Jewish war in 66 C.E. What we are left with are fragmentary clues to a group that resided in Jerusalem for a relatively short period of time. Piecing these clues together, it seems that James, who was Jesus' brother, together with Peter and others, made some connections between Jesus' teaching about the kingdom of God and the temple-kingdom in Jerusalem. What those connections may have been is unclear. Since they regarded the purity codes as compatible with Jesus' teaching, a position with which Matthew, writing much later, would agree, they may have appeared to many merely as a Pharisaic sect. But taking up residence in Jerusalem adds a touch of seriousness that indicates some political agenda. Perhaps they thought of themselves as a leaven, appropriately placed in Jerusalem to lift up the ideals of piety and thus contribute to its sustenance or regeneration as the city of the great king. The lament over Jerusalem in Q was written from just such a perspective, so we know that thoughts such as these were possible within the Jesus movements, even if not everyone held them. Unfortunately for the pillars, supposing that they thought Jesus' teachings about the kingdom were most appropriate for a school in Jerusalem, the destruction of the city meant the end of their mission as well.

CONCLUSION

Many other groups may have formed in the wake of the historical Jesus. The few we have discussed are enough, however, to let us see what the first forty years of the Jesus movement was like. At the beginning, Jesus was remembered as a teacher who challenged individuals to think of themselves as citizens of the kingdom of God. The concept of the kingdom of God was apparently timely. It brought people together who were aware of the troubled times and gave them a forum for both talk and action. But the concept of the kingdom, though drawing upon notions that were already in the air and thus not completely vacuous, was nevertheless vague and inviting rather than clear and programmatic. Thus the various groups that formed in the schools of Jesus were experimental. They experienced rapid change as they attracted others by their talk of the kingdom, developed their own social practices and group identities, and responded to the pressures of giving an account of themselves as a little society with big ideas. The common strategy was to attribute the wisdom they had achieved to Jesus, putting it in the form of instruction from him by revising his teachings to match the school of thought they were developing. They did this just as any Hellenistic school of philosophy would have done. And the result of such a development was that the voice and thus the image of Jesus, their founder, was repeatedly recast as well. As we have seen, the portrayals of Jesus are strikingly different as one moves from group to group within the Jesus movement.

The need to imagine Jesus as an authority for what a group had become is not difficult to understand. And the way in which that was handled by most Jesus groups, namely by attributing their teachings to him, can be explained as Hellenistic practice. But one other dimension of this early form of mythmaking is a bit less obvious and thus deserves a final observation. It was the way in which each of these groups tried to link its picture of Jesus to the grand traditions of Israel. Attributing the group's current teaching to the founder of its school of thought was not enough to grant the kind of authority required of a new movement that thought of itself as more than a school of philosophy. The Jesus movements were being guided by a comprehensive social vision to which persons found themselves granting funda- mental loyalties and from which they were demanding a full range of identification as members of "a people." To be legitimate as "a people" meant that Jesus had to be imagined as more than a teacher. He had somehow to be authorized to offer the kind of radical instruction he gave for thinking of oneself differently, as if one be- longed to a society or *ethnos* (race, tribe, nation) other than one's own. And so, for these reasons, and for others which we shall come across in the course of our inves- tigation, models from the past, both of Israel and of the roles of Israel's leaders, soon came to mind.

The ways the early Jesus groups thought of themselves as reconstituting Israel not only gave them illustrious social models to work with, but it gave them a sense of heritage as well. The ways in which Jesus was associated with images from the past not only enhanced his stature as an important person but also laid claim to the au- thority such roles had in the history of the people Israel. Although these early at- tempts to align Jesus and the Jesus movements with the history of Israel were ad hoc, experimental, and tentative, they tell us that the investments people were making in these new social formations were serious business. That is because the attempt to align themselves with the history of Israel was not a simple task. It required consider- able ingenuity. It should be seen as a remarkable intellectual achievement, for it was mythmaking against great odds, achieved under tense and trying circumstances. Sug- gestions had to click into place with only brief periods of time to test them and find them acceptable. And these mythic ideas had to be accepted not only as appropriate to the self-understanding of the group, but also as plausible. These early Jesus people were engaged in a form of mythmaking that can be called epic revision.

The revision of Israel's epic history will become a theme as we proceed with our investigation of early Christian literary and mythmaking activity. We can already see that epic revision began at a very early period in all forms of the Jesus move- ment. The Q community started with memories of Jesus as a Cynic-like sage, found it helpful to expand that to the role of a prophet, then further enhanced that role in order to account for all the knowledge being attributed to him. They ended by thinking of him as the envoy of divine wisdom and the son of God, two roles that had the effect of turning the historical teacher into the appearance of a divine being and his teachings into a revelation of cosmic arrangements. Before they were fin- ished, the Q people had positioned themselves toward the end of a sweeping view of history from its beginning at the creation of the world to its ending with a judgment scene in which either God or Jesus would use the Book of Q as the standard for ad- mission to the final form and manifestation of the kingdom of God.

Mythmaking in the Jesus School, among those who produced the pronounce- ment stories, did not proceed as rapidly or entertain such extravagant claims as within the Community of Q. Belonging to Israel was apparently taken for granted by the Jesus School, or at least had not become a serious issue for them until they ran into trouble by rejecting the Pharisaic purity codes. When that happened, they responded by thinking of Jesus as more than a match for the Pharisees. That resulted, however, in turning Jesus into an interpreter of the legal aspects of the epic in its function as Torah or constitution. They may have thought of Jesus as a super interpreter with extraordinary wisdom, but they do not seem to have gotten very far with finding precedent in the scriptures for the epic importance of such a figure, or for themselves as a legitimate form of God's people. They had just finished a round of argumentation in which Jesus won by rejecting the (Pharisaic interpretation of the) law. That was hardly a firm foundation for making a claim to be the legitimate heirs of the epic's promise. They did toy with comparing David and Jesus in the story about plucking grain on the sabbath (Mark 2:23–28) and they discovered the conundrum in Psalm 110:1 about who it was that David referred to as "my lord" (Mark 12:35–37). But forays such as these into the scriptures were desperate attempts to argue for independence from the Pharisees by finding contradictions within the Pharisees' own scriptures. The figures with which Jesus was implicitly associated, king David and a scribe of the Pharisees, actually canceled each other out because kings and scribes played different roles. They did not produce a mythic role for Jesus appropriate for the claims to legitimacy that would have to be made by the Jesus School. We will have to wait for Matthew's time before the role of Jesus as an interpreter of the law could be successfully combined with a mythology of his role as wisdom's child and both seen as a fulfillment of the goal toward which the epic of Israel had been moving.

The True Disciples who produced the Gospel of Thomas were much more interested in reconceiving the nature of the cosmos than in revising the history of Israel. But they too found it necessary to take a position against Pharisaic codes and ward off associations with major Jewish symbols such as the temple and its sacrificial system. If we note the incidence of androgynous images throughout the gospel, and their positive valence, it does appear that the Thomas people thought of Adam, the first human being, as God's intention for humankind, an ideal status that was lost when the "fall" happened as the story in Genesis relates. They had taken a big, imaginary leap over the entire history of Israel to land at the beginning when the world was first conceived in the mind of God. If Jesus' wisdom helped an individual to see himself or herself as part of the cosmos as originally designed, that must have counted as a kind of epic revision as well as a moment of gnostic enlightenment and transformation. The Thomas people had, in effect, "revised" the Israel epic by rejecting it.

And as for the myth of origin constructed of miracle stories, we have seen how different it was from either the apocalyptic history of the Community of Q, the reinterpretation of the ethical intention of the Torah within the Jesus School, or the cosmic anthropology of the Thomas community. The Congregation of Israel picked up on the exodus story and delighted in the thought that, though their group was an unlikely bunch compared to contemporary notions of Israel as defined by ethnically pure Jews, the Jesus movement in their time was like the formation of Israel in Moses' time. They seized on miracle stories to recall epic precedent and to dramatize the change that was taking place in their lives as they came in contact with the Jesus people. This challenged them to think of themselves differently, as if they had found a new social identity.

So serious mythmaking had begun. But none of these early attempts to associate Jesus with the history of Israel was systematic, as if a programmatic concept of the Jesus movement were being matched by a complex conception of Israel. They were instead suggestions based on single associations. They said, in effect, "Think of Jesus as a prophet" or "Think of us as a congregation-in-the-making on the model of Israel-in-the-wilderness." And each group came up with suggestions that differed from the others. This finding is significant. It means that the Jesus movement attracted new people on some basis other than its attempt to revise, reform, or revolutionize Judaism. The attractiveness of the movement was based on its invitation to experiment with the notion of the kingdom of God in the teachings of Jesus, and it flowed from the energies people were investing in the groups that began to form. And yet, just because the social notion had its roots in Jewish mentality and its lineage in the epic of Israel, the attempts to revise that epic in the interest of finding precedent for the kingdom of God would have to be part of the mythmaking enterprise that defined Christianity. We shall see that epic revision was a constant factor in early Christian mythmaking for the next three hundred years.

3

FRAGMENTS FROM THE CHRIST CULT

Social movements change over time. They do so in response to new circumstances and also because experience within a group often introduces new patterns of behavior and thinking. Leaders rise and fall. Moods ebb and quicken. And strategies shift, sometimes abruptly. We watch, fascinated, because living in groups defines the human enterprise, and a people in the process of changing their patterns of life and thought always catches our attention. We might learn something, both about others and ourselves. The learning would be especially meaningful if it were focused on the formation of a pristine community whose strategies for living together still haunt us as a legacy left over from the foundational chapters of our own cultural history. Such a process of social formation is exactly what we are privileged to observe as the Christ cult emerged from the Jesus movement.

Beginning somewhere in northern Syria, probably in the city of Antioch, and spreading through Asia Minor into Greece, the Jesus movement underwent a change of historic consequence. It was a change that turned the Jesus movement into a cult of a god called Jesus Christ. At first sight it is difficult to imagine that the Christ cult was at one time a Jesus movement, for the change was so drastic and appears to have happened so suddenly. But if we spread the process out, taking our time to move slowly through the complex developments of about twenty-five years of social experimentation, noting the clues that scholars have discovered for the reasons that underlay the transformations that took place, a very understandable history comes into view.

The Christ cult differed from the Jesus movements in two major respects. One was a focus upon the significance of Jesus' death and destiny. Jesus' death was understood to have been an event that brought a new community into being. This focus on Jesus' death had the result of shifting attention away from the teachings of Jesus and away from a sense of belonging to his school. It engendered instead an elaborate preoccupation with notions of martyrdom, resurrection, and the transformation of Jesus into a divine, spiritual presence. The other major difference was the forming of a cult oriented to that spiritual presence. Hymns, prayers, acclamations, and doxologies were composed and performed when Christians met together in Jesus' name. Meals and other rituals of congregating celebrated both Jesus' memory and the presence of his spirit. These features are distinctive and mark the Christ cult as strikingly different from all the Jesus movements we have observed. How to account for that difference has been our task as scholars, and we have finally learned enough to track the shift from a Jesus movement to the Christ cult. This chapter will tell the story of that transition and offer an explanation for the myths and rituals these Christ people produced.

Evidence for the Christ cult comes mainly from the letters of Paul written during the 50s. Were it not for his correspondence with these congregations we might never have known that such a cult existed, at least not at such an early period and surely not as the vigorous and spirited communities scholars have been able to reconstruct. We would not have known because even the slightly later forms of community that continued the Christ cult tradition were not able to comprehend the complex mythologies of the early Christ cult reflected in the letters of Paul, or to sustain its exuberant spirit. And had we only the early Jesus traditions from which to construct Christian origins, no modern scholar would have imagined that anything like the Christ cult would have or could have developed from them. So the letters of Paul are a precious bit of evidence for a first-century social experiment otherwise unimaginable. His letters are as important for our knowledge of the Christ cult as, for instance, the Dead Sea Scrolls are for our knowledge of the Qumran community.

However, Paul's letters tell us much more about Paul and his own understanding of the Christ than about the cult to which he was converted. So we need to distinguish between the two if we want to understand the Christ cult as a development that was already in existence before Paul encountered it. The Christ people must have been making their presence felt in a way that aroused Paul's hostility when first he encountered them. And yet, they must have been attractive enough to have occasioned his later conversion. We shall explore the letters and the mind of Paul in the next two chapters. In the present chapter it is the Christ cult reflected in these letters that we want to understand.

Fortunately, quite a bit of textual material from the Christ cult is available to us from the letters of Paul. That may seem strange, given the fact that the letters are clearly Paul's own compositions. But the happy circumstance is that Paul incorporated in his letters, not only the ideas he had gotten from these Christians, but also fragments from their literary production. These fragments of literary composition cannot be pieced together to give us a single, larger composition of any kind, so we have no composite text from these early communities. But the small units that have been preserved share a tenor and manifest other literary features such as poetic conventions that make of them a coherent set. This set of poetic fragments gives us enough information to paint a most interesting picture of the people Paul hated but couldn't resist. Because these people were the ones who first used the term *Christ* when referring to Jesus, we may think of them as the first Christians.

To isolate these fragments from the letters of Paul, one must pay close attention to Paul's own ideas and distinctive use of language. When a small unit of composition occurs in one of his letters that varies from Paul's customary ways of expressing himself, a closer look at the smaller textual unit is necessary. Especially in those cases where the smaller unit resembles poetry in keeping with ancient rules of composition, the suspicion can hardly be avoided that Paul engaged in a bit of creative borrowing to make his points. By using material familiar to these congregations, even while reshaping it for his own purposes, Paul was performing as an accomplished rhetor. That would not have been unusual for the times. As a matter of fact, using traditional material in a speech or treatise without crediting the source was customary practice for Greco-Roman authors. How to do it was taught in school, and doing it well brought high honors. Thus it has been possible to identify and collect a sizable number of small literary units that reflect the views and literary accomplishments of the Christian congregations with whom Paul was in conversation. When one looks at all these smaller literary units together, a comprehensive picture of the Christ cult comes into view.

Among those units, we find small creedal formulas about the meaning of Jesus' death and resurrection (as in Rom. 3:24–26 and Rom. 4:25) as well as highly crafted summaries of the Christ myth (as in 1 Cor. 15:3–5). Poems in praise of Christ as a god (Phil. 2:6–11) and of *agape* (love) as a spiritual power (1 Cor. 13:1–13) also occur. Acclamations ("Jesus Christ is Lord," Phil. 2:11), mottoes (such as "Everything is lawful," 1 Cor. 10:23), and doxologies abound (as, for instance, "To our God and Father be glory for ever," Phil. 4:20). And there are snippets of scriptural allegorization that reveal energetic scribal and intellectual activity (such as the allegory of the story of the exodus in 1 Corinthians 10:1–5 and that of the children of Abraham in Galatians 4:22–26). The importance of these bits of literary composition is enormous, not only because they provide evidence for the congregations of the Christ to which Paul was converted, but also because they hold the hints we need to account for the transformation of a Jesus movement into a Christ cult.

Briefly, what happened was that the Jesus movement spread to the cities of Syria, Asia Minor, and Greece, where it attracted Jews living in the diaspora as well as gentiles. Cells were formed by those who met together regularly to discuss the kingdom of God. Patrons emerged who were able to host these meetings at their homes. Following common custom for associations such as these, meals became the occasion for gathering, and eating together became the sign of belonging to the new fellowship. The new fellowship challenged erstwhile ethnic and social prejudices because its constituency was mixed, and it unleashed heady thoughts about new ways to experience human community. What if such a fellowship was exactly what Jesus had meant by his talk of the kingdom of God (or so these Christians seem to have framed the question)?

The claim was made. Participating in the fellowship that talked about the kingdom of God was the same as belonging to the kingdom of God. And that fellowship included everyone, irrespective of customary social identities. Thus a novel notion was born. It was the thought that full participation in a community might be defined on the basis of a shared social vision rather than on the traditional markings of ethnic identity and social status. In retrospect we might want to call such a thought utopian, an idealistic social anthropology with a multicultural flair. But given the social uncertainties and ethnic tensions of the times, a fellowship cultivating such a notion may certainly have been experienced by many as rewarding. It was, in any case, this feature of the new social formation that Paul would find irresistible. The way he put it, once he had gotten over his antagonism to the idea, was, "There is no longer Jew or Greek, there is no longer slave or free, there is no longer male and female; for all of you are one in Christ Jesus" (Gal. 3:28). Such a statement is, of course, pure hyperbole, but it does get to the heart of the matter (Boyarin 1994). It is a rather unguarded admission of the new community's essential attraction, and it does reveal the degree of enthusiasm possible when one accepted the grandiose claims being made.

But making such a claim was one thing, and convincing oneself and others that it was true was quite another. There were no models for such a novel grouping of disparate individuals, no names or concepts to use in defining their social entity, except for the vague notion of the kingdom of God. The first attempt to be more precise about the kingdom being the "people of God" ran into trouble. That is because this notion was rooted in the concept of Israel, and the concept of Israel belonged to the Jews. What about the gentiles? What about the erasure of ethnic boundaries? What about an ethnically mixed group being one of the attractions? How could the notion of Israel help if it made second-class citizens of the gentiles? And supposing the notion of Israel could be expanded to include the gentiles, what about the traditional codes of Jewish piety and observance? Would they still apply? Even to gentiles? Would all of them still apply? If they did not, would the new Christian community find itself in embarrassing competition with diaspora synagogues where Jews and god-fearing gentiles had much greater claim on the name of Israel? If so, how could the case be made that the Christian claim was reasonable and right? And what, then, should the codes of behavior be? What would be the distinctive marks of belonging to the Christian community? What, in fact, should the Christians be doing when they got together? The questions must have rushed to the surface and created quite a stir. Making the claim that a mixed group of Jesus people represented God's plan for restructuring human society was not a simple matter.

We have no written records of the way in which these debates were conducted. What we do have is the result of the first round of agreements. These agreements are contained in the fragments from the Christ cult to which we can now turn. The fragments reveal an elaborate mythology that may at first seem extravagant as an answer to the questions of self-identification outlined above. The mythology was rooted in the logic of martyrdom, or the Greek tradition of the noble death, but it drew as well upon a number of other myths that were current at the time. These included a Jewish wisdom tale about the vindication of a falsely charged righteous man, the Greek concepts of hero and divine man, ancient Near Eastern myths of the king as God's son, and the story of Israel as a people who lived constantly under the eye of God. The resulting Christ myth strikes us as an uncalled for overreaction. And it certainly comes as a surprise when first encountered against the background of the Jesus movements from which the Christ cult developed. But we should not let the fantastic imagery of this mythology keep us from analyzing its logic and appropriateness for the self-definition of this community-in-the-making. The myths this group borrowed were not strangers to the Greco-Roman age, and the process of merging myths to create new symbols was standard practice. So the sense we have that the Christ myth is far-fetched and thus excessive as the foundation for a group's claim to a place in the sun is best redirected. It is not only the extravagance of the myth that we should keep in view but the incredible ideal of human community it was thought to justify. The one complements the other, and both together give us some idea of the huge investment people had made to belong to the new social arrangement.

THE CHRIST MYTH

The most important texts for working out the logic of the Christ myth are found in Paul's letters to the Corinthians (1 Cor. 15:3–5) and Romans (Rom. 3:24–26 and 4:25). All focus on the significance that early Christians attributed to Jesus' death, and each brings to expression a distinctive if complementary view of the meaning of his death. Taken together, they contain all the clues we need to discover the rationale for their myth. Each deserves a closer look.

1 Corinthians 15:3–5

This fragment has been called the *kerygma* (proclamation or gospel) of the early Christian community in keeping with Paul's description of it as the content of his preaching (1 Cor. 15:1–3). He also said that it was a "tradition" he had received and passed on in his preaching. The tradition was:

> That Christ died for our sins
> > according to the scriptures;
> > > and that he was buried;
> and that he was raised on the third day
> > according to the scriptures;
> > > and that he appeared
> > > (to Cephas, then to the twelve . . .).

The first thing to notice is that this text is formulaic and carefully composed. Four events are in view (death, burial, resurrection, appearance), two of which are fundamental, namely the death and the raising of the Christ. Each of these introduces a unit of composition that offers an interpretation of the event. The two units are balanced formally, that is they are composed of lines or thoughts that correspond to similar lines in the other unit. This feature is clearest in the reference to the scriptures, which is repeated in each unit, but it is also true of the rhetorical function of each subordinate event. The burial underscores the reality of Christ's death, just as the appearance underscores the reality of his having been raised. Only in the case of the primary significance of the death and the raising is there a slight bit of imbalance, namely that the death occurred "for our sins," while the raising occurred "on the third day." What we have is poetry, and it is polished. This kerygmatic formula was not created in a moment of inspiration. It reflects a lengthy period of collective, intellectual labor, including agreements about the value of focusing on Jesus' death as the event of significance for the community, what that significance was, the use of the name *Christ* (instead of Jesus), the thought that Christ had been raised, the importance of the reference to the scriptures, and the kind of argument that would make the two pivotal events seem real (burial and appearances).

In order to get at the thinking packed into this creedal formulation, two mythologies that provide the logic underlying the entire enterprise need to be explained. One is the Greek myth of the noble death. The other is the Jewish myth of the persecuted sage, which has sometimes been called a wisdom tale. The concept of the noble death can be traced back through the history of Greek thought to its origin in the honor due the warrior who died for his country (or people, city, or its laws). With Socrates the application of the honor broadened to include philosophers and teachers who suffered banishment or death because of their teachings. In this case death was considered honorable if the teacher remained true to his teachings and died for them. This concept of the noble death was absolutely fundamental to Greek views of citizenship, honor, and virtue. It was prevalent during the first century, and examples quickly came to mind whenever a person of repute was condemned for his views by a government that found him inconvenient and sought to put him aside.

The shift from warrior to teacher enhanced the significance of the noble death by turning the person who died nobly into a martyr for a cause. The standard for assessing the virtue of such a death was a person's integrity (with respect to the teaching or cause for which one was willing to die) and endurance (or loyalty to the cause, even unto death). And so it was that martyrdom came to represent the ultimate test of virtue, and obedience unto death the ultimate display of one's strength of character. As for the cause, it also was ennobled by having engendered such integrity. Stoics, Cynics, and other schools of popular ethical philosophy claimed and cultivated the image of Socrates and other martyrs who had died for the truth of a teaching rejected by the politicians of their time. Thus the image of the martyr was available during the Greco-Roman period as a template for assessing the strength or truth of a teaching, school of thought, political philosophy, or an embattled or disenfranchised cause (Seeley 1990).

Within Jewish circles the concept of martyrdom took yet another turn. Drawing upon the older image of the warrior who died for his country and the significance of such a death as a sacrifice offered in defense of one's people, the idea occurred to some that a martyr's death might be effective. Perhaps it could actually bring to an end the circumstances that had occasioned the death and so establish or strengthen the cause for which the martyr had died. Thus the history of the Maccabees who had fought for Judean independence from the Seleucids during the mid–second century B.C.E. was gradually turned into a martyrology of the seven brothers who "died for the law" (or the land, people, traditions of their elders) and thus assured the defeat of the foreign power against which they had fought. According to the story in 4 Maccabees, the tyrant Antiochus was "defeated" because he was not able to dissuade them from violating their law, even by threatening them with death. Thus, by putting together the idea of an effective martyrdom with the memory of the Maccabees' victory against the Seleucids, a Jewish martyr mythology was produced. As the authors of 4 Maccabees put it, the martyrs "purified the land," meaning that the country was freed from foreign domination, "having become as it were a ransom for our nation's sin," meaning that their deaths exemplified and thus made possible a return to self-rule and Torah piety (4 Macc. 1:11–12; 6:28–29; 17:20–22). The language of sacrifice is purely metaphorical ("as it were"), just as the stories of their martyrdom are purely legendary. But the fact that the image of the martyr could be used to write the recent history of the Maccabees, founders of the Hasmonean dynasty that ruled the second-temple kingdom of Judea, is strong evidence for the pervasive influence of the martyr theme. The way the significance of Jesus' death is expressed throughout the Pauline correspondence is strongly reminiscent of the stories of the martyrs found in 2 and 4 Maccabees.

The Jewish myth of the persecuted sage, sometimes called the story of wisdom's child, was also popular at this time. Older variants of the myth included the stories of Joseph, Esther, and Daniel, as well as many of the Psalms that turn on the moment of rescue for the pious in distress. The plot included two major episodes. The first was the unjust charge of disloyalty that put the sage "into the hands of" a foreign despot who threatened to kill him. This was the "trial" gone wrong. The second episode was the revelation or discovery of the sage's piety and loyalty by the despot. This revelation resulted in the rescue of the righteous man and his elevation to a position of honor. This was the "trial" gone rightly, the "vindication" of his righteousness. The social history of the Jews during the late period of the second temple sorely challenged the happy ending of the old wisdom tale. But what other story was there to keep alive the hope that justice would finally prevail? And so, although honesty demanded the recognition that the righteous were not always rescued from persecution, foreign powers, and death, the tale was revised by granting the righteous a postmortem destiny and by imagining that the scene of vindication would take place at some other time and place (in some other world) after death (Nickelsburg 1972). A striking example of an elaborate meditation on this story is found in the treatise called the Wisdom of Solomon, a priceless document of Jewish thought and literary accomplishment that found its way into the Christian Bible. A careful study of the Wisdom of Solomon is indispensable for students who want to understand early Christian mythology, whether in its form as the Christ myth or as the passion narrative of the narrative gospels (to be discussed in chapter 6).

Both myths, the story of the martyr and the revised story of the persecuted righteous man, turned on the event of the protagonist's death. One sees how easily they might be combined and, as a matter of fact, some features of the stories in 4 Maccabees and the Wisdom of Solomon suggest that a tentative merging of both plots had already been imagined. The Christ myth also is rooted in a combination of these two stories, with the meaning of Jesus' death drawing primarily upon the logic of martyrdom and the significance of the raising taken from the wisdom tale. The slight imbalance between the two episodes, noted above in the *kerygma*, is partly due to the difference in the logic of the two tales. Note that the meaning of Jesus' death is said to be its effectiveness for the community ("for our sins"), while the significance of the raising is related only to Jesus' own destiny and honor.

Three features of the text indicate that the martyr myth was in mind while the Christ myth was being imagined. The first is the critical significance of the phrase "died for." It is the only indication of what the *kerygma* is about. It is the only statement of the purpose, motivation, or effectiveness of the event. Without it one would not know why Jesus' death had attracted any attention. It is not just one interpretation from among other ways of viewing his death in the Christ cult. It is the only interpretation, and it occurs repeatedly throughout the Pauline letters whenever reference is made to the meaning of Christ's death. "To die for" was a technical term for expressing the purpose of a martyrdom. It occurs repeatedly in the Maccabean martyrologies and makes sense only in such a context. It has no other meaning.

The second feature of the Christ myth that marks it as a martyrology is the fact that the purpose of the death was to achieve some effect for the Christian community as a whole. In this case the purpose had something to do with "our sins." The plural formulation is extremely important, indicating as it does that the martyrology was being thought of in relation to the community as a social unit. The aspect of the community that called for a martyr's defense was referred to as "sins." The use of the term *sins* has caused no end of trouble in understanding the *kerygma*, for it is so easily read in the light of later Christian views of sin, guilt, and the forgiveness or redemption of individuals. Perspective on its original intention is gained when it is noticed that, in other references to Jesus' death, the purpose can be expressed simply as "for you" (plural) without any mention of "sins" (1 Cor. 11:24; Rom. 8:32). What then may have been the intention of describing the Christian community in terms of their sins?

The word *sin* occurs frequently in early Jewish texts in reference to behavior that did not accord with Torah, a concept encompassing ethical instruction, rules for ritual observance, and scriptural legislation for the sacrificial system of the second temple society. *Torah* referred to the Jewish way of life, and *sin* referred to disregard of its laws, rules, or codes of etiquette. It did not refer to an individual's religious experience or sense of wrongdoing, though psychological considerations could be used to distinguish between intentional and unintentional failures to keep the conventions or laws, and violations could be ranked to indicate more serious and less serious infractions. Nevertheless, both sin, or the failure to keep the law, and piety, or the faithful keeping of the law, were objective matters, and the term *sinners* could therefore be used to classify people whose deeds or patterns of behavior were known not to correspond to Torah. One finds, for instance, that the entire priestly establishment were "sinners" in the eyes of Jews who viewed it as in violation of Torah. And one also finds that gentiles as a class were called "sinners" simply because their way of life was not governed by Jewish law. So it does appear that the use of the term *sins* in the context of a martyrology such as the Christ myth referred to the group's lifestyle, constituency, or sheer fact of existence as problematic with respect to Jewish norms. Perhaps it was all three. And as we shall see, that is exactly where the problems lay to which the Christ myth offered an answer.

The third feature of this *kerygma* that is best understood as part of a martyrology is the reference to Christ's being "raised." The Greek word for *raised* had no mythological connotation. Heroes and divine men became gods in other ways, and people entered the afterlife without resurrections. *To raise* meant only to awaken someone from sleep or get someone up. Used here as a euphemism to bring Christ back from the dead, or resuscitate a corpse, the response of most people, including both Jews and Greeks, would have been "What?" (or worse, perhaps, "Yuk"). That is because, for the Greeks, the notion of immortality did not include the body. Immortality was thought of, if at all, as a matter of one's spirit (mind, psyche, wisdom) leaving the body. For the Jews, personal immortality was a troubling idea, not easily integrated with their social anthropology, and a corpse signaled uncleanness and death. The spirits of the dead were supposed to leave, not hang around, and an encounter with a living corpse would not have been a pleasant experience. There was only one story world in which the idea of bodily resurrection was thought appropriate, and that was the scene at the end of the world where, in some Jewish apocalypses, people were raised from their graves in order to be present for the final judgment. So fright and aversion would have been the natural responses for both Greeks and Jews upon hearing about a person waking up after having been dead and buried. Why then the emphasis upon Christ's having been raised? Martyrology did not require such a sequel in order to portray the nobility and effectiveness of a person's death. And where the wisdom tale began to merge with the martyr myth, as it seems to have done in both 4 Maccabees and the Wisdom of Solomon, the postmortem vindication of the martyr was cast in terms of spiritual, not physical, transformation.

This means that the thought of Jesus' death as a martyrdom for the Christian cause forced a new and unusual thought. Martyrs died for causes already in place; Jesus would have to die for a cause yet to be realized. Martyrs died at the hands of external powers; Jesus would have to confront a condition within the community for which he would then die. And to think that both the cause and the condition were highly questionable, one characterized by sins and sinners, made the matter even worse. So using the logic of a martyrdom to claim vindication for the rightness of the cause was not enough. It had to be matched by clear signs of vindication for the martyr as well. That was a difficult assignment, for Jesus was a most unlikely martyr dying for a quite unthinkable cause. The only way to overcome the implicit contradictions was to exaggerate the drama and consider the event from God's point of view. What better way than to have God himself involved in the action? And so, since the question that had started it all had to do with being okay in the sight of the God of Israel, telling the story from his point of view was crucial. As with the mythologies of other peoples, we need not ask how the early Christians knew the mind of God in the matter. The important thing is to see just how integral this theological perspective was to the making of the myth. Four features of the *kerygma* are direct results of this imagination.

One aspect of the myth's theology is the use of the term *Christ*, meaning that Jesus was imagined as having been "anointed" or approved by God for divine service (*christos* being a translation of *messiah*, meaning anointed, a mark of dedication to an office or social role, such as that of a prophet, priest, or king). Another is the characterization of the community as "sinners," a category that focused on its standing before God. A third is the appeal to "the scriptures," an implicit claim that the marvelous events of the Christ were fully in keeping with the way in which God had designed and engaged the history of his people. And the fourth is that this God had proven his approval of both Jesus and Jesus' cause by raising him from the dead. The passive "he was raised" contrasts with the active "he died for," indicating that considerable thought had been given to matters of agency in the drama. In the case of Jesus, his motivation was the important consideration, while God's involvement called for a demonstration of divine power and activity. It was that need to imagine God's involvement in an otherwise implausible martyrdom for a very problematic cause that resulted in the odd and grotesque notion of God raising Jesus from the dead. As we shall see, the myth of Jesus' resurrection achieved its purpose and became a winner, but not a single early Christian community was satisfied to leave it at the literal level. It was much too gross for that, and besides, the real stakes had little to do with questions about ghosts and bodies. What mattered was the cause for which Jesus Christ had died.

Romans 3:21–26

This text from Paul's letter to the Romans puts us in touch with a very early period in the development of the Christ myth. It documents a stage in the thinking of the first Christians that predates the refined formulations of the *kerygma*. The death of Jesus was in view, and its significance as a martyrdom had been worked out without any need to imagine a resurrection. Paul found the formulation of these ideas much to his liking, and he all but erased the original saying in the way in which he cited it. Fortunately, scholars have been able to reconstruct the gist of the pre-Pauline fragment. I cite the reconstruction worked out in a detailed study by Sam Williams (1975). The parentheses are his; I have added the material in brackets for clarity:

> In times past God overlooked the sins of the gentiles.
>> But now God has regarded Jesus' death as a means of expiation because of his faith(fulness).
> He [God] did this to show his righteousness,
>> and to justify (or make righteous) the one whose faith[fulness] stems from Jesus' own faith(fulness).

Four ideas converge in this interpretation of Jesus' death. The first is that God took note of the problem facing the new community, namely that the inclusion of gentiles had to be justified. The second is that God worked it out by regarding Jesus' death as an expiation for their sins. The third is that the effectiveness of Jesus' death was due to his faith(fulness). And the fourth is that one who learns to be faithful on the model of Jesus' faithfulness is justified in the sight of God.

The logic of this mythology is extremely interesting. It is based on a martyrology, for Jesus is said to have been "faithful," and the word for that is *pistis*, a term that occurs in the stories of the martyrs to express their essential virtue. It means something like "committed," and, along with the term *endurance*, refers to the martyr's steadfastness even in the face of death. The cause to which Jesus was faithful is not expressed, but it is possible that the early Christians started down this line of thought by imagining Jesus to have been loyal to his own teachings and/or vision of the kingdom of God. That would have been an easy step to take, imagining the manner of death befitting a founder figure whose integrity was unquestioned. If so, we can see how the transition from a Jesus movement to the Christ myth may have been accomplished. In any case, this early martyrology is about Jesus, not the Christ. The factor that turned his martyrdom into an event that justified the new community, and so allowed the thought that the new community was the cause for which he had died, was derived not from Jesus' own intentions, but from the way in which God was understood to have viewed the event. Being sure of that must have taken some long and hard thinking. But the important words were there to work it out.

The terms settled upon for justifying the inclusion of gentiles in a movement that thought of itself on the model of Israel, the people of God, were *sins* and *righteousness*. As we have seen, *sinners* was a generic designation for any and all who did not live according to Jewish standards of piety. Those who did were called the righteous. Thus the terms worked as a pair and could distinguish Jew from gentile with respect to acceptance or nonacceptance of Jewish laws as the standard for righteousness. As such, the terms were completely appropriate to the situation of a group troubled about its mixed constituency. All we need to do is see that the words for *righteous*, *righteousness*, and *justify* (acquit as righteous), the terms that are used in this mythology to register God's judgment upon the community, are all cognates of the Greek *dikaios*, meaning "lawful" or "right." The image was that of a trial in which God, the righteous judge, "vindicated" the gentiles as rightful members of the community if only they regarded Jesus' death as the mythology portrayed it. We begin to see something of the power of this persuasion that caught Paul's attention. These, at least, are the very terms of the argument that Paul would embellish as his gospel.

The notion of sacrifice is also present. This adds yet another nuance to the imagery, building upon the "sacrificial" aspect of a martyr's death by using metaphors from the sacrificial system of the second temple. To integrate the logic of temple sacrifice to that of the council chambers of God was a deft move, for the argument now encompassed the entire horizon of Jewish theology, at least with respect to God's role in the social and religious history of his people. The only notion of God not yet tapped for the new mythology was that of God the creator and ruler of the cosmic order, but that was soon to follow. As noted above, the Maccabean martyrologies also used metaphors of sacrifice from the temple cult to describe the effectiveness of the martyrs' deaths, including *purification, ransom, propitiation,* and *sacrifice*. The problem underlying the situation was twofold. The more obvious was that a foreign power threatened the purity of the temple-state. The other problem was that the "nation's sin" had allowed the foreign power to enter the land. By analogy, it is possible that the "sins" of the Christian community for which Christ died, as the *kerygma* would express it, were also understood to implicate both Jews and gentiles. This, at any rate, is what Paul would argue.

The essential logic of the Christ myth should now be clear, and the intellectual labor invested in its construction should be obvious. It was not a product of playful speculation, the fantasy of unbridled imagination, or based on the personal religious experience of mystics. It was hard work in the interest of a social experiment thought to be worth the effort. The myth was generated by the need to justify a fundamental feature of the group's constitution that threatened its sense of rightly representing the kingdom of God. It was put together by merging mythologies with which both these Christians and their potential critics were familiar, mythologies that were most appropriate for the issues in need of resolution. We have not yet caught sight of the cultic consequences of this mythology, but we can already sense the potential it had for thinking further about the divine status of the transformed Jesus. We see the myth developing just at that point where a Jesus movement was turning into a cult of the Christ. The need to justify the inclusion of gentiles called forth a venture in mythmaking that shifted attention away from Jesus the teacher and his teachings to focus on his death as a dramatic event that established the movement's claim to be the people of God.

We may now look in on one of the activities of the new community, its practice of meeting together for meals. But before we do, the point should be made that the

Christ myth was not a narrative of Jesus' passion as we find in the later gospels. As a martyrology, and especially in its kergymatic form, the Christ myth does have the potential for becoming a story. But its first conception had little to do with historical reminiscence and no interest at all in setting the event in any historical context. Only the figure of Jesus, the indications of his martyrdom, God's involvement in the event, and its meaning for the community are of interest and in view. To imagine more would rob the *kerygma* of its logic. It would, in fact, destroy its logic. Given the purpose of the myth, any fleshing out of the story to include the social circumstances that led to Jesus' death, who put him to death, why they did so, and what happened to Jesus and those around him would have turned the rehearsal of the Christ myth into a forum for political debate with ethnic distinctions and questions of blame dangerously close to the surface. These were the very issues the myth was designed to overcome. Thus only the motivations of God and his martyr were allowed to play any role in this story. There is not the slightest hint in any text of the Pauline corpus that he or the Christians to which he was converted thought of Jesus or themselves in opposition to the temple establishment in Jerusalem, as Mark will say in his gospel. The *kerygma* and the passion narrative of Mark's gospel are two different, incongruous myths.

We may also note that, since these myths are the first references we have to the death of Jesus as a crucifixion, and since Mark's story is dependent upon the martyr myth in the *kerygma*, we really have no way of knowing anything about the historical circumstances of Jesus' death. There is no reference to Jesus' death as a crucifixion in the pre-Markan Jesus material. The one possible exception is the saying about "carrying one's own cross" in Q 14:27 (Seeley 1992). But since "the cross," among Stoics and Cynics, had become a metaphor for having one's mettle tested, this saying cannot be used as positive proof that the Q people knew that Jesus had been crucified.

THE RITUAL MEAL

Another important window into the congregations of the Christ is the picture Paul paints of the community at meal in 1 Corinthians 11. The text is familiar to Christians for, along with the story of Jesus' last supper with his disciples in the synoptic gospels, it provides the script for the Christian celebration of the Eucharist, or Mass. In the Christian imagination, the Pauline text is based upon a memory of the last supper at which Jesus anticipated his sacrificial death by giving the bread and wine symbolic meanings and instructed his disciples to continue the practice as his proper memorial (the so-called words of institution). A close look suggests another interpretation, one that fits better in the setting of the Christ cult than that of the imagined time of Jesus with his disciples.

1 Corinthians 11:23–25

This is another text that Paul called a "tradition" he had "received" and passed on to the Corinthians at some earlier time. The tradition reads as follows:

> that the Lord Jesus on the night he was handed over took bread,
>   and when he had given thanks, he broke it, and said,
>   "This is my body which is for you.
>   Do this in remembrance of me."
>   In the same way also the cup, after supper, saying,
>   "This cup is the new covenant in my blood.
>   Do this, as often as you drink it, in remembrance of me."

Astonishment may well be the first response of any modern reader of this text. Even after coming to terms with the grisly imagery and tortured logic of the Christ myth, one is hardly prepared for this shocking portrayal of Jesus calmly announcing his imminent immolation. And New Testament scholars have not been much help in making sense of it. Part of the problem is that the history of Christian liturgy and iconography has overloaded the scene with pious depictions of a totally divine persona representing absolute serenity at the thought of sacrificing himself to save the world from perdition. That image tends to frustrate critical analysis. But another part of the problem is that the dominant scenario for Christian origins automatically places this scene in the narrative context of the gospels and treats it as historical. If one does that, the task of analysis will be to imagine how it could have happened, how it could possibly fit with what we know of the historical Jesus, how his followers could have understood it, and what Jesus could have meant by it. This set of questions, arising from the assumption that it must have happened, has led nowhere. So the first thing to notice about the scene depicted in this text is that it does not make sense as history. The scene assumes that the death of "the Lord Jesus" was a martyrdom and, as we now know, that thought was an interpretation specific to the Christ cult. The scene is not historical but imaginary. It was a creation of the congregations of the Christ in keeping with their mythology. The reasons for the mythology are clear. What we now need to understand are the reasons for imagining the icon of Jesus at the table.

The place to begin is with the observation that the icon depicts a meal. Since early Christians gathered for meals, and since Paul used this supper text to say some things about the way in which the Corinthians were behaving when they gathered for meals, the suspicion would be that the Jesus icon might have something to do with early Christian meal practice. Note that the words of Jesus are spoken over the breaking of bread and the drinking of a cup of wine. Bread and wine were shorthand for food and drink, the two natural symbols that everyone used when referring to common meals. And note, also, that the text separates the moments of recognition by placing the word about the bread at the beginning of the meal, and the word about the wine "after supper." This means that the icon had its setting in normal meal practice and would have been recognized as such.

We know less about the meal practices of early Jesus people and Christ congregations than we would like. Food, begging, and eating at homes where one was welcomed seem to have been given much attention among the Q and Thomas peoples, leading one to believe that eating together may have played a significant role in their social formations. But we can't be sure. Neither do we know the circumstances under which eating together came to be recognized as a practice that defined Christian congregation. What we can be sure about is that eating together was practiced by several groups in the Jesus and Christ movements from a fairly early time. There is also evidence that some of these groups developed rather elaborate rituals and symbols by which to recognize and celebrate the significance of their gathering for a meal. The icon of the Christ congregations is not the only instance of such ritualization. And none of the others of which we have some evidence (such as the feeding stories in the miracle chains, the meal scenes in the pronouncement stories, and the liturgical prayers in an early church manual of instruction called the Didache) portray the meal as a memorial of Jesus' death. This means that we need to understand meal practice in general before asking about the particular significance given to their meals by these early Christians.

As mentioned briefly in the introduction, the Hellenistic period saw the emergence of free associations that took the form of clubs or fellowships. These followed a basic pattern of gathering for meals, conducting business, and engaging in social activity. The pattern was rooted in ancient practices of hospitality, developed by the Greeks into a highly refined and self-conscious social convention called a *symposium*. When the pattern became a model for free association during the Greco-Roman period, meals continued to be the occasion for gathering. Clubs formed with members, officers, and patrons who were able to host the group in much the same way as an estate owner or head of the household would have entertained his guests. But now membership was defined by the interests shared by the group, and these interests set the tone of the meetings. Of some importance for our understanding of early Christian practice is the fact that it was customary for an association to take the name of a patron deity ("The Fellowship of Hercules"; "The Company of Dionysos") and to acknowledge the purpose of its gathering by making some reference to the god at an appropriate juncture. At the beginning of the meal was one such appropriate moment. Another was when a round of wine was poured and toasts were to be made. It was then that a small libation to the god was in order and some form of invocation could be uttered.

It is not surprising that Christian meetings followed the same pattern (D. Smith 1980). There was no other model available. Thus we can understand the emergence of "house churches" with their "elders" and patrons, the frequency of the terms *fellowship* (*koinonia*) and *gathering* (*ekklesia*) to describe their congregations, the use of *christos* to name their patron deity, and the fact that they gathered for common meals. So all we need to do in order to understand the supper text is recognize that social formation had taken place on the association model, that meeting together had been recognized as the moment when the purpose of the group was experienced, and that the symbols chosen were natural to this setting. There is no sense in looking for the secret, allegorical meaning of bread and wine that must have evoked Jesus' words. Both bread and wine, as well as breaking bread and drinking wine, were basic symbols (of the sources of life in all its connotations) with a large range of metaphoric significance. That should cause no surprise. The reason they were taken up as symbols with a special reference was first and foremost because they were already there, repeatedly marking the significant moments of the common meal. It is not the symbols themselves but the odd way in which martyrological meanings were given to them that makes the icon so astounding.

The explanation must be that the martyr myth was in mind as the supper symbols evolved. "My body for you" contains the telltale, kerygmatic phrase "for you," and it is precisely the body that martyrological literature focused upon. It was the body, and only the body (not the person, soul, or flesh), over which the tyrant had any power. The martyrological significance of "the new covenant in my blood" is a bit more difficult to explain. But *blood* was the key term for describing the death of a martyr, and to defend or purify the people with one's blood was a way of expressing the vicarious effect of a martyr's death (4 Macc. 6:29; 7:8). In this case the sacrificial connotation of the Christ myth was expanded by association with the archaic custom of sealing an agreement (or covenant) with a sacrifice, an allusion that makes no sense unless it was intended as a reference to stories of covenants and sacrifice in the Hebrew scriptures (cf. Exod. 24:8). Apparently the earlier notion that Christ died "in accordance with the scriptures" had given rise to further research! One sees here how eager and active the early Christian imagination was, busily following the tracers that shot out in all directions once the primary associations of wine and blood, martyr and sacrifice, myth and its ritual started to spark. It was quite an explosion of intellectual energy, one that resulted in a stupendous claim, but one that was perfectly in accord with the basic self-understanding of the community and the meaning of its myth. Jesus' death was a "sacrifice" that sealed a "covenant" that founded the Christian community, and the Christian community acknowledged that foundation by making of their common meal a memorial of that sacrifice.

This does not mean that early Christians were overly sobered by the icon they created. Paul's description of the Corinthians' behavior at suppertime shows they were not. So our use of the term *cult* should not be confused with the highly refined aesthetic experience associated with the term *worship*. That was a Christian cultivation from a much later time. Nor should cult be thought of in the current sense of obsession with a charismatic leader. What the text shows is that early Christians had thought about their common meal and noticed that it was the right thing for people of the kingdom to do. They had found a way to recognize that by associating the meal with their myth. The myth would briefly be recalled at the two important moments of the afternoon's activities, and the meal would therefore count as a "memorial" of the founding event of the community gathered. It is this focus upon two moments of the meal and the symbolization of those two moments that suggests an early ritual. How that ritual was actually performed we do not know. However, two things are clear: (1) The supper texts in 1 Corinthians (and Mark) were not intended as scripts for dramatic reenactment. The notion of a priest taking the place of Jesus in the reenactment of the "last supper" did not even occur until sometime during the third century. (2) The icon in 1 Corinthians has the unmistakable marks of an etiology, a myth that tells how something happened for the first time and explains why it continues to be done. In this case the mythic features are that Jesus himself explained the symbols and that it happened "on the night he was handed over." *Handed over* was a term taken from the history of warfare and used in martyrologies to indicate the shift in power that set the situation up for a martyrdom. It did not need any narrative elaboration.

And yet, the story is about the "Lord Jesus." That makes a big difference in the way it was intended to be taken. *Jesus* meant one thing, *Christ* another, and *lord* another still. *Jesus* referred to the man that we now call the historical Jesus. *Christ* referred to the martyr whose cause God regarded as right. And *Jesus Christ* soon became his proper name. Thinking of Jesus as a lord was something altogether different. It referred to a new status imagined for Jesus as the Christ, the role assigned to him by virtue of his obedient death and subsequent resurrection. That role was one of sovereignty, a role otherwise thought of as appropriate only for gods and kings. If this supper was the supper of the lord Jesus, and if this lord was now imagined a sovereign god, we really would be watching a process that might become a new religion. That it was such a process is documented in another fragment called a Christ hymn.

THE CHRIST HYMN

Christ hymn is a name that modern scholars have given to a genre of praise poetry that apparently was quite popular in early Christian circles. There are several examples in the New Testament (Phil. 2:6–11; Col. 1:15–20; Eph. 2:14–16; 1 Tim. 3:16; 1 Pet. 3:18–22; Heb. 1:3; and John 1:1–18) and many more from later Christian literature, including rather large collections such as the Odes of Solomon. The earliest example is the poem in Philippians 2:6–11, another pre-Pauline fragment:

> Although he was in the form of God
> > he did not think equality with God was anything worth grasping,
> But emptied himself and took the form of a slave,
> > born in the likeness of humankind.
> And when he appeared on earth as a man
> > he humbled himself and was obedient to the point of death.
>
> Therefore God exalted him on high
> > and gave him the name above every other name,

That at the name of Jesus every knee should bow,
>   in heaven and on earth and under the earth,
And every tongue should confess that
>   "Jesus Christ is Lord," to the glory of God the Father.

The hymn contains two stanzas, each having three double lines. The stanzas balance one another in a pattern of composition called a *chiasm* (from the Greek letter *chi*, X). The *chiasm* was an outline whereby a progression of thought narrowed, took a turn, then opened up again, retracing the pattern in reverse order to end with a line that matched the first line of the first stanza. In this case the first stanza describes three stages in the "descent" (or "humiliation") of a person "in the form of God," whereas the second stanza describes three stages in his "exaltation" (or "ascent"). The pattern reminds one of the Christ *kerygma* with its shift from death to resurrection, but the focus here in the Christ hymn is no longer on a martyrdom. To be sure, the line about being "obedient to the point of death" shows that the Christ myth was in the background and still in mind. But reflection upon the death as a crucifixion and the resurrection as a vindication of the martyr is no longer the primary interest. (Some scholars have thought so because of the phrase "even death on a cross" in verse 8, but most agree that it was Paul who added that line.) According to the Christ myth, Jesus *became* the Christ by virtue of his obedience unto death. Here, in the Christ hymn, Jesus is the incarnation of a divine figure who possessed "equality with God" already at the very beginning of the drama and had every opportunity to be lord simply by "taking" possession of his kingdom. His glory, however, is that he did not "grasp" that opportunity (or take advantage of it for himself) but took the form of an obedient slave. Because of this, God exalted him to an even higher lordship, one that was higher than any other imaginable. This new myth with the descent/ascent pattern all but erased the *kerygma*. Instead of a martyrology, the early Christians now had a myth of cosmic destiny on their hands. Thus the poem is not really about Christ; it is a hymn about Jesus Christ as *lord*.

This is mythmaking on the cosmic scale. Throughout the Greco-Roman world *lord* meant sovereign. One needed only to know the name of the lord in question in order to locate his or her domain. The God of Israel was the lord for Jews. Serapis was the lord of his mystery cult. Other gods were lords of their people. Egyptian kings and queens ruled as lords by virtue of their divinity. And the Roman emperors, unable to withstand the seductive notion of being regarded and treated as gods, were also encouraging obeisance and allowing themselves to be addressed as lords. The poem says that Jesus Christ is the name of the lord that is above every other lord. That is an absolutely stupendous claim. Just the thought is mind-boggling. Think of *every* knee bowing, *every* tongue confessing, that the Christians' martyr by the name of *Iesous Christos* was lord of all, and that if such homage should actually happen throughout the cosmos, including the heavens and the underworld, God the Father would be pleased to receive the glory for it. What a picture!

The audacity of this poem is only partially due to the exaggerations of its imagery. In the cultural turmoil of the Greco-Roman age even the gods had to compete, and in order to outrank other deities extravagant claims had to be made. Isis, for example, claimed to be the "lord of every land," and her devotees claimed that Isis was the "true name" of every female deity with whom she had been identified in all of these lands (Grant 1953, 128–33). So the Christ hymn does not contain thoughts that others would have found strange or outlandish per se, if they were claims made in the name of a known god. The audacity, rather, was to think of Jesus as such a god in the first place. To make such claims for Jesus the martyr would certainly have turned some heads. So we need to ask what caused the thought that Jesus had been or was a god.

The clues are available in the myths that were merged in this poem about Jesus. Scholars have identified at least three mythological backgrounds to the poem. One is the wisdom tale with which we are already familiar, the story of wisdom's child who is rescued from powers that imprisoned it. That Jesus was wisdom's child was not a new idea, for it was present already in Jesus traditions such as Q, and it was also a basic ingredient of the kerygmatic Christ myth. In the Jesus traditions, the idea of Jesus as wisdom's child was not part of a martyrology. It was based on the range of his knowledge, knowledge that only a divine man could have. This idea developed naturally in the Jesus movements as a result of new sayings and knowledge attributed to Jesus as the founder of the movement. In the Christ myth, a merger of the wisdom tale with a martyrology suggested the further thought that Jesus had been "faithful" (to his teachings and to God) and so was vindicated by being raised from the dead. In the Philippians hymn we see that the additional step was taken to think of his postmortem destiny as an "exaltation" to a position of sovereignty. This thought would not have been completely outrageous for people accustomed to the wisdom tale. In the Wisdom of Solomon there are some examples of the wisdom tale that take this form (Wisdom 10). But that does not tell us why these early Christians would have wanted to press the wisdom tale so far.

A second mythology in play was a romantic picture about the ideal king or ruler. According to this romance, one that developed during the Hellenistic period, the "true" ruler would not take advantage of his godly appearance and power, but would set them aside in order to "serve" the interests of his people. In the Christ hymn, the references to "appearance," "form," "grasping," "emptying," "obeisance," "exaltation," and "ruling" have all been traced to this royal romance. For a ruler to have the "appearance" of a god was a common notion. There are even descriptions of some rulers who actually dressed like slaves and mingled with their people as a way to enact the romantic ideal (Seeley, "Philippians Hymn" 1994). Note that the royal romance shares the pattern of humiliation/exaltation with the wisdom tale.

A third source for the Christ hymn was a pattern of myth common to most cultures of the time, namely that the gods would descend from heaven, appear to persons as messengers, and then return to heaven. In gnostic mythology this pattern was highly developed. The son of the high god, sometimes called a "second god," would be sent to earth, appear to the chosen as a guide or teacher of the "way" through the world, and then return to his father where he might well inherit his father's kingdom. The myth in the Christ hymn is not that fully developed, but ears accustomed to the stories of the gods (and whose ears would not have been?) would have sensed the common myth lurking in the background. Again, the descent/ascent pattern is the point of correspondence with the first two mythologies.

There is also the possibility that the book of Isaiah may have been a fourth source for some of the imagery in this Christ hymn (Georgi 1964). The "suffering servant" depicted in Isaiah 52:13–53:12 had the form of a servant, was humiliated, killed, and exalted. And the heightened style of "every knee bowing" and "every tongue swearing" closely parallels a claim made by God himself in Isaiah 45 (v. 23), a long and powerful poem about the sovereignty of Yahweh as Lord and Cyrus (the Persian sovereign who let the Jews return from Babylon) as the Lord's *messiah* (or christ).

If we see that the Christ hymn is an amalgam of these three (or four) mythologies, easily merged because they shared a common pattern of humiliation/exaltation, the thoughtful meditation that must have occurred begins to surface. The kerygmatic form of the Christ myth was enhanced by further reflection upon the transformed nature of the resurrected one. The idea that commended itself was to think of resurrection as an exaltation to a position of sovereignty. Mythologies were available to consider such a thought, and the motifs from several mythic patterns of destiny were combined in a single poem about the Christ Jesus. It was the merger of these myths that resulted in two novel ideas. One was to think of Jesus Christ as having become a sovereign, divine ruler, one who was destined to such a position of authority by virtue of his essential divinity. That happened along the way, when all the mythic beings in view, from the righteous one to the son of God, were compressed into a single figure. The other was to imagine that his realm of authority encompassed (or was destined to encompass) all peoples. The graphics for that were easy. Jesus was given a place "higher" than the other rulers, and his domain was imagined to be "larger." The result was that Jesus' position of authority now encompassed all the kingdoms imaginable within a single cosmic horizon. Thus Jesus Christ could be hymned as lord of all.

However, this clarifies only the process of mythmaking at the level of thinking about this or that arrangement of ideas to produce an organic poetic image. It does not engage the critical factors of social circumstance or group interest that may have motivated or called for such a myth. It does not yet answer the question of why early Christian congregations would have wanted to merge these myths. Thus we need to see that the Christ cult had encountered a set of embarrassing questions that called for such extravagant claims. If they were no longer living in accordance with the customs of their inherited cultures, what about their loyalty to the powers that actually prevailed? Should Christians heed the rules, rulers, and systems of authority that expected their allegiance? If not, what authority could these early Christians claim for living as if they belonged to another world, another social order? The Christ hymn was their answer to those questions. It is the song of a congregation that had come to see itself as part of a "kingdom" that was superior to and independent from the kingdoms of the world. This new myth was not a result of mere speculation or of a burning desire to have a patron deity. Neither was it the result of the personal religious experience of some visionary who may have "seen (the god) Jesus," as some modern Christians interpret Paul. No. The myth emerged while struggling with a conflict of authority. It was an answer to the burning question of who had the right to tell them how to behave, to control their allegiances and loyalties. We can be sure of this because the common denominator for all these myths was not the divinity of the mythic figures involved but their sovereignty. The very absurdity of the claim that Jesus was lord of all signals the degree of embarrassment that the question of authority first posed for these Christians.

What the Christ hymn reveals, then, is that Christians had taken themselves very seriously as an alternative society. They had thought about the ways in which their congregations differed from other social formations, and had looked for ways to say how much better their vision of human community was for people to live together in the world. The Christ hymn was the result of such critical thought. Comparing, contrasting, and evaluating were involved. Naturally, the model they used for thinking about themselves in relation to other societies was that of a kingdom. In keeping with that model, the question of authority had to be worked out in terms of the relation of their king to other kings, as well as to the world as a whole and to God. Any theologian of a mystery cult would have done the same, as Plutarch did for Isis and Osiris, for example, in his treatise by that name. And the result of such thinking would have to be expressed in terms of the position their ruler held in the ranked hierarchy of the gods and kings who presently ruled the world. Thus the Christ hymn was the result of a Christian protestation to have no king but Jesus.

But what an audacious claim! Compared with other kingdoms of the world, or even with other groups with roots in ancient ethnic, national, or religious traditions (such as the mystery cults, associations, or Jewish synagogues), these Christians were nothing more than little ad hoc cells of unlikely people experimenting with a novel social notion. They had no status, no power, no cultural tradition of their own. And yet here they were, no longer thinking of themselves on the model of an association, content to promote a teaching, philosophy, or social vision. They were thinking of themselves as congregations that belonged to a kingdom, one that was independent from and superior to all the other kingdoms of the world. Some kingdom! With a lord more exalted than the Roman emperor? Yes. With a lord as exalted as the God of Israel? Yes. Quite a claim, one that must have sounded absurd, pretentious, and downright dangerous for good relations with friendly neighbors. And yet it was just this audacious notion that commended itself to early Christians as the best way to express their identity and say what it was they represented.

To consider belonging to such a kingdom may have been a very attractive option for dislocated and disenfranchised people. Christian congregations provided a place for excited debates about the significance of this newly imagined cosmic kingdom. Questions were raised about how to understand its spiritual reality and the form of its presence in a world not yet aware of its power and ultimate destiny. It was a marvelous forum for intellectuals and poets to share creative thoughts and compositions about the event of its revelation. Sensitive souls experienced spiritual transformations. And a cult developed to celebrate their loyalty to Jesus Christ as lord.

It would be wrong to think of early Christians congregating for "worship" on the model of later Christian practice. But a sense of "knowing," experiencing, or wanting to experience the power of this kingdom as a present reality is evident. Doxologies (poetic expressions ascribing "glory to God") abound in the Pauline letters, and some of them have the marks of congregational discourse. Sometimes a doxology is appended to a short creedal statement, as in Galatians 1:3–5:

> Grace to you and peace from God our Father and the Lord Jesus Christ,
>> who gave himself for our sins to set us free from the present evil age,
>>> according to the will of our God and Father,
>>>> to whom be glory forever and ever. Amen.

There are also acclamations (such as "Jesus is Lord," Rom. 10:9), hymns to divine love as a cosmic power (1 Cor. 13), blessings (2 Cor. 1:3–4), thanksgivings, prayers, and invocations (such as "Our Lord, come," 1 Cor. 16:22). What happened, apparently, was the transformation of a Jesus movement into a religious association on the model of a mystery cult with political overtones. The lord's presence was understood to be "spiritual," easily associated with the "spirit" of the congregation, the spirited tenor of its activities, and even the spirit by which God created and continued to be at work in the cosmos. As Paul was to put it in one of his letters to the Corinthians (2 Cor. 3:17): "Now the Lord is the Spirit, and where the Spirit of the Lord is, there is freedom."

The transformation of a Jesus movement into the Christ cult, where the Christ was acclaimed as the lord of the universe, marks an important juncture at the beginning of Christianity. It was that transition that laid the foundations for a distinctly Christian mentality, a way of understanding one's place in, but not of, the world. Several notions converged in this complicated mental construct. They are: (1) the sense that the kingdom of God (or the divine order of things to which Christians belonged) was universal; (2) the sense that an actual Christian congregation was independent from its social and political milieu; and (3) the sense that some combination of Christian congregation and the spiritual kingdom of God stood over against the kingdoms of the world as a reminder of what they should be like. The startling feature of this amazing sense of presence in the world is that it did not include an obligation to produce an actual working society of its own.

PART 2

Christ and the Hinge of History

4

PAUL AND
HIS GOSPEL

After Jesus, a single personality dominates the traditional picture of the way Christianity began. This person, an intellectual Jew named Paul, looms so large in the pages of the New Testament that what he called his gospel has served for the Christian church as the definition of the new religion. Unfortunately, many scholars also continue to imagine Christian origins in keeping with Paul's views. The reasons for this impression are obvious. His (partially pseudonymous) authorship accounts for over one-half the books in the New Testament. His letters from the 50s are the earliest Christian writings for which we have manuscript documentation. These are the only texts from the first century that scholars consider authentic, which means that they were actually written or signed by the author whose name was attached to them. All the many other writings and text fragments from the first century were either written anonymously or lost to the vicissitudes of history. From Paul's letters, moreover, the first autobiographical sketch of the life and thought of a real live Christian emerges. So Paul has counted as the first convert to Christianity, the first Christian who did not know Jesus "after the flesh," as he said, and thus the first witness to the faith that must have started with Jesus' resurrection from the dead.

There are two problems with this view. One is that Paul's conception of Christianity is not evident among the many texts from the early Jesus movements. The other is that Paul's gospel was not comprehensible and persuasive for most people of his time, including many other Christians, as we shall see. For historians this means that the traditional picture of Christian origins derived from Paul's letters is suspect and needs to be revised. Instead of reading the material from the Jesus movements through the eyes of Paul, we need to read Paul as a remarkable moment in the history of some Jesus movement. It is the difference between the picture painted by the Jesus movements and the picture painted by Paul that requires explanation. The groundwork for doing that has already been laid in the last chapter. Now we need to revise the traditional understanding of Paul's own conversion, mission, and message.

Paul was converted to a Jesus movement that had already become a congregation of the Christ. That much is clear from his own account. It was, he said, a "revelation" from God that Jesus Christ was God's son (Gal. 1:12, 15–16). That must refer to the Christ myth, not to any of the views of Jesus from the other Jesus movements. He also said that before he changed his mind about Christians, he "pursued" them as a threat to his own religious convictions (Gal. 1:13). If that is so, we need to understand the reasons for his hostility and subsequent change of mind in order to appreciate his gospel and the reason for its place of privilege in the New Testament.

We may start with a clue from his letter to the Philippians. He was, he said:

> . . . circumcised on the eighth day, a member of the people of Israel, of the tribe of Benjamin, a Hebrew born of Hebrews; as to the law, a Pharisee; as to zeal, a persecutor of the church; as to righteousness under the law, blameless. (Phil. 3:5–6)

There is no reason to doubt this personal profile. Paul clearly identified himself as a Jew who knew his lineage and was proud of it. His understanding of Jewish law agrees with what we know about Jews living in the diaspora, namely that the emphasis was upon lineage and prescriptions for personal behavior, not upon the law as a legal constitution for the second temple. Paul's statement also reveals his agreement with a particular school of thought about the codes that governed Jewish piety. He was, he said, a Pharisee, which means that he aspired to the regular observance of a specific set of practices. These must have been the purity codes discussed in chapter 1. Keeping them guaranteed a person's cleanness, or righteousness. This was the mark of a Jew who was zealous about being Jewish and convinced of the importance of Judaism's presence in the larger world of peoples and cultures. That Paul announced his pre-Christian manner of life in just this way, mentioning as proofs of his piety both his hostility to the Christian congregation (*ekklesia*) and his careful observance of the law as a Pharisee, is an extremely important bit of information. We need to know only one or two additional features of the pre-Christian Paul in order to understand the significance of his conversion.

One additional feature is the degree of education or learning that Paul achieved. Judging from his letters he was highly educated, not only in Greek language, literature, and rhetoric, but also in what he called "the traditions of my fathers" (Gal. 1:14). This must have included rigorous training in the reading and interpretation of the Jewish scriptures, for he constantly referred to this literature in his letters, used it when arguing for the new Christian religion, and was polished in the exegetical methods of interpretation typical of Jewish teachers. This means that Paul lived in the crosscurrents of the two major intellectual traditions of his time and that he was thoroughly prepared to engage in thinking with others about social issues. But the more important question is what he may have been doing with his education or what his vocation may have been. The clues from his letter to the Galatians are the following: He was "advanced in Judaism" and "zealous for the traditions" (Gal.

1:14); he was an itinerant acquainted with both the diaspora synagogues in Syria and the congregations of the Christ; and he had once "preached circumcision" (Gal. 5:11). The conclusion must be that Paul was a leading figure among Jewish synagogues in Syria, conspicuously involved in their intellectual life as a proponent of Pharisaic standards.

We do not know of any office that Paul may have held as he worked to further his conservative view of Judaism, but it is not difficult to imagine that the role he played as a trained Jewish intellectual must have been similar to his subsequent vocation as a Christian missionary. That he once "preached circumcision" can only mean that Paul was actively engaged in discussions of policy with regard to gentiles joining Hellenistic synagogues. He must have known that gentiles wanted to join these Jewish schools and community centers. He must have realized how attractive Judaism could be in the eyes of gentiles because of its social values and network of synagogues in the midst of the social fragmentation of the times. We know that the gentile issue was widely debated among Jewish intellectuals during this period and that the proposed solutions were many. Paul thought that gentiles who wanted to join a synagogue should be circumcised. That was the most conservative position, and it says several things about Paul's understanding of himself and his world. Consider the problems involved in taking such a position. The first problem was that Judaism was both a way of life and an ethnic heritage. Supposing gentiles found the Jewish way of life attractive, on what basis could they hope to participate if they did not share the ethnic heritage? To make matters worse, circumcision was taken for granted as the mark of being Jewish. So how could gentiles hope to be Jewish without becoming circumcised? You can see the problem escalating. Now add the persuasion that attracting gentiles was not something that had happened accidentally because of recent social history, but that it had always belonged to God's plan and purpose for Israel. Israel was supposed to be attractive. Its destiny was to be a "light to the nations," as one of the prophets had put it. What then? Then the conservative position was inviting in one respect (nonethnic gentiles *could* become full-fledged Jews by being circumcised) but troublesome in another (could circumcision really erase an ethnic difference?). And what about gentiles who did not want to be circumcised but who nevertheless had learned to honor the God of Israel? Enter the Jesus people who had inadvertently worked out an answer to this question with their acceptance of gentiles into the Christ cult.

Paul's hostility toward the Christ congregations is thoroughly understandable, for the Christian solution to the gentile problem countered his own position and threatened the integrity and mission of the diaspora synagogue. *Synagogue* meant "gathering," and *church* (*ekklesia*) meant "gathering." Two congregations of Israel in the same town meant schism, and that was troublesome. So Paul ran into Christians on his own turf and, as he said, "was violently persecuting [or pursuing] the church of God and was trying to destroy it" (Gal. 1:13). What, possibly, could have changed his mind? Only two thoughts were necessary, one of which would have been extremely painful for a Jew such as Paul, but possible nonetheless, and the other quite attractive once assent had been given to the first. The first thought was that the Christians might be right. What *if* they were right? What if gentiles did not need to be circumcised in order to belong to the people of God? *That* thought would have been revolutionary for such a person as Paul. The other was that, if so, the time had come and the door was opened for a concerted mission to the nations. *That* thought must have been electrifying. Suddenly the importance Paul had been attaching to the presence of Judaism in the greater Greco-Roman world would have turned incandescent. Think of it. Think of everyone taking his or her place in the one big family of Israel's God without demanding that the gentiles be circumcised. Paul switched. He decided that the Christians were right and that because he had seen the truth of God's plan he was called to be the "apostle to the gentiles." It was a rather simple proposition, after all, admitting that circumcision would not really turn a gentile into a Jew and that the Christians had been right all along not to demand it. But what a new horizon! Paul's concept of Israel suddenly expanded to include both Jews and gentiles in the one great family of God.

As Paul expressed it, his conversion was radical. He described it in terms of a revelation from God that Jesus was God's son, and as a call to take this message to the gentiles (Gal. 1:15–16). It is very important to see that the "revelation" and the "call" were two ways of expressing a single change of mind. Unfortunately, the New Revised Standard Version continues a long tradition of sloppy translation by suggesting that God "was pleased to reveal his Son *to* me" (Gal. 1:15–16, emphasis added). The Greek term is *en*, which means "in" or "by means of," not "to." Instead, Paul was saying that God "was pleased to make his son known by means of me." He was not claiming a personal, private experience of encounter with God's son. He was reporting a sense of divine commission resulting from his insight (or "revelation") that the Christians' claim about Jesus had significance for Israel's mission and that he, Paul, would have to lead the way. Naturally, Paul wanted to claim this revelation as the sole reason for changing his mind about the Christians. As he said, "I did not receive it [the gospel] from other human beings, nor was I taught it, but I received it through a revelation of Jesus Christ" (Gal. 1:12). This is a remarkable statement, and it underscores the importance Paul placed upon his own personal experience in coming to his new persuasion. But it cannot be the whole story because Paul certainly knew about the Christ myth before he had his revelation. It was the Christ myth that he had been fighting against and, on another occasion, would say that he *had* "received" (1 Cor. 15:1). Thus, using the same term on both occasions (*paralambano*, receive), Paul said both that he did and that he did not receive the gospel by learning it from others. This should not be a problem for us, as long as we see that Paul's insistence about the revelation being directly from God was his way of underscoring the importance of his own change of view. It was a personal "seeing" that the Christ myth was "true."

We dare not think of Luke's account of the blinding light that knocked Paul down on the road to Damascus (Acts 22:6–11). The traditional view of Paul's conversion as a personal encounter with the resurrected Jesus is based on Luke's story, and that story is a legend written some eighty years after the event. If we want to see what Paul himself thought about his revelation and its effects, we must pay attention to his own reports. According to Paul, he waited fourteen years after receiving his revelation before making a visit to the "pillars" in Jerusalem (James, Peter, and John). He made that trip, he said, for the purpose of "laying before them the gospel I proclaim among the gentiles, in order to make sure that I was not running, or had not run, in vain" (Gal. 2:1–2). This sounds as if Paul was still actively engaged in definitive ideological debates about his gospel for the gentiles. What might they have discussed in Jerusalem?

Paul's report of the meeting in Jerusalem and of an incident in Antioch shortly thereafter mentions two issues under discussion, both of which had to do with the gentile question: (1) Must gentiles be circumcised? and (2) Should Jews share table fellowship with gentiles? (Gal. 1–2). From the report as a whole, it appears that the pillars had not given much thought to these questions and that Peter was confused about what to say and do. Paul's report of these encounters, and Peter's waffling on the issues, fits the suspicion that the Jesus movement in Jerusalem was not a congregation of the Christ cult kind. Instead, the Jerusalem group had drawn the conclusion that Jesus' teaching about the kingdom of God was best understood in combination with some form of Jewish piety. Confronted with Paul and his gentile gospel, the Jesus people at Jerusalem were extremely troubled and opposed him. Many scholars think that Paul lost the argument on both the occasions he reported, for his accounts are obvious attempts to put the best construction possible upon unpleasant encounters. What he said was (1) that Titus, a Greek who had accompanied him, was not compelled to be circumcised (as if the pillars would have wanted to do that on the spot!), and (2) that he and the pillars agreed to disagree and shook hands on it. Peter would be "entrusted" with the gospel for the circumcised (whatever *that* "gospel" was); Paul would be entrusted with the gospel for the uncircumcised (Gal. 2:3–14). If we ask why Paul felt the need to make this visit to Jerusalem fourteen years after his revelation, it does appear that Paul may have taken some time to cogitate on the Christ myth and work out the implications of its logic for his own sense of mission. He mentions going into the regions of Cilicia and Syria as a missionary sometime before the meeting at Jerusalem (Gal. 1:21–24), but we have no record from that period to tell us what he preached. His missionary activity in Asia Minor, Macedonia, and Greece, from which we do have his correspondence, began after the meeting as if that was the occasion when Paul finally decided to launch out on his own. The meeting can be dated to the year 48; his letters are all from the 50s. The point is that Paul's persuasion was the result of many years of thinking, not some mystic moment of instantaneous vision.

Paul nowhere describes his missionary strategies or activities. The traditional picture of Paul on the move, landing at the local synagogue in a new town to gain a hearing, is from Luke. In general, Luke's stories of Paul's mission are questionable. They were told in support of Luke's own theory of Christian beginnings and do not agree with what Paul says about the same places and events. Nevertheless, one feature of Luke's portrayal is helpful. It is the suggestion that Paul found his converts mainly among "godfearers," that is, gentiles who were already associated with Jewish synagogues. Since Paul does not describe his missionary strategy, we cannot be sure. But it is very difficult to imagine the early spread of the Christ cult other than among Jews and gentiles already clustered around diaspora synagogues. As discussed in the last chapter, the Christ myth was essentially a Greek answer to a Jewish question about the mixed constituency of a nondescript Jesus movement that had come to think of itself as Israel. Before the Jesus people found themselves in the midst of that Jewish-gentile dilemma, the Jesus people had not needed a Christ myth. Only gentile "godfearers," who already thought that belonging to Israel was a thing to be desired, would have been impressed with the logic of this Christ myth. And only Jews who shared the social vision of the kingdom of God as a call to expand the borders of Judaism would have been excited about the thought that God's *christos* had died for such a cause. So the Christ myth would have made most sense where Jews and gentiles were already congregating. And in that mix the Christ myth was capable of generating heat as well as light. The rub that created the sparks, both of the incendiary and the incandescent kind, was already there in the mutual attraction and resulting ethnic tension between Jews and Greeks in search of community. Paul's conversion to the Christ myth is best understood as switching sides in a social and ideological battle on the growing edge of a Judaism in the process of Hellenization. And Paul's mission is best understood with such an audience in mind. Only such a ready mix would account for the willingness of some to entertain Paul's gospel as well as for the constant rumble of others who opposed him.

In his letters, Paul poses as the founding father of Christian congregations, and it must be that he was the primary missionary for some of them. It is quite clear, however, that other leaders were also involved in the spread of the Christ cult. Paul was not the founder of the congregations in Corinth or Rome, for instance, and it is questionable whether Paul was the first to introduce the Christ gospel to Athens, Ephesus, and other cities in Asia Minor for which Luke gave him full credit. The Christ cult spread because of its own inherent attraction, and many missionaries as well as local leaders were actively caught up in the excitement. One can imagine how many solutions there must have been to the issues that soon surfaced, with what intellectual energies they were pursued, and how vociferous the exchanges of opinion were when different judgments fell. Paul is an example of an extremely intelligent, highly educated Jew who changed his mind about the Christ myth in the midst of these battles. This shows how deeply in touch the Christ myth was with strongly felt social sensibilities. A broadly based intellectual exploration was under way, and Paul's gospel was not the only one to gather adherents. As he himself reports, a full spectrum of options for gentiles was in play, from various proposals for gentiles to become Jewish to completely personalized invitations to individual spiritual transformation. The Christian combination of Jewish synagogue and Greek school, which took the form of small cells on the model of the Hellenistic fellowship (*koinonia*, association or club), apparently produced an arena for unheard-of social experimentation and a forum for the display and discussion of very avant-garde ideas. The Christ cult was not a worshiping community with an orthodox creed. It was a social space for those who wanted to create a brave new world.

In this arena, Paul's particular contribution was to turn the Christ myth into a proclamation. When the Jesus people first entertained the Christ myth, it was not intended as a proclamation to the rest of the world. It was their own myth of origin, their way of justifying what they had become as a group that had been attractive for other reasons. Paul must have understood that. When he tumbled to its logic, however, Paul could not resist seeing the Christ myth, not only as a justification for including gentiles within the Christian congregations of Israel, its original and essential rationale, but as a charge to set about expanding the very borders of Israel to include all gentiles. He construed his conversion as a call to become a missionary for this new gospel, and that resulted in the notion that the Christ myth should be taken to other people and places, that it should be proclaimed, and that the message would bring about the conversion of other gentiles. Gentiles were now to be summoned as well as welcomed into the house of Israel. From Paul's Jewish point of view that was a very big deal. It does not seem to have crossed his mind that all gentiles may not have been impressed. For him, however, the thought of a gentile mission was irresistible because it more than solved a social issue for Jewish synagogues in the diaspora by turning their situation into a historic opportunity for the glory of Israel's God. To think that the God of Israel had finally gotten his plan across to visionaries such as Jesus and Paul was already wondrous. To think that the point of the plan was a divine invitation to all the nations to join the house of Israel was simply overwhelming. Think of it! Gentiles did not need to be circumcised in order to sit at the same table with the "saints."

The slogan for Paul's gospel was "freedom from the law." By that he meant that gentiles could become Christians and join the house of Israel without keeping the Jewish law. That, of course, was bound to create trouble. Those with Jewish sensibilities were certain to take offense at the cavalier dismissal of the law. The law was the very foundation upon which the house of Israel had to be constructed. And those gentiles who may have delighted in having no law at all were sure to end up wondering why they needed to bother with such a gospel in the first place. So Paul had to battle constantly on these two fronts. That he persevered is more to his own credit as a man of social vision than it is to the logic of his proclamation. In order to make the Christ myth work as a call for Christian conversion, Paul had to perform some amazing feats of intellectual sophistry. He became, in fact, the first dialectical thinker in the history of Christian theology.

At first, the law Paul had in mind, from which Christ set one free, was probably limited to a short list of items. These were the codes of Jewish identity that created the greatest obstacles for full gentile participation in the Hellenistic synagogues: ethnicity, genealogy, and circumcision. At no time did Paul take freedom from the law to mean that Christians need not pay attention to the high standards of the Mosaic ethic for which the Jews were known and respected throughout the empire. But as his gospel gained a hearing and became the target for opposing views, Paul found himself confronted with an ever growing list of items for consideration as "laws" from which Christians had been set "free." These soon included some purity rules, such as table fellowship, as we have seen (Gal. 2:11–14), and then the feasts and fasts that marked the calendrical celebration of the ancient epic of Israel. Such feasts and fasts also kept the Christian gospel shackled, according to Paul (Gal. 4:8–11). And finally, raising the issue of law and freedom to the level of theory and abstraction, Paul actually constructed a dualistic view of the world and human existence to the effect that all things legal could be ranked as prior, and therefore inferior, to the world of Christian existence.

Our task is to follow the development of Paul's thought with regard to his gospel and his concept of law. If we do not take the time to do that, the conventional picture of Christian origins will retain its mystique and resist revision. That is because Paul's view of the world, its need of salvation, and the gospel's answer have deeply influenced the modern imagination of the Christian message. A mysterious aura surrounds the concepts basic to Paul's theology, such as law, gospel, freedom, redemption, spirit, body of Christ, judgment, and salvation. If these cannot be explained as products of Paul's intellectual labor in the interest of a particular social vision, the sense that Christian origins are really inexplicable cannot be resolved. We need to see that Paul was a mythmaker along with many other early Christian mythmakers, and that the concepts he coined were attempts to put a certain construction upon the Christian movement he had joined.

In this chapter we will look at Paul's letters to the Thessalonians and Galatians. In the next chapter I shall discuss the rest of his correspondence. First Thessalonians is important for three reasons. It is (1) the earliest document we have for Paul's activity, (2) proof that Paul was successful in his plan to proclaim the Christ myth and win converts, and (3) the primary text for the modern theory that Christianity was born of an apocalyptic persuasion. Galatians is important as the primary text for the conventional view that Christianity was born of a law-gospel conflict and that the gospel made it possible to be "justified by faith" instead of "by works." If we want to revise the conventional picture of Christian origins, we must take a hard look at this correspondence.

THE THESSALONIAN CORRESPONDENCE

First Thessalonians is the earliest letter we have from Paul, and it is the very first Christian writing for which we have an independent manuscript. From the letter we learn that Paul had spent some time at Philippi before arriving at Thessalonica (1 Thess. 2:2), after which he and his co-worker Timothy had gone on to Athens where he had decided to send Timothy back to Thessalonica to encourage the newly formed congregation in their "faith" (1 Thess. 3:1–2). The letter was written later, probably from Corinth in the year 50 C.E., after Timothy's return with the good news that the Thessalonians were indeed keeping the faith (1 Thess. 3:6–7). The letter is important, for it gives us both a sketch of Paul's missionary activity far from home and, by indirect reflection, a glimpse of the people who had been attracted to his gospel. Paul was apparently the founder of this congregation, for he refers to their becoming Christians as a result of his gospel (1 Thess. 1:5–6), and he refers to himself as an apostle of Christ among them (1 Thess. 2:7) who behaved "like a father with his children" (1 Thess. 2:11).

Thessalonica was a large, prosperous seaport on the main overland trade route from the Adriatic to the Bosporus (*Via Egnatia*). It was a thoroughly Hellenistic city, founded by Cassander, one of the successors to Alexander the Great, and it had played an important role as a city of power in the politics of the empires that had clashed during the three hundred years of its existence. When Paul arrived, it was the capital city of the Roman province of Macedonia, a city where Pompey had made his headquarters during the Roman civil war. Strong and rich, with a worldly-wise air and a mixed population of peoples and cultures, Thessalonica was apparently ready to entertain an itinerant evangelist talking about a new association that had sprouted from the roots of a known and respected ancient religious tradition.

Paul's letter is priceless evidence that his mission in Macedonia was successful. Were it not for the letter, we would never have imagined that people in Thessalonica would have found Paul's gospel attractive. That they did is evident from the signs of the Christ cult visible in Paul's offhand references to the congregation there. They were "called" into God's kingdom, had "turned" to God from idols, knew themselves to be "chosen," recognized Jesus Christ as lord, "imitated" the lord "in spite of persecution," were inspired by the spirit, regarded one another as brothers and sisters in the new family of God, and received instruction on how to live together in accord with a high standard of morality. Even if we allow for a Pauline perspective and a bit of exaggeration in the rhetoric, it does appear that the Thessalonians had formed a Christian congregation.

Paul's plan had succeeded. He had turned the Christ myth into a gospel capable of proclamation, and the proclamation had proven capable of winning adherents to form a congregation. It is the formation of the congregation that is telling, and the fact that it saw itself as the family or kingdom of God. The essential attraction must therefore have been similar to that for both the Jesus movements and the Christ congregations to which Paul had been converted, namely the invitation to join with others in the pursuit of a new social arrangement that dramatically expanded the (fictive) family of Israel's Father God. This fits with Paul's sense of mission, the urban setting of Thessalonica, and the presence of a Jewish colony there. And his emphasis throughout the letter on holiness, blamelessness, purity, and the Jewish ethical codes of sexual morality, honest labor, respect for parents, and love for "brothers" and "sisters" is exactly what one would have expected Paul to have urged upon a new congregation of the Christ.

The occasion for the letter was first of all to register Paul's joy at hearing the good news about the faithfulness of the Thessalonian congregation. But the letter also includes vague references to opposition, mistreatment, and "persecution" that both he and they had suffered, as well as questions that apparently had been raised about Paul's credibility. Whether these were flashbacks to Paul's earlier anxieties about the well-being of the new congregation or were triggered by Timothy's report is not certain. What does seem clear is that Paul learned about two additional questions that were apparently under discussion among the Thessalonians. One was the question of proper conduct for Christians (1 Thess. 4:1–12). The other was what to think about "those who had died" (1 Thess. 4:13). Paul responded by (1) commending the Thessalonians for their reception of the gospel (1 Thess. 1:1–10), (2) distinguishing his activity from the more familiar itinerant philosophers who "sold" their wisdom by flattery and rhetorical trickery (1 Thess. 2:1–3:13), (3) exhorting the congregation to aspire to a life of blamelessness and "holiness" (1 Thess. 4:1–12; 5:12–22), and (4) offering an apocalyptic instruction about the "day of the Lord" (1 Thess. 4:13–5:11). The exhortation to a life of holiness was Paul's answer to the question about proper conduct. The apocalyptic instruction was his answer to the question about those who had died.

The issues addressed in Paul's letter now begin to make some sense. Rearranging patterns of social identity around a novel religious loyalty would, in the bumpy, vociferous, catcalling world of the Greco-Roman age, naturally have created ridicule from onlookers and opposition from those immediately affected by shifts in personal relationships. Note that there is no indication of an ideological battle with Jewish synagogue leaders or other Christian missionaries (as will be encountered in Paul's letter to the Galatians). In Thessalonica it was the credibility of the novel gospel that must have called forth consternation. The question of Paul's own credibility also is closely intertwined with his remarks about those who "opposed" his mission and "afflicted" the Thessalonian Christians. He had apparently been slandered as just another itinerant peddler of philosophies, a familiar figure throughout the Greco-Roman world. Frequently called sophists, these wandering teachers were known for their clever rhetoric and preposterous offers of special teachings, insights, and knowledge. Paul's self-defense was an attempt to strike a strong contrast between his own motivations, behavior, and authority with the standard caricature of the sophist. So Paul and his converts both must have suffered derision or worse as the new community formed. Such derision can easily account for the escalation in the claims Paul had to marshal in support of the new social vision.

But what, then, was the concern about "those who have died"? Paul's answer, that God would "bring with him those who have died" at the "coming of the Lord" (1 Thess. 4:14–15), has always been taken as an indication that the Thessalonians were worried about the personal salvation of fellow Christians who had died since Paul was among them and thus would not be alive when the Lord returned. This view would mean that the Thessalonians had indeed become apocalyptic Christians in order to answer a desire for personal salvation and that they thought of being saved rather soon, before any had died, when the imminent end of the world occurred. Given the history of the Jesus movements and the Christ cult preceding this moment, that would be an astonishing interpretation of the Christ myth for Macedonians to have managed by the year 50 C.E. Was that really their understanding of the gospel and the reason for their question about those who had died?

The Christ myth was not based upon an apocalyptic message. The entertainment of an apocalyptic imagination is always a defensive move designed to protect a prior and more fundamental ideological investment that has run into serious trouble. Apocalyptic projections of judgments calculated to destroy the bad and reward the good have no attraction of their own. One needs already to belong to that which is "good," and for reasons that are not rooted in an apocalyptic mentality. It is a people's investment in their traditions, institutions, culture, and ideals that determines what is "good." Only when the good is in danger of being overwhelmed by external circumstances does an apocalyptic rationale begin to make sense (J. Z. Smith 1978). Jewish apocalyptic literature worked that way. The turn to an apocalyptic idiom in the Q community was a defensive and self-protective move. And in the other letters of Paul, apocalyptic language always occurs as an addendum to the gospel itself. It serves as a kind of threat to his listeners to shape up and keep the faith in view of a final accounting. It may be, of course, that Paul had already learned to add an apocalyptic finale to his preaching of the Christ myth. That, at least, is what Paul said when he reminded the Thessalonians that they had "turned to God from idols, to serve a living and true God, . . . *and* to wait for his Son from heaven, whom he raised from the dead—Jesus, who rescues us from the wrath that is coming" (1 Thess. 1:9–10, emphasis added). But it would be strange, indeed, to think that Paul's gospel to the Thessalonians had emphasized an apocalyptic salvation and that they had been persuaded to become Christians in order to be rescued from the wrath of a god who offered to save them from it. Is there not another, more plausible way to understand their query about those who had died?

Concern for the dead was a distinctive feature of all Eastern Mediterranean cultures. Each had a slightly different concept of the nature and abode of the dead, and each had developed different forms of funerary rites. Burial was the common practice, and the rite was surrounded with elaborate taboos. Each culture also had its own ways of honoring the dead at their burial sites. In some cases, such as the patronymic hero shrines of the Greeks or the tombs of the Egyptian pharaohs, forms of burial and memorial prevailed that distinguished the great figures of myth and history from the common populace. But proper burial and memorial were not reserved for kings and heroes. Every family aspired to provide honorable burial for their dead and cultivate the memory of their ancestors by means of yearly rites. It was at the ancestral tombs that the Greeks gathered to perform their "sacrifices" and reconstitute the lines of political power and authority in a district (Stowers 1995). As for ways of thinking about afterlife, many ideas were in the air during the cultural confusion of the Greco-Roman age. Greek concepts of the immortality of the soul were being explored and refined by philosophers. Jewish intellectuals had recently begun to imagine different scenarios of translation into the heavenly world as well as resurrection at the end of time. And the notion of eternal life with roots in Egyptian mythologies of the afterdeath journey of the soul (or *ba*) was exciting early gnostic thinkers. But judging from the funerary iconography of the time and from the typical inscriptions about remembering the one who had departed and mourning the shortness of life, it was not the guarantee of personal salvation that exercised the Greco-Roman age. Discussions about the destiny of the dead were symptoms of a much deeper sense of dis-ease triggered by the incidence of death. What all had in common was a concern for continuity, not just between the life and afterlife of an individual, but from generation to generation of a people. It was a people's land, traditions, and ancestors that gave them their identity and culture. And it was the shrines of the dead that marked the land as belonging to a people. The dis-ease that emerged during the Greco-Roman age resulted from dislocation from one's traditional territory where burial made most sense. Ruptures were taking place between generations, and small groups were separated from their own land and people. What if joining the Christ cult exacerbated the problem instead of solving it? What if joining the Christ cult had inadvertently threatened one's sense of belonging to the ancestral traditions lodged in the local cult of the dead? Could that have been the occasion for the question in Thessalonica about those who had died?

Paul's answer suggests that the question was not really about the "personal salvation" either of the living or of the dead. The question was about belonging. It was about incorporation into the family of God, or how to imagine the place and destiny of the dead in relation to the kingdom of God now that their own people, the Thessalonians, had become a new people. The Thessalonians were not to worry, Paul said, because God would bring those who had died *with* him on the day of the Lord; "so we [all] will be *with* the Lord forever"; "so that whether we are awake or asleep we may live *with* him" (1 Thess. 4:14–17; 5:10, emphasis added). We can almost hear the discussion the Thessalonians had been having: Given the new "family" we have joined, they were asking, do our dead still belong to us and we to them? Or have we lost contact with our dead and they with us? What about genealogy? Have we as Christians lost our rootedness in the people to which we belonged, in our land and our ancestral lineage? Do the old traditional rites take our dead away from us? What about those who have died? What does belonging to the kingdom of God mean for us who still have our dead to consider? And what about Christians who die? If we imagine the Thessalonians being concerned about such questions, we can see that their question about the dead was a fairly astute way of getting to the heart of the new social anthropology they had entertained by becoming Christians.

Paul chose to answer their question by spinning out an elaborate scenario that is clearly apocalyptic. The question is how integral any apocalyptic persuasion may have been to the gospel as the Thessalonians had first understood and accepted it, and whether they would have thought that Paul's apocalyptic answer was satisfactory. His first statement indicates that his answer contained new information (1 Thess. 4:13). As a matter of fact, the apocalyptic scenario that follows is very strange when compared with other apocalyptic visions of the time, including other scenarios that Paul himself projected. It does not fit easily with other ways Paul found to talk about "departing and being with Christ" (Phil. 1:23) or imagining the end of history when "all Israel will be saved" (Rom. 11:25–27). The scene in 1 Thessalonians includes the Lord himself coming as a thief in the night, descending from heaven with a military commander's cry (to "charge"), an archangel's wake-up call with the sound of "God's trumpet," and a "rising" from the earth of both the dead and the living to "meet the Lord in the clouds" and be with him forever (1 Thess. 4:16–5:3). What an astounding imagination! We can almost see Paul working it out on the spot, desperately trying to find a way to answer the question about those who had died.

Paul was caught between a Jewish notion of resurrection and the Greek idea of immortality. He was also caught between an apocalyptic imagination of the end of history and a gnosticlike scenario of the ascent of the soul. He was struggling with the problem of bringing two eschatologies together in a single graphic portrayal. The one had to do with the finale of the Christian mission driven by an essentially social concept and concern. The other had to do with the personal destiny of individuals. Looking ahead, we can see that Paul continued to work on this problem, addressing the conceptual issues that this apocalyptic vision introduced. In the Philippian correspondence, for instance, he anticipated that he would "depart and be with Christ" (Phil. 1:23). In his correspondence to the Corinthian community, where questions had been raised about the notion of resurrection, he toyed with the idea that the bodies of Christians would be transformed into spirits at the *eschaton* (1 Cor. 15:42–57; cf. Phil. 3:21). His exchange with the Thessalonians reveals that he was just beginning to think about the significance of the Christ myth for those who had died. It is the first attempt to work out a specifically Christian concept of eternal life of which we have any record. In order to imagine it, Paul had to integrate several views of the dead with his apocalyptic vision.

That Paul worked out an apocalyptic scenario as the way to answer the question about the dead was historic. It was hardly the easiest way to express convictions about the attainment of eternal life. The reason he did so was grounded in the logic of the Christ myth as he understood it. His mission to the gentiles was generated by a social vision that called for historical actualization. That actualization, however, could be imagined only for the future. When confronted with questions about the dead, therefore, an apocalyptic vision won out over other ways of thinking about postmortem destiny. The destiny of the dead could not be imagined except in relation to the eventual success of the Christian mission and the gathering together of all Christians, both those who had died and those who were still alive. The Christian dead would not depart to have their place in the ancestral past of the traditional collective imaginations. They would instead have a future, one that was linked with the future of the Christian mission itself. Thus the Christian concept of eternal life was born: eternal life would be attained only at the end of time. The lord of the story would gather his children together, not in Jerusalem, and not to form an earthly kingdom, but in some cosmic realm of eternal bliss at the end of time. What an extraordinary scene for Christians to imagine as an ending to the history of God and his people. It ends, as Paul said, "in the air" (1 Thess. 4:17). The Thessalonians, Paul said, were to "encourage one another with these words" (1 Thess. 4:18).

A second letter to the Thessalonians is not Pauline. It lacks the personal warmth, reminiscences, and references characteristic of the authentic letters of Paul (Schmidt 1990). Almost one-third of it is a verbatim copy from the first letter. The signature is suspicious. And the eschatology reflects a development of Christian apocalyptic thinking of the kind that took place only after the Roman-Jewish war around the turn of the first century. I mention it here as the most appropriate place for its discussion, but it adds nothing to our knowledge of Paul's gospel. Its only importance is in documenting the fact that Paul's letters continued to be copied and read after his time in the churches of Greece and Asia Minor and that those who belonged to his school continued to write letters in his name. This phenomenon, called pseudonymous writing, was a common practice and will be thoroughly explored in chapter 8. At this point it is enough to emphasize that, although the author of 2 Thessalonians belonged to the school of Paul, his concept of the *eschaton* was not Pauline.

In 1 Thessalonians there is mention of rescue "from the wrath that is coming" (1 Thess. 1:10) and the promise that "God has destined us not for wrath but for . . . salvation" (1 Thess. 5:9). A contrast between the rescue of some and the destruction of others was standard in many Jewish apocalypses, where the point was always a theodicy in favor of the righteous. Paul's mention of God's wrath must have been derived from this apocalyptic dualism. But Paul did not say with whom God was angry, nor would it have made much sense to the Thessalonians had he been more specific. Wrath was mentioned merely as the other face of God, the one that did not countenance immorality and uncleanness. This view of God's wrath changes dramatically in the second letter to the Thessalonians, where "the Lord Jesus is revealed from heaven with his mighty angels in flaming fire, inflicting vengeance . . . on those who do not obey the gospel of our Lord Jesus. These will suffer the punishment of eternal destruction. . . ." (2 Thess. 1:7–9). This does not sound like Paul, and it tells us that those who continued to work as preachers and teachers in the Pauline tradition had no trouble attributing new ideas to him. It was written by someone who was willing to name the target of God's wrath and who, contrary to Paul's own caution about timetables (1 Thess. 5:1), was eager to spell out a sequence of events that had to take place before the end finally arrived (2 Thess. 2:1–12). This person was apparently intrigued with Paul's apocalyptic scenario in the first letter to the Thessalonians, perhaps because it was an unusually graphic depiction, and he thought to use Paul's authority to validate his own version of the *eschaton*.

Another indication of editorial activity in the Pauline school should be mentioned. It has to do with the addition of some material to the first letter (1 Thess. 2:14–16). The person who made this change was interested in directing Paul's apocalyptic preachments against those who opposed the Christian mission and did so by inserting a small unit aimed specifically at the Jews who "killed Jesus" and "drove us out," for which reason "God's wrath has overtaken them at last." Nothing in all of Paul's letters comes close to such a pronouncement (Pearson 1971). The idea seriously tarnishes the inclusive logic of the Christ myth, and it presupposes the logic of Mark's passion narrative which, as we shall see, runs counter to that of the Christ myth. And since, according to this addition, it was the Jews upon whom God's wrath had (already) fallen, the reference must surely be to the destruction of the temple in 70 C.E., an event that Paul did not live to see. So Paul's first letter to the Thessalonians, written only as an occasional instruction, picked up layers of interpretation on its way into the New Testament. It was supplemented by the addition of a second letter to form a Thessalonian correspondence, copied many times over, edited as we have just seen, and used to claim Paul's authority for later versions of the Christian view of history and its apocalyptic finale. Looking back, it is doubtful that Paul would have been pleased.

THE LETTER TO THE GALATIANS

Paul's letter to the Galatians is much more important to our project than the Thessalonian correspondence. That is because the concerns addressed in the Thessalonian correspondence, though real, were ancillary to the core logic of the Christ myth. In Galatians, however, a situation developed that involved a critical challenge to Paul's gospel at the very center of its basic rationale. Other persons had entered the picture with "another gospel" (Gal. 1:6–7; 4:17) and, like some nightmare for Paul, were saying that the Galatian Christians would have to be circumcised (Gal. 5:2–12; 6:13). "Damn them," Paul wrote, "damn them" (Gal. 1:8–9). "I wish those who unsettle you would castrate themselves!" (Gal. 5:12). It is clear that a central Pauline nerve had been pinched.

We can't be sure exactly where this happened. The letter is addressed to a number of churches in Galatia, the Roman province in central Asia Minor (Gal. 1:2), a region in which Paul must have been active before reaching Philippi and Thessalonica, though the only record we have of that is Luke's later account in Acts. Exactly when he was there, whether on the journey that took him to Macedonia or earlier, how he discovered the situation that developed subsequently, and from where he wrote the letter are all matters of uncertainty. However, many scholars have concluded that the letter was written from Ephesus sometime between 52 and 54 C.E., shortly before Paul's Corinthian correspondence, also written from Ephesus. One thing is obvious from the letter, namely that Paul was well acquainted with the church or churches he addressed, for he felt no need to begin with the usual thanksgiving and commendation. He got down to business immediately, repeatedly alluded to specific aspects of the persons and views that had enraged him, and even dared to charge the Galatians with folly: "You foolish Galatians," he said, "who has bewitched you?" (Gal. 3:1).

Who were these "bewitchers"? They have often been called "Judaizers," a term that scholars have used to refer to Jewish Christian missionaries who followed in Paul's footsteps to counter his gentile mission of freedom from the law. There is very little evidence for such a movement, although part of Paul's argument does seem to implicate some connection with the Jesus people in Jerusalem. He mentions both "false brothers" at Jerusalem (Gal. 2:4) and "people from James" in Antioch (Gal. 2:12), both of whom insisted on the keeping of Jewish purity codes. But we need not think of a movement in general that was propagating such a view, much less one that was organized to hound Paul in particular. The question of what to do with gentile proselytes was, as we have seen, a burning issue throughout the Jewish diaspora, including Asia Minor. And wherever a Christian congregation formed in proximity to a diaspora synagogue, the question would have been raised by Jews and new Christians alike. It was to Paul's own advantage to insinuate that those who held such views had, in every case, infiltrated Christian circles from outside. The important observation is that in Galatia the issue had been raised after Paul had moved on. And at least some of the Galatians had apparently been persuaded that Christians should keep the Jewish laws.

This does not mean that Galatian gentiles were overjoyed at the prospect of being circumcised. Circumcision was the price they would have to pay for the benefits of full membership in the Jewish community. But that was Paul's point. If that's what they wanted, there was no need to be Christian (Gal. 5:2–4). So the issue was not just about circumcision but about really becoming a Jew in order to enjoy the benefits of belonging to the people of Israel. There is mention of the Galatians wanting to keep the law (Gal. 3:2; 4:21), their observance of special days, months, and years (a reference to the cycle of Jewish feasts and festivals; Gal. 4:10), and even the working of miracles (presumably by means of the power and protection granted by the Jewish God; Gal. 3:5). Thus the situation was serious. It is the first indication we have that gentile Christians, not Jews, questioned the credibility of Paul's gospel of freedom from the law. No wonder he was furious.

Paul developed two arguments in response to this issue. The first was that he had successfully defended his gospel in debate with James and Peter, the leaders of the Jesus people at Jerusalem. We have already noted the importance of this account for reconstructing Paul's conversion. The point he made of it in relation to the Galatian issue was that both his authority as an "apostle" and the content of his "gospel for the uncircumcised" had been accepted even by the "pillars" in Jerusalem. We have to imagine that the Galatians already knew something about the Jesus people at Jerusalem and that the point of Paul's argument would have been understood, whether they accepted it or not.

The second argument was much more complex. And it is of enormous interest for our project, for it tackled the Galatian challenge to Paul's gospel straightfor-wardly, and it forced Paul to attempt a major revision of the Israel epic. If gentiles did not need to become Jews and live like Jews, so the question can be phrased, how in the world could they claim to *be* Jews? Paul's strategy was to go back to the stories of Abraham where the beginning of Israel's promise and election were lodged. If Christians could not claim to be Jews, perhaps they could claim to be "children of Abraham." The thought was ingenious. If Paul could pull it off, he would have rede-fined the constitution of Israel and found a way to anchor the once upon a time of the Christ myth both in recent human history *and* in the epic of Israel. Paul's letter to the Galatians is actually a lengthy, passionate, and convoluted argument in sup-port of that claim. It is the earliest recorded revision of Israel's history that tries to align the Christ myth with that history. It is the first systematic argumentation that the covenants foundational to Israel were set in anticipation of the coming of the Christ. It is the first elaboration of the Christ myth's logic that gentiles could belong to the people called Israel. And it documents the first serious effort to research the Hebrew scriptures as the way to support such a claim.

Briefly, Paul started with Abraham as the acknowledged patriarch of Israel, and among the stories of Abraham he found repeated mention of a promise God made to him that "his seed," or children, would be without number and that "all the nations would be blessed in him" (Gen. 12:1–3, 7; 15:5–7; 17:1–8; 18:17–19; 22:17–18). Never mind that the obvious reference here was to physical lineage. Never mind that the promise was made to Abraham and his children, while the blessing was for the nations. Notice, Paul said, that the *blessing* was *promised* because of Abraham's *faith* and *righteousness*, for "Abraham *believed* God," it says, "and it was reckoned to him as *righteousness*" (Gen. 15:6; Gal. 3:6–9, emphasis added). What happened, Paul asked, to the promise and the blessing? The promise to Abraham occurred 430 years prior to the revelation of the Mosaic law (Gal. 3:17). That means that the law was "added" to the promise, Paul said. Why? Because of transgressions (Gal. 3:19). The law, he said, could not make anyone righteous; it was a curse to those who relied upon it and served only as a guardian "until the offspring would come to whom the promise had been made" (Gal. 3:10–24). And who do you sup-pose that was? Since the law could not abrogate the promise, he concluded, the promise to Abraham must have been fulfilled in the person of Jesus Christ who, like Abraham, was "faithful" and "righteous," and because of whom God had regarded the nations (gentiles) as "faithful" and "righteous" as well.

As one can see, subjects, objects, antecedents, and the plain sense of the passages in Genesis were all violated in order to put the construction upon them that Paul did. To make the argument sound plausible, Paul had to turn the Jewish scriptures inside out. He had pored over the scriptures, and not just those that rehearsed the stories of Abraham. He selected texts from throughout the Pentateuch and even found a few citations from the prophets that he could use to advantage. He scrutinized all of them with an extremely sharp eye and shrewdly arranged them for effect. The methods of interpretation he used ranged from observations on historical sequence, through the logic of legal transactions, to outright allegorization. It was an extremely brave attempt to give cognitive and conceptual support to the vision Paul had when he tumbled to the Christ myth.

Sustaining such an argument was no easy task, as one can imagine, and the jumble of rapid-fire, ad hoc assertions Paul makes, though they do follow certain rules of Hellenistic rhetoric here and there, are tortuous (Mack 1990, 66–73). The modern reader is fully justified in being put off by the way Paul used contrasting pairs of powerful words and stacked them up like metaphors in search of a symbol to mark the distinction between Christians and Jews: "promise" and "law," "blessing" and "cursing," "faith" and "works," "righteousness" and "sin," "life" and "death," "sons" and "slaves," "heirs" and "disinherited," "free born" and "slave born," "spirit" and "flesh." It does help to see that the avalanche of strong statements was intended to come crashing down in support of a single assertion, namely that gentile Christians did *not* have to keep the law. That was the bottom line and, though we cannot be sure that the Galatians were convinced, they may have been overwhelmed. It is at least the case that Christian theologians down through history have not been known to call Paul's hand. They have in fact appeared not to have had any trouble thinking that Paul's arguments about "law" and "gospel" were persuasive. But that won't do and, though we do not have the leisure to follow all of the argument and pit Paul's fundamental convictions against the stretch of all his imaginative moves, we can isolate the linchpin on which the entire chain of associations relies. We must do this if we want to test the logic of Paul's claim and ponder its chances of being accepted by the Galatians, as well as by those bewitching them, and other Christian intellectuals interested in the logic of the Christ myth from a gentile's point of view.

Paul found the linchpin in the Greek translation of the Hebrew scriptures where the term for Abraham's "seed" was in the singular (*sperma*; Gen. 12:17; 22:17–18). Struggling to connect Abraham's children and gentile Christians, Paul said two things about that singular "seed." One was that, because it was in the singular, the seed to which God had given the promise could not be the children of Israel, a "many," but only "one person, who is Christ" (Gal. 3:16). The other thing Paul said to make this connection work was, "If you belong to Christ, then you are Abraham's seed, heirs according to the promise" (Gal. 3:29). It does not require any training in logic to see how weak this argument is. It does not require any sophistication in linguistics to notice how weird the imagery appears. It is not just that the two applications of the "seed" as a collective symbol are contradictory, denying its reference to Jews and affirming it for Christians, or that the notion of a singular "seed" wiggling all the way from Abraham to Jesus can hardly be put out of mind, or that Paul had to overlook the fact that Abraham was reckoned righteous because he performed the covenant of circumcision, or that the idea of Christians being the children of the Christ was inadvertently suggested. The main problem was that the thought itself was patently absurd. And yet, the entire argument of Paul's letter to the Galatians rode on taking that thought seriously.

It is clear that Paul was in conceptual trouble. That is because the questions raised by the Galatian crisis were absolutely critical to his program, and the Christ myth was not really designed to answer such questions. According to the Christ myth, God said yes to Jesus because of Jesus' faithfulness to the idea of the kingdom of God, and God said yes to gentiles if only they learned to be faithful to the kingdom idea as Jesus was. Both Paul and the Galatians understood and accepted that as the fundamental persuasion of Christians. But what if you changed the metaphor? What if the concept of a family, "house," or children of God seemed more appropriate than the idea of a kingdom? What if alignment with the people of God (Israel) raised questions about the manner of life appropriate to the children of God, and about the appropriateness of celebrating the festivals in commemoration of the old covenants that had established the family of God in the first place? What if it made sense to the Galatians to realize their newly won citizenship in the kingdom of God by fully participating in the patterned life of a real Jewish community? Paul thought such a position would undercut the point of the *kerygma* as the basis for gentile admission to the family. But what could Paul say? The Christ myth had no guidance for answering questions such as these. Thus, reasons other than the logic of the myth would have to be found if Paul wanted to argue that a Christian congregation should not follow Jewish practices and laws. He would have to find some way to align both the Christ of the *kerygma* and the Christian congregation with the epic history of Israel and argue that Christians could belong to the family of God without being Jewish. He thought he hit pay dirt with the stories about Abraham.

Abraham was the founding figure for the epic history of Israel, and all who saw themselves as heirs of that tradition called themselves his children. To argue simply that gentiles might be included among the children of Abraham would have been an understandable, magnanimous, and potentially acceptable metaphoric license if left unexplored. The problem with Paul's argument was that, under the pressure of the challenge to gentile freedom from the law, he decided to claim the promise of the epic for gentile Christians at the expense of the Jews. This radical revision of the epic was forced by Paul's attempt to find a moment of divine revelation at the beginning of Israel's history to match the moment of divine revelation recounted in the Christ myth. Instead of leaving the mythology of the Christ myth at the level of God's intentions, however, matching the two stories meant messing with historical imagination. We can see just how radical Paul's revision was by noting what he had to leave out. Adam is not in the picture. The early history of the covenants is missing. The covenant with Moses is negated. The Leviticus charter for the system of feasts, festivals, and sacrifices is completely overlooked. David and Solomon do not appear. The kingdom ideal and history are not mentioned. The predictions of the prophets do not play a role. Messianic ideology is not the bridge. And there is only the slightest mention of an apocalyptic end of history (Gal. 5:5; 6:9), the ending of the epic that played such a large role in Paul's letter to the Thessalonians. Everything hinges on the Abraham-Christ connection. This is a marvelous example of myth-making strategy, seeking a pristine point of contact with a foundational moment of the past and making a connection that brackets all the intervening and recent histories of failure to achieve that ideal. In order to make his case, however, Paul had to press both the logic of the Christ myth and the plain sense of the Abraham stories much too far.

Nevertheless, Paul's radical hermeneutic may have inadvertently resulted in a concept of major consequence for his subsequent work. Christ as the "seed" of Abraham was forced to become a symbol for the "source" of the common life that Christians shared because of "belonging" to him (Gal. 3:29). In the Hebrew Bible and in early Jewish literature, an ideal human figure could be storied as a person and at the same time understood as a corporate symbol. Thus Adam, the first man, was pictured as a person but understood to represent all humankind. The term *Adam* means "humankind." And the patriarch Jacob could be storied as a historic person but called "Israel" and understood to represent the people of Israel stemming from him. In the case of Abraham, the metaphor of his seed encompassed many Semitic peoples who claimed to be his children. Such figures functioned for thought both as patronymic ancestors and as collective symbols for the people in their line. In Galatians, the figure of Christ is not fully developed as a corporate symbol in this sense, but there are nudges in that direction. These nudges prepare us for Paul's concept of the "body of Christ," to which Christians are said to belong in the Corinthian correspondence, as well as the concept of the cosmic Christ as the "head of the body, the church" in the post-Pauline letter to the Colossians. Since Paul's letter to the Galatians is the first occurrence of this concept, the suspicion would be that making a pair of Abraham and Christ encouraged that kind of thinking.

The critical expression is the term *in Christ* (*en christo*), which occurs several times in the letter. The preposition *en* can mean "in" or "by means of" or both at the same time. It is not always clear which nuance is intended. The same problem exists with the promise to Abraham, cited by Paul, that "all the nations [gentiles] will be blessed *in you*" (Gen. 12:3; 18:18; Gal. 3:8, emphasis added). The ambiguity exists in both the Hebrew Bible and the Greek translation that Paul was using. We should therefore not press this expression too far, especially not in the direction of being incorporated into a mystical figure. It is best to translate the phrase "in you" with "by means of you," for according to Jewish interpretation during the Greco-Roman period, the "promise" went to Israel while the "blessing" was intended for "the nations." The role Israel would play in the world would constitute the blessing to the nations. It was this distinction between the promise and the blessing that Paul deliberately erased. Christ was the promised "seed," and he was also the source of the blessing upon the gentiles. This means that Christians had become the "children of Abraham" by virtue of "belonging" to Christ. The critical expression *en christo* could therefore mean either "by means of Christ" or "in Christ."

The New Revised Standard Version regularly translates *en christo* as "in Christ," influenced no doubt by the cliché as it occurs in Christian theology. In most cases, however, the occurrence of *en christo* in Galatians should be understood in the sense of "by means of" or "because of." This would be true for "the freedom we have in Christ" (Gal. 2:4), the phrase "justified in Christ" (Gal. 2:27), mention of "the churches of Judea that are in Christ" (Gal. 1:22), and the statement that "in Christ the blessing of Abraham might come to the gentiles" (Gal. 3:14). Nevertheless, there are three statements in which the phrase *en christo* teases the reader to imagine "being in Christ," as if Christ were a symbol for the collective. In each of the three statements that follow, I have added the emphasis:

For *in Christ Jesus* you are all children of God through faith. (Gal. 3:26)

There is no longer Jew or Greek, there is no longer slave or free, there is no longer male and female; for all of you are one *in Christ Jesus*. (Gal. 3:28)

For *in Christ Jesus* neither circumcision nor uncircumcision counts for anything. (Gal. 5:6)

It is difficult to make sense of these statements without thinking of the promise to Abraham, that the nations would be blessed "in him." If we remember that the purpose of the entire argument was to claim legitimate status for gentile Christians as the "children of Abraham," without demanding that they be circumcised and keep the law, it does seem probable that Paul had begun to imagine the relationship of Christ to Christians on the model of the relationship of Abraham to his children. If so, the statements underscore the length to which Paul was willing to go in making the equation between Abraham and Christ.

That he had already gone that far seems to be clear from other statements he made about being "baptized into Christ" and having "clothed yourselves with Christ" (Gal. 3:27), as well as the strange expression that, since Paul had been "crucified with Christ," "it is no longer I who live, but it is Christ who lives in me" (Gal. 2:20). These are truly extraordinary expressions. Christ was no longer being thought of as a historical person, a martyr, or a god, but as a spiritual field of force and divine agency. Christ in this conception combines the notions of personal deity, tribal patriarch, genealogical agent, ethnic principle, cultural spirit, and cosmic power. Such extravagance alerts us to look further, asking whether the notion of being Christ's children did not occur to Paul, and wondering what he may have made of it. We are not disappointed, for at the point of arguing that Christians were the "heirs according to the promise" (Gal. 3:29), Paul found himself having to deal with the implicit suggestion that Christians were Christ's "children." He had already said that Christians were the children of God (Gal. 3:26) and the children of

Abraham (Gal. 3:29). He now turned to their relationship to Christ and, while staying with the notion of being children, broke the metaphor in the following way:

> But when the fullness of time had come, God sent his Son, born of a woman, born under the law, in order to redeem those who were under the law, so that we might receive adoption as children. And because you are children, God has sent the Spirit of his Son into your hearts, crying, "Abba! Father!" So you are no longer a slave but a child, and if a child then also an heir, through God. (Gal. 4:4–7)

This is an amazing tour de force. It was acceptable, indeed necessary to the argument as a whole, to think of Christians as the children of Abraham and also of God. But it was clearly embarrassing to extend the metaphor of paternity to Christ. Paul therefore switched to Christ's role as God's son, allowed the Christ myth to hover in the background, picked up on the notion of the spirit that was associated with the resurrection, and concluded that, by sending that spirit into their hearts, God had "adopted" them as his children. So Christians were the children of God by virtue of having the spirit of God's son in their hearts. If it was the spirit Christians experienced when they met together that proved they were God's children, why was that not enough? Why the lengthy and difficult argumentation? And if the lengthy argumentation actually breaks down as logical reasoning, devolving into a desperate stacking up of images to create an impression, who was fooling whom? It would be no wonder if the modern reader's eyes began to roll. Paul's persuasiveness ultimately rides on the swiftness with which he was able to move from metaphor to metaphor, not giving the reader time to reflect on any momentary association long enough to assess its plausibility. We can conclude only that the strange jumble of condensed imagery must have been impelled by a very serious challenge to Paul's gospel, a challenge that, in the last analysis, Paul was unable to counter.

Even Paul must have known that he had gone too far, that his passion had outstripped his reason. In his later letters he backed off completely from the seed argument, for instance, and he worked hard to take the harsh edge off many of the claims he had made in Galatians. One such claim was that those who lived under the Jewish law were enslaved, under a curse, and in need of redemption (Gal. 3:13, 23; 4:4). Later he would emphasize that sin was the real culprit, not the law, and that the law was "holy and just and good" (Rom. 7:12). Another brash assertion was that Jews were excluded from the covenant with Abraham in the allegory of Sarah and Hagar, who stood for the two covenants (Gal. 4:21–31). Paul inverted the obvious intention of the story to insist that the Mosaic covenant was represented by Hagar, not Sarah, and that the point of the story was to "drive out the slave and her child," referring to Jews who honored the law, "for the child of the slave will not share the inheritance with the child of the free woman," meaning the gentile Christians (Gen. 21:9–12; Gal. 4:30). Later in Romans 9–11, Paul would argue that God had *not* rejected his people and that "all Israel would be saved" (Rom. 11:1, 26). So although the story of Abraham's faith and righteousness would continue to occupy a major niche in Paul's epic imagination, as in the fourth chapter of Romans, he would not again mention that Christ was Abraham's "seed."

Despite the weakness of its logic, however, the dialectic Paul worked out, favorably comparing Christ and Abraham while setting Jews in opposition to Christians, was destined to play a decisive role in the history of Christian thought. Paul's particular solution to the question of how Christians might be heirs of the promises to Israel would not become the dominant mythology of Catholic Christianity, but in its milder form in his letter to the Romans, it would emerge again and again as a powerful alternative Christian persuasion. Its influence is obvious in Marcion's challenge to Christian thinkers of the second century and in the biblical theologies of Augustine, Luther, Karl Barth, and American evangelicals. Here the bottom line has always been the contrast between "law" and "gospel," or Judaism as a legal religion and Christianity as a living "faith." Paul's letter to the Galatians is where this dialectic roots, for the contrast between the "law" as the definition of Judaism and the "spirit of Christ" as the definition of gentile Christianity is also the core of Paul's argument. All other aspects of Paul's epic mythology were invented to claim access to Israel's God even while maintaining that contrast.

5

PAUL'S LETTERS TO
GREEKS AND ROMANS

We have learned three things about Paul and his gospel from his letters to the Thessalonians and Galatians. The first is that he understood the logic at the heart of the Christ myth, a mythology aimed at justifying a mixed congregation of Jews and gentiles as the children of the God of Israel. The second is that, as he worked out the implications of that myth for his own mission to the gentiles, Paul's Jewish mentality determined every new construction he put upon it. This included such moves as appealing to the Abraham legends, arguing from the Jewish scriptures, imposing Jewish ethics, and creating apocalyptic scenarios in order to spell out the significance he saw in the *kerygma* at the bedrock of his gospel. And the third thing we have learned is that Paul's gospel was his very own construction. It was not the way that others in the Jesus movements or the congregations of the Christ understood the import of Jesus and God's plan for a kingdom.

And so, while Paul was preaching his gospel and trying to keep his congregations in line, the Jesus Christ movement was attracting adherents on its own initiative without much concern for the problem Jewish intellectuals were having with their law. And once the Christ myth was in place, in support of a novel social vision, Christian congregations found themselves with a most interesting myth on their hands. Social experimentation exploded, and the Christ myth spiraled out of control. It did not take long for those familiar with Greek mythology and Hellenistic mystery cults to catch the spirit of the resurrected Christ. And it did not take long for people with some knowledge of Greek psychology to translate the Christ myth into a symbol of personal transformation via contact with the spirit of Christ. If spirit (*pneuma*) was the all-pervasive element that gave the cosmos its structure and soul, as well as the primal principle that generated the spark of divinity in humans, and if the spirit of Christ was available to those who joined a congregation of the Christ, the sky was the limit as far as personal Christian experience was concerned. At Corinth, for instance, the Christian congregation became a place for a most amazing display of extravagant spiritual behavior, including ecstatic utterance, sexual license, mystical experience, poetic gifts, ritual power, and baptisms for the dead.

Paul was not prepared for such a display of personal spiritual aggrandizement. It made him nervous. It threatened both his Jewish sense of community and his Christian vision of the kingdom of God. He had to counter this trend, and in the shift of focus that occurred, from the gentile mission to the governance of the Christian congregation, Paul gave the Christ myth yet another twist. The Christ myth does set the pattern for Christian experience, he said. But notice that the crucifixion precedes the resurrection, and that, while the Christian may experience the "deaths" of past commitments, identities, practices, and desires, being "resurrected" to eternal life must wait until the *eschaton*. In the meantime, the cross of Christ should set the pattern for humility and service to one another in the interest of "building up" the congregation. And by the way, at the *eschaton* there would be a judgment to see whether everyone had lived in accord with this new ethic of service to the Christian community.

The Christ myth was not born of considerations such as these, nor did its elaboration demand them. It was Paul who focused attention on "the cross" (1 Cor. 1:18) instead of the resurrection and who added an apocalyptic framework to the mythology of Jesus Christ as lord. He did this to counter a fascination with the mythology of the resurrection he thought dangerous. It was a fascination many early Christians found irresistible. If one thought of the myth as a pattern to be imitated, it suggested an offer of spiritual transformation and transcendence. Paul thought such a cultivation of the Christ myth gave rise to personal religious experiences that ranked and divided the community by allowing some individuals to claim superior spiritual status. Paul had to be careful, of course. He had argued for apostolic authority on the basis of his own personal call. But that was a call, not an experience of the resurrected Christ. What if he put the two together, his call experience and the Corinthians' claim to experience the risen lord? Then he could argue that his call was an experience of seeing the risen lord, and that *their* experience should also be understood as a call to serve the Christian mission. And what was the Christian mission but the formation of Christian congregations? He did it, and it seemed to work.

Paul's Jewish sensibility placed high value on community. His concern was that the Christ congregations manifest a community ethic befitting the ideal of Israel as the people of God. In order to make that preachment stick, he forced a shift in focus from the Corinthians' fascination with the resurrection of the Christ to the moment of Christ's crucifixion. He then turned the cross of Christ into a major metaphor for the lifestyle appropriate to a Christian congregation. He not only proclaimed the cross as the event that changed the course of history and made it possible for gentiles to be justified in the house of Israel, he now used it to imagine all the transformations involved in becoming a Christian: joining a Christian congregation, receiving baptism, sharing the common meal, resolving conflicts within the Christian community, and cultivating an ethic of self-sacrifice and service. According to Paul, Christ's obedience unto death exemplified the attitude that was definitive for the Christian community. And lest this purpose of the Christian gospel not be taken as seriously as it should be, Paul reminded his converts that a final judgment was still a part of God's plan.

Thus, starting with the revelation that Jesus Christ was the son of God and that his death and resurrection marked the great hinge of social and epic history, Paul set out on two grand adventures. One was what he called his mission to the gentiles. The other was constructing a complete theology on the basis of the Christ myth. His quest would be to comprehend the "wisdom and knowledge of God" or God's "inscrutable ways" (Rom. 11:33). His letters to the Corinthians and Romans do not provide us with a complete record of Paul's intellectual quest, but they do document major moments in his elaboration of the Christ myth. And in the case of Romans, we have a very well-crafted and comprehensive statement of his theological system. Since it was "Christ Jesus," as he said, "who has become for us the wisdom from God" (1 Cor. 1:30), it was the Christ myth that focused and generated his quest to comprehend what he called God's "ways." We should not be surprised, therefore, to find that every feature of Paul's worldview was eventually touched by the symbol of the Christ. That, naturally, would have some consequences for the shape of the symbol itself.

THE CORINTHIAN CORRESPONDENCE

At Corinth, Paul's gospel of freedom from the law and new life by means of the spirit of Christ spun out of control. Corinth was a lively new city, Greek to the core and thoroughly Hellenistic in spirit, although Roman in recent design. Its long and illustrious history as a prominent, independent, and smart Greek city, the city that watched over the crossing between Achaea and the Peloponnese, had come to an end at the hands of the Romans in 146 B.C.E. During the next one hundred years the Romans realized their role as a colonial power, and Julius Caesar rebuilt Corinth as a Roman colony in 44 B.C.E. It flourished, and in 27 B.C.E. Caesar, now Augustus, designated Corinth as the capital city of the Roman province of Greece. Corinth was hardly a match for Athens as a center for the continued cultivation of classical Greek philosophy and learning, but it was the city where Greek thought and culture poured into the mixing bowl of peoples and ideas that had been thrown together during the Greco-Roman age. It was a busy seaport and a center for commerce, industry, and the Isthmian games. There were temples and sanctuaries for Apollo, Aphrodite, Asclepius, Poseidon, and Demeter, as well as for Isis, Serapis, and the Asian Mother of the gods. Sailors, merchants, philosophers, and travelers passed through. Roman government officials, craftsmen, merchants, and performers contributed to a bright and bustling public life. And prostitutes brought Corinth fame as the city of sex, pleasure, and immorality. The temple of Aphrodite Pandemos

("Goddess of love for all the people") overlooked the city from a massive acropolis and blessed the intercourse below.

Paul was hardly prepared for Corinth. He did receive an eager hearing for his gospel there, apparently, and he did find himself deeply involved in the life of this new congregation, returning to it again and again in person, spirit, and by letter, as he said, long after he had moved on to Ephesus and other places to continue his gentile mission. But Paul was not the only teacher to which these Christians were listening, and it is clear that his views on the meaning of the "cross of Christ" and the "law of Christ" were difficult for the Corinthians to accept and understand. They were impressed rather with the chance to experience the spirit of the new god called Christ and to manifest the spiritual signs that proved they had entered his kingdom. The way the Corinthian Christians displayed these signs of spiritual power produced a remarkable congregational behavior. Nothing we know about the Jesus movements or the congregations of the Christ prior to Paul's Corinthian correspondence, as fanciful as some of these other movements and mythologies were, is enough to explain what happened in Corinth. What the Corinthians did with the Christ myth therefore comes as a great surprise. Paul himself hardly knew what to make of it. The Corinthians saw the Christ myth as an invitation to experience the spirit of that spiritual realm over which Christ ruled, and they took delight in various forms of public display aimed at demonstrating their immediate contact with that spirit. Paul was alarmed. It was certainly not the kind of congregation he had in mind. We can see him backpedaling on freedom, changing his mind about the spirit, and being forced to take positions that seem to contradict his earlier views. Obviously, the problem Paul faced in Corinth was due to the fact that these Corinthians were thoroughly at home in the Hellenistic environment of Greek life and thought. Their reasons for being interested in the Christ myth were not the same as Paul's.

Thus the window Paul provides into this Christian congregation is an exceptional treat. The Corinthians are the first example we have of a thoroughly Hellenistic, mainly gentile, urban Christ cult in the heart of Greece. Their experience of the Christ, the kingdom of God, freedom from the past, and the spirit of God is so far removed from the persuasions of the Jesus movement that the rapid development from the one to the other is simply stunning.

Paul was active in Corinth for about eighteen months around the year 50 C.E. From there he went to Ephesus where he and some co-workers set up a center for his Christian mission. From Ephesus Paul wrote much of his correspondence with the Corinthians, and from there he made at least one interim visit to Corinth in the course of about four years of an exceptionally stormy relationship. The two letters of Paul to the Corinthians in the New Testament are actually a collection of six different communications. First Corinthians is a single letter relatively intact, written in response to a report Paul had received from "Chloe's people" about issues over which the Corinthians were divided (1 Cor. 1:11) as well as in regard to some other "matters" about which the Corinthians had written to him (1 Cor. 7:1). An even earlier letter of Paul's to the Corinthians, now lost, is mentioned in 1 Corinthians 5:9. Portions of a second surviving letter are contained in 2 Corinthians 2:14–6:13 and 7:2–4. It was written some time later, after Paul had learned that his authority as an apostle needed to be clarified and defended. After a visit to contend with the influence that other apostles were having in Corinth, a visit that did not go well, Paul wrote a "severe letter," a portion of which is contained in 2 Corinthians 10–13. This letter included a warning that Paul intended to return to Corinth to discipline certain members of the congregation who were divisive and had not repented of some sexual license that Paul had condemned. This plan did not materialize, for Paul apparently ran into trouble with the authorities in Ephesus, was imprisoned, then released, and left to wend his way to Corinth via Troas and Macedonia, the long way around. It was probably in Macedonia that Paul received word from Titus, a coworker whom he had sent to Corinth with the severe letter, that the Corinthians were anxious to be reconciled with Paul. Paul then wrote a fourth letter to the Corinthians, from which a portion has survived as 2 Corinthians 1:1–2:13 and 7:5–16. It may have been the cover for two additional letters of solicitation regarding a collection of money for the "poor saints in Jerusalem," a project Paul now felt comfortable in urging upon the Corinthians. One letter was intended for distribution among the churches in Achaea (2 Corinthians 9), the other for the congregation at Corinth (2 Corinthians 8). We thus have an exceptionally rich documentation of a Christian mission in Greece not more than twenty years after the time of Jesus.

Why were these Corinthians attracted to the Christian gospel? That is the first question raised by this evidence for a mainly gentile congregation. Given the logic at the core of the Christ myth, a logic of "justification" in which the Corinthians apparently were not at all interested, what possibly could they have made of the myth that so excited them? Unfortunately, Paul's letters were not intended to provide us with a full description of the Corinthians and their beliefs, and we have no texts written by the Corinthians themselves. There are, however, enough clues in Paul's correspondence to paint a picture of these people, if we pay attention to the topics discussed and the reasons Paul gave for seeing things a certain way.

Four types of material can be distinguished. The first may be called agreements on matters of belief and practice that Paul assumed the Corinthians shared with him. These include such things as their reception of the gospel, their meeting regularly, their knowing about the kingdom of God, their practice of baptism, their memorial meals, and their interest in the spirit of Christ. These agreements tell us that the Corinthians had indeed formed a congregation on the model of the Christ cult. The second type of material indicates differences in the ways Paul and the Corinthians understood the Christ cult. Paul was troubled by a large number of their views and practices. Some of these he criticized, such as their behavior when meeting together for the association meal; some he mentioned sarcastically, such as the Corinthians' claim to be "rich" and "wise." We do have to be careful not to let

Paul determine our view of the Corinthians, but even his sarcastic references must have been somewhat on target or he could never have hoped for a hearing. The third type of material is new instruction from Paul. Questions had arisen about behavior appropriate to the new community, and he gave his advice. Here we can see Paul squirming, struggling with the problem of having been misunderstood, trying to accommodate the Corinthians' views as far as he could, but insisting nevertheless that the Christ myth (according to *his* gospel) provide the answers. A fourth type of material is the defense Paul gave for his authority to say what the Christ myth implied. By paying close attention to each of these types of material it is possible to construct a fairly full description of the Corinthian Christians.

It seems that the Corinthians had indeed gotten excited about the report of a god recently crucified who was then transformed into the lord of the spiritual kingdom he represented and revealed. They apparently had no trouble thinking of this kingdom as a spiritual realm. Perhaps they understood it on the model of the world of the gods with which they were familiar from Greek mythology, or perhaps they understood it as a cosmic essence or sphere, as taught by their philosophers. And the Corinthians apparently had no trouble thinking that the god Jesus Christ had appeared as a man, suffered a human fate, and been transformed into a spiritual being. That may have sounded a bit strange at first, for it combined features of their stories about the gods with events that were usually reserved for their hero tales. But perhaps the very combination of the two kinds of spiritual beings created its own intrigue. It was also the case that, being good Greeks, they naturally assumed that human spirit and divine spirit were very closely related, if not part and parcel of the same cosmic substance. So what the Christ myth suggested to them was on one level novel and new; on another it did not contain anything new or strange at all.

What was the novelty that attracted their attention? It was something about the concept of the spirit that came along with the Christ myth. The Greeks thought of spirit as an elemental substance of the cosmos; Christians imagined a spirit with agency and power. What if the Christ myth made it possible to imagine a spiritual realm as a domain, complete with its lord Jesus Christ? What if, moreover, it also provided a way to experience that spirit by devotion to its lord? The Greeks had always thought that something like mind or spirit was the common bond between human nature and the nature of the cosmos itself. What if the Christians were right? What if that spirit were less an elemental substance and more a divinity? What if the spirit of the cosmos could be imagined as a divine agent who cared about people? And what if devotion to the new god could actually awaken the spirit within a person to make contact with the deep, hidden spirit of the cosmos?

Such a shift in thinking about the world and the gods was timely. The Greek gods had grown old and tired. They and the people with whom they trafficked were no match either for the Roman legions marching from the west or the ancient gods and cultures invading from the east. All these gods from the east, whether the God of Israel, Isis of the Egyptians, or the Christians' lord, shared a fundamental advantage in comparison with the gods of the Greeks, including Zeus. They were sovereign, transcendent, and in charge. They ruled imperiously over creation and history in the interest of governing human destinies, peoples, kings, and their fates. And in the case of the Jews, the character of their one God was thoroughly high-minded, ethical, and trustworthy. The gods of the Greeks, on the other hand, were fickle beings, feared and in some ways revered, but hardly loved, and not to be trusted. Their world was too much a grotesque mirror of Greek history and social life with the messy side turned up for review. No one would have wanted to live in that world of the gods or would have thought that the gods' primary interest was focused on the well-being of individual Greeks and their society. Greek gods were partial, took sides, and often played the trickster. A visit by a god or a goddess was not welcomed as a sign of unambiguous portent. And when one pondered the world of the gods and asked how it affected and fit into the elemental structures of the cosmos, as all Greek philosophers did, the natural order always won. The gods were inevitably reduced to allegories of the inorganic elements from which the world was constructed, or at most treated as personifications of the physical forces that shaped the empirical world.

Christians invaded the thought world of the Greeks with a message about a different kind of God, one who was not only the creator of the world, revealer of law, and guarantor of justice, but whose primary concern was the well-being of his people. Encountering Christian missionaries who announced that the true and living God could now be known because of Jesus Christ would not have been the introduction of just another god to the Greek pantheon. It would have challenged the way the gods had been imagined to have inhabited the world, and it would have called for a major reconfiguration of the way the world was put together and how humans fit into the picture. The attraction of the Christian message was that one might have contact with the highest God, and that such contact would be inspiring, not frightening. The new theology implied that the cosmos was energized by an extension of God's spirit. Such a thought resulted in an altogether different kind of spiritual universe than was possible with traditional Greek cosmologies. How heady it must have been to think of the spiritual order of the cosmos as a domain of agency and power with its face turned toward persons, inviting them to talk back to the universe in which they found themselves estranged. How disgusting those old Greek gods now appeared, how boring the natural world when seen as their habitat, and how ineffectual they were for helping humans find their place and way in the chaotic world of alienation from one's land and people. So the thought of Jesus Christ as the son of that high God, sent to make his will, kingdom, and spirit known, and now installed as lord of the kingdom, may have been quite attractive for some. Just think. A gift of the spirit of God from Christ his son could awaken one's own true spiritual self and put one in contact with the spiritual kingdom over which Christ ruled! How was this spirit experienced? It was experienced when Christians gathered in the name of Jesus Christ their lord and called upon his name. And the signs of its presence? How about inspired discourse, ecstatic experience, and charismatic performances?

Paul was appalled. He had not expected the Christ myth to call forth such a public display of personal religious experience. It may be that he had underestimated the way the Greek mentality would respond to his message about the freedom and power available through the spirit of Christ. To think of the Christian spirit as a sign of freedom from the law was one thing. That is what Paul had intended by the term *spirit* in his letter to the Galatians. But freedom from any and all physical and cultural constraints because of spiritual contact with cosmic powers was another thing altogether. Paul's consternation is registered in the biting sarcasm he used to call the Corinthians to task.

His sarcasm is most obvious in the way Paul treated a number of slogans that must have been Corinthian catchwords. If we discount Paul's rhetorical innuendoes, these slogans can tell us what the Corinthians were experiencing as Christians. They include the following: "We are rich" ; "We are free"; "We are kings" (1 Cor. 4:8); "We are wise" ; "We are strong" (1 Cor. 4:10); "All things are lawful" (1 Cor. 6:12; 10:23); "It is well for a man not to touch a woman" (1 Cor. 7:1); "Food will not bring us close to God" (1 Cor. 8:8); "Food is meant for the stomach, and the stomach for food" (1 Cor. 6:13); "We all possess knowledge" (1 Cor. 8:1); "No idol really exists" ; "There is no God but one" (1 Cor. 8:4); "There is no resurrection of the dead" (1 Cor. 15:12); "We have all we want" (1 Cor. 4:8); "We have spiritual gifts and power" (1 Corinthians 12–14).

These sayings show that the Corinthians had cleverly combined clichés from Greek traditions of popular philosophy with some new terminology learned from the Christ myth. A popular saying among the Stoics is not too difficult to discern in the background, namely, "Only the wise are kings." The Cynics' virtue of living with little was regularly turned into a conceit about having it better than those who were rich. And freedom from social pressures to conform, as well as strength of personal integrity, was the standard, bottom-line ideal among most schools of popular ethical philosophy. There was even a strong stream of Cynic tradition to the effect that it did not matter whether one was ascetic or indulgent with regard to such things as sex and food, as long as one knew that such things did not really matter. So the peculiar tenor of these Corinthian sayings is that the claim to freedom, sufficiency, wisdom, strength, and power was now being attributed to the spirit of Christ and interpreted as a sign of belonging to his kingdom. This can only mean that the Corinthians thought the Christ myth a remarkable justification for being free spirits on the one hand, and an invitation to upgrade spirited behavior as a sign of superior spirituality on the other. This may have been a brand new notion. It was the idea of being energized by or "filled with" the spirit of a god who was actively engaged in recruiting individuals for his countercultural kingdom. What an intoxicating experience! What unexpected access to immortality! Thus the congregation of the Christ at Corinth was the place where the Greek desire for personal honor was raised to the level of spiritual manifestation. In modern terms, it was a cross between participation theater and the personal display of ecstatic experience. It was this display, construed as spiritual achievement, that Paul thought of as inappropriate self-conceit. The Corinthians were cultivating "spiritual gifts" such as "speaking in tongues" and "prophesying." They were allowing women to prophesy without covering their heads. And their freedoms extended to breaking standard taboos on sexuality, marriage, and sacrificial meals. The Corinthians were having quite a good time of it, apparently, exploring all the possibilities that came with the new mythology of the spirit of the Christ. It may even be that this cultivation of the spirit had let some Corinthians say, "Let Jesus be damned" (1 Cor. 12:3). No wonder Paul was deeply troubled.

Actually, it was Paul's Jewish sensibility that was offended. He found himself confronted with a social arena in which individuals were showing off their different spiritual gifts, differences of opinion were taken for granted, and competition motivated the drive for superior achievement in knowledge or spiritual power. None of that would have violated traditional Greek sensibilities. But it did violate Paul's Jewish anthropology and sense of propriety that underlay his social ethic. It was not what Paul had intended by inviting gentiles into the family of God. It was not what he had meant by proclaiming that the spirit of God, manifest in the world through his son Jesus Christ, set Christians free from the law. He still thought of the Christian congregation on the model of Israel and of Israel, as a people of purity and holiness, living in community according to high ethical standards. It was one thing to say that gentiles need not be circumcised and that adherence to the rituals of purity did not automatically confirm either Jew or gentile in the new kingdom of God. But it was quite another to behave as if common codes of morality no longer applied. The Corinthians had not understood the importance of being the children of Abraham. They did not seem to understand that the kingdom of God, though available now to gentiles, was supposed to look like a congregation of God's chosen people, Israel. They were acting as if personal experience of the divine spirit was all that mattered and as if one's body did not matter at all. Paul thought them arrogant and licentious. It just would not do for Christians to behave that way.

So Paul responded with a vociferous and sustained argument about the importance of "body" for Christian ethic and belief. He developed the metaphor in order to bring three different figures into close relationship with one another: the individual human being, the Christ, and the Christian congregation. In the first place, Paul said, what one did with one's body was important. Actions had consequences. Behavior was the standard by which the individual would be judged. In the second place, he said, the true significance of the crucifixion and the resurrection of Christ could only be discerned by realizing that both were "bodily" events, by which he meant that they really happened. And in the third place, the purpose of these bodily events was to create the "body of Christ," a congregation of individuals who were knit together as an organic, social unit. Talk about mythmaking! You can almost hear the wheels whirling in Paul's head as he struggled to merge some disposition of the Christ myth with the shape of the Christian congregation he had in mind.

The ethical issues under discussion were many: sexual immorality, marriage, children, celibacy, circumcision, women prophets, food offered to idols, the display of spiritual gifts, dissensions, class distinctions, ranking at the common meal, and lawsuits. After reading the Corinthian correspondence, no one can say that early Christians were not involved in experimental social formation. But Paul thought that the congregation was about to fly apart, not come together. So he dealt with all of these issues as signs that the integrity of the Corinthian congregation was in danger. His concern at each point was to foster organic unity, and he handled each issue as if it could be traced to a difference of opinion about the importance one attached to the body.

The positions Paul took were all rooted in his Jewish convictions about the importance of purity for the people of God. In Jewish circles the discussion of purity would have taken for granted the fact that humans have bodies and turned instead to the question of codes. The important thing to get straight would have been the standards, authorities, and ideals by which behavior might be judged. Paul could not start down that path, for he had consigned the law to an unhelpful past. And he could not take the importance of the body for granted, because the behavior he wished to counter derived its power from the thoroughly Greek notion of body-soul dualism that regarded the soul as superior to the body. It was the soul or the spirit that defined human identity. As for the body, the common saying was, "The body is the tomb" (*soma sema*). So Paul, caught in the middle between two cultural attitudes with respect to the body, was reduced to manipulating tortured metaphors, some taken from his Jewish culture, some from the Greek, and all intended to emphasize just how important it was for Christians to focus on "the body" instead of celebrating only "in the spirit." "Do you not know," Paul wrote, "that your bodies are members of Christ? . . . Do you not know that whoever is united to a prostitute becomes one body with her? Do you not know that your body is a temple of the Holy Spirit within you, which you have from God, and that you are not your own? For you were bought with a price; therefore glorify God in your body" (1 Cor. 6:15–20). The tempo tells of the passion with which Paul wrote. And the point is clear. But the argument rides on a very shaky clustering of incompatible images.

The same is true of Paul's attempt to ground his ethic in the Christ myth and ritual by using the body metaphor. The crucifixion was a "bodily" event, according to Paul. It was, moreover, a sacrifice for others, one that should establish the pattern for ethical behavior in the new community. Christians should live in accord with that pattern by keeping in mind the effect of their behavior on others. They should "serve" one another and so "build up" the community rather than seek their own interests. That would be the correct way to imitate the true meaning of Christ's obedience unto death. To "discern the body" would be the proper way to come together to "eat the Lord's supper" (1 Cor. 11:20, 27–29).

At this point one might think that Paul had pressed the body metaphor as far as it could go. To focus on the term *body* in the Christian myth and ritual was appropriate to the martyrology at its core. And to call for imitating the myth as a pattern or example of ethical behavior would not have sounded strange to Greek ears. But Paul could not leave it there. The Corinthians might still go on thinking of themselves as essentially individualistic spiritual beings and so not grasp the significance of belonging to a social group. So Paul pressed on.

Now concerning the resurrection, he said, it should also be understood as a bodily transformation. The Corinthians had gone so far as to say, "There is no resurrection of the dead" (1 Cor. 15:12). Of course not. "Resurrection of the dead" was a Jewish, apocalyptic notion that did not make sense to Greeks. The Corinthians had understood the Christ myth, not in terms of a bodily resurrection "from the dead," but in terms of translation, metamorphosis, or exaltation into a purely spiritual mode of existence. So Paul was really in trouble. He certainly did not want to renege on the gospel of the spirit, but he had to counter the Corinthians' enthusiasm for experiences of the spirit that discounted the body. And he had to do it by interpreting the resurrection from the dead as an eschatological event, though in such a way as to challenge the Corinthians' fascination with the spirit. He therefore proposed what surely must be the most preposterous conceptual equation of all his attempts to bridge the intellectual traditions of Jewish and Greek cultures. He came up with the notion of a "spiritual body"! His argument in 1 Corinthians 15 was that (1) there are many kinds of bodies among animals and human beings; (2) the "bodies" of plants are different from the "bodies" of the seeds from which they come; (3) there are earthly bodies and "heavenly bodies" (with reference to sun, moon, and stars); (4) the first man, Adam, had a "physical body"; the "man from heaven" (Christ) had a "spiritual body"; (5) the resurrection of Christ was the "first fruits" of the general resurrection of Christians which would take place at the *eschaton;* and (6) at the general resurrection the bodies of the dead would be changed into imperishable bodies just like the heavenly body of Christ. And that's it. The argument is only a bizarre assortment of metaphors strung together by ad hoc associations, this time in order to create the impression of "spiritual body." It was the best Paul could do. He did not want the Corinthians to think that their Christian existence could ever be imagined as a matter of pure spirit, even in the heavenly kingdom of God.

The passion that drove Paul to such intellectual extravagance and absurdity was not a flair for imaginative speculation but the need to defend a social anthropology in the face of the Corinthians' individualistic views. Thus, as far-fetched as the notion of a spiritual body was, it was not yet enough. To imagine having a "spiritual body" even in heaven countered their body-soul dualism, but it did not immediately underscore Paul's critique of their individualism. The latter point would have to be made by still another application of the body metaphor, this time to the Christian congregation itself. In the Greek tradition, a city or other social unit could be referred to as a "body," quite similar in meaning to our own references to a "body politic." Paul eagerly used this metaphor to upgrade his notion of being "in Christ." To be "in Christ" was the way in which he had phrased the collective in his letter to the Galatians. But that was imagined on the model of the Jewish concept of an ancestor as both a personal figure and a collective symbol. By using the term *body of Christ*, it was now possible to merge the image of being "*in* Christ" with the Greek concept of a social organism *into* which Christians had been called. There is more than a touch of the grotesque to this metaphor, to be sure, conjuring up as it does the image of many Christian "bodies" wiggling around inside a large, spiritual "body" (Christ). And since the Christian bodies are imagined as both earthly and spiritual, the application of the metaphor to the local congregation is even more difficult to control as a concept than if used only of a cosmic, spiritual "body of Christ." Nevertheless, despite its grotesque features, Paul used the image of the "body of Christ" to great advantage at every turn in his instructions to the Corinthians.

In his discussion of Christian ethics, for instance, Paul could say that "your bodies are members of Christ" (1 Cor. 6:15). Concerning the bread as the symbol of the body of Christ (1 Cor. 10:16; 11:24, 29) he said, "Because there is one bread, we who are many are one body, for we all partake of the one bread" (1 Cor. 10:17). To counter the individualism of the Corinthians' understanding of spiritual gifts, Paul said that "in one Spirit we were all baptized into one body" (1 Cor. 12:13). And after he had detailed the ways in which the Christian congregation should be seen as an organic unity, he concluded with the statement, "You (plural) are the body of Christ and individually members of it" (1 Cor. 12:27). Thus the incredible concept of the church as the body of Christ was born. It was born of Paul's attempt to express his dream of an Israel made up of non-Jewish Christians. It was called for by the success of the gentile mission among those who thought, not as Jews, but as Greeks. It violated cultural sensibilities on both sides of the line and packed a motley collection of convictions into a dense and contorted symbol. But never mind the mental stretch. It apparently did the trick for some Paulinists, for it actually became an object of devotion in the post-Pauline school, as a hymn to Christ as the "head of the body" shows (Col. 1:15–20). And Christians are still using this language to express what they call the mystery of the church as a cosmic entity and order.

Thus Paul's mission had taken him much further into the heart of Greek culture and thought than he may have planned. Inviting gentiles to join God's people was not the end of the cultural encounter. After the proclamation and its reception came the much larger, time-consuming task of explaining, instructing, and inculcating a strictly Christian mentality. This task took its toll on Paul, and two shifts took place in his thinking. One was that he was forced to tone down his earlier views on the freedom Christians had in Christ. In his letter to the Galatians, Paul had been adamant about the freedom of Christians from any sense of being beholden to the Jewish law, and he had been forceful in his assertion that the experience of the spirit was a sufficient basis for guidance in living the Christian life. In the Corinthian correspondence that confidence is no longer obvious. In its place is a studied attempt to

interject the language of sobriety, considerateness, constraint, law, loyalty, obedience, and judgment into his discourse about the spirit, the body, and the Christian
life. The other shift was that he was forced to rework the way in which he viewed
the Jewish scriptures. His pastoral assignments now required a rather different approach to the scriptures than is evident in the Galatian letter. He now could say that
"obeying the commandments of God is everything" (1 Cor. 7:19). That's new, as is
his repeated and positive use of the scriptures to find illustrations, examples, oracles,
and even maxims that scored the points Paul wished to make. It is obvious that he
wanted the Corinthian Christians to take seriously the God of Israel's history. This
is an extremely important feature of the change in Paul's thinking. It lets us see that
arguing for a reinterpretation of the Christ myth and revising one's view of the epic
of Israel went hand in hand. What may have happened at Corinth to make these appeals to the scriptures sound plausible?

At some point after leaving Corinth, and after the writing of 1 Corinthians, some
other apostles who did not belong to the Pauline school entered the picture in
Corinth, and the Corinthians apparently found themselves enchanted. Reading between Paul's lines as he describes them in 2 Corinthians, it appears that these
"super-apostles," as he called them (2 Cor. 11:5), were clever with words, charismat-
ics who performed signs and wonders, and visionaries whose esoteric knowledge
was such that the Corinthians paid them to learn about it. Paul was horrified and reacted as if the entire project of the gentile mission had been threatened. These apostles prided themselves in being "Hebrews," "Israelites," "children of Abraham," as
well as "ministers of Christ" (2 Cor. 11:22–23). Their ultimate appeal to authority,
moreover, was the Jewish scriptures. That is startling. It is the earliest evidence we
have for Jewish Christians who combined the display of charismatic powers with
skill in scriptural interpretation as their means of persuasion (Georgi 1986). Paul
was understandably upset, because he and they were too much alike at one level (as
Jewish Christian missionaries) yet too far apart at another (differing with respect to
their interpretation of scripture and attitudes toward charismatic display). What
competition. When they compared him with these missionaries, the Corinthians
thought Paul's former presence had been "weak." So Paul found himself in the embarrassing position of having to "boast" of his ministry, credentials, and his own visionary experiences (2 Corinthians 10–13). And he also had to explain what he
thought about the authority of the Jewish scriptures for his gospel and work (2 Cor.
2:14–6:13; 7:2–4).

The pressure was on. Paul could not compete as a charismatic. But he was
bright. Perhaps he could beat them at their own game of scriptural interpretation.
The problem in this case was that linking the Christ myth to the Abraham stories
would not be enough. He would have to find the reflection of the Christ in many
more places and develop a much more comprehensive reading of the scriptures
from his own Christian point of view. And so he took it on as a research assignment
and came up with three exegetical novelties. These would have a lasting effect upon

Christian thought, irrespective of what the Corinthians may have thought of them. One was the use of the terminology of an "old" and a "new covenant." A second was the pairing of Adam and Christ as representative figures of the two epochs. And the third was a clever use of allegory to turn the old covenant into a story of the Christ. Each of these developments can be accounted for as mythmaking in the interest of anchoring Paul's gentile mission in the epic traditions of Israel. Each can be viewed as a remarkably clever intellectual play. And each was fraught with potential for later Christian elaboration.

In 2 Corinthians, chapter 3, Paul distinguished between the old Mosaic covenant written on stone tablets and the new Christian covenant "written" by the spirit on human hearts. The notion of a new covenant written on the hearts of the people was taken from Jeremiah (31:31–34), where it simply meant that God would put it in the hearts of the people to actually keep the (old) covenant. Without reference to Jeremiah, Paul applied the concept to the Christian experience of the spirit of Christ, thereby implying that God had made a new covenant with Christians, thus relegating the Mosaic covenant to the past as old. We dare not think that Paul was referring to the New Testament, for the texts of the New Testament were not written yet, much less collected together as the new covenant. Paul's audacity was not only to take the notion of covenant, fundamental for Jewish epic mythology, and apply it to the Christ myth as the basis for the Christian-gentile mission, but to pit the oral proclamation of the gospel against the textual form of the old covenant and call the textual form passé. "To this very day," Paul wrote, "whenever Moses is read, a veil lies over their minds; but when one turns to the Lord, the veil is removed. Now the Lord is the Spirit" (2 Cor. 3:15–17). The allusion was to Moses' veil at Sinai, which Moses used to cover his face against the brilliance of the glory of Yahweh when receiving the law (Exodus 34). Paul misused the metaphor on purpose to (1) rank oral communication and personal presence above written forms of communication, and (2) claim superiority for the Christian knowledge of God over the views of those who regularly read the books of Moses. As one can see, with this masterful move Paul made it possible for Christians to acquire the books of Moses without having to read them the way they were read in the synagogues. The books of Moses could now represent for Christians both a covenant that was passé and a text that contained a deeper meaning. The true meaning of the text would depend upon seeing in it the glory of the new covenant in Christ.

The Adam-Christ comparison in 1 Corinthians 15:45–49 is the second innovation of importance for our study. Instead of drawing the link between the epic of Israel and the new gentile mission by working with the Abraham-Christ figure, as he did in Galatians, Paul now turned to the story of the first human being, Adam. With Adam as the figure comparable to Christ, the horizon of Christ's effectiveness was automatically expanded in two significant respects. Not only the whole human race, but the entire creation came immediately into view. This move was particularly appropriate for the Corinthian situation where a Greek philosophical view of humankind prevailed. Simply by drawing the comparison with Adam, Paul was able to put a universal, representative, cosmic, and creative connotation on the figure of Christ. And by drawing the contrast between Adam as human creature and Christ as divine spirit, the two epochs of human history over which each presided were immediately ranked in terms of a new Christian dualism between the old (= earthly, literal, written) and the new (= heavenly, spiritual, allegorical). One might well be astonished at the rapidity with which Paul was able to set up this equation between the "old" and the "new" and have it work to the advantage of the Christ myth. Do you suppose that the Corinthians, watching Paul and the super-apostles fight it out over the Jewish scriptures, were duly mystified? Apparently they were.

With the distinction between letter and spirit in mind, as well as that between the old and the new "covenants," it is not surprising to find that Paul quickly moved to take advantage of an allegorical interpretation of the Jewish scriptures. We may call Paul's strategy a Christ allegory, for the primary thrust was to find some association between the image of Christ and other important figures or symbols from the epic. Note the difference it makes when one moves away from comparing Christ with Abraham or Adam, both of whom were anthropological symbols similar to the Christ, to hear Paul say that the *rock* from which the children of Israel drank in the wilderness "was Christ" (1 Cor. 10:4), that "our *paschal lamb*, Christ, has been sacrificed" (1 Cor. 5:7, emphasis added), or that "God, in Christ, always leads us in triumphal procession, and through us spreads in every place the fragrance that comes from knowing him" (a play on temple pageantry and sacrifice; 2 Cor. 2:14). Suddenly, as with the waving of a wand, Paul was able to redeem every image in the Jewish scriptures, not just the anthropological figures, for Christian instruction, even while continuing to relegate the history they recounted to the "ministry of death" (2 Cor. 3:7). Using allegory, the scriptures could be read as Christian texts by allowing the image of Christ to become a symbol large and complex enough to encompass the entire sweep of the epic they contained. As we shall see, the allegorical setup established a precedent that later became the canonical method for the Christian reading of the Hebrew scriptures, known to Christians as the "Old Testament."

THE LETTER TO THE ROMANS

Paul's letter to the Romans is a theological essay, quite different in content and style from his letters to other Christian congregations. One reason for the difference is that the occasion for writing this letter was not the same as with the others. The other letters were written to Christian communities where Paul had been active, and several of them had been written in response to questions that had arisen after Paul's departure. Most scholars agree that Paul intended to visit Rome, as he said, and that he wrote the letter to the Christian congregation there in preparation for his visit (Rom. 1:7, 15; 15:23–24, 28–29, 32). But he had not yet been to Rome, had not founded the congregation there, and thus was not personally acquainted with it.

Another reason for the difference in style and content is that, based on his remarks in chapter 15 about finishing his work in Asia Minor and Greece and preparing to take the offering he had raised there to the saints in Jerusalem (Rom. 15:19–26), Paul was at a point in his career where setting forth a summary of his views would have been an understandable desire. In any case, the Romans essay is the most mature statement we have of Paul's religious ideas, and it must have been written with all his co-workers and congregations in mind, not just the Christians in Rome.

The letter is actually a comprehensive elaboration of Paul's gospel and thus the earliest systematic treatise we have of a rationale for Christian myth and ritual. Systematic theologians have often regarded it as the most important text in the New Testament, and it has played a profoundly influential role in the history of Christian thought from Augustine at the turn of the fifth century, through Martin Luther and the reformers in the sixteenth century, to Karl Barth and other Protestant theologians of the twentieth century. We need to remind ourselves that later theologians interpreted Paul's letter in the light of later Christian thought. What we now want to understand is Paul's own theology. And since the letter was not addressed to a specific congregational situation, the only background we have against which to highlight its conceptual achievements is the earlier work, views, and letters of Paul.

From the letter it is clear that Paul's purpose was to make the case for his gospel to the gentiles, and that he had gentile ears in mind no matter where they happened to reside. Romans is thus a programmatic essay of the type the Greeks would have called a *protreptic*, or reasoned argumentation for a particular philosophical position. The rhetorical style of the letter bears this out, for it moves through a set of theses elaborated according to Greek rules of argumentation, and it sets up straw men as opponents, which was customary practice in Greek schools of rhetoric and philosophy (Stowers 1981). This means that Romans gives us a marvelous opportunity to see Paul at work on the logic and significance of his gospel project as a philosophical or theological enterprise. The familiar Pauline building blocks are all present: the promise to Abraham; God's plan to include gentiles among his children; the argument against circumcision; the proclamation of the Christ myth; the contrast between living under the law and living by faith; the spirit of life; the body of Christ; the ethic of holiness; and the day of judgment. In each case, however, a change in nuance has taken place when compared with earlier letters. These conceptual refinements give an entirely new tenor to Paul's emerging system of thought. Some are changes in terminology, emphasis, or the interpretation of the significance of some feature of his gospel. Other shifts in Paul's thinking can be detected in the softening of sharp edges characteristic of earlier polemics. All of these turns are related to a single factor, namely Paul's desire to make his gospel understandable to gentiles. That was not an easy task, given the decidedly Jewish mentality in the core logic of the Christ myth. After all, the claim to know what the God of Israel intended for the world of Jews and gentiles lay at the heart of the whole intellectual enterprise. So spelling out his gospel plan of salvation for Greek ears to hear may not have impressed Greek philosophers uninterested in Jewish theological questions. But for gentile Christians who had been attracted to the congregations of the Christ for other reasons, Paul's attempt to translate the logic of the Christ myth into recognizable philosophical concepts may have given them something to think about. At least Paul had to hope so.

The first conceptual advance was developed in the first three chapters where Paul rephrased the human problem to which the gospel provided an answer. The problem was no longer stated in terms of gentile ethnicity or Jewish failure to keep the law. The problem, Paul said, was the power of sin. This was a brand new concept, a concept that Paul developed in order to include both Jew and gentile, or all humankind, within the same horizon and in need of the Christian gospel. Instead of referring to sins in the plural, a notion that would have recalled the Jewish concept of transgressions or sins that were committed specifically in relation to particular commandments, Paul used the singular and thus turned the concept of sin into a universal feature of human existence. More than that, he personified sin as an objective power or field of force that determined the whole of human existence "before" the coming of Christ. In order to make this shift, the "law" that served as the standard by which sin could be judged was also reconceptualized as an ethical norm built into the very structure of the universe, a "natural law" that had to be obvious to all in the ordering of the created world. Since that was so, according to Paul, the licentious and unethical behavior that prevailed among humans everywhere demonstrated their sinful condition and left them without excuse. What a projection of Jewish ethical categories onto the cosmos as an all-encompassing domain! Jews would have winced; Greeks would have shivered. But gentile Christians may have been caught off guard, hard-pressed to argue against the clever merger of the two laws, the law of nature and the law of Moses. So the familiar consignment of all human beings to a sinful state, and thus a need for the gospel, was conceived. It was Paul's own invention. To think such a thought had not occurred to other Christians or Jesus people. And notice the direction of the argument. Paul presupposed the solution when he conjured up the problem. Some would say that was cheating. And yet, to this day, Christian theologians have used his concept of sin as a neutral and apt category to describe what they call "the human problem."

For Paul, the gospel was still defined by the myth of Christ's death and resurrection, of course, and various formulations of the Christ myth occur throughout the essay. When compared with earlier expressions, however, these references to the founding event are curiously less dramatic than one expects from Paul. He does not dwell on images of the crucifixion, does not emphasize the proclamation of the cross, and does not say that it is "foolish" when compared with Greek philosophy or Jewish wisdom as in the Corinthian correspondence (1 Cor. 1:18–25). In Romans there is only one elaborate declaration on the significance of the death of Jesus. It is the important statement in Romans 3:21–26, the pre-Pauline core of which we have already considered in chapter 3. Paul's elaboration of this core is a dense compression of terms asserting that Jesus' death was a convincing demonstration of Jesus' faithfulness and God's righteousness with regard to some divine plan. The divine plan, "attested by the law and the prophets," was to offer "all who had sinned" grace, redemption, and justification in the eyes of God. Before Jesus' death God had "overlooked" sins in order to demonstrate his "forbearance," but now, by regarding Jesus' death as a sacrificial atonement, God's righteousness had been disclosed in his willingness to "justify" anyone who came to faith and faithfulness because of Jesus. One can see how closely Paul stayed to the fundamental logic of the Christ myth even while expanding upon the divine plan behind it. The only surprise is the mention of the death as a "sacrifice," but this can be explained. Because Paul had defined the human condition as one of enslavement to sin, he had to slip into the metaphors of redemption and sacrifice in order to suggest the effect of Christ's death as "release" and "freedom." It is important to see that he did not develop these sacrificial metaphors, preferring instead the language of justification and martyrdom (Rom. 1:16–17; 5:6–11). This shows that Paul knowingly appealed to the Greek notion of the noble death as the way to understand the significance of the Christ myth.

As for explaining the resurrection from the dead, a problematic notion for Greek mentality, Paul switched from his earlier attempts to describe an eschatological event to the mythic notions of ascension and transformation. He did this by linking the idea of Jesus' being "raised" to the concepts of spirit, power, and life. He no longer insisted on the idea of a spiritual body raised from the dead as he did in answer to the Corinthians' rejection of the notion of resurrection (Rom. 1:3–4; 4:25; 6:4–11; 8:11; 8:34; 10:9; 14:9). So Paul took a very big step toward accommodating Greek mentality. In effect, Paul reinterpreted the Christ myth as an understandable transformation from the human condition of being determined by "sin," "flesh," and "death," to "life" in the spiritual kingdom of God. On this model, what happened to Jesus could also be experienced by Christians, according to Paul, except that in their case it was more a transfer of citizenship, a transfer from the domain of sin and death to the spiritual kingdom over which Christ now ruled as lord. Believers experienced this transfer by conversion and by being baptized into the Christian community. Thus the Christ myth could now be seen as: (1) a founding event that created or revealed a new spiritual domain; (2) a demonstration of the power required to create that new spiritual domain; (3) a disclosure of the path by which access was gained to the new kingdom; and (4) the establishment of a pattern that people could imitate or follow in order to be transferred from one's "old" or customary world into that new domain. And as for the notion of the spirit, which had gotten so out of hand in the Corinthian congregation, Paul boxed it in with great precision by making sure that its activity was to be understood only in relation to this interpretation of the Christ myth and always within the arena of the spiritual kingdom over which Christ ruled. So the Greek concept of the spirit was being tamed by the Christ even as the Christ was being transformed into a Hellenistic deity.

Paul's taming of the spirit had a very precise objective in view. The concept of sin colored the horizon against which the Christ event glistened and the new spiritual kingdom came into view. This was Paul's vision of a Christian "Israel" composed of both Jews and gentiles living together in purity, holiness, and righteousness, and it was this vision that drove his entire mission and mythmaking enterprise. He knew from his experiences with the Corinthians that Greeks had a difficult time understanding the social and ethical dimensions of his Christian vision. So his challenge was to translate his concern for social ethics into terms that Greeks could understand. He did so by working with the term *righteousness*, a term that allowed a bridge to be built between the logic of the Christ myth and Greek ethical philosophy. Paul intentionally forced a play between two connotations of the Greek word *dikaiosyne*, one of which stemmed from the verb *dikaioō* (to make right, declare right, or vindicate), the other of which stemmed from the adjective *dikaios* (to be right, to be just). By allowing the term *dikaiosyne* to mean both "justification" and "righteousness," Paul was able to anchor his concern for ethics (righteousness) right there in the core logic of the Christ myth where justification or vindication was the theme. He did have to overlook the fact that the Christ myth was about justifying the *un*righteous, not about establishing righteousness as the standard for being welcomed into the kingdom of God. But since "declaring right" was what the Christ myth was about, it was easy to suggest that living according to the standard of righteousness must therefore be the mark of the purity and holiness required of the people of God. He worked this out in Romans 6:11–23, where we finally catch sight of Paul's purpose in setting up the contrast between sin and righteousness in the first three chapters. That purpose was to describe righteousness as the solution to the human problem of being enslaved to sin. The absolutely astonishing result of this chain of associations is that the Christian corner on righteousness started to look very much like the answer to what the Greeks called the problem of self-control (Stowers 1994).

Self-control was the uppermost goal of most popular Greek philosophies of the time. With the world whirling around without and the passions stirring up desires within, all agreed that the mark of the truly superior person was self-control. It was the mark of excellence for judging one's character, education, virtue, composure, integrity, and self-esteem. Stoics preached it. Cynics worked it out according to their own assessment of life's challenges. Even Epicureans found ways of combining the idea of self-control with their views on the importance of pleasure. For the Greeks, self-control was the same as being able to control one's passions. According to Paul, living in sin was the same as being "handed over" to "lusts" and "passions" (Rom. 1:24–32), the very condition that, according to the Greeks, was in need of being brought under control. And throughout the essay, Paul set up the contrasts between sin and righteousness, flesh and spirit, enslavement and the disciplined life on the model of the Greek contrast between enslavement to the passions and self-control. And so, having set things up to suggest that the righteousness available to Christians by virtue of the Christ event was, in effect, not just a matter of status in the eyes of God, as the original logic intended, but the power to live a disciplined life, Paul was ready to see if he could actually put such thoughts into words.

Chapter 7 of Romans offers a marvelous soliloquy of despair by someone unable to bring the passions under control. It was written from a thoroughly Greek point of view except that Paul used the language of law, sin, and death instead of the Greek notions of passion and desire to establish the need for Christ as the way to achieve self-control. It concludes with a cry of thanksgiving for being rescued by Christ from such a horrible fate. Greeks may have done tailspins trying to grasp the new language of Christ's redemptive power that Paul asserted as the answer to one's powerlessness to control the passions, but they would easily have recognized the assertion involved. Paul simply said that the spirit of Christ was the solution to the Greek quest to achieve virtue. The corollary was that, since virtue was not a personal achievement, there was no room for "boasting" about one's righteousness, the theme that Paul developed in the interest of turning the notion of discipline into a Christian social ethic.

As for the apocalyptic threat of God's judgment upon sinners, Paul also found a way to tone it down for Greek ears to comprehend. He did this by isolating the various functions of the traditional apocalyptic scenario and relocating them. God's wrath was already "revealed from heaven," according to Paul, forming a contrast with God's righteousness, which also was already "revealed" in the Christ myth (Rom. 1:17–18). The "day of wrath" could still be mentioned in passing as a caution about a future day of reckoning (Rom. 2:5), but God's response to human sinfulness had already been "revealed" in the obvious fact of human enslavement to the passions. According to Paul, this was an act of God, who "gave them up" or "handed them over" to their sinful condition (Rom. 1:24, 26, 28). This left the apocalyptic scenario of the end time open for a more constructive proposal, the imagining of a time when the Christian mission would reach its completion in the glorious reunion of Jews and gentiles in the one kingdom of God (Rom. 9–11, especially 11:25–32). This was hardly the intention of the traditional apocalyptic imagination, and it shows the degree to which Paul's own conception of the gospel for the gentiles, an invitation to belong to the children of Abraham, was the motivation and guiding principle for his mission from beginning to end.

It was this vision of a kingdom that had determined every new extrapolation in Paul's revisions of the Christ myth. It was also this vision that determined all the attempts he made to revise the history of Israel. And now we can see that it was this vision as well that forced a most fantastic stretch of the imagination in order to picture the way the story of God and his people would end. Thus, what Paul achieved in his essay to the Romans was not merely an exposition of his system of thought, whether as a philosophy, theology, or mythic worldview. It was a comprehensive revision and expansion of the history of Israel as the story of God's desire to bless humankind with righteousness. According to Paul, the story encompasses all of creation and all of history. It pivots on three dramatic moments: the creation of Adam, the coming of Christ, and the final reconciliation of the wayward world to God (Rom. 11:15). Adam represents humankind as well as the first human being. Because of his transgression, sin and death entered into the world. Christ also represents humankind as well as the man whose act of righteousness made justification and life possible for all (Rom. 5:12–21). The story of Israel fills the history between Adam and Christ; the story of the gentile mission fills the history between Christ and the *eschaton*. But the story of Israel no longer ends with Christ, and the story of the gentile mission no longer ends with all the nations being saved. At the end "all Israel will be saved" by being "grafted" back into the great family tree of the justified children of God (Rom. 11:17–24). Some story. It cannot solve the many conceptual contradictions it creates. But it does reveal the criteria that Paul had used all along when elaborating and revising his view of the gospel, and it does soften some of the more offensive hyperboles that Paul had fallen into on previous occasions. The absurd argument that Christ was the "seed" of Abraham no longer appears. The children now included the faithful Jews as well as the gentiles. And one no longer finds the harsh polemic against the law characteristic of earlier letters. Instead, Paul could now say that the Israelites are his own people and that "to them belong the adoption, the glory, the covenants, the giving of the law, the worship, and the promises; to them belong the patriarchs, and from them, according to the flesh, comes the Christ, who is over all, God be blessed forever" (Rom. 9:4–5). That is quite a relocation of emphasis. Apparently the significant contrast now was not that between Jews and gentiles, or even between Jews and Christians, but between "sinners" and those whose righteousness came from faith. The scene is a bold and striking projection. And what an unexpected coincidence. Paul turned the Jewish scriptures into a Christian epic in the course of laying out a programmatic argument for the gentile mission. But he ended it with a fundamentally Jewish vision of the victory of righteousness. One wonders what the gentile Christians in Rome thought of Paul's inclusive vision.

THE LETTER TO PHILEMON

A runaway slave, Onesimus, joined Paul's company in Ephesus and became a Christian. What was Paul to do? He was personally acquainted with the slave's master, Philemon, also a Christian and apparently the host of a house-church in Colossae where Paul had been active (Philem. 1–2; cf. Col. 4:9). "In Christ" there was no longer slave and free (Gal. 3:28), but only "brothers and sisters" in the new family of God's children. In the Roman world, however, the institution of slavery was not in question, and the laws that governed the treatment of slaves were clear. Paul was in danger of abetting a runaway, and that meant full legal and financial responsibility for damages due to the owner for the loss of his slave. So Paul was faced with a serious dilemma. The question was not only what to do, but how to live in the Roman world as a Christian. What real difference did it make for a slave to join the fictive family of God? Paul the apostle and Paul the citizen were at odds, as were the kingdom of God and the Roman Empire, when faced with Onesimus.

Paul's response was both practical and sage. In the last analysis, social relations in the new Christian community were a matter of attitude and regard, not a rejection of the social institutions and codes that governed life in the real world. So Paul sent Onesimus back to Philemon with this letter, asking Philemon to receive him without punishment as a "brother" and as Paul's own "child." Paul told him that Onesimus had been of service to him in his imprisonment (*onesimos* means useful), and for that reason Paul was thankfully indebted to Philemon even as Philemon was now indebted to Paul. Paul hoped that Philemon would welcome Onesimus even as he would welcome Paul.

This letter is an extremely valuable document. It spotlights an actual situation in which Christians had to confront the gap between the kingdom of God as a mythic ideal and Roman society as the real world in which they lived. After spending so much time in the fantastic worlds of Paul's lively imagination, seeing him struggle with practical considerations comes as a great relief. Here we learn that he fully understood the place Christians occupied as a religious association or a philosophical school within a larger, working society. He somehow understood what we would call the social function of myth. As with myths in general, the Christian myth was a projection onto the cosmic screen whose purpose was to imagine ideals, canvass desires, and create a space for reflecting upon the actual state of affairs. When confronted with this concrete case, however, Paul did not use the notion of the one body of Christ to question the institution of slavery. As he would put it in his correspondence to the Philippians, also written from prison at about the same time, Christians should be "blameless and innocent, children of God without blemish in the midst of a crooked and perverse generation, in which you shine like stars in the world," because "our citizenship is in heaven" (Philem. 2:15; 3:20). There is no indication that the Christ cult developed a social program aimed at calling the institutions of the Greco-Roman world into question. Paul's letter to Philemon shows only that the Christ cult fostered a certain circumspection with respect to the Roman world and that it could encourage critical thinking about social relations with the Christian ideal in mind.

THE PHILIPPIAN CORRESPONDENCE

Paul's letter to the Philippians is the icing on the Pauline cake. Paul is off guard. Preachments, polemics, and defensiveness are at a minimum. An especially close and friendly relationship with the Christian congregation at Philippi sets a tone of intimacy. Paul writes freely about his desires, joys, and sorrows. It is the closest we can get to an inside view of Paul's personal experience of the Christ.

The letter is actually composed of three letter fragments, accidentally saved as it appears and crudely joined together at some later time by those who collected the letters of Paul in the name of the Pauline school (Phil. 4:10–20; 1:1–3:1; 3:2–4:9). The first two seem to have been written from Ephesus around the time of Paul's imprisonment there (ca. 54–55 C.E.), or five to eight years after Paul first established the congregation in Philippi. Epaphroditus had arrived with gifts from Philippi for

Paul's support, and Paul looked back on earlier occasions when the Philippians had sent their gifts to him (Phil. 4:15–18). Epaphroditus stayed with Paul for a while and suffered an illness before Paul sent him back to Philippi with Timothy, bearing a letter of thanks (Phil. 2:19–30). The third letter fragment is more difficult to place (Phil. 3:2–4:9). The address is missing and there is no express mention of the Philippian congregation. The situation addressed is also difficult to place, for Paul writes against persons who were pestering the congregation with the need to be circumcised and perhaps with extravagant views about spiritual perfection. It is possible that this third letter fragment was not originally addressed to Philippi at all but inserted between the other two letter fragments because of the personal tone. In any case, the Philippian correspondence is marked by unguarded statements about Paul's personal feelings.

What strikes the reader most is the contrast between the way Paul refers to the Christ myth and the way he writes about himself. The Christ myth is referred to matter-of-factly; Paul's own involvement with it is passionate. What we see is the extent to which Paul the apostle and preacher convinced Paul the person of the reality of the imaginary world he had constructed. The Christ myth fills the horizon even as he writes about himself, his imprisonment, his concern for the well-being of the Philippians, his conversion, his manner of life, and his desire to reach the goal at the end of his life, namely to "attain the resurrection from the dead," "the heavenly call of God in Christ Jesus" (Phil. 3:11, 14). What a remarkable attestation of personal conviction in the objective reality of his gospel! It is also a remarkable self-disclosure for a Jewish Christian at the end of a twenty-year mission under the banner of a collective, corporate, social vision. Paul the person wanted to be saved! "I want," he said, "to know Christ and the power of his resurrection . . . ; not that I have already obtained this or have already reached the goal; but . . . I press on toward the goal for the prize of the heavenly call . . ." (Phil. 3:10–14). Paul actually wanted to experience personally the power of Christ's resurrection, an event of transformation that he had proclaimed as a unique occurrence in the case of Christ and as an eschatological drama in the case of the collective destiny of Christians. How could Paul have become so enrapt in the thought of personally stepping into the mythic world of Christ's death and resurrection, "sharing his sufferings by becoming like him in his death, if somehow I may attain the resurrection from the dead" (Phil. 3:10–11)?

The answer is that Paul's intellectual efforts to accommodate both Greek and Jewish ways of thinking in the interest of his gospel had affected both his imagination of the Christ myth and his own relation to it. He had been a missionary and broker of cultural merger since his conversion, a call to be an apostle to the gentiles, inviting them into the kingdom of Israel's God. But as the mission advanced, Paul's lofty vision of a single family of God for both Jews and gentiles had to be defended against those who championed conflicting values on both cultural fronts. Caught in the middle, Paul worked out his own definitions of the gospel by drawing upon each cultural tradition even as he drew the line against what he considered views and practices that endangered the balance of cultures basic to the vision. In the course of this mythmaking, the figure of the Christ became a dense, symbolic repository of two cultural mentalities and their patterns of thought. As we have seen, the Christ was overlaid with mythic and anthropological concepts from both the Semitic and the Hellenistic worlds. In Paul's mind, the Christ was now a historic person, now the son of God, a "corporate personality" representing a collective humanity, a cosmic king, a spiritual power pervading the cosmos, the hidden meaning behind the significant events of Israel's history, and the incarnation of the very mind, promise, and intention of God for humankind. That is an extremely dense symbol. A Jewish penchant for personified abstractions and divine agency merged with a Greek predilection for conceptual abstractions and cosmic order. The Christ had become an overwhelming, all-encompassing symbol of the agency of a Jewish God in a Greek world.

We need to add only one other ingredient to the picture in order to understand Paul's desire. It is the Greek notion of *mimesis*, or "imitation." Paul's discourse in Philippians turns on the desire for *mimesis*. He set forth the Christ hymn as a pattern to be imitated (Phil. 2:6–11). He described his own pattern of life as an example, to be imitated (Phil. 3:7–17). He wanted the Philippians to imitate the "mind . . . that was in Christ Jesus" (Phil. 2:5). He wanted the Philippians to imitate his example (Phil. 3:17). And he himself wanted to "become like" Christ in his death and resurrection (Phil. 3:10–21). The concept of *mimesis*, to copy a pattern or an example, strikes deeply into the Greek tradition of philosophy, education, and ethical teaching (Castelli 1992). The English terms *imitation* and *copy* do not get at the significance of the concept. Pattern expressed structure, character, and the very being of things. To imitate the pattern of an example meant to become like it, to share its character and being. What had happened to the Christ symbol in the cultural merger was that a representative human figure had been deified as a cosmic spirit. And the Christ myth was the story of its transformation from the one to the other. The combination was apparently overpowering. Paul continued to resist the Corinthian temptation of claiming to experience the spirit of the resurrection before the *eschaton*. But he could not withstand the thought of becoming so like Christ in his death that he would personally experience the power of his resurrection. The question was, when would that resurrection happen? A close reading shows that Paul cleverly avoided the problem this created for his customary reservation of "the" resurrection for the final, collective apocalyptic drama. But the euphemism of "straining forward to what lies ahead . . . [to] press on toward the goal for the prize of the heavenly call of God in Christ Jesus" belies the seduction of anticipating a personal resurrection in the near future. Paul would not be the only Christian unable to resist such a desire, as we shall see. Personal salvation as spiritual transformation, offered by imitating the Christ of the cosmos, would become the hallmark of a major stream of Christianity.

6

GOSPELS OF JESUS
THE CHRIST

War broke out in Palestine in the year 66 C.E. A ridiculous Roman procurator, Gessius Florus, was not able to control street fighting in Caesarea between Jews and Greeks over a property dispute next to the synagogue, or a public demonstration in Jerusalem to mock his pilfering of temple treasury funds. Two little sparks are all these were, but they landed in a tinderbox, and Florus left Jerusalem in retreat to Caesarea.

The political mood of Jews throughout the empire had been growing tense since the reign of Gaius Caligula, emperor from 37 to 41 C.E. Caligula had offended the Jews by planning to have his image placed in the temple at Jerusalem. Under Claudius (41–54 C.E.) and Nero (54–68 C.E.), who actively intervened in Palestinian politics without much wisdom, the situation worsened. The last Herodian king of Palestine, Agrippa I, who was knowledgeable enough about Jewish affairs to keep the peace in Judea, died in 44 C.E. A famine in 46 C.E., deteriorating economic conditions, a series of seven Roman procurators who were inept and hated, aristocratic family intrigues in Jerusalem, collaborations with the Romans, unpopular political appointments to the high priesthood, internal Jewish religious party strife, the emergence of several resistance groups, and a series of ruthless executions by the Romans set the stage for a popular uprising. No king, the wrong high priest, a compromised aristocracy, and a hated foreign power meant that the traditional structure of Jewish society had all but vanished.

Leaders of armed guerrilla movements took advantage of Florus' retreat from Jerusalem and vied for control of fortresses in Jerusalem, Judea, Idumea, and Galilee. Attempts to put down the resistance by Gallus, the governor of Syria, and Agrippa II, client king of cities in the north Transjordan, were not successful. In February of 67 C.E., Nero appointed Vespasian as special commander of Roman troops to suppress the Jewish rebellion, and Vespasian started his march toward Jerusalem. His troops easily routed what must have been a pitiful army of defenders in Galilee, quickly organized under Josephus who had been sent there by remnants of the temple establishment in Jerusalem. Galilean villages were razed, and the fortress at Jotapata, a few miles north of Sepphoris where Josephus and his men had taken refuge, was overrun. Josephus survived the slaughter at Jotapata by deserting to the Romans, and Vespasian moved on to take control of Perea in the Transjordan and western Judea. He might then have taken Jerusalem except for a strategy of containment to let the several warring parties wear each other down. When Nero died in 68 C.E., Vespasian was acclaimed emperor by his troops and returned to Rome. The command of the Jewish war was then transferred to Titus, his son. In the meantime, chaos reigned in Jerusalem.

In *The Jewish War*, Josephus describes the confusion in Jerusalem during the temple's last two years (68–70 C.E.). Political factions were at war within the city. Leaders of various groups representing the aristocracy, the high priesthood, an Idumean party, Hasidic movements, and guerrilla bands from the several countrysides, including Galilee, had taken advantage of the confusion following Florus' retreat and converged on Jerusalem in the attempt to take control of the city. The reasons for the long list of intrigues, collaborations, betrayals, and internecine slaughters recounted by Josephus are difficult to follow. But one thing is clear. All factions were driven to desperate measures in the face of the Roman threat and the complete breakdown of social order throughout the land of Palestine. Many residents fled Jerusalem during these years, leaving the city to armed bands who fought each other to gain control of the temple and the citadel. It is also clear that, in addition to the uncontrollable surge of desires to press grievances, right wrongs, and gain political power, the reinstatement of the second temple was in everyone's mind. The office of the high priesthood was contested, and contenders were slain. Faction leaders assumed the role of the king of the Jews and were killed. At the very end, when Titus invaded Jerusalem, he found only two faction leaders left, a certain John of Gischala who was hiding in a cave and Simon bar Giora, the ruthless leader of the Idumean faction who had come out on top. Titus found Simon standing in the temple clothed in purple robes. He leveled Jerusalem, sentenced John to life imprisonment, and took Simon back to Rome in chains for the traditional triumphal procession. After the procession, Simon was executed as the king of the Jews, Titus was deified, and the story of Rome's conquest of Jerusalem was memorialized on Titus' arch, still standing at the top of the Sacra Via in the ruins of the old Roman forum.

The Roman-Jewish war destroyed more than a city, citadel, and temple. It brought to an end the history of the second temple. Jews of all persuasions had assumed the temple-state to be God's design for Jerusalem. But now the sacrifices ceased. The sacrificial system of priests, scribes, and courts came to its end. The establishment of the priestly aristocracies was gone. Dissenters such as the sect at Qumran no longer had any reason to exist, for they had hoped for an end to the current establishment of tainted priests, not for an end to the temple system itself. Now the temple lay in ruins. The city was desolate. The inhabitants who had not fled were sold into slavery, and the land became a Roman province.

The end of the second temple meant that all the grand traditions of Israel were in question. Israel's epic was supposed to end with the Jewish occupation of the land and the establishment of a temple-state at Jerusalem. The covenants with the patriarchs, the promises to Abraham, the Mosaic traditions of the exodus, law, and wilderness trek, the history of the kings and prophets had all been interpreted as constitutional history for the establishment of a temple theocracy in Jerusalem. Even Jews in the diaspora, such as Philo of Alexandria, could not imagine the continued existence of the Jewish people throughout the world should the temple-state in Jerusalem ever be destroyed. The temple at Jerusalem served as the symbol of Jewish presence in the world. It was the place of pilgrimage and festival, the recipient of a tax that all Jews everywhere paid into its treasury, the center of a Jewish banking network, and site of important schools. Without a temple-state centered in Jerusalem, what were Jews to think about the glorious history of Israel? What were they to think about themselves and their presence in the Greco-Roman world?

The trauma is evident in Jewish attempts to accept and understand what had happened, and in the subsequent scramble to save some pieces from the past and put them back together again. The apocalypses of 2 Baruch and 4 Ezra from the time after the war are full of laments over Jerusalem as a desolate city, expressions of despair in the face of God's incomprehensible failure to protect it, struggles with guilt for the sins that surely must have been the cause of the disaster, and prayers that cry out for some way to imagine a future for Israel despite the destruction of the city. "I went to the holy place, sat down upon the ruins and wept" (2 Bar. 35:1). "Why has Israel been given over to the gentiles for reproach? . . . Why has the law of our fathers been made of no effect? . . . Why do the written covenants no longer exist? . . ." (4 Ezra 4:23). "O Adam, what have you done? For though it was you that sinned, the fall was not yours alone, but ours also who are your descendants. How does it profit us that the eternal age is promised to us when we have done the works that bring death?" (4 Ezra 7:118–19). Thus the laments were written, imagined from the mouths of figures crying out of the past, from the time of the first destruction of the city, as if to take courage from the fact that the first exile of the children of Israel had not been the last. But what did these laments suggest for the present time? What was there to do in the meantime, in the aftermath?

Some despaired of any restoration as long as Rome was in power. That was the realistic answer. Some projected a time when Rome would reap its just deserts. That was the apocalyptic answer: "Endure with patience the wrath that has come upon you from God. Your enemy has overtaken you, but you will soon see their destruction and will tread upon their necks. . . . Just as she [Rome] rejoiced at your fall and was glad for your ruin, so she will be grieved at her own desolation" (Bar. 4:25, 33). Some gave up on history as the arena of salvation and projected a destiny for the righteous in heaven. That was the gnostic answer. Some mustered the strength for one last, belated attempt to regain Jewish control of Jerusalem and went down to humiliating defeat. This happened under Simon bar Kochba in 132–135 C.E., after which Hadrian renamed Jerusalem Aelia Capitolina, rebuilt the city as a Roman provincial capital, and declared it off-limits to Judeans on pain of death. And others still, such as Johanan ben Zakkai the Pharisee, carried the Torah of Moses with them as they fled Jerusalem to take up residence in other towns and cities of Palestine. There they addressed the question of how to keep the law in the absence of the sacrificial system. From them would eventually arise the academies of rabbinic Judaism, the mishnaic codes of purity, and the regulation of liturgy for diaspora synagogues.

The war was traumatic as well for the early Jesus movements. In the prewar materials from the Jesus movements discussed in chapter 2, there is not the slightest hint of interest in or concern about the temple-state in Jerusalem. It was simply there, taken for granted. After the war, reflections on the fate of the temple show that Jesus people also had been deeply affected by the war, and that they had been just as confused as other Jews about what to do, whose side to be on, and what to make of the dreadful destruction. The lament over Jerusalem in Q is full of sorrow and sadness. "O Jerusalem . . . your house is left desolate" (Q 13:34–35). The little apocalypse in the Gospel of Mark, chapter 13, "predicts" in retrospect the destruction of the temple, counsels flight, and cautions against following false prophets and false messiahs. Thus the Markan community had experienced the war in ways that recall Josephus' account. Later traditions tell of the flight of the Jesus people from Jerusalem to Pella, in the Tranjordan. We are not told why they fled, but it must have been occasioned by the outbreak of violence that precipitated the war. Unfortunately, we do not know enough about the Jesus people in Jerusalem to trace their loyalties and history during this troubled time. However, all the evidence points to an understanding of the Jesus legacy that was able to accommodate Jewish piety and perhaps some kind of loyalty to the temple as an institution or at least an ideal. There is a report in Josephus that James, the brother of Jesus and the "leader" of the Jesus group in Jerusalem, was killed along with others by an overzealous high priest in 62 C.E. as the prewar violence began (*Jewish Antiquities* 20.200). According to Josephus, Ananus, the high priest, accused them of having transgressed the law, but what specifically that may have been is unclear. In any case, it was probably about this time that the Jesus people in Jerusalem disbanded.

Very serious reflection had to set in when the war ended. As we have seen, both the Jesus movements and those engaged in the Christian mission had been eagerly seeking ways to justify their existence as heirs to the grand traditions of Israel. The burning questions had to do with how Jesus fit into the picture, where to locate the kingdom of God, and how to relate the new, unlikely communities of Jesus and Christ people to the various forms of being Jewish in the first century. Now that the temple-state was no longer the central institutional form of Judaism, the epic would have to be revised, for it could no longer be read as if its promise had been fulfilled in Jerusalem. And since the failure of the second-temple establishment was easily laid to the account of its sins, the stage was set for others more righteous to take its place as the rightful heirs of the epic's promise. We have just considered a few of the ways Jews responded to this bewildering situation. We now need to recognize the options taken by Christians.

The congregations of the Christ were not as deeply affected by the Roman-Jewish war as were the Jesus people. The Christian congregations had quickly developed their own system of myth and ritual on the model of a Hellenistic cult of a dying and rising god. But the Jesus movements had thought of themselves on the model of schools and had stayed in touch with their Galilean origins and generally Jewish cultural environment. These movements were caught in the confusion created by the catastrophic events and found themselves forced to rethink everything. It must have been a distressing time but also one of great, exhilarating intellectual challenge. The thought that commended itself to several of these groups was to distance themselves from the "sins" of the recent Jewish past and reread the epic of Israel to end with Jesus instead of with the temple-state. That thought was revolutionary, and the reasons for bringing judgment upon the recent Jewish establishment began to take on a very critical edge.

The lament in Q accounts for the desolation by referring to the fathers' killing the prophets in whose line the people of Q understood themselves to stand. Another saying in Q, attributed to the Wisdom of God, explains that ". . . the blood of all the prophets, shed from the foundation of the world, [will] be required of this generation . . . ," a censure intended to account for the terrible slaughters in Jerusalem (Q 11:50). That the Thomas people were wrenched by the war, its violence, and the apocalyptic climate it engendered is traceable throughout the Gospel of Thomas and especially in references to the "vineyard," "cornerstone," and "house" (that is, temple) that, in their view, justly came to an end (GTh 65, 66, 71). The addition to Paul's letter to the Thessalonians shows that some early Jesus people, or perhaps Christians, were angered by their exclusion from some synagogue, charged the Jews with killing Jesus and the prophets, and concluded that God's "wrath" had come upon them at last, apparently with reference to the destruction of Jerusalem (1 Thess. 2:16). And the author of the Gospel of Mark took full advantage of the situation by writing the story of Jesus' life as if the destruction of the temple had been God's answer to the Jews' rejection and crucifixion of Jesus. Thus the war changed everything, both for Jews and the Jesus people. Everything had to be rethought, explained again, and each group had to find its anchor in the past in some new way.

For the history of Christianity, the most important shift in postwar thinking took place in the Markan community. It was there that a dramatic change took place in the memory and imagination of Jesus, one that laid the mythic foundation for the Christian religion. The change is documented in the Gospel of Mark, a literary achievement of incomparable historical significance. Before Mark there was no such story of the life of Jesus. Neither the earlier Jesus movements nor the congregations of the Christ had imagined such a portrayal of Jesus' life. It was Mark's composition that gathered together earlier traditions, used the recent history of Jerusalem to set the stage for Jesus' time, crafted the plot, spelled out the motivations, and so created the story of Jesus that was to become the gospel truth for Christianity. All the other narrative gospels would start with Mark. None would change his basic plot. And the plot would become the standard account of Christian origins for the traditional Christian imagination. What an achievement! Mark succeeded in collapsing the time between Jesus in the 30s and the destruction of the temple in 70 C.E. Ever after, Christians would imagine Mark's fiction as history and allow this erasure of time as a wink in the mind of Israel's God. And yet, Mark's fiction could not have been conceived before the war. It would not have made sense before the war had run its course and the tragic fate of the city was known. Why Mark imagined the life of Jesus as he did, and how he came to write his gospel, are the questions that now need to be addressed.

THE GOSPEL OF MARK

Mark's portrayal of Jesus is strikingly different from other, earlier images, whether of the Christ or of Jesus the teacher. His story of Jesus was not a gospel of the Pauline kind, proclaiming an event and interpreting it as a message of justification. His portrait of Jesus was also quite different from those created by small sets of stories about a divine man or an imposing sage as some Jesus people had imagined him. And his portrayal differed from the person behind the voice of a collection of sayings such as Q or the Gospel of Thomas. Mark's story was what the Greeks would have called a "life" (*bios*). It was a biography. Just as the Greeks would have done, Mark took the many little sayings and stories of Jesus that were available to him from earlier traditions and used them to create a new image of Jesus. Then he arranged these stories to develop some themes, such as that of Jesus' power or the plot to have him killed, and he brought the story to focus on a conflict that Jesus and God had with the Jerusalem establishment. As for the story of Jesus' crucifixion and resurrection, Mark took the basic ideas from the Christ myth but dared to imagine how the crucifixion and resurrection of the Christ might look if played out as a historical event in Jerusalem, something the Christ myth resisted. Thus Mark's story is best understood as a studied combination of Jesus traditions with the Christ myth. The combination enhanced Jesus' importance as a historical figure by casting him as the son of God or the Christ and by working out an elaborate plot to link his fate to the history of Mark's community. We may therefore call Mark's gospel a myth of origin for the Markan community. It was imagined in order to understand how history could have gone the way it had and the Jesus movement still be right about its loyalties and views.

Catching sight of the Markan community has not been easy. The story is set in the past and filled with people who were no longer present. The lines from Jesus' time to Mark's time are not clearly drawn. The Markan community is not described, not directly addressed, and only reflected opaquely in the story as if in a dark reflecting pool whose waters have been troubled. And yet, it is also clear that the story was written for readers who wanted to be sure that their kingdom movement was still alive and well, that they were still in touch with their prewar commitments, and that they still had a glorious future. If we read their story from their point of view, perhaps we can find some clues that will let us sketch a profile of the people whose story this was.

As for the author, we know only that we do not know who it was. The Mark to whom the gospel was attributed is a legendary figure from the second century. The legend may have started when someone looked for an author for the anonymous gospel among the circles of named apostles and their friends. A Mark had been mentioned by Paul as one of his fellow workers in his letter to Philemon (Philem. 24) and by Luke in the Acts of the Apostles. Then, in the first epistle of Peter, a pseudonymous document from the second century, a Mark is mentioned as Peter's son (1 Pet. 5:13). Papias, bishop of Hieropolis in Asia Minor (ca. 130), named Mark the author of the gospel and the "interpreter" of Peter, presumably as if Mark had written from Peter's memory and notes as his secretary (Eusebius, *Ecclesiastical History* 3.39). These are traces of a developing legend of a kind common for the early second century. We shall explore the reasons for these legends later in chapters 8 and 9. For now it is enough to see that the gospel was not signed by its author. This agrees with what we know about all of the gospels. Writing one was a communal process in which stories were told, polished, changed, and rearranged many times in the course of several generations. Some creative author must have credit for the final composition of each, however, for the signs of literary skill and design are obvious in all of them. I will continue the tradition of referring to Mark as the author of the Gospel of Mark, for there is no other name to use.

According to Mark, John the Baptizer was preaching about a man of power who was to come and baptize the people with the holy spirit when Jesus showed up to be baptized. The holy spirit descended, the voice of God said that Jesus was his son, and Jesus started out on his mission, preaching the gospel of God's kingdom, healing the sick, and casting out demons. Disciples, crowds, and Jewish leaders watched and reacted as Jesus moved through Galilee, withdrew to Caesarea Philippi at the northern border of the old kingdom of David and Solomon for a little talk with his disciples, then swept down through Galilee, Samaria, and Judea on a march to Jerusalem. There he confronted the religious establishment and was put to death. His death, however, was not the end of the story. That is because Jesus had been destined to come into conflict with the rulers of the world. He was God's son, and God had a controversy with Judaism of spiritual and cosmic proportions. The controversy was about God's kingdom which the scribes, Pharisees, high priests, and Herodians had botched and Jesus had come to set right. When Jesus entered their synagogues and confronted the unclean spirits there, the Jewish leaders decided to get rid of him. The same thing happened when Jesus entered Jerusalem, and then the temple. So when they killed him, they mocked him as the "king of the Jews" (Mark 15:2, 9, 12, 18, 26, 32); the veil of the temple was mysteriously rent in two "from top to bottom" (Mark 15:38); and the divine response was set in motion just as Jesus had predicted. First there would be a resurrection to vindicate Jesus (Mark 8:31; 9:31; 10:34). Then the temple would be destroyed to vindicate his message and prediction (Mark 13:2; 14:58). And finally, Jesus as the "son of man" would appear to inaugurate the kingdom of God with glory and power as a vindication and realization of God's great plan for the people (Mark 14:62). At the time of Mark's writing, everything predicted had happened on schedule except the final appearance of Jesus as the glorious king of the kingdom of God.

That is certainly a hard-hitting story. It is stunning in its realistic depiction of fabulous events, in its matter-of-fact handling of cosmic designs, and in the brevity with which it turns a few miracle stories into the only events that count in the whole history of humankind. Were it not for the fact that it was immediately popular as the gospel truth, you might think it was not to be taken very seriously. And yet it was taken seriously, so seriously in fact, that we have to regard it as a major achievement in early Christian mythmaking. We do not usually think of mythmaking as the achievement of a moment or the work of a single writer no matter how brilliant. But in Mark's case we have an obvious fiction, masterfully composed by someone who had to be doing his work at a desk as any author would. It was Mark's fiction that soon became the accepted story of the way to imagine Jesus appearing in the world. We can follow his design by noting what he did to change and reinterpret his sources. The sources we can be sure of are the sayings source Q, some parables of Jesus, many of the pronouncement stories, two sets of miracle stories, some form of the Christ myth (1 Cor. 15:3–5), the Christian meal text (1 Cor. 11:23–26), and a number of Hebrew scriptures.

A comparison of the teachings of Jesus in Mark with the collection in Q is enlightening. Mark preferred the prophetic and apocalyptic sayings from the second layer of Q and made it clear that Jesus' instruction was not for the general public but only for his disciples and followers. It was esoteric teaching about the kingdom of God yet to come. This is a very different notion of the content of Jesus' teaching from what one finds in Q or in the Gospel of Thomas. And even his disciples, to whom the "mystery of the kingdom" is expressly given (Mark 4:11), are not able to comprehend it fully. Only Mark's readers had enough perspective to understand what Jesus intended, why the disciples did not understand, and what the coded messages meant, such as those about the cup (Mark 10:38) or the temple (Mark 13:2). And as for the disciples, to whom the secret of the kingdom was given and who figure in the story as Jesus' understudies, they were Mark's addition to the picture of the "historical Jesus." Named disciples do not appear anywhere in Q. In Mark, the disciples are Jesus' "followers," but they are not set forth as positive examples to be imitated. That is because they fail to understand who Jesus was and what Jesus taught them. They are negative examples, letting the reader see that one could be a better disciple of Jesus by "following" the story in Mark's time than the disciples who "followed" Jesus in Jesus' time.

Mark treated the parables of Jesus the same way. The original point of the pre-Markan parables in chapter 4 was not about a future, eschatological kingdom, as a comparison with the parables in the Gospel of Thomas shows (Crossan 1973). Mark is the one who put that construction upon them and interpreted their message as a secret given only to the disciples.

Mark also changed the point of the miracle stories. As discussed in chapter 2, the original intention of the miracle story chains was a myth of origin for some Jesus group. It allowed an unlikely collection of Jesus' followers to think of themselves as the people of God with a leader (Jesus) something like Moses and something like Elijah, both of whom figured importantly in the formation of Israel. Mark was not interested in continuing such a notion. Instead he used the miracle stories to create the impression of Jesus' power and authority as the divine son of God. He did that by erasing the marks that identified the two chains of miracle stories as distinct literary units, and by creating other miracle stories, exaggerating the miraculous, and making miracles programmatic for all of Jesus' activity in Galilee. He emphasized exorcisms, accentuated the amazement of the crowds, and introduced demons as characters in the story who knew that Jesus' power came from God. It is the miracles in Mark that dramatize Jesus' appearance as a man of power who was really the son of God. It is the exorcisms that create the impression of a cosmic battle under way between the spirits of uncleanness that are loose in the world and the holy spirit that came upon Jesus as empowerment to announce a new world order. It has sometimes been thought that, with such a display of power in the first half of the story, the leaders in Jerusalem should not have had such power over Jesus in the second half of the story. Mark handled this problem very creatively. One device he used has been called the "messianic secret," a narrative motif in which only the demons really knew how powerful Jesus was. Another stratagem was to continue the theme of the miraculous in the second half of the story but present it in a different form. The miraculous was now evident in the accuracy of Jesus' foreknowledge and prediction of future events. But most of all, miracles were appropriate to the apocalyptic drama that started with Jesus. They set the scene for seeing Jesus' crucifixion as a first episode in a series of conflicts between God and the rulers of this world. Even though Jesus gets killed in the first battle, the series would eventuate, naturally, in victory for both the king and the kingdom.

A close look at Mark's use of the pronouncement stories yields two other important observations. One is that the plot to kill Jesus started with the conflicts portrayed in the pronouncement stories. This is clear from the announcement of the plot at the conclusion of the first cycle of pronouncement stories (Mark 2:1–3:6). This observation helps to position Mark's community as a group of Jesus people who, until recently, had close contact with a Jewish group influenced by the Pharisaic codes of purity.

The other observation is that the authority of Jesus to make pronouncements was of considerable interest to Mark. He enhanced this authority by calling it *exousia*, the Greek term for the power to make things happen. He then illustrated it by crafting a new kind of story. This Markan creation, a combination of miracle story and pronouncement story, made it appear that Jesus' power to perform miracles and his authority to make pronouncements were manifestations of the same *exousia* (Mark 1:21–28; 2:1–12; 3:1–6). Mark created this impression in the very first account of Jesus' public activity, an exorcism that took place in the synagogue at Capernaum. Jesus' authority then becomes a theme that triggers the plot to have him killed (Mark 2:10; 3:15; 6:7; 11:28–33; 13:34). It is this new kind of authority that conflicts with the authority of the scribes and Pharisees. From the reader's point of view, what Jesus said about anything was not merely true, his saying it made it happen. Even his teachings now come across as fiat. And one can also be sure that, since most of what Jesus predicted came true, the rest would also surely happen. When Jesus finally enters the temple, it is the question of his authority that is raised by "the chief priests, the scribes, and the elders" (Mark 11:28), a challenge gives rise to another set of pronouncement stories (Mark 12) and Jesus' apocalyptic predictions (Mark 13) before the pace quickens with events that will lead to his crucifixion. Merging miracle stories and pronouncement stories was a very clever device. It created a novel concept of authority befitting the novel appearance of Mark's son of God. Christians have been mesmerized ever since with the haunting suggestion that words spoken by a divinely inspired person might have the power to effect miraculous change.

Mark also drew upon the Christ myth and the lord's supper etiology from the congregations of the Christ. That Mark knew about the Christ myth is especially clear from the formulaic style of the three so-called predictions of the passion that Jesus makes on his way to Jerusalem (Mark 8:31; 9:31; 10:33). That Mark knew about the meal tradition is clear from his stylized account of the last supper (Mark 14:22–25). However, Mark was not interested in the cult of divine presence that had developed in the congregations of the Christ. He did not include the command to repeat the meal as a memorial of Jesus' death, and he shied away from the symbolism of the bread as the body of Christ, preferring instead to emphasize the cup as a symbol of the martyr's blood "poured out for many" (Mark 14:24). His supper story was not intended as an "institution" for ritual reenactment. In Mark's hand it became simply the last supper that Jesus had with his disciples. And just to make that clear, Mark had Jesus say that he would *not* celebrate a meal again until the kingdom of God arrived. For Mark, the death and resurrection of Jesus did not inaugurate a cult of spiritual presence; it signaled his departure and absence until his return as the son of man with power (Mark 14:62). Why then did Mark bring his story to a climax with a narrative of Jesus' dramatic death and departure?

Mark got his ideas about the crucifixion and resurrection from the Christ myth, but his interest in the Christ myth was limited to the martyrology at its core. That

Mark saw its fundamental logic, and that he was able to avoid the cultic interpretations it had received, was a truly remarkable intellectual achievement. He could use the notion of Jesus as a martyr, for it fit his project of accounting for the troubled history of his Jesus group. And the notion of the resurrection, if linked to an apocalyptic finale, made it possible to project a future vindication for both his group and for Jesus. To imagine that Jesus would be back in the picture again as the son of man with power would mean that the present time of troubles was survivable, since it would be bracketed by events of God's intervention. In order to make this schema work, however, Mark was faced with two imposing conceptual problems. He had to find some way of combining the Jesus traditions with which he and his group were familiar with the new thought of Jesus as a martyr. And he had to figure out how to transpose the Christ myth into historical narrative. Both problems meant that rather drastic innovations were called for. The Jesus people had not felt the need to account for Jesus' death. In the Jesus material before Mark there is no hint of any lore about Jesus' death, much less a vicarious death that was necessary in order to justify the Jesus movements. His teachings and the stories about him contained nothing that could be imagined as a cause for his being crucified by anyone. As for the Christ myth, it resisted historical explanation. Its logic of justification for a mixed community required that the motives for the vicarious death be limited to God's recognition of Jesus' willingness to die for that cause. Were all of the historical factors accounted for, other reasons would have to be given for Jesus' willingness to die, and the motivations of those who killed him would have to be insinuated. That would have undercut the effectiveness and purpose of the myth as a rationale for overcoming just such social and cultural conflicts.

Mark's community was not dependent upon a theology of justification. And Mark was not averse to accounting for the social and cultural conflict experienced by the Jesus movement. So translating the Christ myth into a story of Jesus' martyrdom was thinkable, if only he could find a way to make it plausible. We have already considered the way he recast the Jesus traditions to trigger a plot on the part of the scribes and Pharisees to have Jesus killed. Tracing the appearance of Jewish leaders throughout the story, it becomes obvious that Mark found a way to insinuate complicity for Jesus' death on the part, not only of the Pharisees, but of the priests, Sadducees, high priests, and Herodians as well. Thus the "tyrant" was in place, but the story of the martyrdom itself was yet to be told. There would have to be a provocation, an arrest, a charge, an ideological confrontation, some stories that made the executioners look both reasonable and wrong at the same time, some stories that revealed both Jesus' innocence and his willingness to die, some stories that showed how the disciples and the crowds responded to these last public events, an account of the execution, and some way to end the story after the crucifixion. Quite a challenge.

I have explored Mark's extraordinary attention to detail in crafting a plausible narrative of Jesus' martyrdom in my book *A Myth of Innocence* (1988). Here it will have to be sufficient to note the most important feature of Mark's strategy. It was the use of the old wisdom tale of the wrongly accused righteous man as a pattern for the sequence of episodes leading up to the trials and crucifixion of Jesus. This Jewish story was easily merged with the noble death pattern of the Greco-Roman martyrology, and it provided a marvelous sequel of vindication that could easily accommodate both the resurrection of Jesus and his final appearance as the son of man who would turn the tables on his former persecutors and rule over them as judge. Every episode in Mark's story can be explained as a play on motifs essential to this wisdom tale, interwoven with scenes and details that bring the earlier theme of Jesus and the disciples to a fitting conclusion as an encounter with the crucifixion.

The usual approach to Mark's so-called passion narrative has been to regard it as a historical account of what really happened, but then to fret about features of it that are difficult to accept. The list of improbable features is quite long and includes such things as the trial by night, which would have been illegal; the basis for the charge of blasphemy, which is very unclear if not completely trumped up; the failure of the witnesses to agree, which would have called for a mistrial; the right of the Sanhedrin to charge with death, a sanction that they probably did not have at the time; the insinuation of the crucifixion taking place on Passover, which would have been an outrage; Jesus' anticipation of his death as a covenant sacrifice, which might be all right for a bacchic god but hardly for the historical Jesus; the disciples falling asleep in the midst of it all; Pilate's having Jesus executed as the "king of the Jews" without a good reason to consider him so; the high priests (in the plural!) joining in the mocking; and so on. The better approach is to recognize the whole story as Mark's fiction, written forty years after Jesus' time in the wake of the Roman-Jewish war. If we first read Josephus' account of the war, we can see that Mark's retrospective on Jesus in Jerusalem would not have sounded a bit far-fetched. The temple and palace ethos Mark painted may even have seemed somewhat staid by comparison. And besides, not a single one of the principal players was still around to say it wasn't so.

Mark's interest in such a story would be the same as his interest in imagining how his group of Jesus people could still project a future. After all, they had experienced a very rocky period of their own history. Not only had some Jesus people found themselves confused about prophets, messiahs, Jesus' fate, and their own loyalties, as mentioned in Mark 13, it also appears that a break with Jewish roots and relations had recently taken place. This is clear from the pronouncement stories where the running debate with the Pharisees concerned purity codes. Members of the Markan community had taken the issue of purity very seriously, despite their insistence that the rules did not apply to them. This can mean only that they were very close to those with whom they disagreed and that the parting of the ways had been painful. It was, as we have seen, still painful enough in Mark's own mind and memory to imagine that something like it had sparked a plot to kill Jesus.

The separation of the Markan community from a Jewish community probably took place somewhere in northern Palestine or southern Syria. That is where a Jesus group most likely would have been involved with synagogues, felt the influence of Pharisaic standards, and experienced the war as troubled spectators. In his story, Mark emphasized that Jesus was a Galilean with interests in the surrounding lands and people as far away as Tyre, Sidon, Caesarea Philippi, the upper Transjordan, and the Decapolis. He also emphasized Jesus' confrontation with the scribes and Pharisees in synagogues. Since the synagogue was a diaspora institution, Mark's interest in these settings fits with his reasons for telling the story the way he did. If Markan interest in seeing his own social situation reflected in the Jesus story is right, it would solve a problem scholars have always had with Mark's presumption that there were synagogues throughout Galilee during Jesus' time (Mark 1:21, 39; 3:1), an assumption that archeologists and historians have not been able to substantiate. Mark's fiction demanded it, however, and a bit of distance from Galilee would have kept the fiction from raising too many eyebrows. For this and other reasons, Tyre and Sidon have been suggested as probable locations for Mark and his community. Placing Mark in these cities makes good sense. Everything would fit, including the educational level and resources needed to write such a gospel, as well as Mark's acquaintance with the Christian traditions of northern Syria, though without an interest in their cult. The older assumption that Mark lived in Rome makes absolutely no sense at all.

Assuming such a recent, painful separation from some diaspora synagogue would help account for the overly dramatic and excessively pugnacious features of Mark's story. It would also explain one final feature of Mark's composition that is important for our own project. It is the way Mark set his story about Jesus in relation to the tradition of Israel. Having thought of themselves as part of the heritage of Israel by virtue of participating in a diaspora synagogue, Mark's Jesus people may not have worked out a completely independent rationale for belonging to God's people. But now, no longer able to count on being part of a diaspora synagogue, they needed to create their own link to the grand traditions of Israel. Because the temple was gone, and thus the ending of the epic was in frightful disarray, Mark was free to imagine the Jesus movement taking the place of the erstwhile institutions of Judaism. That would have been a daring thought, to be sure, especially in light of the fact that Pharisees, synagogues, and other configurations of Jewish presence in the world had not just vanished when the temple disappeared. It was, however, Mark's first thought and, audacious as it was, he carried it out to a remarkable degree in the way he shaped his story.

Mark was not the first to think about Jesus' relation to Jewish tradition as a way to comprehend the importance of a Jesus movement. As we have seen, the people of Q had already found ways to suggest an association of Jesus with the best of Israel's wisdom and prophetic traditions in order to pit him and his teachings against the Pharisees in their own time. The miracle chains were more constructive, leaving the illustrious figures of Moses and Elijah in place while claiming a similar importance for Jesus. Those who worked with the pronouncement story genre took another tack altogether. They had found themselves at odds with Pharisaic codes over matters of behavior, so they looked for stories in the scriptures that they thought might counter the Pharisaic critique. They found stories to embarrass their critics as well as suggest that the behavior of Jesus and his disciples was not much different from that of others throughout Israel's history.

In contrast to these views, Mark insisted that Jesus and his program displaced earlier forms of being Jewish. Jesus should be aligned with the traditions of Israel, but seen as more than the successor to these traditions. He was instead their replacement, demanding a new orientation that rendered passé all older ways of being Jewish and thinking about Israel. Mark was hardly able to carry through with such a program in a systematic way. But the principle was clearly in mind, and he found some clever ways to make the same point at every turn in the story. He set the pattern at the beginning with the stories of John and Jesus, taken from Q. There it is made clear that Jesus was the successor to John in the line of prophets, but also qualitatively different from him in that God called him his "beloved son." The motif of the prophets being killed, also from Q, was upgraded in Mark and combined with the theme of John and Jesus. John the Baptizer is killed, for instance, as a premonition of Jesus' fate, and then Jesus is killed not only as the last of the line of prophets but also as the son of God. This is made clear in the allegory of the vineyard workers where the point is made that God "will come and destroy the tenants and give the vineyard to others" (Mark 12:9). So Jesus' death is qualitatively different from all the deaths of the prophets who went before. And the reason it is different is that Jesus was the son of God.

After his baptism by John, Jesus steps forth to announce the imminent arrival of the kingdom of God, an arrangement of power destined to confront, destroy, and supersede all Jewish institutions. In the synagogue, Jesus' authority surpasses that of the scribes. When Jesus heals the leper, Mark makes the point that he did what the priests could not do. And then he trumps the Pharisees on the very issue of doing what was lawful on the sabbath. So the scribes, the priests, and the Pharisees, those who represent the social institutions of first-century Judaism, are all overshadowed by Jesus. Who is this who outperforms the professionals in every capacity? Has he any right to best them? Has he any credentials to take their place? At the transfiguration Jesus is seen in the company of Moses and Elijah, the two figures of epic importance who gave the miracle story chains their mythic rationale. But again, as in the comparison with John the Baptizer, Mark lets their aura settle about Jesus, only to brush them aside with a voice from heaven telling the disciples, "This is my Son. . . . Listen [only] to him" (Mark 9:7). Then, as Jesus approaches Jerusalem, the crowds welcome him as the messiah, the son of David, and Mark lets the reader think for a moment that maybe the crowds have it right. The reader soon learns, however, that they are mistaken. As Jesus explains while teaching in the temple, the messiah is not David's son, he is David's lord (Mark 12:35–37). It is the same with all the other figures used to characterize Jesus. All are used only as facets of a brand new image. Mark's Jesus combines features of many mythic and ideal figures, and he performs the functions of many social roles. The list is truly staggering: child of wisdom, suffering righteous one, prophet, scribe, legislator, teacher, divine man, messiah, son of man, son of God, resurrected lord, final judge, and king of the kingdom of God. Such a figure needs no credentials except the voice of God's approval as his father. And how does the reader know of that approval? The voice is heard as part of the story. If the story holds together and is good enough to enchant its readers, the credentials will have been given. It was Mark's genius to create just such a story. It was Mark's story, in the final analysis, that created the truly incomparable figure of Jesus the Christ and son of God that Christians have always had in mind.

One final observation about Mark's workshop has to do with his reading of the Jewish scriptures. It occurred to him to turn to the texts of the prophets as a resource for his story about Jesus. He was not the first to think of the prophetic texts in this way, for the authors of Q had already engaged in a bit of playful textual reference to couple the roles of John and Jesus (Q 7:22, 27). But Mark was the first we know of who turned with some seriousness to the books of the prophets to complement the otherwise largely oral and popular motif of the killing of the prophets. It was this motif that allowed the Jesus people to align Jesus with the epic history of Israel without losing the critical edge he had come to represent for them. And as we have seen, Mark's story can actually be viewed as a mythmaking endeavor that worked with the prophet motif as its fundamental point of departure. We can now note that the prophet motif and characterization must have induced an interest in the books of the prophets. Mark combed through these books for images he could apply to Jesus as a prophet, as if the prophets had somehow anticipated Jesus' coming. He actually cited Isaiah, Jeremiah, Zechariah, Malachi, and Daniel to create or interpret events crucial to the story line, and throughout the story there are numerous turns of phrase that repeat or echo prophetic texts. It is also the case that other scriptural repetitions, especially from the Psalms, are given the force of prophetic fulfillment. So Mark turned the prophet motif into a narrative theme, then used the books of the prophets as a narrative device, in order to link Jesus with the story of Israel as its destined agent of change. This was a way of treating the Jewish scriptures that differed significantly from any earlier revision of the Israel epic, including that of Q, the pronouncement stories, the miracle story chains, and Paul. If Mark's overbold strokes fail to startle us, it is because Christians have become so accustomed to the logic of his story line. Without this story, one would have to say, the emergence of Christianity as we know it would not have happened.

THE GOSPEL OF MATTHEW

Matthew's gospel appeared in the late 80s and comes as a complete surprise. The surprise is not due to another fantastic flight of early Christian mythic imagination, additional extravagant claims upon the Israelite legacy, the hostility of its polemics, or its apocalyptic temper. The surprise is that, with that kind of buzz in the air, the

Matthean community had not been overly excited or impressed with the cosmic destinies of Jesus or the thought that it had become a brand new kind of human race. Its gospel succeeded in reducing the Jesus Christ drama to everyday proportions, and they had obviously settled in for the long haul. The Gospel of Matthew is a handbook of instructions for a Jesus movement that had made its peace with the world and with its Jewish neighbors.

It has long been recognized that the Gospel of Matthew is a document of Jewish Christianity, a form of the Jesus legacy that may have been more prevalent during the first centuries than the histories of early Christianity recorded in the New Testament let us see. Since this form of the Jesus movement did not survive the emergence of "orthodox" Christianity in the fourth century C.E., there is a touch of irony in the fact that Matthew's gospel became the preferred "gospel of the church," and that it was given the privilege of first place in the canon of the New Testament. That is because, by that time, the church had clearly distinguished itself from the contemporary form of (rabbinic-synagogue) Judaism, had succeeded in appropriating all the Jewish scriptures as the Christian Old Testament, and had developed a rich anti-Jewish (*adversus Judaios*) literature. How the author managed to compose such a winner is the question before us. Fortunately for our purposes, his strategies were few and simple, and they are easily discerned and described. As our discussion of these strategies unfolds, a rather clear picture will come into view, not only of the author at work, but of the Matthean community as well. Catching sight of this community may come as something of a relief amidst the swirl of intemperate rhetoric and behavior characteristic of other groups we have reviewed. It lets us see that, for some followers of Jesus at least, his teachings continued to be the primary attraction of his legacy and a sufficiently important reason to be loyal to his school. I will refer to the author of this gospel as Matthew, in keeping with the gospel's later attribution to one of the named disciples. In fact, however, all we know about the person who wrote this gospel is that he thought of himself as a "scribe trained for the kingdom" (Matt. 13:52).

Matthew composed his gospel by interweaving the teachings of Jesus from the book of Q into Mark's story of Jesus, then adding some sayings and stories of his own. Though he made a few editorial changes to Mark's story, and left out three or four little stories he could not use, he reproduced the whole gospel very much as Mark had written it. And in the case of Q, though he rearranged much of the material to compress it into five speeches that he had Jesus deliver at significant junctures, Matthew used all of it as well. The material special to Matthew consists primarily of the stories of Jesus' birth and infancy, a few additions to the Q material in the first speech of Jesus, the so-called sermon on the mount (Matt. 5–7), a number of parables, four of which were added to a collection of parables taken from Mark 4, and two postresurrection appearance stories. The remarkable thing about Matthew's story is that, though completely dependent on Q and Mark for the bulk of its material, it achieved a character for Jesus and a tenor for his teachings that were totally different from either precursor. In Matthew's mind, Jesus appeared as the very flowering of the wisdom and spirit intrinsic to the Jewish tradition and religion. He stepped forth as a teacher in the tradition of Moses and his Torah, not to set it aside, but to explicate its significance as an ethic of personal piety, a call to holiness at the level of attitude and motivation. In Matthew's language, Jesus said that one could and should be "pure in heart" (Matt. 5:8).

Knowing what we do about the prehistory of Q and about the way Mark treated the teachings of Jesus as esoteric, apocalyptic instruction, Matthew's understanding of these very same teachings is astounding. He had to counter Mark's picture of an enigmatic teacher whose instruction was given in "parables" so that the public would *not* be able to understand (Mark 4:12), and he had to reinterpret the aphoristic and apocalyptic sayings of Q as if they were coded for personal piety. That would have been quite a challenge. His counter to Mark was first and foremost that he included all of Q in his story of Jesus the teacher and portrayed Jesus as a public figure whose teaching was intended to be understood and accepted by any and all who heard him. In Matthew, the crowds hear more than parables, the disciples understand the instruction, and Peter is not put down. He is blessed, pronounced the "rock" on which Jesus will build his church, and given the "keys of the kingdom" (Matt. 16:17–19).

This change in characterization can be seen from the way Matthew substituted the sermon on the mount for Mark's story of Jesus' first public appearance in the synagogue at Capernaum (Mark 1:21–28). For Mark, that incident was programmatic, a display of Jesus' power, and the crowds responded in amazement because "he taught them as one who had authority, and not as their scribes." Matthew could not use that story and did not repeat it. Instead, he doffed his hat at Mark's beginning by making up a little notice about Jesus moving to Capernaum to make his home there (Matt. 4:12–16), and he summarized Mark's account of Jesus' teaching activity and fame throughout Galilee (Matt. 4:23–25). He was then able to focus instead on the sermon as the first major event in Jesus' public appearances (Matthew 5–7). It was only at the end of this sermon that Matthew cited the response of the people that "he taught them as one having authority, and not as their scribes" (Matt. 7:29).

Thus, in distinction from Mark's picture, Matthew's Jesus does not make his first impression upon the crowds by doing exorcisms. He makes it by presenting a programmatic speech. The sermon on the mount is Matthew's extremely well-crafted statement of what he wanted the reader to understand about Jesus' teaching. Taking Q's lead, he started with the beatitudes but then brought together sayings from throughout the book of Q in order to compose what the Greeks would have called an epitome of the teachings of a philosophical school. Matthew's epitome follows the rules of rhetoric, comes to a clear conclusion, and must have been considered quite a persuasive speech. For our purposes it will be enough to notice the radically new interpretation of the teachings of Jesus in Matthew when compared to the book of Q. In Q, the teachings of Jesus had little to do with the Mosaic Torah. Matthew's contention was that a translation of the Torah into an ethic of subjective piety was exactly what Jesus intended. Three features of Matthew's text can illustrate that change.

The first feature is a series of contrasts between what the people "heard" had been "said to those of ancient times," Matthew's euphemism for the Mosaic law, and what Jesus said. In each case he used the formula, "But I say unto you . . ." (Matt. 5:21–22, 27–28, 31–32, 33–34, 38–39, 43–44). Scholars have often called these "antitheses," making of the contrast an opposition between law and gospel. That is wrong. Matthew cleverly found a way to relate some of Jesus' teachings from Q with some Mosaic proscriptions in order to demonstrate their alignment and show that Jesus' teachings struck to the heart of the matter. The Mosaic Torah was not being scuttled. The contrast was between the way the law had been "heard" by Matthew's contemporaries and should be understood by the Jesus people. That contrast is certainly straightforward and very strongly put. Matthew was clearly convinced of the historic significance of Jesus' appearance as a teacher of the piety required by God. One dare not brush him aside. But the teaching was not to be understood in opposition to, or as a substitute for, the law of Moses. Instead, the teaching of Jesus was the very standard by which true adherence to the law of Moses would be judged.

This point is expressly made in the introductory statement just preceding the series of contrasts, and this is the second feature of the sermon to notice. Jesus says that he "did not come to abolish the law and the prophets . . . but to fulfill" them, that not one letter or accent mark would be erased as long as the world remained, and that the standard for judging status in the kingdom would be the degree to which one observed even the most insignificant of the commandments (Matt. 5:17–19). And then, just to make sure that the difference was clear between Jesus' interpretation of these commandments and the usual understanding associated with the scribes and Pharisees, Matthew added the warning: "Unless your righteousness exceeds that of the scribes and Pharisees, you will never enter the kingdom of heaven" (Matt. 5:20).

The third observation is that Matthew did take the liberty of adding a few instructions of his own to the teachings of Jesus. I have already discussed this practice of attribution as normal for school traditions in antiquity, so the fact that Matthew made additions to the corpus of Jesus' teachings should not be considered audacious. What is of interest about them is that they take up matters that were basic to the Pharisaic codes of ritual purity: almsgiving, prayer, and fasting (Matt. 6:1–6, 16–18). In each case the point is the same. The codes are to be kept, but not as the Pharisees keep them. The Pharisees do them "outwardly," for show. Jesus demands purity of the heart. His followers are to be "perfect . . . as your heavenly Father is perfect" (Matt. 5:48).

So the old distinction between the Jesus people and the Pharisees was still in place, but the conflict now was about the proper observance of the Torah. Amazing. Somewhere between the last codification of Q and the writings of Matthew's gospel, the law of Moses slipped into the picture as the common ground between the two movements. From the point of view of Matthew's community, the worst thing that could be said about the Pharisees was that they were hypocrites, people who did not live by what they espoused. What seems to have happened is that, in the aftermath of the Roman-Jewish war, Jesus people of the Matthean variety had second thoughts about participating in cultural critique of the Q variety and about entertaining grandiose apocalyptic hopes and fears of the kind projected by Mark's gospel. With the temple's destruction fifteen or twenty years behind them, and the Torah coming into prominence as that artifact of the grand traditions still available for any group interested in alignment with the epic of Israel, Jesus people in the tradition of both Q and Mark had no other choice than to come to terms with Moses. They were not Jesus people of the Thomas kind, and they were not Christians on the model of the gentile Christ cult. Thus a retreat into cultivating personal enlightenment or cosmic salvation was not an option. What to do? Why not think of Jesus as a latter-day Moses? Maybe, given the recent, wrenching history of foreign powers threatening to squash the people of God, Jesus *was* like Moses, God's man of the hour with God's instructions for the people. And not just *like* Moses, but a teacher whose teachings were actually based on Moses' Torah interpreted for the new time. Maybe that was it, or so the thinking seems to have been.

So Matthew added the Torah to his growing collection of texts, and Q now read through Matthew's eyes would never sound the same again. But what about Mark? Even with Q added to Mark, Jesus would come on pretty strong, and the impression would still be left of a prophet with fire in his eyes, an exorcist zapping demons, or an apocalyptic seer who expected a quick return to take care of those who killed him. That did not fit. So Matthew devised yet another strategy to play down the sudden, overly dramatic appearance and exit of Mark's son of God. In this case he did it mainly by changing the way the story begins and ends.

To start his story differently, Matthew had to engage in a bit of scribal research. It is obvious that he spent some time studying the prophets, for instance, looking for anything that might suggest details he could use to flesh out the early history of Jesus that Mark had not mentioned. He also gave some thought to constructing a genealogy appropriate for such an important figure as Jesus. Then he gathered some information in general about legendary births of illustrious men, and he did some thinking about what Herod's court may have looked like at the time of Jesus' birth. His strategy was to steal Mark's thunder by suggesting that Jesus must have had spectacular Jewish credentials, so much so that not only would the prophets have had some inkling about his coming, but that angels and stars would have signaled his birth, and sages and kings taken note. And so he came up with the following account (Matthew 1–2).

Jesus, he wrote, was born from the line of Abraham and David with an unbroken genealogy that continued right through the exile and restoration to end with Joseph and Mary. His birth was miraculous and portentous, naturally, given the fact that he was God's messiah, and also given the fact that the details of Isaiah's announcement didn't quite square with his genealogy. Then there was the understandable fright of King Herod, whose slaughter of the infants in and around Bethlehem, predicted by Jeremiah, did not succeed in killing the baby Jesus. That must have been because Jesus wasn't there, not because he was not born in Bethlehem, as Micah rightly predicted, but because Joseph and Mary had taken him to Egypt even as Hosea knew would happen. The appropriateness of a slight sojourn in Egypt was fitting for other reasons as well, for it was just what had happened to other illustrious Israelites with whom God had special dealings (think of Joseph, Israel, Moses, and Jeremiah, for instance), and it explained what happened between Bethlehem, where Jesus was said to have been born, and Nazareth, where everyone knew Jesus had grown up.

Scholars have frequently remarked on these stories of Jesus' birth and infancy. They have been noted as incredible, implausible, far-fetched fictions that signal Matthew's naïveté with regard to legendary material. But exactly the opposite seems to be the case. Matthew was fighting fire with fire, and legends surrounding the birth of the hero were much, much better than Mark's opener, especially if the hero was a scion of the houses of Abraham and Moses. So Matthew did it. It was an extremely clever move and very well done. Forever after, Christians would imagine the story of Jesus starting with his birth.

To end the story was less of a problem. Mark had left the ending open on purpose, to let the chimera of the *eschaton* flash before the mind as the next event of significance in his dramatic story. Matthew needed only to redirect the readers' attention away from that apocalyptic twinkle and toward the long haul of history. He did it by adding two brief reports. One was an account of the bribe paid by the chief priests to the guards at the tomb in exchange for their promise to say that the disciples had stolen the body of Jesus while they were asleep (Matt. 28:11–15). This was an artful touch, supporting the story of the empty tomb even while acknowledging the problem of its credibility. More to the point, however, is the last story, the so-called great commission (Matt. 28:16–20). In some ways it does not seem to fit well as a conclusion to Matthew's story. This is especially the case with the mention that the disciples worshiped him, the notion of a mission to the gentiles, the language of Father, son, and holy spirit, and the statement that Jesus would always be present with them to the end of the age. The preceding gospel account does not prepare the reader well for any of these ideas, for they seem to be more at home in the Christ cult than in Matthew's community. They work quite nicely, however, as soon as one sees that Matthew was working hard to counter Mark's conclusion about the absence of Jesus from the disciples until the apocalyptic appearance of the kingdom of God. What Matthew did was to borrow a few ideas from the Christ cult that were not apocalyptic in orientation, reduce their cosmic and cultic connotations as best he could, and use them to counteract Mark's ending. The significance of the great commission should not be taken from the way this language would sound if coming from the Christ cult, but from the way Matthew used it to end with a theme that was entirely in keeping with his gospel. That theme is the point of the commission, namely that the disciples are to "make disciples . . . teaching them to obey everything that I have commanded you." What a scribe Matthew was! That is not the way Q would have put it, or what Mark would have said, or Paul, gentile Christians, or the Thomas people. That is what Matthew and his community said they heard. Keeping the new commandments is what Jewish Christianity thought Jesus' teachings were all about.

THE GOSPEL ACCORDING TO LUKE

Somewhere in the Aegean, around the year 120 C.E., a great two-volume work appeared that expanded upon the gospel story of Jesus by adding a sequel called the Acts of the Apostles. As with the other narrative gospels, we do not know anything about the author except what can be inferred from the writing itself. Later in the second century, the work was attributed to Luke, the co-worker of Paul (mentioned in Philemon 24; Col. 4:14; and 2 Tim. 4:11), just as other anonymous literature from earlier times was attributed to either the apostles or their companions in order to validate their truth. It has thus become customary to refer to the author as Luke, even though the Luke mentioned by Paul cannot have been the one who wrote this work.

From the writing it is clear that mythmaking in early Christian circles was no longer fixed solely on Jesus. Instead, interest had turned to focus on the apostles. The figure of Jesus was receding into the past, and the apostles provided the link between Jesus and the bishops, leaders of Christian congregations who were responsible for instructing the people. Luke understood what it meant for the bishops to be dependent upon the apostles for their teachings and how important it was for the apostles to have received their instructions from Jesus. As a historian, he also knew how important it was to fit Jesus and his appearance into the history of Israel and so imagine history as a whole to have had a rhyme and reason capable of accounting for the emergence of the Christian churches and their role as ethical leaven in the Roman Empire. So his story about Jesus could not highlight the sudden entrance into history of God's son, as Mark pictured it. It would have to be a chapter in a much greater sweep of history in which God had always commissioned agents to carry out his work.

Luke's theory was that God had always been actively engaged in a quest for an obedient people. God's method was also clear. He had always commissioned teachers to instruct his people to be good. Luke recognized these teachers in the roles played by the Hebrew prophets and noted that they were always inspired by God's spirit. He drew the conclusion that the holy spirit had been God's agent throughout history, and that the holy spirit had always worked by inspiring prophet-teachers to call the people to remembrance when they forgot God's instructions and to teach them anew when they repented. Some of the people always listened to them and obeyed, while others turned to persecute them. This had happened over and over again since the beginning. It was the same during the time of Israel, with Jesus, with the apostles, and presumably for Luke's time as well.

For Luke, the life of Jesus was a significant moment in history because it marked the point when God's spirit became available to all peoples, not just the Jews. It was also significant because it revealed, by the example set by Jesus, just how good people could be if they listened to the holy spirit and obeyed. It is not surprising, then, to find that the important thing about Jesus, according to Luke, was that the holy spirit was especially active in his life. It was the holy spirit that prepared for his coming in the person of John the Baptist (Luke 1:15–17, 67). It was the holy spirit that "overshadowed" Mary his mother (Luke 1:35). And it was the holy spirit that inspired the devout Simeon in the temple to foretell the child's destiny as "the Lord's messiah" and a "light to the gentiles" (Luke 2:25–26). It was the holy spirit that descended upon him in baptism (Luke 3:22), led him into the wilderness for testing (Luke 4:1), and filled him for his return to Galilee (Luke 4:14). There, in his first public appearance in the synagogue at Nazareth, Jesus stood up and read from the prophet Isaiah, "The Spirit of the Lord is upon me . . ." (Luke 4:16–21). Thus Luke set the theme for his life of Jesus. Jesus was important because the spirit was upon him.

As the story unfolds, however, there is not much evidence of the activity of the holy spirit. One reason is that, from this point on, Luke used material from Mark and Q in which the notion of the holy spirit had not been developed. Another is that Luke viewed Jesus as the full manifestation of obedience to the spirit. Jesus' life was a golden age, and his story was a picture of what human history would be like if there were no temptation, testing, conflict, or evil in the world. It was a time when Satan "departed from him until an opportune time" (Luke 4:13), not to appear again until he "entered into Judas" to betray Jesus (Luke 22:3). Thus Luke did not need to emphasize the agency of the holy spirit during Jesus' life. At the end of Jesus' life, Luke returned to his theme with Jesus' announcement to his disciples that he would send "what my Father promised" (Luke 24:49). At first that announcement seems to be a riddle. But turning the page to the second part of Luke's history, we find out what it was, namely the promise of the holy spirit that "came upon" the disciples at Pentecost (Acts 1–2). That is how the disciples became apostles and, filled with the holy spirit, they went out to preach the gospel among all the nations, beginning from Jerusalem and ending in Rome (Luke 24:47; Acts 1:4, 8; 28:16–28). I shall explore Luke's story of the apostles in chapter 8. In the present chapter it is the effect of Luke's grand history of salvation upon the way he told the story of Jesus that deserves some attention.

Luke wrote his story of Jesus with a grand scheme in mind, a history of salvation that started with Adam at the beginning of the world, coursed through the history of Israel, peaked in the life of Jesus, spread out to the nations at Pentecost, and found its new center at Rome when Paul, the apostle to the nations, arrived there. No wonder Luke's Jesus looks a bit tame in comparison with the portraits painted by the other gospels. History had larger horizons now, another divine agent capable of filling those horizons, and a lively chapter of apostolic exploits that had intervened between the time of Jesus and Luke's own time. Notice that Luke's history accounts only for the first fifty years of the first century. Between the time of Paul in the 50s at the end of Luke's history and the time of Luke's writing in the early second century, there are yet another fifty or sixty years to consider. So the truly remarkable thing about Luke is that he was able to write such a full and fresh account of Jesus' life.

As was the case with Matthew's gospel, a writing that Luke does not appear to have known, Luke's life of Jesus was composed by merging Mark and Q and then adding some special material of his own. Luke is evidence that a copy of Q was still in circulation in the early second century. As Luke's use of Q shows, however, and as many other gospels that were being written during the early second century document, Q was by then all but passé in Christian circles. Luke is the last evidence we have for the circulation of Q as a separate text, and he incorporated its sayings into his story of Jesus in a very matter-of-fact manner. He was not as concerned as Mark was to put a spin on Jesus' teachings in order to make them relevant to his readers, as if the voice of Jesus were speaking directly to them and their immediate situation. And he does not portray Jesus laying down the law for all time, as Matthew did for his readers. Luke invited his readers to look on from afar as Jesus walked and talked with those of his own time. The teachings in Q were now to be viewed from a distance.

The way Luke treated Q lets us see what he thought of Jesus' teachings. He did not rearrange the sequence of Q, as Matthew did, but inserted it into Mark's story as if Mark had merely left it out of account. The early Q material on John and Jesus, and the first unit of Jesus' teachings, which begins with the beatitudes, are appropriately placed early in the story (Luke 6–7). But most of Q occurs later in the story as Jesus journeys to Jerusalem. This has been called Luke's special section (Luke 9:51–18:14). He not only created the impression of a leisurely journey by suggesting a series of stops along the way for Jesus to engage in teaching, he introduced questioners and scenes so that Jesus could explain his teachings as he traveled along. Luke actually went to some length to translate much of Q into commonsense moralisms, and this is where he added the famous Lukan parables, such as the good Samaritan (Luke 10:29–37), Mary and Martha (Luke 10:38–42), the rich fool (Luke 12:13–21), and the prodigal son (Luke 15:11–32). The overall impression is that of an irenic, popular philosopher with his disciples, making their way through village marketplaces, stopping here and there to accept an invitation to a meal. He was, as Peter will later be heard to say, a man "who went about doing good" (Acts 10:38), or, as Luke has the centurion say at the crucifixion, "This man was surely a righteous person" (Luke 23:47). The way Luke's Jesus appears in the world is quite a contrast to the sense of confrontation in Mark or the serious tone of the instructional speeches in Matthew.

The ambiance of Jesus' teaching in Luke's gospel also contrasts markedly with the sharp edge characteristic of the sermons in Acts. This is a telling difference. It means that, for Luke, Jesus' significance was no longer located in the enduring importance of his teachings. His teachings were important for his own task and time; it was his life as a whole that was important for all time. It was a life that, even though it had changed the course of history, could be properly assessed only in retrospect. It was an ideal life to be summarized in sermons and used to call Luke's contemporaries to task and to repentance. There is, for instance, a much sharper polemic against the Jews in the sermons in Acts than in Jesus' teaching about them, or even than in the way Luke portrayed their responses to Jesus during his lifetime. The sermons in Acts are the clue to Luke's understanding of the life of Jesus in retrospect. It was important; it was the hinge of history; but it was past, and its importance could be seen only when one looked back and realized the difference it had made for all subsequent history. Luke's lasting achievement with regard to views of the "historical" Jesus was that his story created the Christian sense of Jesus' importance as historical.

Luke's accomplishment is remarkable when one realizes that he based his life of Jesus on the Gospel of Mark, for the difference in the ways in which each affects the imagination of the reader is radical. What changes did he have to make to Mark's story, other than inserting the teachings from Q? One change that made a big difference is that Luke dispensed with one of the two series of miracle stories in Mark (Mark 6:45–8:26). That cut down on the impression Mark created of Jesus as the man of power. Luke also substituted his story of Jesus reading from Isaiah and teaching in the Nazareth synagogue (Luke 4:16–30) for Mark's story of the exorcism in the synagogue at Capernaum (Mark 1:21–28). Instead of the Pharisees always being cast as bad guys, as in Mark, Luke has Jesus dining with one, as if the Pharisees could do right if only they would, and he revised Mark's story of the anointing of Jesus by the woman to make this point (Mark 14:3–9; Luke 7:36–50). Luke also left out or changed anti-Pharisaic material that he apparently thought unhelpful or too damning. One example is the controversy story about washings in Mark 7:1–23 that Luke did not repeat. Another is that he rephrased Mark's announcement of the Pharisees' plot "to destroy" Jesus (Mark 3:6). According to Luke, "They discussed with one another what they might do to Jesus" (Luke 6:11). So although Luke used almost all of Mark and did not alter the basic story line, he modulated the feeling of the story by making many small changes to Mark's text. By making these changes, he erased the sense of urgency in Mark's story and scrubbed Mark's dramatic characterization of Jesus as the son of God in conflict with society. Instead of Jesus suddenly appearing on the scene with the power to cast out demons, as Mark pictured him, Luke's Jesus comes slowly into view as a child emerging from the old, old story of God and his people Israel, a story that was destined to continue long after Jesus' death, albeit with God's attention now directed toward gentiles. And as Jesus grows up and takes his place among the people of his time, a time Luke knew to be one of great historical transition with or without Jesus, Jesus' cool demeanor and philosophic discourse lets you know that he knew his place in that larger story.

In order to encase Mark's plot within that larger history, Luke added an extraordinary set of stories and poems to both the beginning and the ending of his life of Jesus. Many of these stories have become deeply etched in Christian imagination, such as what happened on the road to Emmaus (Luke 24:13–35). The poems actually became part of the Christian liturgy, such as Mary's song of praise that came to be called the Magnificat (Luke 1:46–55). These additions to Mark's gospel are more elaborate than those Matthew appended, although the strategy in both cases was the same. Once the strategy is seen, a closer look at this material reveals Luke's genius and the reasons for the success of his fictional historiography.

Three themes dominate this Lukan material surrounding the birth of Jesus and his appearances after the resurrection: the role of John the Baptizer, the temple in Jerusalem, and the Jewish scriptures. John the Baptizer is given an absolutely new role to play when compared with Q, Mark, or Matthew. In Luke, John's birth is linked to that of Jesus, and the stories of each follow the same pattern. There is an auspicious announcement by the angel Gabriel, a response of incredulity, miraculous recognitions of the significance of the two children on the parts of their mothers, fathers, and others, and songs of praise for each that burst forth with detailed information about their historic significance. John will prepare the way for Jesus in the spirit and power of Elijah by turning "the disobedient to the wisdom of the righteous" and so "make ready a people prepared for the Lord" (Luke 1:16–17, 76–79). Jesus will be the "Son of the Most High," "a mighty savior" in the house of David, and "a light for revelation to the gentiles" (Luke 1:32, 69; 2:32). Both John and Jesus are circumcised in accordance with the law of Moses and named in accordance with the instructions of the angel. The temple with its priests, services, and sacrifices is constantly in the background, taken for granted as it were, not only as the only scene appropriate for such historic moments, but also as the place where the oaths sworn to Abraham, the promises to the ancestors, the holy covenants, and the salvation of Israel should rightly find their fulfillment. This interlocking of Jesus, John, Jerusalem, the temple, and the epic of Israel as recorded in the scriptures was Luke's way of fitting Mark's story of Jesus into the great sweep of God's history that Luke had in mind. For Luke, that history was glorious from start to finish. The appearances of John and Jesus may have been more wondrous than some of the other moments because of the new direction God's story would take, but the wonder of their appearances could not be seen apart from their place in the grand traditions of Israel. In order to tack these stories on to Mark's gospel, Luke did have to change a few features of Mark's account that collided with the new ethos Luke wanted to create. The story of John's beheading, for instance, was now too gross for Luke's taste, and so he simply deleted it. But much of the change was accomplished by Luke's skill in crafting these stories he appended at the beginning.

Luke's fiction was possible because he was an accomplished scholar and poet, but also because he and his readers were far removed from the times and places about which he wrote. Luke's skill as a historian has made it difficult for modern scholars to locate him and his community. He wrote about the past with matter-of-fact vividness and never allowed a sidelong glance at his own contemporary circumstances to intervene. The few clues that we have, such as his knowledge of Paul's missions and his interest in gentile Christianity, point to a location near the Aegean Sea. But that is the best we can do. If we place Luke there, say in Ephesus, which became an important center for second-century Christianity, who would have raised so much as an eyebrow when reading his accounts of John, Jesus, and their parents visiting the temple in Jerusalem during Herod's reign? Not only was the temple no longer there, and its destruction also a thing of the distant past, Luke's depiction of the way it was before that time borders on fairy tale. Real life in Jerusalem during Luke's own time was conveniently left out of the account. Instead, he laced the scenes he wanted his readers to imagine with language highly charged with scriptural allusions. There are hints of the old stories of divine visitation to the barren matriarch, the wondrous events surrounding the calling of Samuel in the temple of old, the staged sequence of prophets and kings that repeated itself time after time in the history of Israel, and the generative moments of significance for such concepts as promise, covenant, messiah, and redemption. Luke's poetry was so good, so polished, so evocative of the grandeur of Israel's idealized history that his readers would have willingly suspended any disbelief. It was the kind of fiction that one could easily delight in and eventually come to believe as true.

It is the same with the stories at the end of Luke's life of Jesus. Jerusalem is still in the picture, as it will continue to be until the birthday of the church forty days later at Pentecost. But the reader has been reminded of the eventual fate of the city by means of Jesus' lament as he first approached it (Luke 19:41–44), and thus knows already that Jerusalem will not be able to retain the honor and glory it had at the beginning of the story. Jesus is still in the picture as well, but only to make an appearance or two before he also "withdraws" and, without fanfare, is "carried up into heaven" (Luke 24:51). So history is in transition and will now come to focus on five figures to carry the future: the apostles, the holy spirit, the scriptures, the message of salvation for the gentiles, and Christians meeting together for meals. For Luke these are the things that define the Christian community as a church. One can see how far along he was in his conception of Christianity as a social institution with its traditions and authorities in place.

By Luke's time, of course, the apostles were also figures of the past, roles that had to be played in order to complete the transition from Israel to the church that Jesus had made possible. One does wonder as well, now that the holy spirit had been successful in making God's plan clear to the apostles, whether Luke intended for its dramatic and miraculous role also to be consigned to an illustrious past. If so, that leaves the Christians gathered for meals, their meditations on the scriptures, and the message of salvation for gentiles. We might want to sneak a look ahead at the sermons in Acts to see just how enmeshed the scriptures were with the message, in Luke's mind, and how both the message and the scriptures focused on the coupling of Jesus' life with the epic history of Israel. But already in the Emmaus story the point is that, though his followers realized who Jesus was as he broke bread with them at the table, it was on the road as Jesus "opened the scriptures" to them that their hearts were first made to "burn." What was the point? "Beginning with Moses and all the prophets, he interpreted to them the things about himself in all the scriptures," namely that it was "necessary that the messiah should suffer these things and then enter into his glory" (Luke 24:26–27, 32).

What a storyteller Luke was! Who would have wanted to doubt the Emmaus story? It read so well, and sounded so good, just like the stories at the beginning of the gospel. And so Luke won the minds and the hearts of his readers and subsequent Christians. Forever after Christians would think of Luke, not as a storyteller, but as a historian or even as a reporter of historic events. They would always think that Luke knew something they did not know. Only those who turned to search the scriptures, trying to find the place where the messiah had to die, would ever wonder how Luke had managed such a marvelous fiction. Perhaps it was because he and his readers wanted to imagine the past that way.

7

VISIONS OF THE COSMIC LORD

What a somersault, turning the page between Luke's life of Jesus and the Gospel of John. You land in the presence of God before the world was made, watching as his powerful *logos* (word) begins to move and create the life and light that streak through the universe changing darkness into day. And then, it isn't long before we read that Jesus was that *logos*! This is a totally different imaginary world from that projected by Luke's plan of history, or the law of perfection that would never change until the end of time in Matthew's gospel, or the Markan vision of the kingdom of God that would only be revealed at the *eschaton*. We are now in the presence of a cosmic power that pulsates throughout the world making all of time and space eternally present around us.

This is the world of the cosmic Christ, one of the mythmaking options that several early Christian groups found attractive. In the texts and traditions so far encountered, we have had only a glimpse or two of the first stages of this mythmaking process. In the Gospel of Thomas, Jesus' words had become an invitation to personal enlightenment in harmony with the cosmic kingdom Jesus had revealed. And in the Christ cult, the martyr myth was soon transformed by imagining the resurrected Christ installed as cosmic lord. In both of these cases, we had occasion to note the interesting combination of Jewish wisdom thought and Greek philosophical concepts that merged in the new mythologies. In this chapter we shall look at four fully developed systems of cosmic worldview, each governed by the concept of the cosmic Christ. In the Gospel of John, Jesus as the son and *logos* of God reveals the structure of the cosmos. In the post-Pauline school tradition, documented in the letters to the Colossians and Ephesians, the wisdom of God invites the reader to see and praise the cosmic Christ. In the letter to the Hebrews, Jesus is depicted as the great high priest performing an eternal sacrifice in the cosmic temple of God. And in the Revelation to John, the dominant cosmic image is that of the city of God. A closer look at each of these will help us understand the thought invested in this kind of mythmaking and the rewards that early Christians reaped by imagining the Christ as a cosmic power.

Please keep in mind that the mythmaking process always includes a reconfiguration of the "world" in which one lives. That is the way we measure the fit between our social circumstances and the place we would like to imagine for ourselves in the larger scheme of things. That early Christians thought of their world as an organism (*cosmos*), a universe pulsating with powers that both threatened to break it apart and pulled it back together, should not be thought strange. That was the way the Greeks thought of it, and everyone influenced by Greek thought had learned to do the same. The critical questions were how the cosmos was structured, how the powers were imagined to function, and whether such a view seemed reasonable in light of the schools of science and philosophy that were in charge of knowledge about the natural orders.

We will therefore have to proceed with caution, for these early Christian cosmic visions will surely strike us as vagaries unless we see them against the backdrop of the world of late antiquity. They all stem from a time when the first flush of excitement had subsided in the Jesus movements and Christian congregations. The imagined kingdom of God had been postponed or displaced, projected onto locations at the far ends of human imagination in heaven above, in the deep structure of the universe, at the creation of the world, or at the *eschaton*. The vision was still at work, however, and the investments people had made in the social movements were still strong. Some had even found ways to make contact with the mysteries hidden since the foundation of the world that were now revealed because of Christ. And on that cosmic screen, as we shall see, early Christians learned to simulate the conflicts they experienced and the victories they hoped for in the real world.

THE GOSPEL OF JOHN

John started his story of Jesus with a poem in praise of the *logos*, God's son and active agent in the creation of the world (John 1:1–18). According to his poem, which begins before the world was made, this *logos* circles around and around through a series of interlocking lines, leaving in his wake created things, life, light, and finally humankind. Then, picking up speed and spiraling down through all of troubled time and darkened space, the *logos* finally takes the form of a human being, and behold, it was Jesus! "We," John wrote, "have seen his glory, the glory as of the Father's only Son" (John 1:14). As for those of us who did not see that glory, we might want to ask where and when that happened, since it seems to be a sighting that other early Jesus people and Christians did not have. Who besides the author was included in the "we," and did they keep the vision to themselves?

Scholars date the Gospel of John in the 90s and see it as evidence for a distinct Christian community that developed its own views of Jesus more or less independently. It has long been recognized that this gospel differs from the other three New

Testament gospels and that it must be studied separately. The other three are known as the "synoptic gospels" because they have so much material in common that they can profitably be "viewed together" (from *synopsis*). The Jesus, setting, and story line of the fourth gospel, however, cannot be aligned with the synoptics. John's Jesus appears from heaven, speaks only in self-referential terms, knows that this confounds his listeners, but insists nevertheless that they accept his assertions about himself. He is the son from the Father, the bread of life, the water of life, the way to the Father, and so forth. Those who want to make sure are brushed aside or worse. Those who "see" who he is, mainly his disciples, are told, "Whoever has seen me has seen the Father" (John 14:9). So it has not been possible to meld John's Jesus with that of the synoptics as if each had merely emphasized different features of the same historical figure. John's Jesus is an altogether different kind of being.

In the Gospel of John, the story of Jesus' baptism is missing, there is no account of the transfiguration, and instead of a last supper of Jesus with his disciples there is a scene in which Jesus washes their feet. At the beginning of the story, instead of Jesus' calling the disciples to be "fishers of men," as in Mark, he invites them to "come and see" who he is and where he lives. Instead of his miracles creating astonishment among the crowds, they provide occasions for Jesus to interpret them as "signs" of the spiritual gifts he can give. In the synoptics there is a clear distinction between Jesus' activity in Galilee and his one-time visit to Jerusalem. In John, Jerusalem is ever present in the background, as is the cycle of Jewish festivals, and Jesus visits the city three times before the final appearance, each time for the express purpose of revealing himself on the occasion of a Jewish festival (John 2:13; 5:1; 7:14; 10:22; 12:12). In the synoptics, the story of Jesus' entering the temple to drive out the money changers is an act of provocation at the end of the gospel (Mark 11:15–17); in John this story is told at the very beginning, combined with Jesus' prediction of the temple's destruction, and interpreted as a coded reference to Jesus' own body (John 2:13–22). It is as if the whole story in John is about the "transfigured" Jesus popping in and out of the temple at Jerusalem. And the material special to John is also highly mythic: the hymn to the *logos*, the miracle stories that invite lengthy monologues of the I-am-the-son-from-the-Father variety, the allegorized parables of the good shepherd (John 10) and the vine (John 15), the foot washing (John 13), the "upper room" instructions (John 13–16), Jesus' last prayer (John 17), and his after-death appearances. All told, John's story seems to be about the manifestation of a god, not about the historical Jesus or even the Jesus of the synoptics.

And yet, John's gospel does share some features with the synoptics. John the Baptizer introduces Jesus at the beginning, there are miracle stories in the middle, the Pharisees and others develop a plot to kill Jesus, and there is a trial and crucifixion at the end, all of which is reminiscent of Mark's outline. The call of the disciples, the cleansing of the temple, and a last meeting of Jesus with his disciples are all included, though in each case the stories have been radically changed and relocated when compared with the synoptic accounts. Some scholars are saying that John must have known about the Gospel of Mark because his account of the trial and crucifixion follows Mark so closely that some form of textual dependence is probable. Surely that is correct. The passion plot was a postwar Markan creation, and it is improbable that John would have come up with the same plot independently. This means that John's community cannot have developed in complete isolation from other Jesus groups and Christ congregations. But it certainly did go its own way, probably from an early time, and it put its own distinctive interpretation on the Jesus materials and Christ traditions that it shared with other groups.

Of the various kinds of material that left their mark in the composition of the Gospel of John, the miracle stories stand out as the basic building blocks. Scholars call these stories the "signs source," because the miracles are called "signs" (*semeia*) in John's gospel, and because at some point in the history of their interpretation they were numbered. The wine miracle at Cana is still called "the first sign" (John 2:11), and the healing of the official's son is called the "second sign" that Jesus performed (John 4:54). There are seven sign miracles that scholars regard as belonging to the signs source. They put us in touch with the earliest phase of the community's history, and a careful study shows that they were interpreted in different ways at different times in the history of the community. By tracing this history of interpretation we are able to reconstruct stages in the social history of the community. The seven stories are the following:

1. The wedding at Cana (2:1–11)
2. The official's son (4:46–54)
3. The lame at Bethesda (5:1–9)
4. Feeding the five thousand (6:1–14)
5. Walking on water (6:16–21)
6. Healing the blind man (9:1–38)
7. The resurrection of Lazarus (11:1–44)

This set of miracle stories is reminiscent of the two sets that Mark used in composing his gospel, except that it consists of seven stories, whereas the Markan sets had five stories each. However, five of the seven stories in John do follow the Markan pattern. There is a story about crossing the water, one about feeding five thousand, and three healing miracles, one of which features the healing of a gentile. It is the first and last stories of John's set that do not fit the pre-Markan pattern. They are quite different from the other five. The Cana story is different because the problem is not a life-threatening matter or an impossible condition; it is merely a potential embarrassment. The point of the story is couched in the symbolism of the wine, a symbolism that sets Jesus as a kind of Dionysus over against the Jewish rites of purification on the occasion of a wedding. Even the steward of the feast did not know that Jesus had performed a miracle, though he recognized the quality of the wine it produced. So Jesus' "glory" was reserved solely for the disciples to see. This is a strange departure from the way miracle stories work in Mark. And in the case of

Lazarus, the miracle is so extravagant, the tale so macabre and yet so humorous in its depiction of Jewish burial rites, and the description so suggestive of Jesus' own resurrection to come, that it also must have been added to the set when the miracles were interpreted symbolically and numbered as signs. With a wedding at the beginning of a series of seven miracles, five in the middle that correspond to the pattern of the miracle sets in the pre-Markan tradition, and a funeral at the end, we have reason to suspect that the miracle stories passed through an interesting history of reinterpretation in the Johannine community.

As discussed in chapter 1, a set of five miracle stories functioned as an early myth of origin for some Jesus group. The myth was that, though they were an unlikely collection of people, coming together as followers of Jesus was a bit like what happened during the exodus and the early history of Israel when Moses and Elijah performed their miracles for the people. The Jesus people did not imagine this myth in order to stand over against Jewish institutions of the time, as if Jesus had been a reformer of Judaism or as if his followers thought of themselves as the true Israel under a new Moses. They simply delighted in thinking of themselves as a new congregation that was as important in their time as the formation of Israel was in its time. To come to this understanding of the importance of the Jesus movement would have required a few years of social experience and a great deal of talk, self-reflection, and intellectual ingenuity. But it would have been thoroughly in keeping with what we are able to reconstruct of the historical Jesus, his teachings, and the early history of the movements that emerged in his name. It thus appears that the roots of the Johannine community go back to a Jesus movement that told miracle stories about Jesus as a way to celebrate their sense of legitimacy and importance as a novel congregation. If so, they must have gathered around the notion of the kingdom of God and the teachings of Jesus, just as all early Jesus people did. And this means that, by noting the changes that took place in their interpretation of the miracle stories, we should be able to chart the history of this community for a period of at least fifty years, from about 45 C.E. to 95 C.E. As we have seen, much could happen to a Jesus group during this time, and in the case of the Johannine community much did.

Four distinct types of miracle interpretation occur in the Gospel of John, and each can be assigned to a specific level in a logical sequence of development. The earliest level of interpretation is the meaning given to a story simply by being included in the original set of five stories as part of the group's myth of origin. The second level of interpretation is the use of the miracle stories to trigger some controversy with Pharisees. The third level of interpretation happened when the set of five was expanded to seven stories and imagined to have taken place on the occasion of Jewish feasts or festivals. And the fourth level is their use in the extant gospel story. As we shall see, each miracle story serves as a point of departure for Jesus to deliver a little speech about himself as the true form of the "gift" just given in the miracle. With such a history of interpretation, it is not surprising that each of these stories became layered with complex clusters of descriptive material to reset the scenes, and discourse material to intertwine the themes. This stacking of interpretive material can be illustrated in the story of Jesus healing the man born blind.

The story of the man born blind occurs in chapter 9. The story was apparently popular, for it gave rise to lengthy elaboration. The parable of the good shepherd was inserted to further enhance the dialogue about a controversy it had engendered. The original story must have been brief, one of three stories that exemplified the unlikely origins and wonder of the Jesus movement. Then, at a somewhat later time, this story was retold as the occasion for a controversy with the Pharisees. They took offense, it was said, because Jesus had "worked" on the sabbath (John 9:14, 16). One is reminded of the way miracle stories were used to represent conflict with the Pharisees in Q and Mark, the Beelzebul story in Q, for example (Q 11:14–23), or Mark's merger of miracle stories with pronouncement stories to create controversy stories. This happened sometime during the 50s or 60s, and that would be about the right time for the Johannine community also to have turned their miracle myth into a set of conflict stories. At the third stage of the story's reinterpretations, the symbolic significance of the sight miracle was noticed, and the story was set on the occasion of the Jewish Feast of Dedication or feast of lights (John 10:22). Now the story turned on the question of "seeing" who Jesus was against that background, and the story was expanded so that the man who was healed could both "see" and "believe," while the Pharisees and "the Jews" were cast as "blind" because they wouldn't believe (John 9:35–41). At the fourth stage of interpretation, the themes of sight and light were focused upon Jesus as the very "light of the world" who was able to give "sight" to those in darkness (John 9:4–5, 39). This is the type of interpretation given to all of the miracle stories at the level of John's gospel, where the symbolic significance of the wine, word, work, bread, water, light, and life that figure in the stories is transferred to Jesus as the real miracle of the story. Jesus is the miraculous manifestation and revealer of God's gift of "light" and "life," or enlightenment and spiritual being.

It is not too difficult to see that the several levels of miracle interpretation correspond to stages in the life of this community. It began as a Jesus movement with characteristic élan, found itself invested in the social formation of a group that thought of itself as a new congregation of Israel, the people of God, and then ran into trouble with the Pharisees because the Jesus people were not observing the codes of ritual purity. This conflict was traumatic and the Johannine community never fully recovered from it. Though their tryst with the Pharisees was long past by the time the gospel was written, the community still thought of itself in opposition to Pharisees. In the meantime, however, it had learned to consign, not just the Pharisees, but all of "the Jews" to the realm of darkness as the necessary contrast to their own world of enlightenment. This development is documented in the third level of reinterpretation, the expansion of the miracle set from five to seven with its implicit suggestion that the cycle of Jewish feasts and festivals had been superseded by the coming of Jesus into the world. This severance of all ties with "the Jews" was radical. It was not accompanied by any sense of mission, either to Jews or to the world. Instead, the Johannine community retreated to form an enclave of the enlightened ones. As Jesus taught his disciples before he returned to his "Father," he had come into the world so that they might know the Father, stay together as a close-knit community, and "love one another just as I have loved you" (John 13:34). The vast expanse of the cosmos these followers envisioned contrasted with the small and strictly bounded community in which they lived. They were the enlightened ones in the midst of a huge and darkened universe, a universe that was dark because "the Jews" had not "received" the "*logos*" (John 1:10–11).

One of the more interesting features of this community is the way in which they retained the remnants of materials from their past experiences and previous myth-making. The author of the gospel was much more comfortable with this jumble of memory traditions than it is possible for the modern reader to be, and he apparently had great fun working each against the other in what amounts to a very involuted discourse. An example of this is the way he playfully treated the theme of signs. The Greek word for sign (*semeion*) was not the normal term for a miracle, but it could be used for one that had some special significance in distinction from, or in addition to, being a sheer manifestation of power, or *dynamis*, the usual term. The Johannine community used the term *semeion* in this sense. Their miracle stories were not just stories of miracles; they were signs of something else.

It is not quite clear when these people started using the term *signs* to signal the significance of their miracle stories, for it would have been an appropriate designation from the very beginning. That is because the set of five miracles alluded to the exodus story, and the miracles of the exodus were regularly referred to as "signs and wonders" in Jewish literature. At the second level of interpretation the miracles signaled Jesus' special role as their founder and God's son. At this level, a game seems to have been played at the expense of the Pharisees similar to that recorded in the synoptic tradition, namely that the Pharisees were imagined to request a sign, and Jesus would retort that no sign would be given to them (John 6:30). The significance of the miracles at the third level of interpretation was that Jesus himself embodied the meaning of the Jewish feasts and festivals. And at the level of the gospel story, the miracles were signs of Jesus' identity as the *logos* of God. The author knew about all these connotations and turned the subject of the signs into a paradoxical theme. Sometimes the signs are not seen and should be (John 2:1–11; 7:31; 10:37–38; 12:37). At other times the signs are believed but do not result in seeing (John 2:23–24; 4:48; 6:26, 30; 10:32). And lest we think that the story is about the blessed disciples who were fortunate enough actually to see the *logos* of God in the flesh, Jesus' last word to Thomas, to whom Jesus made a special appearance so he *could* see him, was, "Blessed are those who have *not* seen and yet have come to believe" (John 20:29, emphasis added). That is really rubbing it in.

The author's overall plan is clear. He took the series of seven miracle stories as his starting point, retold the stories in all their realism and earthiness, then found a way to let Jesus start talking about himself as the true manifestation of the gift of "life" storied in the miracles. At this point, he had the Jews object with questions to the effect that Jesus' statements did not make any sense. These questions were then used to turn Jesus' monologues into the semblance of dialogues, and that allowed Jesus to introduce two important Johannine themes: those of witness and judgment. The Jews, Jesus says, want to make a judgment about the truth of any matter on the basis of signs or on the basis of a second witness. But believing in Jesus on the basis of the signs does not go far enough. One has to see the (symbolic) significance of the signs. And as for a second witness, there is none. One has to see that Jesus' witness about himself is true without demanding any other attestation. This naturally confounds "the Jews" and always leads to another round of miracle working and self-revelation. That Jesus claims to be the son from the Father, while knowing that his listeners will not be able to prove or accept his claim, has also frustrated modern interpreters who have spoken of the logical paradox that lies at the heart of the Johannine christology (view of Jesus as divine). For those within the community, however, the series of miracles and monologues must have created knowing smiles. That is because they had already seen the truth, namely that Jesus was the *logos*, the son of God, and that they belonged to him as his "sheep," "vine," or "friends" (John 10, 15).

At one level of experience they "knew" that Jesus was the son of God because they knew the mythology they had developed. It was a variant of the old, standard descent-ascent pattern, whereby a god comes down into the world from the heavenly realm on a mission or with a message and then returns. In this case, the John people may have taken the mythology of Jesus as the son of God from other Christian groups, such as the Christ cult or the post-Markan Jesus people, and used it to enhance their own miracle myth of origin. Along with the myth of Jesus as God's son came both the notion of a redemptive death, as in the Christ cult, and that of an apocalyptic encounter with the establishment in Jerusalem, as in the Gospel of Mark. Telltale fragments of both the Pauline and the Markan traditions let us know that the John people got their mythology of Jesus as the son of God from sources such as these. But they were not interested in either a redemptive death or an apocalyptic confrontation. Jesus returns to the Father by dying, but his death is not a martyrdom. It is simply his hour of "glorification," the author playing on the dialectic of being "raised" on the cross (John 12:27–36). As Jesus said, "No one takes my life from me, I lay it down of my own accord" (John 10:18). So even the standard mythology of Jesus' death as a martyrdom was set aside in favor of the myth of a god's appearance in the world and return to his heavenly abode. All of John's gospel is governed by this mythology. Couched between the descent of the *logos* and Jesus' return to the Father, the miracle stories and the dialogues they spawn are simply seven chances for the Johannine Christians to watch and enjoy the collision of the world of enlightenment and the world of darkness, a collision they experienced every day.

This can only mean that the Johannine community cultivated the image of the mythological Jesus and his words as coded invitations to personal enlightenment in much the same way as the Thomas people had done. The big difference between the two groups was that the Johannine community treasured their sense of being a social unity with a claim upon the heritage of Israel and found themselves traumatized by their conflict with the Pharisees. They had more in common with the Jesus groups that produced the pronouncement stories and the synoptic gospels than the Thomas people. But they did not take either the Markan turn to an apocalyptic enclave mentality or the Matthean turn to acquiescence as a subcultural Jewish sect. And, like Mark, they were not interested in becoming a congregation of the Christ on the model of a Hellenistic association or mystery cult. Instead, aware of all these options, they cultivated their miracle myth of origin and developed a mythology of their founder to correspond with their own sense of being a beloved community in the midst of a hostile environment. They apparently were not interested in baptism and memorial rituals, but they may have met for meals, washed one another's feet, prayed together, and sung hymns of praise to the *logos* and to Jesus as the son of God. The monologue material, famous for its repetitious "I am" sayings, is suspiciously poetic in ways similar to the opening poem in praise of the *logos*. Interlocking lines pick up on a term just used, add to it another, then circle back in a rhythmic pattern that overloads the meaning of terms and frustrates clear, conceptual definitions. It gives one the impression of having been produced by collective chanting, and, as a matter of fact, one is not always sure where the voice of Jesus leaves off and the voice of the Johannine community takes over. For John, the "I" of the mythological Jesus, the light of the world, and the "I" of the Johannine Christian, the enlightened one who "abides in Jesus" and "in whom Jesus' words abide," are, in the last analysis, one and the same.

THE LETTERS TO THE COLOSSIANS AND EPHESIANS

Paul's letters to the Colossians and Ephesians are not authentic. There is not a suggestion of the personal Paul in either of them. The styles are different, the vocabulary is different, and the rhetoric is different from authentic Pauline letters. Paul may not always have been convincing in his letters to the churches, but he was always passionately engaged and intellectually sharp. The letters to the Colossians and Ephesians are flaccid and, to tell the truth, quite boring. So why are they among the letters of Paul in the New Testament?

The first answer is that, by the time the church started drawing up lists of literature acceptable for public reading in the third and fourth centuries, Colossians and Ephesians were already part of the "letters of Paul" and so came along for the ride. The second answer is that they were written in Paul's name after his death by leaders loyal to the school that survived him. Writing in the name of the founder of a school was common practice at this time, so the scholars' conclusion that these letters are pseudonymous (written under a false name) should not suggest dishonesty on the part of those who wrote them. On the contrary, these letters are proof that

Paul's influence took the form of generating a school that looked to him as its founder. The letter to the Colossians, written sometime during the 70s or 80s, shows that the authority of the apostle could be called upon to address a sectarian conflict that had arisen in Asia Minor. That it was written as if during his lifetime would not have damaged the argument. The letter to the Ephesians, which lacks the local address "to the Ephesians" in the earliest manuscripts, appears to have been a cover letter for an early collection of Pauline letters addressed to "the church" in general. This would mean that scribes at some center for Christian instruction were busy making copies of Paul's letters for dissemination to a network of churches, perhaps as early as the 80s or 90s. Though we can't be sure, Ephesus comes to mind as a likely location.

Both letters show, however, that the influence of Paul's memory and letters did not extend to his ideas or theological system. He was remembered and honored as the apostle to the gentiles and the founder of Christian congregations. But his gospel had been watered down, if ever it had been understood full strength, to the notion that the death and resurrection of Christ created a new human order into which people could be transferred by means of the Christian rite of baptism. Nothing is left of Paul's heated arguments for freedom from the law, the justification of sinners, faith in Christ, scriptural precedence, epic revisions, or apocalyptic scenarios and threats. For Paul, Christian existence was understood as an imitation of the sufferings and sacrificial death of Christ; full participation in the resurrection of Christ would have to wait until the *eschaton*. In Colossians, by contrast, Christians were addressed as those who had already been "raised with him [Christ] through faith . . . when you were buried with him in baptism" (Col. 2:12). In Ephesians, the author speaks for all Christians, saying, "Even when we were dead through our trespasses, [God] made us alive together with Christ and raised us up with him and seated us with him in the heavenly places in Christ Jesus" (Eph. 2:5–6). This is transfer terminology devoid of transformational drama, ethnic identity conflict, or apocalyptic consequence. Something must have happened to the Pauline Christ.

What happened to Paul's Christ was that he became an imaginary world the size of the cosmos. With a little help from the Stoics, Christians of the Christ cult had reconceived the image of Christ as cosmic lord by thinking of his kingdom as the hidden structure of the cosmos and he himself as the creative power that brought it into being and continued to sustain it. The Greek penchant for correlating anthropology with cosmology had, in this case, the weird result of imagining the Christ-cosmos in the monstrous form of a person, with Christ as the "head" and both the world and the church as his "body." As the Christ hymn puts it (Col. 1:15–20):

> He is the image of the invisible God, the firstborn of all creation;
> For in him all things in heaven and on earth were created,
>> Things visible and invisible,
>> whether thrones or dominions or rulers or powers—
>> all things have been created through him.

He himself is before all things, and in him all things hold together.
He is the head of the body, the church;
He is the beginning, the firstborn from the dead,
So that he might come to have first place in everything.
For in him all the fullness of God was pleased to dwell,
And through him God was pleased to reconcile to himself all things,
      whether on earth or in heaven,
      By making peace through the blood of his cross.

Paul would not have liked this hymn. Christ was now imagined as the power that created the world and held it together. The grand event of reconciling any and all tensions, fractures, or oppositions in either the cosmic realm or the realm of human history had already been accomplished according to this hymn. Since all had already been accomplished, induction into this peaceable kingdom need not be traumatic. As the author of Ephesians puts it (Eph. 2:19–22):

So then you are no longer strangers and aliens, but you are citizens with the saints and also members of the household of God, built upon the foundation of the apostles and prophets, with Christ Jesus himself as the cornerstone. In him the whole structure is joined together and grows into a holy temple in the Lord; in whom you also are built together spiritually into a dwelling place for God.

"What about conversion," Paul would ask, "what about holiness, what about suffering and service, what about the Romans, what about Jews, what about the real world, and what about the final judgment of God?" "What is the problem?" these Paulinists would say:

Remember that you were at that time without Christ, being aliens from the commonwealth of Israel, and strangers to the covenants of promise, having no hope and without God in the world. But now in Christ Jesus you who once were far off have been brought near by the blood of Christ. For he is our peace; in his flesh he has made both groups into one and has broken down the dividing wall, that is, the hostility between us. He has abolished the law with its commandments and ordinances, that he might create in himself one new humanity in place of the two, thus making peace, and might reconcile both groups to God in one body through the cross, thus putting to death that hostility through it. (Eph. 2:12–16)

It sounds good. But it could have had meaning only for Christians who had found the Christ cult and its congregations a large enough world in which to live and not feel threatened by social forces in the world outside the cult. The rhetoric of reconciliation is particularly hollow if listened to through Jewish ears, or even if read in the light of the Christian polemics against the Jews that began to pop up in other literature around this time. The authors of these letters represent a development in the Christ cult that can only be called philosophical or perhaps even gnostic. They had actually succeeded in mastering thoughts about such things as hostility, ideology, social distinctions, martyrdom, death, and the declarations of guilt and innocence by imagining a little cosmic drama to have played itself out in which Christ "made peace by the blood of his cross." In order to live in such a world, to belong to the "body of Christ," as they would have said, one need not struggle any longer with the issues of faith and faithfulness (*pistis*); one would need only a fertile mind and constant intellectual stimulation to keep the body of Christ in view and explore its hidden recesses, to keep feeling sure that it was present and that one really did belong to it. And that, of course, is what the letters are all about. The authors called this mental effort "wisdom":

> Let the word of Christ dwell in you richly; teach and admonish one another in all wisdom; and with gratitude in your hearts sing psalms, hymns, and spiritual songs to God. (Col. 3:16)

> I want their hearts to be encouraged and united in love, so that they may have all the riches of assured understanding and have the knowledge of God's mystery, that is Christ himself, in whom are hidden all the treasures of wisdom and knowledge. (Col. 2:2–3)

> I pray that the God of our Lord Jesus Christ, the Father of glory, may give you a spirit of wisdom and revelation as you come to know him, so that, with the eyes of your heart enlightened, you may know what is the hope to which he has called you, what are the riches of his glorious inheritance among the saints, and what is the immeasurable greatness of his power for us who believe, according to the working of his great power. God put this power to work in Christ when he raised him from the dead and seated him at his right hand in the heavenly places, far above all rule and authority and power and dominion, and above every name that is named, not only in this age but also in the age to come. And he has put all things under his feet and has made him the head over all things for the church, which is his body, the fullness of him who fills all in all. (Eph. 1:17–23)

Living in such an imaginary world, having to keep it in place by constant reminder, one wonders what these Christians did for excitement, or even what they did not do in order to be thought good citizens of such a kingdom. Taking another look at the letters with such questions in mind, answers are not immediately forthcoming, but the questions do help us focus our observations. Excitements had become a problem, it seems, and had to be countered, not fostered. To judge from the concerns expressed by the author of the letter to the Christians at Colossae, at any rate, the Colossians were observing "festivals, new moons, and sabbaths," keeping taboos on food and other matters, performing ascetic practices, and cultivating the vision and worship of angels (Col. 2:16–23). These practices would not have been strange behavior for Asia Minor. The list outlines a set of standard practices designed to launch a person into the cosmos by means of ecstatic and visionary experiences. The particular features of the list, such as the sabbaths and the vision of angels, show that this form of asceticism had been appropriated by Christians intrigued with the mysteries of some Jewish mythologies and practices. It does not mean that these Christians had turned away from orthodox Christianity, for nothing of the kind existed. They were interested only in making some contact with the cosmic Christ. Taking one's place with the angels surrounding the heavenly throne where Christ was seated at God's right hand would certainly have been an exhilarating moment.

But what does the author say about this practice? Don't do it!

> If with Christ you died to the elemental spirits of the universe, why do you live as if you still belonged to the world?. . . If you have been raised with Christ, seek the things that are above, where Christ is, seated at the right hand of God. Set your minds on things that are above, not on things that are on earth. (Col. 2:20; 3:1)

Ah. Now the wisdom recommended by the author begins to make some sense. Set your *mind* on the cosmic Christ. You have *already* been raised. You should not keep on practicing visions of ascent into the heavens. Don't you *see*, all you need to do is behave and say your prayers.

As for the way these authors thought about being good citizens of such a commonwealth, one feature distinguishes both letters from those of Paul. It is the occurrence of ethical instructions for ordering the household. Wives should be subject to their husbands, children to their parents, and slaves to their masters. As for the husbands and masters, they should treat their wives, children, and slaves kindly. So then, one might ask, what difference did being a Christian make? These were common standards for the managing of a household in the society at large. And, as the author of Colossians said, adding a considered thought at the end of his household codes, Christians should also "conduct [themselves] wisely toward outsiders" (Col. 4:5). If being a Christian did not make any real difference in lifestyle at home or at the *agora* (market), and if the cultivation of contacts with the angels was thought inappropriate, what might the authors of these letters have been thinking?

It does appear as if second-rate minds were in danger of sapping the Christ cult of its juices. Were these authors not already in positions of leadership, or writing from such a perspective as part of an emerging system of administration, and were some practical social functions of Christian congregations not already working in the welfare vacuum created by the law and order bureaucracy of the Romans, the Christ cult form of the Jesus legacy might have been in trouble. The era of ideological and spiritual experimentation, when energy levels were extremely high and issues were of real consequence for lifestyle and name calling, was obviously past. So why would any Greek of Asia Minor have wanted any longer to be called a "gentile"? Think of being told that you were now a member of the "commonwealth of Israel" and that by "holding fast to the head, from whom the whole body, nourished and held together by its ligaments and sinews," you would "grow into a holy temple in the Lord" (Col. 2:19; Eph. 2:12, 21). The only nerves these letters were touching seem to belong to unimaginative caretakers of a worn-out movement. And yet, there may still have been some rewards.

The letters document a late phase in the history of the Christ cult. Leaders at some center of learning and administration were in the process of creating a network of congregations. They saw themselves as caretakers of the tradition and the truth of Paul's gospel. They understood their "ministry" (*diakonia*, Col. 4:17; Eph. 4:12) to be the supervision of the local leadership of these congregations. The term for supervisor (*episkopos*) is not yet in evidence, but the idea is already there. In contrast to Paul's own use of the term *church* (*ekklesia*, congregation), for instance, a term he used only to refer to a local congregation, the author of Ephesians now used the term in the singular to refer to the church universal. From what we know of "the church" as it took institutional shape in the second century, its members received benefits of a very practical nature. Bishops looked after their flocks to see that they had food, jobs, counseling, courts, and celebrations in addition to the spiritual nourishment of regular meditations on virtues, honor, and the wisdom of the Christ. So perhaps the school of Paul was already pushing in that direction. With such a conception of the church coming into place, one wonders what the next steps will be, and especially whether the effort to keep the cosmic Christ in mind will be enough to satisfy the Christian's quest for knowledge (*gnosis*).

THE EPISTLE TO THE HEBREWS

For the letter to the Hebrews we have to imagine a scholar ensconced in some private scriptorium, rummaging through his stacks of scrolls and papyrus notes, walking pensively in his garden, bent over his stand-up writing desk for hours, poring over fine points of the Greek translation of the Hebrew scriptures, and trying out some ideas with a few other highly educated and sophisticated Christian intellectuals. One suspects that these conversations took place at table, lightly spread with fruits and nuts and a small amphora of modest-quality wine. He, and we know he was male because of a masculine gender self-reference (Heb. 11:32), may not have had as quick and sharp a mind as Paul's or as personal and passionate an approach to public debate and theological argumentation, but he was far superior to Paul in learning, analytical capacity, and systematic thinking. He was capable of keeping in mind large quantities of conceptual detail and working with multiple themes as he wove concepts in and out of a vast Platonic world of ideas and watched the cosmic picture change with each new stitch in what eventually amounted to an elaborate mental tapestry. He was also capable of elegant writing. His treatise leads the reader to ever more complex ideas, triggering unimaginable connotations, to end with a burning exhortation not to give up on the Christian faith. His intellectual labor was not the result of a momentary inspiration, and his treatise was not written in a weekend. The Epistle to the Hebrews is the result of many months, perhaps years, of intense scholarly research and writing.

Unfortunately, we do not know who this author was, either by name, location, or association with a specific tradition of early Christian thought. From our point of view, Hebrews just appears out of the blue, without title, destination, or signature, and its particular conception of the Christian faith does not fit anywhere on our map of early Christian writings. It must have been written sometime between the flowering of Pauline Christianity in the 60s and 70s and the writing of 1 Clement in 96 C.E., because an elaborate Christ myth is the starting point for the author's construction of his Christian cosmos, and the treatise seems to have been known by Clement of Rome, cited in his letter to the Corinthians. A date during the 80s would be plausible. But other clues are extremely sparse, and the content of Hebrews cannot be used to place it because it draws upon so many different intellectual traditions. As far as scholars have been able to tell, the author and the Christian congregation he had in mind might have been located anywhere in the Eastern Mediterranean basin.

The author had a definite proposal to make, and he developed a lengthy and sustained argument to support it. Hebrews is not really a letter. It is what the Greeks called a *protreptic*, or philosophical exhortation, a treatise aimed at persuading its readers to accept a particular philosophical point of view. In this case the point of view was that Christ was the Christians' heavenly high priest, having made an eternal sacrifice of himself for the sins of his people. With such a thesis to propose, it is no wonder that the author had to develop a lengthy argument. None of the Jesus people or Christ cult people we have considered thus far had dared such a thought. But the author was serious about his proposal, apparently, and must have had real Christians in mind. If they were Christians who belonged to the Christ cult, his magnum opus may have been written too soon. The ritual meal in memorial to a martyr was not yet being celebrated as a sin offering.

Judging from the spotty trail of references to Hebrews by writers of the second and third centuries, it did not become a popular and widely read book. Hebrews may therefore be a case of an intellectual taking a wrong turn in the collective process of early Christian mythmaking. If the author did succeed in getting a hearing from the congregation he had in mind, that chapter of Christian history did not leave a trace in the collective memory of the church. His treatise was saved from oblivion by some scribe in the school of Paul who thought it worth adding to the collection of Pauline letters. It was as a part of that collection that the treatise found its way into a list of "apostolic" writings that Athanasius recommended for early

Christian worship in 387 C.E. and so became part of the (Catholic) Christian Bible. When the church finally turned its attention to the theme that governs Hebrews, namely Christ's death as a sacrifice for sins, it was the gospel stories of the supper and the passion, not the book of Hebrews, that laid the mythic foundation. Whether the book of Hebrews played any role in that development is questionable. So Hebrews seems to be the result of an individual's intellectual labor, the exquisite proposal of a brilliant mind, but one that failed to make any difference. What a rare find. Given the rules of what usually is saved and what is dumped in the historical processes of selective collective memory, Hebrews should not have survived. What a treat to observe this disciplined flight of early Christian fantasy that survived only by accident. It tells us more about the philosophical stimulation unleashed by the Christian myth than any of the other texts that were saved from this early period. What, then, was the concern to which this author turned his attention?

Three concerns underlay his treatise. The first was that Christians had grown weary. Some had settled into perfunctory participation in the cult, others had "fallen away." This is the concern most obviously expressed, and it runs as a theme throughout the treatise to climax at the final exhortation (Heb. 3:12; 5:11; 6:4–6; 10:26; 12:3). The second concern was that a "persecution" of some kind had taken place. The author apparently thought that this time of trouble had not been properly understood by these Christians and that their lack of understanding contributed to their fatigue and diminishing interest (Heb. 10:32–35; 12:3–4). And the third concern, not expressly addressed, was the author's own need to see the Christ cult in succession to the second-temple system of sacrifice. Why he needed to do that is part of the puzzle we need to unravel.

The first concern is thoroughly understandable. It points to a circumstance that can be documented for the later decades of the first century: malaise, disaffection, and retrenchment. And why not? The exhilarating period of entertaining novel notions and taking the consequences for brash behavior was past. History had gone its own way, extravagant Christian rhetoric had begun to sound hollow, and those who had risen to positions of leadership among the churches were not encouraging countercultural behavior; they were calling for obedience to the traditions. The author of Hebrews was bright enough to know that would not do. These traditions were only "first principles," he said, and Christians should leave them behind in order to understand just how deep, profound, and eternal the truth of the Christian revelation was. His list of the first principles included "the basic teaching about Christ, . . . repentance from dead works, faith toward God, instruction about baptisms, laying on of hands, resurrection of the dead, and eternal judgment" (Heb. 6:1–2). This is not a bad description of Christianity as the bishops will later define it. For the author of Hebrews, however, it is minimal and insufficient. If that is all there is to it, he said in effect, you don't get it.

As for the author's reference to persecution (Heb. 10:33; 12:3), he does not tell us enough to know what happened and why. In scholarship, attempts have frequently been made to date Hebrews by identifying which of the traditional Roman persecutions of Christians the author intended. This approach has never succeeded, first of all because the evidence for that history of persecutions is so meager and misleading, and second because there is no description of the persecution mentioned in Hebrews. Early Christians may have created local disturbances for a variety of reasons and, depending upon the issue and how the local governors responded, Christians may well have been "publicly exposed to abuse and affliction" as the author says (Heb. 10:33). What is often overlooked in reference to this text, however, is that his description is a positive recollection of the "earlier days" when these Christians were learning to struggle with suffering for their faith as a matter of course. His assessment of their response at that time was complimentary, and his point was that to surrender one's confidence because of such suffering *at any time* would be devastating (Heb. 10:35; 12:1–17). It thus appears that the author introduced the theme of persecution to make a point, not because it described the present experience of his readers. Their experience was fatigue and growing disinterest, "drooping hands" and "weak knees," as the author said (Heb. 12:12). The author's hope was that a consideration of *pistis*, a term that meant both "faith" and "faithfulness," would lead to a deeper appreciation of the "basic teaching about Christ," a consideration that might challenge the disaffection about which he was concerned. With *pistis* in view, an appeal could be made for Christian faithfulness as a noble *imitatio* of Christ's own example of endurance unto death (Heb. 12:1–3). And, if that were so, think of what it would mean for Christians to persist in their faith! They would be living in conformity with the deep structure of the cosmos, in agreement with the pattern of self-sacrifice that determined the divine ordering of all creation.

It is rapidly becoming clear that the three concerns just mentioned were all interrelated. Like Paul, the author was personally invested in a thorough conversion to the Christ cult. Unlike Paul, he was living at a later time when the Christ cult was in danger of losing its original sense of urgency and ultimacy. The author wrote as if he wanted to reinspire his fellow Christians, and so he turned to the martyrology basic to the Christ myth and tried to set it forth as an inspirational example of persistence in the faith. But underneath it all, his treatise reads as if he wanted to reconfirm his own sense that the Christ myth was right and that joining the Christians had been the right thing to do. That is why, like Paul, he spent so much time looking for a way to relate the Christ myth to some basic definition of Judaism. Unlike Paul, he decided to compare the Christ myth with the temple system of sacrifice. It was this decision that got him into trouble, but it was one that may have had more merit at the time than anything Paul imagined.

The temple system had been central and definitional for Judaism. Now that it was no longer functioning, the Christ cult could be imagined to have taken its place. The merit of such a comparison was obvious. It would not be necessary to argue for the "old" coming to an end, for that had already happened. It would be necessary only to argue that Christianity was the better form of "sacrificial" worship. And by using the sacrificial metaphor, one could describe the transition without reactivating the bitter competition Christians had with the Pharisees and local synagogues. To set up the comparison, a Platonic model of pattern and copy would work quite well. One would not have to say that the history of Israel as a religious community had been wrong, just that the Jewish temple or sacrificial system had been a poor attempt to copy the heavenly pattern. And the same model of a heavenly pattern and earthly copy could be used with the Christ cult. In this case, however, the superiority of Christ's sacrifice would reside in the access it provided to the divine liturgy. So for this author, the solution to the problem of uncertainty and apathy was solved as soon as he saw that the Christ myth worked both ways, as an example for Christian faithfulness (*pistis*), and as a metaphor for comparing and contrasting Judaism and Christianity ("sacrifice"). Christianity would then be defined as the religion that revealed the cosmic pattern of divine sacrifice.

The author was well equipped to tackle such a project. He was completely at home in the world of Platonic thought and exceptionally skilled in the allegorical interpretation of the Jewish scriptures. He was thoroughly acquainted with the Christ myth and its logic and keenly aware of the ways in which the new Christian congregation might be related to the Judaism of its past. He was highly trained in Greek rhetoric and had no problem with the use of merely rhetorical arguments to build his conceptual system. And he had a fine theoretical mind, capable of inhabiting for long periods the imaginary world he set out to create. What he ended up with may be a philosophical monstrosity, to say nothing of its theological offensiveness. But the treatise he wrote to explain his proposal is such an intriguing exercise in Christian imagination that the unwary reader is quickly swept up into the Platonic world of ideas in which his game was played.

According to our author, the Christ may be compared with the entire system of Israelite religion and shown to be "better." He was superior to the angels by having become "lower," then "higher," than any of them (Hebrews 1–2). He was superior to Moses, because he "was faithful over God's house as a son" instead of as a servant like Moses (Heb. 3:1–6). He was superior to the high priest because he offered himself, not some other victim, as the sacrifice. And he did that for the sake of others, not for himself; once for all, not daily; in the heavenly temple, not in the earthly tabernacle; and so on for several chapters (Hebrews 4–10). Then the author turns to the topic of *pistis* as "faith" and "faithfulness," with a list of examples from Abel through the prophets of those who were indeed faithful but who did not "receive what was promised" (Heb. 11:39). And finally, the exemplar supreme is set forth as "the pioneer and perfecter of our faith, who for the sake of the joy that was set before him endured the cross, disregarding its shame, and has taken his seat at the right hand of the throne of God" (Heb. 12:2). The exhortation that follows is (1) to think of Christ's endurance as a model to be followed, and (2) to understand his accomplishment as making the heavenly sanctuary of God accessible for Christians to enter. One is not quite sure at the end whether the Christian has already arrived for worship in this cosmic sanctuary or is still in danger of losing the way as one approaches the altar far above. In any case, a terrifying thought is appended about being finally rejected by God who is said to be a consuming fire (Heb. 12:19). But either way, "having come to the city of the living God . . . and to Jesus the mediator of a new covenant" (Heb. 12:22–24), or enduring "trials for the sake of discipline" and making "straight paths for your feet" (Heb. 12:7, 12), the reader is to get the following point, namely, "Let us continually offer a sacrifice of praise to God. . . . Do not neglect to do good and to share what you have, for such sacrifices are pleasing to God. Obey your leaders and submit to them, for they are keeping watch over your souls and will give an account" (Heb. 13:15–17). What a dull, insipid conclusion to such a passionate argumentation. If that is what the letter was about, it was certainly an exercise in intellectual overkill. But perhaps the author was one of these leaders. If so, and if his congregations respected him as an erudite scholar, perhaps his effort in imaginative mythmaking enhanced his authority and at least did no harm.

THE REVELATION TO JOHN

One Sunday on the island of Patmos, so reports the author of the Revelation to John, he was "in the spirit," heard a voice, turned and saw a vision of the cosmic Christ with seven stars (angels) in his right hand standing in the midst of seven golden lampstands (churches). The Christ told him what to write to the angels of seven churches, those at Ephesus, Smyrna, Pergamum, Thyatira, Sardis, Philadelphia, and Laodicea. For each there was a commendation, a criticism, and a warning about the imminent return of Jesus. Then a door into heaven opened and the canopy of the cosmos rolled back. John was taken up to the throne of God where twenty-four elders, seven spirits, four living creatures, a scroll with seven seals, a booming voice, a slaughtered lamb with seven horns and seven eyes (which was really the lion of the tribe of Judah), and thousands of angels set the stage for the drama of "what must soon take place" (Revelation 1–5).

The lamb was found worthy to open the seven seals on the scroll that contained the script of what would happen. One after another the seals were broken, and there appeared in sequence the four horsemen of the apocalypse, astronomical disorders, the protective marking of 144,000 servants of God from Israel, and the rapture of a multitude from every nation who had "washed their robes in the blood of the lamb" (Rev. 7:14). As the seventh seal was broken, there was silence in the heavens for half an hour until the seven angels took up their seven trumpets. As each was blown, the world started to come apart. There was hail mixed with fire and blood. A third of the waters became a sea of blood. A third of the waters turned to wormwood. And the moon and the stars ceased to shine. That was what happened when the first four trumpets were blown. Then came three woes. The sound of the fifth trumpet unleashed the first woe: Smoke from the bottomless pit turned to locusts with hair like women's hair, teeth like lions' teeth, scales like iron breastplates, and tails with stingers like scorpions, to torture the people without protective marks. The sound of the sixth trumpet unleashed the second woe: Four angels of death, two hundred million horses of death, and three plagues joined to kill a third of humankind. Then, seven thunders were sealed up in a little scroll that John, our author, had to eat in order later to prophesy. He was also told to measure the temple of God where two witnesses would stand to prophesy, be killed by the beast from the bottomless pit, and be raised again to life in three and one-half days. All of that happened at the sound of the sixth trumpet. When the seventh trumpet sounded, a child was born to a woman who was standing on the moon, clothed with the sun, when a great red dragon appeared to devour the child, and war broke out in heaven with Michael and the angels fighting against the dragon. The cosmic chase was on, but the dragon disappeared for a time. Instead, huge beasts appeared from the sea and the earth, angels flew through the heavens wailing, seven bowls of wrath were poured out, and the whore of Babylon fell. Then the rider on the white horse appeared, the dragon returned, was cornered, and thrown into the pit and sealed. Immediately, the new Jerusalem descended gracefully from heaven with twelve gates to the city. It had no need for a temple because of the lamb in its midst, and no need for the sun because God was its light, a light that would never, never cease to shine.

The point of the vision was that the lord Jesus was coming very soon "to repay according to everyone's work" (Rev. 22:12). This apparently meant inclusion or exclusion from the heavenly Jerusalem, and the faithful should therefore remain faithful until that city appeared, no matter what the whore of Babylon might suggest or the dragon threaten. We might want to ask what on earth propelled our author into the heavens to suffer through such a ghastly vision. Judging from the letters to the seven churches in chapters 2 and 3, John was worried about two things: false teachings and what he called "affliction" (*thlipsis*), sometimes translated as "persecution." These churches, all in western Asia Minor and apparently known to our author, were not behaving properly from his point of view. Some were not taking their Christian vows as seriously as they once did. Others were paying attention to false teachings such as those of "Balaam," "Jezebel" the prophetess, the Nicolaitans, and the "synagogue of Satan." We have no way of knowing what these teachings were, but it is clear that John thought they were not true to Christian teaching and that they were the source of such bad practices as eating food sacrificed to idols and fornication. The letters to the angels, who presumably would carry the messages to the churches, are the words he heard from the cosmic Jesus who once was dead but now was alive with the keys of death and hades (Rev. 1:18). That is fairly ultimate authority. What the lord Jesus wanted John to write was a warning to the churches that they should repent, rekindle their original Christian fervor, and learn to wait patiently for their rewards. Thus their deviance from the faith was a very serious issue in Jesus' mind and in John's mind.

John was also concerned about trials, suffering, and the affliction of Christians. These were experiences for which the churches were not adequately prepared. He intimated that he was on the island of Patmos because of affliction ("persecution," NRSV; Rev. 1:9), referred to a certain Antipas being killed as a "witness" (*martys*) in Pergamum (Rev. 2:13), and predicted imprisonment for some at Smyrna (Rev. 2:10). The question is whether John's concern about affliction and his concern about false teaching were related, and whether there was any real reason for being so concerned. If we discount John's hyperbolic style and vision, the answer seems to be a cautious yes, that there may well have been a set of circumstances where a Christian confession, or staying true to the "true teaching," put one in danger of being "afflicted."

We have, in any case, the exchange of correspondence between Pliny, the governor of Bithynia in northern Asia Minor, and the emperor Trajan, on the question of policy toward Christians charged with disloyalty to the Roman Empire (Bettenson 1967, 3–4). This correspondence took place about 112 C.E., and it documents the fact that Christians were now known to the Romans as a network of independent associations with practices that were potentially disruptive of a town's peace and tranquillity. Pliny says that the local temples and the commerce related to them had suffered because Christians were not supporting them. And he intimates that non-Christians were charging the Christians with disloyalty to the Roman Empire. During this period, loyalty to the empire was being measured by willingness to offer incense to an image of the emperor as divine, something neither Jews nor Christians were supposed to do. Pliny wanted to know Trajan's policy because, when Christians were charged with disloyalty and they refused to recant and prove their loyalty by offering incense, he had no alternative but to have them executed. Trajan's response was that, of course Pliny had to punish the disloyal, but that he was not to seek Christians out as if all of them were disloyal; he was not to allow anonymous pamphlets as evidence against them; and he was always to give them a chance to recant and worship "our gods."

This is an extremely telling bit of information about the circumstances in which Christians found themselves early in the second century. As long as they were thought to be just another Jewish synagogue, they were exempt from having to demonstrate their loyalty in this way, for the Romans had made a number of exceptions for the Jews since the time of Julius Caesar, including exemption from military service and the right to meet together and collect their own temple taxes without suspicion of disloyalty. In return, the Jews promised to pray for the emperor instead of "worshiping" him. But now, apparently, as a distinctly new religion, Christians could no longer count on that protection. It may therefore be significant that two of the false teachings about which John seemed most concerned had something to do with food offered to idols on the one hand, and synagogues on the other, the two alternative religious associations that would have guaranteed escape from execution.

A problem remains, however, with the question of the appropriateness of John's reaction. His revelation still strikes the modern reader as excessive. A rigorous

Christian, frustrated with these new circumstances, turned his guns on the Romans ("Babylon") in a grisly vision of their comeuppance, and used the terrifying image of this bloody destruction as a warning and preachment directed at his fellow Christians. The most one can say in defense of such an action is that the author certainly must have been serious about his commitments. But the loss of perspective is still obvious. Compared with the book of Hebrews, where a similar set of social circumstances prevailed and the attitude of the author was similar with respect to keeping the faith, extending even to an exaggerated fascination with a cosmic image of sacrifice, John's vision is simply macabre. Instead of encompassing the "afflictions" down below with a heavenly altar of access to God and succor in suffering, as in Hebrews, John's vision filled the universe with afflictions that no one would be able to survive except those who had "washed their robes . . . in the blood of the lamb" (Rev. 7:14). And in comparison with Jewish apocalypses of the time, such as 4 Ezra and 2 Baruch, where the overriding mood is one of lament for an unimaginably great social loss, John's revelation seems to delight in the gruesome for the sake of a personal advantage.

Impressed with John's fixation on slaughter, as in the description of the whore of Babylon (Rome) being "drunk with the blood of the saints and the blood of the witnesses to Jesus" (Rev. 17:6), scholars have regularly tried to date this writing during one of the traditional "persecutions of the church." Nero's "persecution" in 64 C.E. doesn't work because (1) it was not a persecution but an ad hoc, localized, scapegoating strategy that everyone understood to be the action of a madman, and (2) in any case was highly exaggerated by Tacitus, who reported it in order to discredit Nero. The second "persecution" under Domitian (emperor 81–96 C.E.) won't do either, although it was then that early Christian legend dated John's Revelation. Modern scholars cannot find any evidence for a Domitian persecution. There were executions aplenty toward the end of his reign, but they were all affairs of the royal house and senate, as far as we know. This violence finally culminated in Domitian's own assassination in 96 C.E. So we know of no official persecution by the Romans to which John may have been reacting (Collins 1984). It must have been the vulnerability of Christians to charges of disloyalty that became apparent around the turn of the first century that so exercised John.

It is overreaction in any case, for literary analysis demonstrates a studied fascination with the torture and torment of martyrdom. The interlocking sevens are clearly a device for prolonging the descriptions of terror. And some of the descriptions would put Hieronymus Bosch to shame. A search for the source of John's imagery turns up a veritable hodgepodge of ancient Near Eastern myths. From verse to verse the historian's mind, in search of parallels, ricochets among myths of creation, sea dragons, holy wars, royal births, Egyptian depictions of the afterlife, Isis of the heavens, Horus and Seth, the divine court, wisdom at the throne of God, the plagues of the exodus, angelic warriors, cosmic conflagrations, and so on. It does not help that, interspersed with the horrific, there are many examples of heightened and holy liturgical language reminiscent of the prayers and psalms of the pious. After twenty-two chapters of blood-soiled linens, beds, and bodies, the concluding exhortation to the thirsty to "take the water of life as a gift" is not very inviting.

John's revelation is an example of cultivating the image of martyrdom as the major metaphor for making sense of a difficult set of circumstances. The metaphor was apt in some ways, given the martyrology at the core of the Christ myth, and given the threat of execution that Christians now faced. But neither the Romans nor the Christians designed such a set of circumstances on purpose or wanted to put loyalties to the test in this way. So the use of the metaphor was not really apt, and the cultivation of its more gory connotations could not have been a very helpful approach to working out a new understanding of relationships. That, however, was not John's concern. He raised the metaphor of the martyrdom of Christians to mythic status solely in order to imagine the ultimate vindication for the truth of the Christian faith. In so doing, he shaped a literary legacy for Western Christian imagination that continues to haunt us.

The immediate effect of John's writing is less traceable. We are not able to follow the early history of its transmission, and the evidence for its being read with appreciation is spotty. At some point, it seems, the Revelation to John of Patmos was associated with the writings of the Johannine school solely because of the common name. And even after it was blessed for posterity by inclusion in Athanasius' list of apostolic writings, there were doctors of the church who questioned its authenticity and groused about its theology. Its importance for the historian is nevertheless immense. That is because, whether this writing had any effect on the immediately subsequent Christian imagination, it documents a shift in Christian thinking of great consequence for mythmaking during the next two centuries. The shift in thinking was occasioned by two changes in social-historical circumstance. Christian congregations surfaced as a social factor in full public view; and the Romans were toying with a cult of the emperor as divine, a cult to be used as a test of loyalty to the empire. The two features of the new social circumstance for Christians did not mix. And the result was the myth of martyrdom as the highest form of Christian confession. The term *martyr* was actually coined by Christians at this time. It comes from the Greek *martyria*, a word that did not mean "martyr" at all, but "witness." It was the curious conflation of being on trial before the Romans and having to "witness" to one's loyalty to Christ, with the consequence of being executed, understood as an imitation of Christ's own martyrdom, that gave the term *martyria* its peculiar Christian connotation. From that time onward, the true "confessor" of the Christian faith would be the martyr for Christ.

8

LETTERS FROM
THE APOSTLES

Early Christian mythmaking changed course around the turn of the second century. A new set of conceptual problems had surfaced for many Christian groups worried about the bewildering variety of ideologies and practices that had emerged in the name of Jesus. Hasidic sectarians, local mystery cults, itinerant magicians, exegetical mystifiers, cosmic philosophers, and gnostic mystagogues were all calling on the name of Jesus to validate the source or the truth of their programs. Not everyone found this confusion of religious experimentation threatening. Many felt it was titillating in much the same way as modern new agers are attracted to the exploration of cosmic and psychic mysteries for personal orientation. But for a certain type of Christian congregation the range of experimentation became increasingly threatening. These were congregations that occupied a broadly centrist position where the Jesus movements and the Christ cults were learning to accommodate one another. They were those who had accepted the Christ myth, but welcomed the narrative gospels; formed networks of Christian congregations, but thought of themselves as heirs of the Israel legacy; imagined an eventual apocalyptic judgment, but organized themselves to take care of one another in the meantime; knew they were a minority within the larger Roman world but harbored universalistic, this-worldly hopes for the kingdom they represented. The leaders from congregations of this type began to be worried about losing their claim to represent the true Christian teaching. Their answer was to anchor the truth of their gospel in the claim that they "received" it directly from a disciple who had known Jesus personally.

This turn toward interest in Jesus' disciples was a natural move. It followed a model that was firmly in place among the schools of Greek philosophy. According to this model, the teachings of a school were understood to have originated with a founder-teacher and then to have been transmitted through a line of leading disciple-teachers. These disciple-teachers were known as successors (*diadochoi*), and the teachings were known as the school's tradition. Diogenes Laertius used this model to trace the entire history of Greek philosophy from its legendary beginnings with the seven sages and thus account for the antiquity of the many schools of Greek thought still active during his time (ca. 200 C.E.).

However, there was a problem with this model for the Christians. The spread of the Jesus and Christ movements had far outpaced the rise of a philosophical school, and the vast majority of first-generation Christians, including the teachers, preachers, and leaders in charge of local congregations, had never known the historical Jesus. Seventy years had passed without keeping track of the *diadochoi* in the schools of Jesus. The first itinerant founders of Christian congregations were dead. Local congregations were under the care and leadership of resident "elders" and patrons, just as any association would have been. And as for the collective memories of Jesus' first disciples, they were very fuzzy and hardly appropriate for the task at hand. The early Jesus movements had not left any record of disciples that Jesus had trained to carry on his program. As we have seen, that is because Jesus did not have such a program and did not train disciples for leadership.

To make matters worse, during the earliest phases of the Jesus movements every new instruction had been attributed to Jesus himself, not to a successor disciple. Paul's converts had never had a "disciple" to guarantee their tradition. And what of the several other groups, such as those who produced the gospel that was eventually attributed to John, groups that had developed intricate systems of myth and ritual without ever thinking it necessary to call on the name of a disciple in order to feel sure about their experience of the cosmic Christ? They had gotten along quite nicely with anonymous and collective literary production, with only the voice of a mythic Jesus ringing in their ears. And why was the literature current among the various Jesus movements, including the book of Q, not signed by any of "the disciples"? Come to think of it, there was very little evidence to support the notion that the teachings of Jesus had been transmitted through disciples whom he himself had taught.

When Mark finally thought to use the model of a teacher with his disciples to write his life of Jesus in the 70s, the only disciples he knew about were very unlikely candidates for the transmission of his gospel. He knew about two different sets of named disciples. One set was the trio of Peter, James, and John, the "pillars," as Paul called them (Gal. 2:9), who had been in Jerusalem before the war. And Mark made a point of portraying them as understudies of Jesus. But as we know, he also made them look very foolish, as if every reader would know that the real Peter and company would never have agreed with Mark's view of the kingdom of God and his novel life of Jesus. Mark also knew something about another set of disciples called "the twelve" and he actually produced a list of names for them (Mark 3:13–19). But now he had two lists of names, one for the pillars and one for the twelve, and where they overlapped they did not agree. The James of the list of twelve and the James of the three pillars in Jerusalem were not the same. The James of Jerusalem had been Jesus' brother (Gal. 1:19), not a disciple, not the son of Zebedee and brother of John, as Mark said (Mark 3:17). So where did Mark get the idea of the twelve disciples in the first place?

The idea of twelve disciples was already in currency when Paul was active in the 50s, for he includes "the twelve" in his list of those to whom Jesus, he said, appeared after his death (1 Cor. 15: 5). And at the later stages of Q's composition a saying was added about disciples sitting on thrones in the kingdom of God, "judging the twelve tribes of Israel" (Q 22:28–30). These references show that the notion "the twelve" was developed in the course of mythic elaborations with the purpose of laying claim to the concept of Israel. Names were not mentioned because the concept was a fiction and would work best without naming names. It was not until Mark wrote his gospel in the 70s that we have a list of names for the twelve disciples, presumably his own short list of names associated with the early phases of the Jesus groups known to him. And it was not until Matthew wrote his gospel in the late 80s that Peter finally emerged as the preeminent leader of the twelve, cast now as the disciple Jesus selected to carry on his work. So for those who started to worry about the truth of their gospel toward the end of the first century, and how the gospel instructions had gotten from Jesus to them, some juggling of the "historical" records was absolutely necessary.

Well, then, if no early writings could be traced to the disciples portrayed in the gospels, second-century Christians would just have to invent them. Imagining that the disciples must have written down their memories of Jesus and kept notes on his instructions to them would not be difficult, for that belonged to the teacher-school model. And, as we have seen, the practice of attributing speech to illustrious persons of the past was a skill learned in school. First-century Jesus people had created and cultivated their "memory" of Jesus on this model. Second-century mythmaking would follow suit. It would simply shift its focus from Jesus and his authority to an interest in his disciples as apostles and missionaries.

The narrative gospels had already taken the first step by imagining that the disciples had been commissioned by Jesus. The term that began to be used in place of *disciples* or *the twelve* was *apostles*. Apostles were messengers who had been commissioned to represent the one who sent them (*apostolos* means sent). Paul had already used this term to refer to himself, but in his case it was God who had commissioned him to preach the gospel, not Jesus. This was Paul's way of claiming authority to speak about Jesus Christ despite the fact that he had *not* been a disciple. He even used the term *apostle* to refer to Peter, James, and John, thus suggesting to his readers that he and they shared the same level of authorization, as if they also had been commissioned by God. But this assertion turns out to have been a clever strategy on Paul's part (Mack 1988, 113), and the point to be made is that he did not refer to the pillars as disciples. They were, as he put it, "those who were already apostles before me" (Gal. 1:17). This bit of evidence from the 50s is extremely important, for it tells us that the idea of an apostle was rooted in the concept of mission, and that the merger of the ideas of disciple and apostle took place at a later time for other reasons. The idea of an apostle may even have been Paul's own contribution to the early Christian language of leadership, for the term *apostle* seems to have taken on the connotation of a very special authorization, limited just to those who had "seen" the risen lord. By confusing the roles of disciple and apostle, those who had been "with Jesus" and those who had seen the risen lord, a confusion of images that took place during the late first century, even Paul could be numbered among those authorized to guarantee the truth of the gospel. But what, then, about the notion of disciples rooted in the Jesus traditions, those who had only been "with him," for whom there were no stories about seeing the risen lord? In order for them to be imagined as apostles, the narrative gospels would have to include a story of their commission as apostles as well as an account of their "seeing" the risen Christ.

Mark took a stab at the idea of disciples being commissioned by Jesus by having the twelve sent out while Jesus was still active in Galilee. That didn't add much to the story of Jesus, of course, or to the enhancement of the disciples as guarantors of the gospel, as Mark knew and made clear in the stories he told of their sad lack of understanding (Mark 6:30–44; 8:14–21). Matthew's so-called great commission was better, coming at the end of the story, mentioning that they "saw" and "worshiped" the risen Jesus, and involving the charge to baptize and make disciples of the nations. This established the authority of the disciples as apostles much better than Mark's story of their commission to preach and cast out demons in Galilee. However, Luke's idea was even better than Matthew's. Luke had Jesus appear to the eleven and tell them to stay in Jerusalem until he sent the holy spirit to empower them, had them elect a twelfth to take the place of Judas, celebrate Pentecost with the whole world looking on, and then had the holy spirit send them out in all directions to tell the story of Jesus as the gospel truth. Others would find additional ways to set the scene for a special instruction from Jesus, such as the secret words spoken to Thomas in the Gospel of Thomas, the private instruction in the Gospel of John, and the postresurrection revelations to only certain disciples typical of gnostic treatises. Secret traditions did not really need an apostle of the missionary kind. But each of these other ways of linking a tradition with a disciple shows that the notion of the twelve disciples as guarantors of authoritative tradition was at work, and each was beholden in some way to the general notion of an apostolic period. The idea behind much of the apostolic literature written around the turn of the second century was that disciples who had known Jesus personally formulated the instructions received from him and passed them on to the next generation of leaders.

Thus they needed texts. And so the writing of texts in the name of some disciple or apostle became standard practice. It is for this reason as well that previously written anonymous literature, such as the New Testament gospels, were now attributed either to a disciple, as in the cases of Matthew and John, or to an associate of a disciple, such as Mark, or to an associate of Paul, as in the case of Luke. A cursory glance at the large collection of early Christian writings traditionally known as the apocryphal New Testament (Elliott 1993) and at the corpus now known as the gnostic scriptures (Layton 1987; Robinson 1988) reveals many texts purportedly written by a disciple as well as many stories about the disciples' acts, missions, and preachments. The favorites include Peter, James, John, and Paul. For each of these there are letters, a collection of acts, and either a gospel or a revelation (apocalypse). Other writings could also be attributed to them, examples being the Preaching of Peter and the Correspondence of Paul and Seneca. For Matthew, we have the gospel attributed to him and lore about an earlier Gospel According to the Hebrews. For Thomas we have the Gospel of Thomas, the Acts of Thomas, an Apocalypse of Thomas, an Infancy Gospel of Thomas, and a Book of Thomas the Contender. There is also a Gospel According to Philip, the Acts of Andrew, and the Questions of Bartholomew, as well as many other writings, such as A Prayer of the Apostle Paul. But that is not all. Literature was also written under the authority of the twelve apostles as a unit, such as the Didache (Teaching) of the Twelve Apostles, the Epistula Apostolorum (Letter of the Apostles), and the Apostolic Constitutions (a manual of instructions for Christian faith and liturgical practices).

This literature, most of which was written during the second, third, and fourth centuries, documents the success of the shift in early Christian mythmaking that took place at the turn of the second century. The shift produced the notion of an apostolic period, a notion that eventually made it possible for the Christian church to imagine the first chapter of early Christian "history" as the assured foundation for its institutions and offices. It also had the effect of turning the disciples into heroes and creating a model for writing subsequent Christian history as a series of exemplars of the faith. And it had the effect of concentrating authority in texts. We shall explore this literature and these apostolic developments more fully in the next chapter. In the present chapter only the pseudonymous letters that eventually found their way into the New Testament will be discussed. They include the letters of Paul to Timothy and Titus, the so-called catholic epistles of Peter and Jude, the letter of James, and three letters of John. Scholars date all of these letters somewhere between 90 C.E. and 140 C.E., thus making it very important to understand the mood and activity of the early second century in order to grasp the circumstances of their composition. Several observations can be made about these letters that will give us guidance as we proceed.

One observation is that these letters, together with the other letters of Paul already discussed, constitute the bulk of the New Testament. There are four gospels in the New Testament collection of texts, one acts of the apostles, one apocalypse, and twenty-one letters! Why are there so many letters? And why do we have letters only from these disciples and apostles? Detailed answers vary from text to text and require the tracing of complex histories of textual composition and transition. Ultimately, the shifting interests of church leaders from the second through the fourth centuries would have to be described. At some point during the third century, for reasons to be discussed in chapter 10, these letters were included in various lists of texts recommended for public Christian reading and so eventually found their way into the collection we know as the New Testament. And yet, merely by noticing the preponderance of letters in the New Testament, we gain an impression of their importance for those who wrote, conserved, and appealed to them as the church emerged from the networks of congregations that began to develop around the beginning of the second century. There must have been something about letters, and about these figures, that interested congregational leaders in the broadly centrist traditions just described. What may it have been?

About this time, the leaders of local Christian congregations began to be called elders (*presbyteroi*) and overseers (*episkopoi*). These were caretakers of congregations with responsibility for the stability, order, and general well-being of their congregations conceptualized as a family or flock. It was time to think about Christians taking their place in the social system of the empire. Interest turned to ordering family life, honoring the dead, caring for the widows, cultivating gospel traditions, and comparing notes with other Christian congregations. And the beginnings of a remarkable development can be discerned. The leaders of congregations in the larger cities began to oversee congregations in other towns throughout their districts. For this purpose, the letter was a perfect form of communication. It could be addressed to a congregation, combine personal, official, and instructional material, be read in lieu of the presence of the sender, and be copied and circulated throughout a network of congregations.

We have six letters of Ignatius, the overseer at Antioch, written around 100 C.E. to Christian congregations at Ephesus, Magnesia, Tralles, Rome, Philadelphia, and Smyrna, as well as one to Polycarp, the overseer at Smyrna. In these letters, Ignatius displays an amazing sense of authority to offer instruction on matters of faith and practice to Christians far beyond the boundaries of his own congregation in Antioch. A recurring theme in this correspondence is instructive. Not only does Ignatius write with the authority of one entrusted with the truth of the gospel tradition, his main concern is that the Christians in each of these other congregations honor and obey their own resident overseers as those who know and have responsibility for guarding the truth of the gospel. The major difference between these letters of Ignatius and those we find in the New Testament is that the New Testament letters were purportedly written by apostles, not by an overseer. The New Testament letters were written to support the apostolic fiction, to insert the authority of the apostles into the chain of tradition that was imagined to have run from Jesus to the overseers. Because of this authorial fiction, the letters in the New Testament cannot compete with the warm, authentic, and personal style of Ignatius's letters. But their message is very much the same, namely, to urge Christians to conform to the teaching and authority of the overseers. Imagine an overseer writing a letter in the name of Peter in which "Peter" says that Christians should obey the overseer. The fiction is obvious in all of these letters, and the circularity of the preachment ridiculous. That Christians have apparently had no trouble regarding these letters as authentic demonstrates just how important the apostolic fiction is to the Christian imagination.

Why letters were written specifically in the names of Paul, Peter, James, John, and Jude is another matter. Paul seems to have been a natural choice, for his legacy already included letters to congregations, references to co-workers such as Timothy and Titus, instructions to local leaders, and a school tradition that could be integrated into a larger network of Christian churches. It may have even been the case that the Pauline precedent established the model for using the letter as a primary vehicle of oversight where we find it developing most clearly, namely among the churches in Asia Minor, Greece, and Rome.

With Peter, James, and John, the situation is quite different. One suspects that these disciples were selected primarily because they are mentioned in the letter of Paul to the Galatians and because of their special role in the synoptic gospels. There may have been local lore attached to each of these figures as well, although the records we have of their being mentioned outside the gospel tradition are very late. These references do not give us substantive information about them and appear to be legends based upon the gospel traditions themselves. Exactly when the name of John came to be associated with the gospel and letters of John, for instance, is most unclear. There is no mention of the disciple John in either the gospel or the letters attributed to him. The earliest attestation that these were regarded as having been written by "John" is found in Irenaeus' *Against Heresies*, dated about 180 C.E. As we shall see, the letters were actually written by an unknown elder who was mightily interested in bringing that gospel tradition into alignment with what I have called the centrist gospel tradition. One way to do that was to claim apostolic authority for the gospel and, as one of the three legendary intimates of Jesus, John could lend great authority to the writings. The situation is much the same with the Letter of James, except that, in this case, the match between the content of the letter and information about James the brother of Jesus may have suggested the authorial fiction. The attribution of a letter to Jude, on the other hand, is inexplicable. But by the time some author thought to gain apostolic authority for his apocalyptic views, there may not have been many names left from which to pick. And it may have been that Jude's credentials included being a brother of both James and Jesus.

With Peter, lore had already turned to legend by the time Luke wrote the Acts of the Apostles. Peter became a prime figure for mythmaking because, if you could recast the Peter of Paul's Galatians and imagine the Peter of the synoptic gospels to represent and validate the Christ myth, centrist interests would gain an exceptionally solid foundation. Just think what it would mean if the leading figure of the Jerusalem congregation had taken the gospel to Rome. So that is what happened. And it apparently happened quite easily. There was certainly no Jesus movement or group of Christian congregations with sole claim to his authority. So many hands were able to get in on the Petrine mythmaking. That factor, plus the fact that it happened at too late a stage to give it a particular contour, determined that the character of the privileged disciple and first bishop of Rome would be very weak and wobbly. The Gospel of Peter, the Preaching of Peter, the Acts of Peter, and the Apocalypse of Peter are filled with idiosyncratic views of later local traditions that do not mix well. The New Testament letters attributed to him, on the other hand, are firmly in the centrist tradition and completely out of character for the Peter that Paul knew. These are the letters that established his authority for the Roman church. The Roman church was soon to become the major player as Christians learned to accommodate the Romans and their empire. It needed both Paul and Peter to make sure of its gospel moorings.

PAUL'S LETTERS TO TIMOTHY AND TITUS

Christian scholars refer to Paul's letters to Timothy and Titus as the *pastorals* because they offer instruction for the overseers of Christian congregations. In the long course of the history of the Christian church, the Greek term for overseer (*episkopos*) was transliterated into Vulgar Latin (*ebiscopus*), Old Saxon (*biskop*), and Old English (*bisceop*), eventually becoming *bishop*, and it was used to refer to the ecclesiastical administrator of a diocese. Since bishops came to be understood as shepherds of their flocks, Paul's letters to Timothy and Titus came to be called "pastoral epistles," and they have taken their place in the Christian imagination as evidence for the early emergence of the episcopal form of church governance. At the time these letters were written, however, *episkopos* did not have the connotation of shepherd, and the office of an overseer was hardly distinct from that of an elder. Nevertheless, the concern for church order and for defining the duties of an overseer is clearly manifest.

The three letters were written at different times, undoubtedly during the first half of the second century. They were not included in Marcion's list of Paul's letters (ca. 140 C.E.), nor do they appear in the earliest manuscript collection of Paul's letters (P46, ca. 200 C.E.). Quotations first appear in Irenaeus' *Against Heresies* (180 C.E.), and their content fits nicely into the situation and thought of the church in the mid–second century. Their attribution to Paul is clearly fictional, for their language, style, and thought are thoroughly un-Pauline, and the "personal" references to particular occasions in the lives of Timothy, Titus, and Paul do not fit with reconstructions of that history taken from the authentic letters of Paul. The mention of Crete in Titus (Titus 1:5, 12–13), of Ephesus in 1 Timothy (1 Tim. 1:3), and clues from the later legends about Paul, make an Aegean provenance likely (MacDonald 1983).

Mythmaking on either flank of the centrist position was apparently proceeding apace. Titus and Timothy are warned against becoming involved in "quarrels about the law" on the one hand (Titus 1:9–16; 1 Tim. 1:4–7), and in the idle talk of ascetics and gnostics on the other (1 Tim. 4:1–3; 6:20; 2 Tim. 2:18). For the author of these letters, conversations with people who did not agree on the "truth" of the gospel "entrusted" to the apostles was dangerous. Titus and Timothy were to stay true to the "sound doctrine" they had received, knowing that the church was the "bulwark of truth" (Titus 1:1–3; 2:1; 1 Tim. 1:10–11; 2:4–5; 3:15). "The mystery of our religion is great," the author wrote, namely that:

> He [Jesus] was revealed in flesh,
>> vindicated in spirit,
>> seen by angels,

proclaimed among Gentiles,
believed in throughout the world,
        taken up in glory. (1 Tim. 3:16)

Period. That is all anyone need know about Jesus. What this "mystery" meant for persons should also be clear. They should "lead a quiet and peaceable life in all godliness and dignity" (1 Tim. 3:7) and so accept the invitation to "eternal life" offered by the gospel (1 Tim. 6:12, 18–19; 2 Tim. 1:10; Titus 1:1–3). And they should learn to obey the instructions of their overseer!

The letters say that Titus and Timothy had been commissioned as overseers of congregations and that Paul was writing to remind them of his instructions to them. But then it appears that just as Paul had been an example for them, they were to be examples for other overseers. These overseers had to be upstanding citizens, "well-thought-of by outsiders," "subject to the kings and authorities," and able to manage their own households (Titus 1:5–9; 1 Tim. 3:1–7). They were also to be charged with managing the congregation just as they managed their own household. Not to be left to their own devices in making judgments about such matters, "Paul" spells out in detail what he expects, demands, allows, and disallows regarding the behavior of overseers, deacons, widows, women, elders, young men, and the slaves in a congregation. Women, for instance, would have to be subject to their husbands, be silent at church, dress modestly, and not wear their hair braided (1 Tim. 2:9–15). There is also instruction for prayers, public reading of the scriptures, enrolling widows on the list of those in need of welfare, teaching, baptism, and the "laying on of hands," a second-century ritual of ordination. Thus the author created a marvelous fiction in order to place a church manual of discipline from the mid–second century at the very beginning of the apostolic tradition. One wonders whether Paul would have been pleased by this honor.

THE EPISTLES OF PETER AND JUDE

The letters attributed to Peter and Jude have been called the catholic epistles (from *katholikos*, general), because they are addressed to Christians in general, not to a particular congregation. First Peter is addressed to the "exiles of the dispersion"; Jude to "those who are called, who are beloved in God the Father and kept safe for Jesus Christ"; and 2 Peter to "those who have received a faith as precious as ours." They were written at different times, most likely during the first half of the second century, but they can be discussed together as Petrine because of the pseudonym common to two of them, and because 2 Peter is related to Jude by incorporating almost all of it in its new rendition.

Exactly when these letters were written cannot be established. Polycarp refers to 1 Peter in his Letter to the Philippians (135 C.E.), so a date earlier in the second century can be assigned to it. But for Jude, the only clues we have are that it matches other early second-century literature and that it was copied by 2 Peter. There is, unfortunately, no reference to 2 Peter in other second-century texts. The first mention of 2 Peter occurs in Origen's Commentary on John from the third century. However, its view of the Christian faith fits well with other Christian literature of the mid-second century, and scholars have traditionally assigned it a date from 124 to 150 C.E. All three letters bear the marks of second-century authorship and erudition: excellent Greek, formal education, facile use of the Greek Old Testament (Septuagint) and other literature, fully developed christologies, a treatment of the sayings of Jesus as if they were standard, Greek-like maxims, and a view toward the past that is clearly one of distance and leisurely contemplation. A close reading of the three is quite instructive, for they document the rise of the Peter myth at Rome, in the course of which the figure of Peter was thoroughly domesticated for the centrist position to serve as the primary apostle of the Christian gospel of the Roman church.

1 Peter

One of the more interesting features of 1 Peter is the concept of the Christian church as a network of sister congregations who know their place as "resident aliens" within the social structure of the Roman Empire and think of themselves on the Jewish model of being in exile, or in the diaspora. That is quite a development for a mere one hundred years of social history. The principal worry was no longer how to relate to Pharisees, synagogues, the temple-state, apocalyptic Jesus people, Jewish Christians, mystery cults, or even the Christian gnostics who would soon become the major alternative and threat to the Roman church. The church now had its eye on Rome. First Peter was written from Rome and, though it euphemistically refers to Rome as Babylon in keeping with the exile theme (1 Pet. 5:13), it is already quite clear that the author would like Christians to behave properly in the eyes of the Romans:

> Conduct yourselves honorably among the gentiles, so that, though they malign you as evildoers, they may see your honorable deeds and glorify God when he comes to judge. For the Lord's sake accept the authority of every human institution, whether of the emperor as supreme, or of governors, as sent by him to punish those who do wrong and to praise those who do right. For it is God's will that by doing right you should silence the ignorance of the foolish. (1 Pet. 2:12–15)

A second feature of importance is the way in which the social model of the household was applied to Christian churches. The concept of the household had its roots in antiquity where the landed estate and its complex stratification of family, servants, friends, and peers was the actual form of social organization in the lands around the eastern Mediterranean. During the Greco-Roman period, this form of social organization became a model for societies of many kinds, including the Roman government itself, which was referred to as Caesar's household. Local

Christian congregations naturally took the form of house-churches and, as we have seen in the pastoral letters of Paul, overseers eventually turned to the very conservative and patriarchal structure of the household as a way to stabilize behavior and control congregational life. At first the move from house-church to household was made by acknowledging the honor due to the elders of a congregation and appropriating the so-called household codes that were common in Greco-Roman society. These codes were based on a widespread cultural definition of honor and shame and were spelled out in a hierarchical ranking of authority. Thus there were certain behavioral requirements for fathers, mothers, children, women, slaves, and friends as they related to one another. In the pastoral letters of Paul, these household codes were set forth as if they were a new instruction. In 1 Peter, however, the household codes seem to be taken for granted as appropriate for Christian ethic. And yet another level of application was also made. The new thought was that the church as a whole should be understood, not only as the family of God (1 Pet. 1:14, 17), a "spiritual house" (temple), or "chosen race" (1 Pet. 2:5–10), all of which were metaphors already in use among Christian congregations since the time of Paul, but as "a holy nation" and as the "household of God" (1 Pet. 2:9; 4:17). What a grandiose idea! Think of the Christian congregation in Rome entertaining such an idea for the Christian churches spread throughout the empire.

The political implications of this new, universal concept of the church are startling. It defined a social role for Christians who, though resident throughout the empire as "aliens and exiles" (1 Pet. 2:11), making sure of their eventual salvation by preparing for the final judgment (1 Pet. 1:4–7, 17; 4:7, 17–19; 5:4), were nevertheless urged to "honor the emperor," "honor everyone," "conduct yourselves honorably," and "live for the rest of your earthly life . . . by the will of God," "like obedient children," "in reverent fear during the time of your exile" (1 Pet. 1:14, 17; 2:12, 17; 4:2). With an elder in charge of the local "flock of God," "exercising the oversight" required of such a social ethic (1 Pet. 5:1–2), how alien, do you suppose, was this new nation? And with Peter himself as the first elder (1 Pet. 5:1), writing in this vein from Rome to the churches in Asia Minor (1 Pet. 1:1), it does appear that these exiles and aliens had become quite accustomed to their residence in this world.

There is one curious embellishment of the Christ myth that deserves notice. If you piece together all of the partial references to the Christ myth in 1 Peter, it is clear that a unified story of the epic-apocalyptic kind had become standard creed. Christ was "destined before the foundation of the world," predicted by the prophets, "revealed at the end of the ages," died an atoning death, was raised from the dead, ascended into heaven, and was expected to be revealed again, bringing grace and salvation to the believers. All is set forth as doctrine which is taken for granted, including the "expectation" of a coming judgment. But as we have seen, the author was much more interested in the present state of the Christian churches than in the end of the world. His desire to co-opt Peter in order to validate the household concept also betrays a concern for alignment with tradition and the past. These interests do not fit with an apocalyptic mentality, and so a new addition to the Christ myth was imagined in order to cut the nerve of a strictly apocalyptic gospel.

The new addition is the statement that, after Jesus had been put to death and before he had ascended into heaven, he was "made alive in the spirit, in which [spirit] also he went and made a proclamation to the spirits in prison [the dead in hades]" (1 Pet. 3:18–19). This strange image, spelled out in narrative form in another second-century ascription to Peter, the Gospel of Peter, was destined to become mythic dogma. In later Christian rehearsals it became the "descent into hell," which took place on Saturday between Good Friday and Easter Sunday. In 1 Peter it appears to be a brand new idea, awkwardly attached to the term *spirit* as that term occurred in opposition to *flesh* in older formulaic expressions of the Christ myth. The new image solved two conceptual problems, both of which would have arisen in the course of imagining the church as a universal "spiritual house" (1 Pet. 2:5). The first was where to imagine those who had died before Christ appeared, "who in former times did not obey" (1 Pet. 3:20). The second was how to account for a fair last judgment on the part of "him who stands ready to judge [*both*] the living and the dead" (1 Pet. 4:5; italics mine). The answer in this case was that "the gospel was proclaimed even to the dead" for the reason that "though they had been judged in the flesh as everyone is judged, they might live in the spirit as God does" (1 Pet. 4:6). This comes perilously close to cutting the nerve of an apocalyptic mentality, offering instead a "spiritual salvation" that need not wait until the *eschaton* to be realized.

Jude

The author calls himself the brother of James, which indicates interest in a particular identification. Unfortunately, we have no way of knowing which James is meant. If James the brother of Jesus is meant, Judas would also be a brother of Jesus (Mark 6:3) as well as Jesus' "servant" (Jude 1). Since that appears to be an odd way to express such a historical imagination, the solution may simply be that the author was content to allow the multiple associations of both names, Jude as brother and/or disciple of Jesus, and James as the brother and/or disciple of Jesus, to work their magic without feeling the need to be exact about it. The content suggests second-century authorship.

The letter is a brief exhortation to stay true to the "faith once for all entrusted to the saints" and to avoid certain people who had "denied our only Master and Lord, Jesus Christ," who are "blemishes" on the Christians' "love feasts" and "pervert the grace of our God into licentiousness" (Jude 3–4, 12). Old Testament examples of the judgments that befell those who "indulged in sexual immorality and pursued unnatural lust" are cited, such as the cities of Sodom and Gomorrah, as well as similar lessons from Jewish apocalyptic texts, to underscore the point that the Lord would destroy those who did not keep believing even though they once had been saved. The tenor is morose and the mythology extremely gross, filling a three-decker universe with angels, heavenly hosts, the devil, fallen angels in "eternal chains in deepest darkness," scoffers who suffer the same fate, and the fire from which some would have to be snatched if they were going to be saved by Jesus.

Except for the fact that such a full-blown apocalyptic mythology could be treated as banal in the second-century church, the only interest this letter has for the historian is the strange historical imagination of the author. Apocalyptic predictions were normally ascribed to figures of the past whose visions of the future were written down to be read by those who found themselves in the midst of the very events predicted. Jude knew this formula by heart, for he referred to an apocalyptic prediction by "Enoch in the seventh generation from Adam" (Jude 14–15) and to one by "the apostles of our Lord Jesus Christ" that "in the last time there will be scoffers, indulging their own ungodly lusts" (Jude 17–18). The oddity is that, instead of sticking with the authorial fiction of Jude the brother of James and writing an apocalyptic exhortation against these scoffers from the vantage point of the past, the author could not resist addressing his readers as a contemporary, writing about "the salvation we share" (Jude 3). The author is one who stands with them and looks toward the past and who says that they, his readers, "must remember the predictions of the apostles of our Lord Jesus Christ." He even goes on to say, "For they [the apostles] said to you, 'In the last time there will be scoffers'" (Jude 17–18). This confusion in the historical placement of the implied author is not due to the difficulty of working with three distinct literary genres (apocalyptic, exhortation, and apostolic pseudonymity). More than one combination of these three genres could be worked out quite easily. And nothing is gained by the confusion of authorial voices. Jude is simply a matter of sloppy literary production.

2 Peter

Even after one grows accustomed to the creative borrowing, pseudonymous attribution, and the putting of words into the mouths of fictional characters typical of Greco-Roman literary practice, 2 Peter catches one's attention. In the first place, the letter was obviously written by a well-educated person with more than grammatical facility in the Greek language. Why would such a person have found the Letter of Jude interesting enough to quote parts of it? In the second place, the changes that this person made to Jude's letter did not erase the basic structure of its message, even though the author of 2 Peter was clearly addressing quite a different situation and taking a much cooler approach. And in the third place, if the purpose was to write an exhortation in the name of Peter, why start with a letter already attributed to Jude? It is very hard to imagine the kind of person and the circumstances that would have produced such a text.

The message of 2 Peter is not much different from that of Jude, the letter that was used as a source. However, some changes made in it deserve attention. The opponents have been specified more clearly, even though labeling continued to be the primary mode of characterization. The opponents now appear to be of a gnostic persuasion that, from the author's point of view, threatened several ideas the author found central to Christian faith: the prophetic interpretation of the Jewish scriptures, the gospel story of a real Jesus who was also the son of God, the Christian ethic of sexual continence and clean living (holiness), and the apocalyptic view of history. Some stylistic features of 2 Peter temper Jude's rough priggery, and the mythology is not quite as offensive. As an example, an attempt was made to put a positive construction on Jude's view of judgment. Jude's emphasis was on the Lord's power and willingness to punish by destruction, while 2 Peter says, "The Lord [also] knows how to rescue the godly from trial" (2 Pet. 2:9). The purely apocalyptic framework is also somewhat meliorated, as it was in 1 Peter, by statements about "having everything needed for life and godliness" because of the divine power given to Christians, escaping "the corruption that is in the world," and becoming "participants of the divine nature" (2 Pet. 1:3–4). And, of course, the switch from Jude to Peter allowed for the introduction of a number of legendary touches that make the letter a bit more interesting for the historical imagination.

These legendary touches are of the "I, Peter . . ." variety, and they are in some ways quite charming, enough so to forgive the author for the other absurdities. At this point it becomes clear that the author knew the gospel traditions about Peter, including the Peter of the Gospel of John, and that he wanted his readers to think of that Peter when reading his letter. "Peter" knows that he is only reminding his readers of things they already know, that his death is approaching, just as the lord Jesus Christ made clear to him (John 21:18–19), and that he is writing the letter "so that after my departure you may be able at any time to recall these things" (2 Pet. 1:12–15). "These things" refers to the instructions in the letter but includes references to Peter's own experiences with Jesus. Peter's account of one of these experiences, his presence at the transfiguration, is the most remarkable feature of the letter. Peter slips into the first person plural to acknowledge that he was there with James and John, and he recalls that they saw Jesus' divinity and heard God's voice calling Jesus his son. That, Peter says, confirmed the message of the prophets (2 Pet. 1:16–19) and should keep the Christian reader on the right track in the face of scoffers who deny the apocalyptic gospel (2 Pet. 1:19; 3:1–4).

This was a very clever stratagem for recasting Peter as an apostolic authority for the centrist gospel. With two deft strokes, the Peter of the gospels comes to speech and confirms that he "saw" the divinity of Jesus, both at the transfiguration and after the resurrection! Paul could not have been more pleased with Peter's agreement with the Christ myth, though this confession was belated by more than one hundred years. And, as if the author knew that the centrist position would require some mutual accommodations between the Pauline legacy and the aura of a Jewish Jesus movement that hovered around the figure of Peter, what does he have Peter say about Paul? Speaking about the need to be patient while waiting for salvation to come and the need to lead lives of holiness and godliness, the author has Peter say, "So also our beloved brother Paul wrote to you according to the wisdom given him, speaking of this as he does in all his letters" (2 Pet. 3:15–16). So, not to worry. With Peter and Paul in agreement on the gospel, surely the scoffers are wrong.

But the infelicity of Jude's fiction, though more charmingly put in 2 Peter, was not overcome. Not only does the "historical" Peter know about all Paul's letters, he writes to his second-century readers as if he is one of them, one of "those who have received a faith as precious as ours" (2 Pet. 1:1). He says, "This is now, beloved, the second letter I am writing to you; in them I am trying to arouse your sincere intention by reminding you that you should remember the words spoken in the past by the holy prophets, and the commandment of the Lord and Savior spoken through your apostles" (2 Pet. 3:1–2). So Peter is an apostle writing to remind his readers that they should remember the words of the apostles! The fiction should be clear.

Need I remind the reader of Peter's importance for the traditional view of Christianity's arrival in Rome? According to this view, Peter was the first disciple to see the risen Jesus, the founder and leader of the first church at Jerusalem, and the apostle who first took the gospel to Rome. Since the documentation for this tradition has always been these letters, it should be clear that the tradition is in reality a myth. The so-called Petrine tradition was created in the second century by means of pseudonymous writings attributed to the Peter pictured in Paul's letters and in the narrative gospels. There is not a shred of historical evidence to support it.

THE LETTER OF JAMES

The Letter of James is another interesting piece of the New Testament puzzle. It consists entirely of moral exhortation in the genre of proverbs, maxims, and ethical imperatives. There is no indication of interest in or concern about getting the Christ myth straight or the narrative gospels in hand. The "Lord Jesus Christ" is mentioned twice, the "coming of the Lord" is in view as a warning at the end of the letter, and the assumption of Christian congregations being "the twelve tribes in the diaspora" is evident. These communities can be addressed as "brothers and sisters," and they have "teachers" among them (James 3:1). But the teaching of the letter is not about the Christian faith. It is about the importance of living a moral life, and the arguments for doing so are set forth as common wisdom. The source and authority of this wisdom are taken for granted by the author. Sayings that remind one of the teachings of Jesus are interspersed with proverbs and imperatives typical of the Jewish wisdom tradition. Greek-style maxims, examples, and small rhetorical units carefully crafted in the style of the Hellenistic art of persuasion also abound. The sayings reminiscent of the teachings of Jesus are not given special privilege and are not even attributed to him as their author or authority. The voice throughout is rather that of the author, and the authority to which he appeals is the wisdom common to ancient Near Eastern ethical instruction.

If there is any other authority to which the author appeals, it is "the perfect law, the law of liberty" or "the royal law according to the scripture" (James 1:25; 2:8–12). This must refer to the Jewish scriptures understood as instruction in wisdom for living a godly life. We know that such a concept was possible in Jewish-Christian circles of the late first century, because Matthew reconceived the Torah by interpreting it in the light of Q or even by taking Q as the true meaning of the Torah. It does appear, then, that the Letter of James represents the thought of a Jewish Jesus movement that had come to see itself as Christian in much the same way as the Matthean community had done. The big difference between the Letter of James and the Gospel of Matthew is that James did not need the authority of Jesus to undergird his Torah instruction, even though it contained teachings that Matthew wanted to hear only from the mouth of Jesus. Instead, James says, "If any of you is lacking in wisdom, ask God, who gives to all generously and ungrudgingly, and it will be given you" (James 1:5). What James and his community thought about the "Lord Jesus Christ" is therefore very uncertain. The real "lord" for these people was not Jesus but the God of the Israel epic. As James puts it, "Was not our ancestor Abraham justified by works when he offered his son Isaac on the altar?. . . Thus the scripture was fulfilled that says, 'Abraham believed God, and it was reckoned to him as righteousness,' and he was called the friend of God" (James 2:21–23).

The Letter of James has been difficult for scholars to place within the various Jesus and Christ traditions of the first and second centuries. There are two reasons for this. One is that the Letter of James seems to have been difficult to place for early Christians as well. It apparently was not read or even noticed by authors in the centrist tradition before Origen in the third century. The other reason is that James sounds like a treatise written against the Pauline notion that the Christian faith opposed the "works of the law." James 2:14–16 is a famous tirade against such an idea, arguing for the insight that "faith by itself, if it has no works, is dead" (James 2:17). How could Christians in the Pauline and centrist traditions have thought that way or accepted a letter that said that? Or so New Testament scholars have wondered. The answer is that Pauline Christians were not the only Christians during the first century, and that centrist Christians of the next two centuries did accommodate the kind of thinking represented by James. Two observations indicate that the Letter of James represents a Jewish-Christian movement that must have been strong and vigorous for at least the first three centuries.

One observation is that, in the course of the first three centuries, the authority of "James," whether in reference to the brother of Jesus or one of his disciples (or both), was attached to a number of Christian writings. He may have become a guarantor for some gnostic groups as well. We have, in any case, an Apocryphon of James, a Protevangelium of James, and an Acts of James. There is also an intriguing reference to James in the Gospel of Thomas to the effect that, when the disciples asked Jesus who would be their leader after his departure, he said they were to "go to James the Just, for whose sake heaven and earth came into being" (GTh 12). Literary evidence of this kind usually means that some group, movement, or school tradition claimed James as the source of their teachings.

The other observation is that the Letter of James was included in the lists of texts that eventually became the New Testament. As we shall see in chapter 11, this indicates an interest in making a place for Jewish Christianity within the spectrum of traditions acceptable to leaders of the church in the fourth century. By itself, the apostolic Letter of James may not have been any more acceptable than the Gospel of Thomas. But it was easier to read in the light of the gospel tradition of Matthew and the instructional literature of the so-called postapostolic period, such as 1 Clement and the Didache. This literature shows that the centrist position turned to Hellenistic-Jewish ethical codes in order to spell out appropriate behavior for Christians. We shall discuss this development in the next chapter. As 1 Clement and the Didache show, the resources for manuals of instruction now included the Jewish scriptures, wisdom traditions common to the cultures of the Greco-Roman age, Hellenistic ethical codes, traditional practices that had arisen in the churches, and the judgments of the bishops themselves. The Letter of James does not look so strange when read in the company of that kind of literature. It was, at any rate, an instructional exhortation with which the bishops could be comfortable, and to re-gard it as an apostolic letter was a sure way to appropriate the authority of James for the church instead of losing him to other groups who would not fit under the cen-trist umbrella.

THE LETTERS OF JOHN

The story behind the three letters of John shares more features with the history of the letters of Paul than with those of Peter, James, or Jude. The similarities are that both sets of letters were written from within a self-conscious community that had already produced written material to which the letters could refer. In each case as well, the vibrancy of the community tradition is demonstrated in the way debates, polemics, and changes of ideology mark the course of their histories. Nothing of the sort is evident in the apostolic letters of Peter, Jude, and James.

However, there are significant differences between the Pauline and the Johan-nine traditions. One is that Paul's legacy was a school tradition for supervising net-works of Christian congregations that were able to harbor differences of opinion and vigorous ideological debates. The community that produced the letters of John was close-knit, more prone to ideological schism. Another difference is that the Pauline school harked back to a real, historical founder figure (Paul) whose activities and writings brought the school into existence. In the case of the so-called Johan-nine community, Jesus was the only founder figure (not John or any other disciple). Written material and patterns of community practice had been produced collec-tively and anonymously under the "signature" of the first person plural "we," a curi-ous feature of both the gospel and the first letter. This feature has caused no end of trouble for scholars in quest of the author or voice behind this literature. As noted in regard to the gospel, the name of John the disciple does not even occur in any of the writings that were eventually attributed to him. And the earliest attestation for such attribution is Irenaeus, writing about 180 C.E. By that time, however, the same gospel had already become popular in gnostic circles where it was said that Cerinthus, the founder of a gnostic school, had written it. So the attribution to John the disciple must have taken place quite late in the second century when the gospel, along with the letters and the apocalypse, became popularly known among centrist leaders as Johannine. In any case, this cannot have happened before 100 C.E., when we find the gospel at a late stage of composition but still lacking any reference to John as its author.

It would be helpful to understand the reasons for the later attribution. Was it done arbitrarily by centrist scholars who wanted to acquire this material for their apostolic tradition? With the other important disciples already "taken," why not assign this literature to John? Or so we might imagine their reasoning. But why would centrists have wanted to do that? Another suggestion would be that there were reasons internal to the community that produced the gospel that pointed to John as the appropriate disciple and apostle for their kind of Christianity. But if so, why would they have wanted to join with the centrists? Why did they not make the attribution more obvious in the literature? And why John?

I will argue that a parting of the ways took place in the Johannine community shortly after the turn of the second century. One faction thought it best to merge with other Christian groups of a more centrist leaning. Another party refused this suggestion, holding to the enlightenment tradition of the community and developing in the direction of a Christian gnosticism. Before the schism, the community tradition had little interest in disciple lore or apostolic mythology. After the schism, those interested in being accepted by centrist Christian groups invented the figure of the "beloved disciple" as the guarantor of their tradition (John 21:20–25). Why they did that, whether it worked to their advantage, and how it may have led to the later attribution of the gospel to John are the questions of importance for our project.

Three clues indicate that the centrist faction within the Johannine community developed a growing interest in attributing the gospel to one of the disciples of Jesus but that they purposely did not lay claim to any of the known (named) disciples. That means that the attribution to John must have taken place at a later time by centrist scholars outside the community. One clue can be taken from the first letter; and two others can be found in the last chapter of the gospel, a chapter that most scholars agree was attached to the gospel at the last stage of its being reworked.

The occasion for writing 1 John was a schism of major proportions in the community. The author of the letter took the position that the other side had "left" the community (1 John 2:19) and wrote to the "little children" of the community that they should stay with the "*logos*" that had been in the community "from the beginning" (1 John 1:5; 2:7; 3:11). But as a matter of fact, both sides had "left" the community that produced the gospel, the author's people moving toward the Christ gospel and centrist mythologies, the other side moving into gnosticism. Comparing the two moves, the author's people had to take the longer step, the gnostics the shorter one. So the author's rhetoric of being left behind includes a good dose of hyperbole and pique. However, there is no doubt that the community did split into two separate camps, and it was natural that each wanted to take the gospel with them. We might want to keep the enlightenment christology of the gospel in mind as we proceed.

Looking at the gnostic side of the schism through the eyes of the author of 1 John, the gnostics had refused to accept the gospel of the Christ with its emphasis upon the death of Jesus as a sacrifice for sins. Their position was that they did not need to believe in such an atoning death because they had already experienced the new life and light brought into the world by the Jesus of the gospel. Their kind of Jesus made it ridiculous to think of his death as a martyrdom or sacrifice for sins. It was really absurd if one said that he died as the Christ or messiah. It was enough to think of his death as the moment when he turned the tables on death, ascended to the Father, and so revealed the truth that the spirit need not be imprisoned forever in the material bodies of this world. If pressed, the gnostics may have said, as the author implies, that the real (divine) Jesus did not "come in the flesh" at all (1 John 4:2–3), that he was not the Christ (1 John 2:22), that the "spirit" he revealed was the main thing, that they had recognized the spirit in him and therefore had knowledge of him (1 John 2:4, 20), that they were "abiding with him" (1 John 2:6), having "fellowship with him" (1 John 1:6), living "in the light" (1 John 2:10), and so were "above" being concerned about such things as commandments, sins, purity codes, or sacrificial atonements (1 John 1:8–10; 3:3–10; 4:20–5:5).

All this has a familiar ring. The terminology and worldview are straight out of the Gospel of John, as is the concept of salvation as enlightenment. First John tells us that the Johannine community had taken Jesus' promises of "abiding in him" seriously. It also lets us see that Jesus talked the way he did in the gospel because the community talked that way in real life. First John lets us see that the first person voice in the gospel, whether in the singular or in the plural, about "knowing the Father," "seeing the light," "having the water of life," and so forth, was the voice of the community echoing the *logos* who brought such knowledge into the world, as well as the voice of the mythic Jesus echoing the songs the community was singing. Were these people serious about enlightenment? Apparently! Did they actually prefer a myth of cosmic descent-ascent to the martyrology of the Christ myth? Yes, indeed. Would they have resisted pressure to conform to myths of Christ's sacrificial death and rituals of a memorial meal? Of course.

For his part, the author of 1 John had been convinced by the centrists' myth and ritual approach to Christian congregation. His personal convictions in this regard were no doubt genuine, and his reasons for wanting to accommodate the centrist Christians may have been well considered. But his polemic against his erstwhile brothers and sisters is vicious and his arguments ridiculous. He was reduced at most points of direct confrontation to labeling his opponents "liars" (1 John 1:6–10; 2:4; 4:20) or consigning them to demonic, cosmic, or divine destruction (1 John 3:4–10). He contends for a definition of Christian life and faith that includes the following: a real, historical Jesus as the Christ (1 John 2:12; 4:15; 5:1); Jesus' death as an atoning sacrifice for sins (1 John 1:7; 2:2; 3:5; 3:16; 4:2, 10; 5:6); the devil as a cosmic power intent on destroying Christians and their faith (1 John 3:8–10; 5:18–19); an apocalyptic day of judgment (1 John 2:18, 28; 3:2–3; 4:17); a righteous God concerned with purity (1 John 2:29–3:7); confession as basic for true faith and as the requirement for the forgiveness of sins (1 John 1:9; 4:2–3, 15); and an emphasis on keeping the "commandments" (1 John 2:4; 3:22–24; 5:3). These notions were not taken from old-community tradition. They sound familiar, but only because they agree so well with the Christ mythology of the centrist position.

The author of 1 John was writing from a stage in the community's development that was much different from the earlier history reflected in the fourth gospel. The community's significant other at the time the gospel was being composed was "the Jews." They represented those "outside" the community who did not accept the group's teaching about Jesus. Now, however, the problem was a battle for Christian self-definition against contenders who had arisen within the community. The author's strategy was to take the concepts rooted in the gospel and reinterpret them in light of his Christian "faith" option. The concepts at issue were knowledge, life, love, *logos*, and abiding. In each case the attempt was made to argue for new connotations as if they were what these words had meant all along. To "know" and "abide" were interpreted as matters of accepting and sticking with the Christian "faith" à la the Christ myth. "Life" was now said to be the "eternal life" made available through faith in the atoning death of Jesus Christ. To "love" meant to remain within the community and treat one another as God the Father treated his son according to the Christ myth. The author did have a bit of trouble expanding the concept of keeping the commandments, because the Jesus of the gospel had already given the community a "new commandment," and that would have to remain untarnished by any additional considerations that might sound like the "old commandments" that should have been left behind (John 13:34; 1 John 2:4, 7–8; 3:22–24; 5:2–3). He also had trouble with the language of sin. He wanted to charge his opponents with being sinners (1 John 1:8–10), but since his new soteriology (doctrine of salvation) was about sin *and forgiveness*, the topic could backfire. He did not want to offer his opponents the promise of forgiveness. This made it necessary to engage in a bit of theological casuistry with regard to sins for which forgiveness was possible in distinction from those for which it was not (1 John 2:1–2; 3:4–10). As one can see, the ways had parted over orientation to knowledge (*gnosis*) versus faith (*pistis*). This issue struck to the heart of an ancient debate between two anthropologies, and it was destined to divide centrist Christianity from gnostic Christianity in a battle that would rage for the next two centuries.

A second clue in the quest for clarity about the attribution of the gospel and letters to John comes from the twenty-first chapter of the gospel. Since chapter 20 provides a clear and appropriate conclusion to the gospel (especially in light of John 20:30–31, which states the purpose for the gospel as a whole), many scholars have noted that chapter 21 must have been tacked on at some later time. It is the story of Jesus' appearance to Peter and the other disciples at the seashore. The point of the story revolves around a special commission to Peter (John 21:15–17), Jesus' prediction that Peter would be crucified (John 21:18–19), and Peter's question to Jesus about what would happen to the beloved disciple, "the one who had reclined next to Jesus at the supper" (John 21:20–23). The significant feature for our purposes is that the end of the chapter contains a signature, and the signature is said to be that of the beloved disciple: "This is the disciple who is testifying to these things and has written them" (John 21:24–25). This means that the person who added chapter 21 also invented the fiction of authorship for the whole gospel. The author was now understood to be one of the disciples. The beloved disciple had not starred in the gospel, however, entering the story at the supper scene as the "disciple whom Jesus loved" and reappearing briefly at the crucifixion before taking on a rather important role here in a postresurrection story (John 13:23; 18:15–16; 19:26–27; 20:1–10). According to the story in chapter 21, Peter, the star disciple throughout the gospel whom one might expect would be the major contender for prime apostolic billing, had just learned two things about his commission. The first was that, if he truly loved Jesus, he must feed the Christian flock. The second was that he should get ready to die as Jesus did, on a cross. As we shall see in chapter 9, this means that Peter was being told that he must be a good shepherd and die like Jesus, images that converge in the apostolic model for a second-century bishop. And what about the beloved disciple? Would he also have to die? That, of course, is exactly what Peter also wanted to know. And Jesus said, "If it is my will that he remain until I come, what is that to you?" Poor Peter. The beloved disciple might not have to die a bishop's death, and apparently he had not, for the subsequent editorial aside suggests that he had already died a natural death (John 21:23). What, pray tell, is going on? Peter gets to be bishop and will be crucified. The beloved disciple gets to live until ripe old age and write his memoirs.

Since it has not been clear to scholars why this story was added, they have looked for clues among other additions to the gospel that also must have been made at the last stage of reworking. The suspicion has been that obvious insertions throughout the gospel were made by the same person who added chapter 21 in order to bring the gospel into line with centrist Christian teachings. These additions include the few sayings of an apocalyptic nature (John 5:28–29; 6:39–40, 44; 12:48), as well as the allusions to a eucharistic ritual in chapter 6 (John 6:52–58), and the odd insertion at John 19:35 that a witness saw both blood and water come out when Jesus was pierced (usually thought to be an allusion to symbols associated with baptism). These additions have created the further suspicion that the last stage of reworking the gospel took place about the time 1 John was written, for the ideological interests correspond exactly. This correspondence extends to such details as the idiosyncratic interest in the blood and water symbolism of John 19:35 which recurs in 1 John 5:6–8. Some scholars have therefore suggested that the person who made the additions throughout the gospel, the person who attached chapter 21 to the gospel, and the author of the first letter of John were all the same person. This stretches the data too far in the interest of too neat a scheme. But whether that was so, or whether this literary activity took place about the same time but with several hands in on the work, it is not difficult to see that the ideological stance is the same for all these bits of writing and that this stance had something to do with shifting the fourth gospel in the direction of a centrist Christian mythology.

The third clue is found at the beginning of chapter 21 where "the disciples" are "gathered" for an appearance of the resurrected Jesus (John 21:1–2). This setting of the scene is similar to the postresurrection appearance stories in chapter 20 and in the other synoptic gospels. It shows that the author was interested in bringing the discipleship theme of the gospel to a climax in which (all?) the disciples were present for the final instruction. They are "Simon Peter, Thomas called the Twin, Nathanael of Cana in Galilee, the sons of Zebedee, and two others of his disciples" (John 21:2). There are several curious features about this scene. One is that the number of disciples is seven, not twelve. Another is that the "sons of Zebedee" (James and John) are included although they had never even been mentioned before in this gospel. A third is that two others are mentioned without giving their names. And a fourth is that the "beloved disciple" is not mentioned although he is featured in the following story and so must be imagined to have been present.

The idea of twelve disciples entered the Johannine tradition at some point, for "the twelve" are mentioned in two of the stories (John 6:67, 70–71; 20:24), but the gospel nowhere lists them by name and does not tell the story of their "commission" and "sending," as is the case in the synoptic gospels. Thus the addition of James and John (as "the sons of Zebedee") was apparently intended as a token recognition of the apostolic tradition associated with the three pillars, Peter, James, and John. They had been mentioned by Paul and were later merged with the lists of the twelve in the synoptic gospels. Of these three pillars, however, only Peter had played a role in the fourth gospel, and there he had been storied, not in the company of James and John, but with Andrew, his brother, Philip, Nathanael, Thomas, Judas (not Iscariot), Judas who betrayed Jesus, and the unnamed "beloved disciple" (John 1:40–51; 6:5–9, 66–68, 71; 11:16; 12:20–22; 13:36; 14:5, 8, 22; 18:5–9; 20:2–10, 24–29). Supposing that the author of chapter 21 started with a list of the seven disciples who had played a role in the gospel story (realizing that counting Judas twice and adding the unnamed "beloved disciple" makes eight and so already presents a problem), the addition of the sons of Zebedee meant that two of the original seven would have to be left unnamed. The two who immediately come to mind are Andrew and Philip. They had played important roles in the gospel and should have been at the final gathering. But if the author had named them, Judas and the beloved disciple would have been missing, and the beloved disciple had to be thought present. So it appears as if the mention of the "two others of his disciples" was intended as a space holder for imagining that, of course, the "others" also must have been there, even though, if one counted carefully, only two of the five left out could be accounted for. By not saying which ones, however, the author allowed the reader to fill in the blanks as one wished. Perhaps inadvertently, the author succeeded in crafting a very clever puzzle for subsequent readers: Who was the beloved disciple? Was he one of the disciples mentioned in the gospel? And which one? The only one he could not have been was Peter, for he and Peter were mentioned together in four stories as contestants.

Why would anyone have wanted to do that? Interest in bringing the fourth gospel into line with centrist ideology dictated the need to introduce an apostolic guarantor into the story of the disciples. But since the people who produced the fourth gospel had never had such a guarantor or needed one, the author was confronted with an embarrassing situation. The solution was to avoid the term *apostle* (it does not appear in the Johannine tradition), include the sons of Zebedee as an accommodation to the apostolic myth, and assign the writing of the gospel to the mysterious, unnamed figure of the beloved disciple. Now the curious role of the beloved disciple begins to make some sense, and the riddle of his identity appears contrived. None of the other named disciples was really appropriate as a guarantor of the community tradition. So it begins to look as if the figure of the beloved disciple was created without a name on purpose to represent the community tradition independently of the other, named disciples.

It is at least obvious that the beloved disciple was made to order. The themes of love, witness, and closeness in the stories about him, and his role as a transmitter of Jesus' speech, created a most appropriate figure to represent and symbolize the community's mythic "memory" of Jesus. Love was the primary language of commandment and community among these people. Witness was a narrative theme throughout the gospel. The witness of the disciples in the gospel to Jesus, moreover, was consistently merged with the "we" voice of the community and the "I" voice of Jesus. There were times when one could not tell when Jesus quit talking and the community came to expression. For instance, in John 3:11 Jesus is talking to Nicodemus and says, "Very truly, *I* tell you, *we* speak of what *we* know and testify to what *we* have seen; yet you do not receive *our* testimony. If *I* have told you about earthly things and you do not believe, how can you believe if *I* tell you about heavenly things?" In the signature at the end of chapter 21 there is also a lovely confusion between the "I," the "we," and the third person singular reference to the beloved disciple: "*This* is the disciple who is testifying to these things and has written them, and *we* know that his testimony is true. But there are also many other things that Jesus did; if every one of them were written down, *I* suppose that the world itself could not contain the books that would be written" (John 21:24–25, emphasis added). The same kind of identity confusion is characteristic of the discourse in 1 John which begins, "*We* declare to you what was from the beginning, what we have heard, what we have seen" (1 John 1:1, emphasis added), then switches to "My little children, *I* am writing these things to you" (1 John 2:1, emphasis added), moving back and forth between first person singular and plural, merged with third person description of the selfsame community along the way. No wonder this community had never needed an apostle, much less one with a proper name! Having to conjure one up as a founder figure in addition to Jesus, just because the community found itself shifting to a centrist position in the early second century, called for some real sleight of hand.

Was the move successful? Did the arguments of 1 John prevail? Did the people represented by this letter succeed in taking their gospel with them as they moved into the mainstream to distance themselves from those who wished to move toward the gnostic camp? The answer seems to be yes. One bit of evidence is that 2 and 3 John, which are signed by "the elder," presuppose a network of congregations on the centrist model, and offer instructions about such things as true tradition, false teachers, and hospitality, all of which sounds very much like the other apostolic letters we have from the second century. A second indication is that centrist leaders did finally accept the fourth gospel and the Johannine letters as apostolic. This means that these writings must have entered into circulation among networks of congregations far beyond the community that produced them. It was probably in the course of copying, reading, and classifying these writings along with other "apostolic" literature that some bright person saw the riddle in chapter 21 and solved it by deciding that, since the "two others" must have been Andrew and Philip, and since James was already taken to represent a distinctly different kind of Jesus tradition, the beloved disciple must have been John. Since the letters were anonymous, they also could be ascribed to John. And then there was the apocalypse signed by (a) John. So the centrists put them all together under the signature of John, and John became the beloved disciple who understood best the "spiritual" meaning of the gospel. Though many third-century scholars found themselves puzzled by the collection and troubled by its attribution to John, they found no way to argue against it. The riddle of John 21 was crafted to perfection and could neither be proven nor disproven. And besides, if one needed a name, and the apostolic myth demanded it, attribution to John did create a subtle mystique. John was the only apostle who did not die a martyr's death. Perhaps he really was the disciple whom Jesus loved most. And so, even today this literature is known as Johannine.

PART 3

History and the Christian Myth

9

INVENTING APOSTOLIC TRADITIONS

Christians imagine the disciples as apostles whenever they picture the way Christianity began. It is as important for the disciples to be apostles as it is for Jesus to be the Christ. Without the apostles, the story of Jesus would recede into the past like a tale told once upon a time without effect in shaping social history. It is the apostles who anchor the story of Jesus in time, attest that it all really happened, and create the impression that history changed then. The apostles are the eyewitnesses of the story of Jesus from beginning to end, the first proclaimers of the story as a gospel or message, the missionaries who took the gospel message to all the other lands and peoples, and those who wrote the New Testament. The apostles are also the first leaders of the congregations of believers that formed in response to their preaching, founding churches and filling in the first chapter of Christian history with their deeds. Without the apostles, the Christian church would not know how to connect its history with Jesus. The apostles are the church's guarantee that, as a social, historical institution of religion, it started right and has its story straight.

Not every Jesus movement, Christ cult, or Christian gnostic community needed the fiction of twelve disciples who became apostles. The fiction resulted from early Christian mythmaking among intellectuals with centrist inclinations and institutional tendencies. And it did not happen overnight. As we have already seen in the last chapter, calling the disciples apostles was one thing, lining them up with particular traditions another, and getting them to agree on fundamental issues yet another. That the apostles agreed would have been as unthinkable at the beginning of the second century as agreement among the many different Christ cults and Jesus movements of the time. Vociferous debate is much too tame a label for the hostile polemics and rhetorical entrenchments that characterized inner-Christian discourse during the second century. And yet, agreement among the apostles is exactly what the author of the Acts of the Apostles set out to show. He wanted to do that in order to demonstrate the apostolic foundations for his own conception of Christianity as a religion of the empire and for the empire centered at Rome. He did it, and his achievement was nothing less than the creation of a basic building block in the formation of the Christian epic.

In retrospect, the author of Acts created the notions of an apostolic council and an apostolic age. This was a period of time like none that had gone before and unlike any that would ever come again. Only the apostles had been with Jesus, and only the apostles could witness to the truth of the gospel. As for the elders, overseers, and bishops that later found themselves in charge of the churches, what did they know that they had not received from the apostles? With the Acts of the Apostles in place, however, they could be sure that the Christian churches throughout the Roman Empire were exactly what Jesus and his apostles had intended. The apostolic age was the golden link that guaranteed a direct line of tradition from Jesus to the churches, especially those churches that recognized the special privilege granted to the congregation at Rome. Thus, the Acts of the Apostles was as important a literary accomplishment for emergent Christianity in the early second century as the Gospel of Mark was in the first.

Unfortunately, the retrospective view glosses over the tumultuous history of the second century, just as Luke's gospel and Acts smooth out the rough edges of the first. We cannot be sure that it was Luke's literary achievement alone that created the historical imagination of an apostolic age for his contemporaries, or even whether his treatment of the apostles affected any of the other apostolic fictions produced during this century. But we can be sure that Luke's Acts of the Apostles fits very well into the mythmaking of the second century and that it does stand out as an early work of genius. If we use it as a guide to the significance of the apostles for second-century Christian thought, it will be possible to organize a large literature for discussion. The Acts of the Apostles marks the shift in focus for second-century mythmaking, away from Jesus and toward the apostles.

Jesus was not dislodged from his place as the primary figure of the Christian gospel, but the apostles were now attracting all the attention. Fascination with the apostles produced stories written about them and literature (purportedly) written by them. Quite naturally, the genres that prevailed were the acts of the apostles, instructions from the apostles, gospels written by the apostles, apostolic letters, and apocalypses. But that is not all. Early Christian authors writing in their own name had to appeal to apostolic tradition, and schools of thought, especially in gnostic circles, had to struggle with the apostolic myth in order to posit the moment when their special teaching was revealed to the world. The emergence of the apostolic myth changed the early Christian imagination of history forever. Not just Jesus, not just his teachings, not just his place in the history of Israel, but the apostles also would have to be in the story as those who received the message, packaged it, and passed it on to later generations. It was the apostolic myth that locked subsequent Christian imagination into the odd persuasion that, for Christians, truth was dependent upon the eyewitness accounts of a past and privileged class of disciples who had personally encountered the divine.

And then something interesting happened. The apostles started to look a lot like Jesus. They were imagined to have performed miracles as he did, preached and taught as he did, confronted the authorities as he did, and died as he did. It was as if the apostles replicated the gospel story of appearing in the world endowed with divine spirit and power. Their preachments caused considerable consternation. Some were converted, others took offense. And in the end the apostles died a martyr's death. Only in the case of John was a martyr's death impossible to imagine, for part of the lore that accompanied the collection of literature attributed to him was that he had died a natural death as an aged man in Ephesus. For the others, a martyr's death was the natural way to end their stories. There was early lore about the martyrdoms of Paul, Peter, and James, but eventually all of the storied apostles were granted a glorious death, including Paul, Peter, Andrew, Thomas, Matthew, Bartholomew, and Philip. This can be understood if we keep in mind the Greek educational model of following or imitating an example. The apostles were cast as the exemplary students of Jesus. And now there were many worthy models in view. Just as Jesus became the example to be followed by his disciples, so the apostles became examples to be followed by other Christians. That is because disciples or students were supposed to be followers of their teachers. Thus Jesus' way to death as a martyr was exemplified in the stories of the apostles, and they became the models for being a true follower of the Christian way.

In gnostic circles, the apostolic myth was used to support claims to esoteric teaching rather than martyrological instructions. The link between Jesus and a particular apostle was storied in the interest of claiming a special revelation from Jesus to account for the special knowledge in the tradition of a particular gnostic school, as if the apostle had passed it on. In the Gospel of Thomas, as we have seen, Jesus took Thomas aside and told him what the other disciples were not able to comprehend (GTh 13). Such scenes became standard in gnostic texts and were frequently specified as postresurrection appearances. Eventually, however, neither the scene nor the apostle to whom the special revelation was given was considered all that important. It was the content of the revelation that interested gnostics and, since the content was a revelation, Jesus came to be seen as the accidental incarnation of the eternally divine revealer. Thus the preferred mythology was the visit of a god from the realms of light to any appropriate guarantor. The Christian apostles were not the only guarantors for such a revelation. Jesus, John, Thomas, and Philip were soon joined by Adam, Seth, Sophia, and the various leaders of gnostic schools of thought, such as Basilides, Valentinus, and Ptolemy. Thus the gnostic notions of truth and revelation seriously challenged the apostolic myth.

Those of the centrist traditions had to counter this gnosticizing tendency. They did so by writing treatises against the gnostic "heresies," appealing to the "historical" Jesus of the gospels, and working hard to appropriate as many of the apostles as they could for their "orthodox" Christian teaching. They did this by writing gospels, letters, sermons, and instructions in the apostles' names. One of the more curious literary phenomena of this period is the appearance of manuals of instruction for church practice in the name of all twelve apostles as a college. Again, Luke seems to have set the pace with his story of the twelve apostles at Pentecost, the birthday of the church. If all of them agreed on what to preach and teach, so the thinking seems to have been, teachings and revelations that diverged from the norm must be mistaken. Luckily for the church, what the apostles agreed upon was known to the bishops and firmly in their hands. And so the story comes full circle, the making of a myth to authorize the makers of the myth—leaders of an emerging institution with claims to historical precedence and presence. Poor bishops, having to appeal to the apostles for their authority. Do they ever get to sign their own names? Of course they do, but only if they are careful not to claim authority based upon a private revelation.

THE ACTS OF THE APOSTLES

The Acts of the Apostles was a work of absolute genius. It was written late in the first quarter of the second century by a highly educated Hellenistic Christian living somewhere around the Aegean Sea. The author was well read in Greek historiography and other, more popular types of literature, such as the novel and the lives of famous men, for he used the techniques peculiar to each of them with skill. He also had copies of first-century texts from the Jesus movements, such as the Gospel of Mark and the Sayings Gospel Q, which he cleverly merged and embellished to serve his own purposes in a new rendition of the gospel story. Since he knew about Paul, Peter, James, and other early Christian leaders, as well as about the spread of Christian congregations throughout Asia Minor and the history of tensions between Christians and Jews in the diaspora, we may assume that he knew about the letters of Paul and had collected other early Christian literature and lore. His plan was to write a history of the Christian movement from the formation of the apostles as a college of twelve in Jerusalem shortly after the death of Jesus to its arrival in Rome in the person of Paul, a period of approximately thirty years. Considering his vantage point in 120 C.E. and keeping in mind all the intervening history and competing traditions that must have been known to this author, his decision to focus on Peter and Paul as the major figures of the apostolic period is telling. The author, whom I will call Luke, in keeping with the tradition of attribution, was obviously committed to the centrist persuasion.

The history begins with a remarkable series of events that take place during the forty days between Passover and Pentecost. These are the festival events that marked the calendar of the Jewish culture destined to be transformed and superseded by the birthday of the church. As Jesus had commanded the disciples before his departure at the end of Luke's gospel, the disciples regroup in Jerusalem, elect Matthias to take the place of Judas, and so constitute themselves as the council of twelve apostles to wait for the spirit Jesus had promised. On the day of Pentecost the spirit comes upon them in the shape of fiery tongues, and the famous story is told of all the apostles speaking in foreign languages to the Jews from every land who had come to Jerusalem for the festival. The story does not explain why the Greek language would not have been sufficient, but it does set the stage for the theme of preaching and the conversion of large numbers of people. Then the focus falls on Peter who delivers the Pentecost sermon and plays the role of major agent and spokesman for a series of events that take place in Jerusalem. Each of these events is about the furor Christians are creating among Jews in Jerusalem, and each ends with Peter preaching, first at the temple (Acts 3:12–26), then before the Jewish rulers (Acts 4:9–12), and finally before the council of the high priest (Acts 5:29–32).

At this point, the conversion of the "Hellenists" has been so successful that the apostles have to ordain seven of them as a special committee to "wait on tables," a curious twist that reveals the author's desire to see table fellowship as practiced in his time established as a Christian practice at the beginning of the church's history. Stephen immediately runs into trouble with leaders of the diaspora synagogues who seize him, take him before the high priest's council, and see that he is stoned to death. So Stephen, representing Hellenistic Christianity, is the first martyr for the church, according to Luke. On the occasion of his martyrdom Stephen delivers a lengthy sermon to the effect that throughout their history the Jews had always opposed the holy spirit and rejected the prophets and leaders God sent to them, just as they were now rejecting Jesus, the "righteous one." And, one might add, just as they were now stoning Stephen to death (Acts 6–7). Thus "the persecution" begins (Acts 8:1; 11:19). The drama then spreads outward to Samaria and Gaza, and Saul, who "approved of their killing him," referring to Stephen, and was "breathing threats and murder against the disciples of the Lord," enters the story (Acts 8:1; 9:1). "Unclean spirits" (Acts 8:7) also enter the story, as well as Simon the magician—all indicative of the resistance that Christians would have to face. But the apostles prevail. Philip is successful in his evangelization of Samaria and Gaza, Saul is converted on the road to Damascus, and Peter moves out to perform miracles and preach in Samaria (Acts 8–9). At Caesarea, Peter has to deal with the conversion of a Roman centurion by the name of Cornelius and learns via a vision that gentiles are not to be excluded from the church, that they may receive the holy spirit and be baptized without being circumcised (Acts 10–11). This is a major turning point in the story, for now we learn that Christianity had already spread to Phoenicia, Cyprus, Antioch, and Cyrene, and that Antioch would be the city to organize the gentile mission (Acts 11:19–30; 13:1–3).

From chapter 13 until the end of the book, the star of the story is the apostle Paul. He makes three missionary journeys to Asia Minor and Greece, each time returning to Antioch to report his success, before he is set upon by angry "Jews from Asia who had seen him in the temple" (Acts 21:27; 24:19), arrested by the Roman authorities, and taken to Rome for trial. One of these reports to the "church and the apostles and elders" in Jerusalem is the account of the famous "apostolic council" at which both Peter and James defend Paul's mission to the gentiles against the demand of some Christian Pharisees that gentiles be circumcised and keep the law of Moses. That Peter and James defend Paul's mission is a marvelous piece of fiction, for every earlier scrap of evidence speaks to the contrary. Luke goes so far as to have Peter take credit for the very idea of gentile Christianity and imagines James citing the scriptures in support of the idea. Peter says, "My brothers, you know that in the early days God made a choice among you, that I should be the one through whom the gentiles would hear the message of good news and become believers" (Acts 15:7, 13–21). Thus the author's strategy is clear. Even Peter and company learned, though God and the holy spirit certainly had to work very hard at this educational task, that the Christian message of salvation was intended for the gentiles from the very first outpouring of the spirit.

Thus the story of the apostles is the story of the spread of the Christian religion throughout the Roman Empire from Jerusalem to Rome. It was also the story of the struggle to wrest the Christian religion away from its Jewish origins and the bad press of civil disobedience that clung to its early history. Luke wanted Christianity to be recognized as a religion that was good for the Roman order and thus worthy of Roman support. Though the "good news" is the same from Peter's first sermon at Pentecost to Paul's final sermon before the leaders of the Jews at Rome (Acts 28:17–28), the tone of the speeches shifts as the story moves away from the earlier sermons addressed to the Jews, through the missionary sermons of Paul where the gospel is preached to the gentiles, to climax in several lengthy speeches in which Paul defends himself before the Roman governors Felix (Acts 24:10–21), Festus (Act 25:8–11), and Agrippa (Acts 26:2–29). In these defenses the author's concept of Christianity as a cultural force for producing good citizens comes to expression. According to the Acts of the Apostles, the apostles were apologists for a civil religion!

The achievement of this fiction, a fiction so well done that it has been read as factual history for nearly two thousand years (Cameron 1994), is marked by great erudition and extremely clever design. What the author had to work with were the standard conventions for composing speeches-in-character, plotting novels, arranging anecdotes for the construction of a famous person's "life," crafting scenes for the miracles and sayings performed by the divine man, and for writing history as an etiology and encomium of some social institution. The history of scholarship on this book is rich in studies that demonstrate the author's knowledge of these literary conventions and his skill in using their techniques. Combining features from each of these literary conventions, he succeeded in describing situations in such a matter-of-fact way, and in providing such innocent and graphic details to his scenes, that the sense of being an eyewitness to the events is very strong. It is so strong, in fact, that the author himself has often been detected lurking behind the famous "we" passages that begin in chapter 16, as if the author had actually been a companion of Paul's on his second and third journeys (Acts 16:10–17; 20:5–15; 21:1–18; 27:1–28:16). Even after one sees that the "we" passages are limited to the journeys in which travel is by sea, and learns that the author was merely following a normal convention for just such description, as Vernon Robbins has taught us (1978), the impression is still strong that the author knew what he knew because he had been there. That is great writing. It is also marvelous fiction. The author could not have been present at the events he describes, except, of course, in the sense of being fully preoccupied with the history he was imagining. It is very important to see that this author was not violating normal conventions of historiography when he invented the history of the apostolic church.

For the writing of lives, novels, and histories, the Hellenistic author always had to work with snippets of oral lore and small units of story, detail, and speech taken from earlier texts. Since these were rarely enough to write a biography or flesh out an unwritten chapter of history, a great deal of imaginative energy was required to fill in the blanks. The trick was to imagine what must have happened on a certain occasion, then create speeches for the agents befitting their characters that both explained and contributed to the situation as an event in the larger story. The characters in the story would be developed by inventing a series of scenes in which the agents repeatedly spoke and acted in character. Creating the background or world in which the story took place was handled by carefully describing scenes in which the same kind of challenge was repeated, thereby becoming an expectation for every new scene. Plot development required the skillful arrangement of these little stories, each complete in itself, so that, with the help of flashbacks and predictions, slight changes in scene, speech, or action would be noticeable. All of this was practiced in the Hellenistic school, with technical terms for each of these narrative functions and the skills required to produce their effects. Thus the description of agents and events in the Acts of the Apostles is highly stylized and repetitive. The same thing happens over and over. The typical event consists of (1) a dramatic action in public performed by the apostle, frequently a miracle, (2) a challenge by those who oppose or fail to understand the significance of the action, (3) the apostle's response, frequently a speech or sermon, and (4) the response of the listeners to the speech or sermon. Some convert and join the Christians; some reject the message and threaten the apostles. The rejection and furor add spice to the stories and provide a good excuse for the apostles to leave the scene and go on to the next story.

The astonishing result of using these common literary conventions for writing the history of the apostles is that the "acts" of the apostles turn out to be speeches and the speeches turn out to be minigospels. The miracles catch the eye and create the impression that the apostles were very powerful persons performing forceful acts that unleashed radical change in the world. But if one stops to ask what the story is really about, what happens at each turn of the story that makes a difference, it has to do with the speech or sermon and the response people make to it. The miracle-effect is important. The author did want to create the impression of dramatic change taking place. But the changes created by the miracles per se are only occasional, provocative, and temporary. The truly significant and lasting change that happens in these stories is one of ideological shift and alignment. What really counts is whether an audience accepts or rejects what the author calls the "good news," and whether people join the church. Thus the drama of prime interest to the author takes place in the minds of the listeners who hear the sermons preached by the apostles. It is the story of a new myth in the process of claiming history and making history.

There are approximately fifteen major speeches in Acts, most of them rather lengthy. About one-half of these are sermons or rehearsals of the gospel; about one-half are reports of personal experience in defense of one's gospel. The latter include Peter's reports of what he learned from the Cornelius episode (Acts 10:34–43; 11:4–17; 15:7–11) and Paul's rehearsals of his conversion and/or way of life (Acts 20:18–35; 22:1–21; 24:10–21; 26:2–23). The personal reports show that both Peter and Paul are talking about the same gospel and that this gospel is the same as that outlined in the sermons that they and Stephen have previously given. The major points of the sermons are that (1) Jesus was exactly what the God of Israel had always wanted in a man, (2) he went about doing good, (3) the Jews killed him, (4) God raised him up, (5) the apostles are witnesses to these things, and (6) the listeners should therefore repent, accept forgiveness, be baptized, and receive the holy spirit. With the exception of point 6, this sermon is a minigospel, that is, a rehearsal of the gospel story about Jesus, slightly overlaid here and there with a bit of salvation theology reminiscent of the Christ cult.

At first it appears that these sermons were to be read as epitomes of the larger, more nuanced gospel that the reader would have in mind. But then it dawns on you that the truncated epitome erased the more complex mythologies of earlier traditions on purpose. The author did not want either a Pauline *kerygma*, a Christ cult salvation, a Jesus movement enlightenment, a Petrine-Jamesian Jewish-Christian ethic, or any of a number of other interpretations of the gospel to surface. His centrist leanings determined that he dilute all these mythologies in the interest of a single articulation of the gospel, a sort of common denominator gospel. Thus Peter is storied as learning not to call the gentiles unclean, James says that the gentiles are not to be bothered about the circumcision debate, Paul undergoes a ritual of purification in order to enter the temple at Jerusalem, and Stephen, the Hellenist, gives the most comprehensive rehearsal of the Jewish epic of them all. In each case, the distinctive features of earlier interpretations of Jesus represented by each of these figures were carefully set aside in order to reach a common denominator. In the case of Paul, for instance, there is not the slightest hint of his passionate arguments for freedom from the law, justification by faith, obedience to the spirit, or the ethic of suffering and service for the body of Christ. That the author wanted to find a middle-ground gospel is understandable, and that he managed to articulate one with as much consistency as he did is something of an accomplishment. But we should not be fooled by his story of the effective force of these sermons. No social, ritual, or mythic logic can be discerned in them that would have made any sense to the audiences to which they were said to be delivered.

Think for a moment of these sermons being addressed to the Jews. Most of them are. The message is: He was your God's choice; you killed him; therefore repent and be baptized, that is, become Christians. That is not good news; it is the insinuation and manipulation of guilt by controlled intimidation. No Jew would have found such a sermon motivating (except, perhaps, as outrage), or the offer of such a conversion attractive. And yet, much more than half of Luke's history turns on the Jew-Christian conflict, and the sermons addressed to Jews are said to win converts as well as create furor. Or think of this gospel as the apostles' defense. They are only telling what they have seen and heard, so how can anyone think them dangerous? What in effect they are saying is that the furors were not their fault. They say this both to the Jewish and to the Roman authorities. Neither Q, nor the Christ myth, nor the narrative gospel had anything to do with justifying the behavior of an apostle. All earlier mythologies were rooted in collective experience and aimed at justifying a particular kind of social formation, one that was called for by a particular vision of the kingdom of God. None of that is evident in Acts. The sermons in Acts serve to validate the authority of the apostles. The apostles are "merely" reporting what they (alone) know, what they (alone) have experienced. But they do expect their listeners to be "cut to the heart" and to ask, "What should we do?" (Acts 2:37). Their answer is, "Repent, and be baptized every one of you in the name of Jesus Christ so that your sins may be forgiven; and you will receive the gift of the Holy Spirit" (Acts 2:38). Why that demand follows from the sermon just preached is not explained. There is no logical link between the story and forgiveness, for instance, the story and baptism, or the story and the gift of the spirit, as there is in other, earlier formulations of the Christ myth. There is nothing in these sermons that would lead anyone to think that Jesus' appearance was about God's desire to forgive anyone's sins, much less forgive the Jews who are said to have killed Jesus. That, however, is what the apostles say the gospel meant. They are the ones who tell the people to repent. And they are the ones who, by means of baptism and the "laying on of hands," two ritual gestures that intertwine and are in the power of the apostles to perform, can offer forgiveness and the gift of the spirit. What was the author thinking?

The author was thinking epic history, and the apostolic age was past. It was much more important to account for the present situation of the church than to explain all the details of a past chapter of history in such a way as to make it plausible. Everyone knew that. Epic, like myth, was granted great license in description as long as it helped to imagine how the present circumstances came to be. And it had to be positive, or even triumphalist, by depicting the great events of the past as a course of history that flowed into the author's present as if the present were the glorious flowering of all that had gone before. To achieve this fiction for the Christian churches of Luke's time, several conceptual problems had to be faced. One was that the church he knew and championed was largely gentile and its mentality increasingly influenced by Greco-Roman culture. How did that fit with the earlier raucous history of conflict with the diaspora synagogue over Jewish questions? Another conceptual problem was that the church's public presence as a social institution made Christian-Roman relations much more poignant an issue than relations with the Jewish diaspora synagogues. Christian congregations were now under the scrutiny of local governors and Roman authorities. And a third was that the intervening history of conflict among the many Christian groups made it difficult to define the core conviction common to them all and present a clear rationale for the new religion to those worried about its influence. A great shift in social history had taken place between the time of Jesus and the author's time. Instead of detailing all the forces, twists, and turns of that history, as we might want to do, the author overlooked the intervening history of the fifty or sixty years since Paul and packed all his explanations into the apostolic age. The thirty years from Peter in Jerusalem to Paul's arrival in Rome would have to account for all the changes that had taken place in the ninety years from Jesus to the author's time.

The big question presented itself: What was it about Jewish history, the Jewish scriptures, the Jewish God, second-temple Judaism, Jesus, and his Jewish disciples that generated Hellenistic Christianity? The author knew that Christianity had emerged from Jewish religion and culture before the end of the second-temple period, and he had the early Jesus material such as Q, the gospel story of Mark, and the legacy of the Christ cult in his possession. All these interpretations of the significance of Jesus drew upon Jewish history and concepts. Writing from the perspective of a second-century Christian church that was gentile in constituency, Greek in mentality, and thoroughly engaged in taking its place in the world of Roman life and governance as a permanent, public, social institution, he was also painfully aware that much of the early history had been marked by Jewish-Christian conflict as the Christian churches slowly broke their ties with diaspora synagogues and distinguished their piety from Pharisaic codes of purity. Thus the major question that was to serve as a guiding principle for his construction of the epic history of Christianity presented itself. He wanted to know what Christianity owed to the Jewish history from which it had emerged. He needed to clarify what Christianity still had in common with the Jewishness of that history now that it had become a Greco-Roman religion. As far as I can tell, Luke was the first to ask that question. It turned the prickly issue of Jewish-Christian identity around, away from the constant marking of distinctions, to interest in the historical question of how they were alike.

The author's answer was influenced by his own assessment of Christianity as a religion of social concern and high ethical standards. He was also convinced that such a religion was good for society as a whole. He therefore found the answer to his question in the Jewish concern for righteousness. He was able to abstract this concern from all the ways in which righteousness had been codified and institutionalized in Jewish history, such as the sacrificial system of the second temple, the Pharisaic rules for purity, and other ways of keeping the law of Moses. He did that in order to equate the Jewish notion of rightness with the Greek concept of virtue. Of the two concepts, it was virtue that he understood best. Thus, according to our author, a single theme ran through the whole of human history, from Adam to the author's time. It was the pleasure God took in people or societies that were virtuous, righteous, or of high ethical integrity. At every significant turn in this history, from the creation of Adam, through Abraham, Moses, David, and the prophets, to Jesus and the apostles, the same divine quest could be discerned. God was at work instructing the people in righteousness by means of his appointed messengers. Luke may not have been far off the mark in this assessment of the attraction that diaspora Judaism held for non-Jews during the Greco-Roman period. It was just this Jewish concern for righteousness and social justice that commended the Jewish-Christian God to gentiles in the first place. None of the Greek gods would have shown such an interest in social justice or personal righteousness, that's for sure.

But how did this God of Israel go about instructing the people? According to Luke, he did it by selecting exemplary leaders and inspiring them with his holy spirit. Exemplary leaders, divine spirit, and powerful speech were not difficult concepts for Greek mentality. It is true that the powerful speech characteristic of the prophets storied in the Jewish scriptures may have sounded harsh to Greek sensibility, for the prophets often ranted and raved about judgment and destruction. But if you toned that down, thought of them as a special kind of teacher, and noted that their message to the people was always about God's concern and call for righteousness, a rather impressive history could be imagined. And if you aligned Jesus and the apostles with the prophets of Israel, a very illustrious, interlocking series of prophet-teachers could surface as the single, most important principle of continuity between the pre-Jesus and the post-Jesus times.

It was Jesus' place in this illustrious history that made him important. He came on the scene quoting from the prophet Isaiah and announcing that the spirit of the Lord was upon him (Luke 4:17–18). Looking back upon his life from the perspective of the apostles, they said that he was "the Holy and Righteous One," "the Righteous One," the one "God anointed . . . with the Holy Spirit and with power; [who] went about doing good" and offering instruction in righteousness (Acts 3:14; 7:52; 10:38). With Jesus, God's desire for a righteous people broadened to include the nations. That was a most dramatic moment, a real change for the story of Israel's God, and Luke had to account for it. But again it was the divine concern for righteousness that made the larger horizon seem reasonable, and it was not difficult to imagine why the one God of righteousness would be interested in instructing all the people in the world in righteousness. Lest that point not be seen from reading the gospel story of Jesus, the story of the apostles made it clear. They were the ones who knew what the appearance of Jesus meant. Jesus was the interlocking link in the chain of God's messengers to humankind, the last of the prophets of Israel, the ideal teacher of righteousness, and the divine son of God who commissioned his disciples to take God's instructions to the gentiles. How did they know that? They knew that because they also were filled with God's holy spirit, the real divine agent in Luke's epic history.

Thus, when the holy spirit "fell" upon the apostles on the day of Pentecost, it meant that they were given their place as the leaders of the people, chosen by God at a significant turn in history, just as all the prophets were, to call the people to repentance and instruct them in righteousness. What happens again and again in this sweep of history is the appearance of the prophet-teacher to call the people to repentance and instruct them in righteousness. As Robert Miller has taught us (1986), each appearance of the prophet-teacher is linked to previous appearances of prophet-teachers by means of reminders. This makes the succession of exemplary leaders interlocking. Each refers to those before in order to make the point that the righteousness called for is nothing new. The history common to Christianity and Judaism was a recursive pattern of ethical instruction and conviction. There was always resistance to God's call for righteousness, but even if a prophet was rejected and killed, it was not the end of the story. It did not mean that the people were evil. It did not mean they could not repent. It did not mean that God would give up in his quest to instruct the people in righteousness. Thus an essential part of the sermons in Acts was always a lesson from history. The apostle would say, in effect, "Look, there have always been prophets, and the prophets have always sounded the same message. God's standards have not changed." And though both the story of Israel and the story of early Christianity had to make room for the rejection of God's messengers, Luke never explained the motivations for such rejection, nor could he without destroying his fiction of continuity. That is why the call to repentance at the end of the sermons preached to the Jews sounds so hollow as history but somehow rings true to the epic Luke portrayed. Rejection was simply a fact of Luke's recurrent scenario. It was unfortunate and not without consequence for redirecting the thrust of history. But it could not threaten the eventual success of God's great plan to educate the nations in virtues fit for social well-being.

Luke's conception of Christianity was very Greek and quite blasé despite the highly mythological language of the holy spirit as the divine agent in history, the fantastic portrayal of the acts of the apostles, and the dramatic intention of the sermons. As a matter of fact, he may have overplayed his hand, for the story of the apostles is so theatrical that alignment with the history of the prophets, or even with the appearance of Jesus, is frequently obscured by the novelty of the apostolic events. But that is the price he had to pay for his fiction of continuity in the interest of rationalizing a drastic change in the course of his epic history. What he achieved was a thoroughly Hellenistic twist to most of the mythological figures and patterns derived from the Jewish scriptures and early Christian thinking. The influence of Greek thought can be detected in the notion of historical continuity, the sequential arrangement of epochs to account for historical change, the notion of change as a shift in social circumstance or an expansion of horizon, and in his way of tracing continuity through a series of exemplary leaders, treating prophets as sages and teachers, using the language of spirit mainly to mark rhetorical moments, and equating righteousness with virtue. The final effect is that, though Jesus stands out as a remarkable moment in the expansion of the spirit's horizon, Jesus did nothing to change the essential human situation. What it meant to be wise and righteous had not changed, according to Luke, just the size of the classroom.

As the story of the apostles comes to its close, the simplicity of Luke's conception of Christianity becomes more and more obvious. The spotlight falls on Paul whose missionary journeys, sermons, and speeches chart the course Christianity has taken. There are four stages, each characterized by a different audience whom Paul addresses. At Antioch in Pisidia, Paul is pictured in the synagogue giving the standard sermon to the Jews (Acts 13:16–41). Later, on the Areopagus in Athens, Paul preaches to the Greeks about coming to know the unknown God (Acts 17:22–31). Later still, at Miletus, Paul speaks to the elders of the Christian congregation from Ephesus (Acts 20:18–35). It is at this point that the careful reader begins to see features of Luke's own situation reflected in apostolic history. Paul reminds the elders of his exemplary life and ministry, knows already that he will be imprisoned and persecuted in Jerusalem, and instructs them, "Keep watch over yourselves and over all the flock, of which the Holy Spirit has made you overseers, to shepherd the church of God that he obtained with the blood of his own Son" (Acts 20:28). He even knows what will happen to the church after he is gone: "I know that after I have gone, savage wolves will come in among you, not sparing the flock. Some even from your own group will come distorting the truth in order to entice the disciples to follow them" (Acts 20:29–30). He then commends them to God, and the elders weep at his departure. All of this is reminiscent of second-century Christianity; none rings true to the Paul of the 50s. It was Luke's way of forging the link to the next chapter of church history, the time of the elders, overseers, shepherds, and bishops.

At last the story puts Paul in the presence of the Roman tribunes, governors, and kings of Palestine, and his speeches in defense of his own life and Christian mission gave Luke a remarkable opportunity to summarize what he thought about the "truth" of the Christians' good news (Acts 22–26). In these speeches Paul rehearses the event of his conversion twice, and biblical scholars have often thought that the account of his conversion was the point of the speeches. This overlooks the fact that Luke's point was to position Paul clearly as a Christian, distance him from Jews who made trouble for the Romans, and depict him as a loyal citizen, one whose exemplary life and character were no threat to the peace and order of Roman society. Paul is uncommonly courteous before these rulers, and they are extremely respectful of Paul and his views. The tribune rescues Paul from the angry Jews and gives Paul a guard to protect him on his transfer to Felix the governor (Acts 21:31–23:30). Felix and his successor Festus are caught in a political bind, wanting to pacify the Jews but not harm Paul. They keep him safe, provide for his needs, and agree with his desire to be tried before the emperor at Rome (Acts 23:31–25:22). From Luke's point of view, that was extremely gracious behavior on the part of Roman rulers toward a Christian. And King Agrippa tells Festus, "This man could have been set free if he had not appealed to the emperor," a precedent for the kind of judicious decision that Luke was hoping for in his own time (Acts 26:32). And there, right in the midst of this series of judicial hearings, Luke quietly inserted a line that contained his own view of the Christian faith. Felix and his wife Drusilla, a Jewess, had sent for Paul to hear him "speak concerning faith in Christ Jesus." Normally, the reader would expect Luke to let Paul come to speech in his own words. In this case, however, Luke summarized Paul's sermon in the third person by saying that "he discussed justice, self-control, and the coming judgment" (Acts 24:25). This is a remarkable sleight of hand, a crisp, momentary intrusion of the author's own face in the story he wrote about Paul, a cleverness that Alfred Hitchcock would surely appreciate. Self-control was the bottom line for Luke, the most prized virtue and most discussed issue among philosophers of the Greco-Roman age. He framed it with justice and judgment, fundamental themes guiding the epic history he had just written for the Christian churches. If God's instruction in righteousness centered on self-control, and God's messenger was capable of discussing justice and judgment with Roman governors, why of course the church's destiny had to be Rome. Sooner or later, the Romans surely would realize just how good Christians could be for the welfare of the empire.

What happened in this shift away from Jesus and toward the apostles is that the gospel story was reduced to a creed and the sign of apostolic authority became the rehearsal of that creed. Apostolic authority supported a distinctive social institution called the church, and the church now had its myth in place: its own founder-teacher, its own divine lord, its own apostles, its own officers and leaders, its own rituals, its own set of practices, and its own body of instructions. Luke's reduction of the "faith in Christ Jesus" to a creedal religion for the inculcation of self-control fits well with other second-century references to the "truth," the "word," the "gospel," the "tradition," or the "faith." All these shorthand clichés referred to the Christ myth and treated it as a symbol for a large cluster of parochial instructions. In this shift, the earlier, first-century myths about Jesus were emptied of their complexity and mythic power to become formulaic statements of faith that signaled one's acceptance of the Christian way.

Then the apostolic myth also suffered demotion. The genre of the acts of the apostles soon lost its orientation to serious epic mythmaking and became a kind of entertainment literature. Puppetlike, the apostles began to pop up here and there in episode after episode in early Christian apocryphal literature to confront the bad guys and their demons, wow the credulous maidens with their miracles, and champion the Christian religion with their amazing rhetorical powers. Not many modern readers have found this literature entertaining. The overbearing presence of a miracle-working apostle who sternly reprimands licentiousness and demands ascetic virtue of his converts does not make captivating reading. However, these legendary figures were the only heroes the average Christian had, and the popularity of their stories, which continued to be created into the fifth and sixth centuries, indicates a kind of curiosity and attraction of the kind that we associate with cults of celebrated personalities. The bishops apparently did not object to this literature, for they themselves were eventually graced with similar legends. But for the practical purposes of congregational leadership, the bishops needed more from the apostles than stories of their escapades. They needed to have their instructions in writing.

APOSTOLIC INSTRUCTIONS

In 1875 a text was discovered in the Patriarchal library of Jerusalem located at Constantinople. It bore the title Didache, or Teaching of the Twelve Apostles, a document that was cited in early Christian literature but thought to have been lost or merged with other, later texts. These later texts were known as the Apostolic Constitutions and Church Ordinances. They were compendia of prayers, hymns, rituals, and rules for administering Christian congregations accumulated during subsequent centuries. Some features of the Didache bore striking resemblance to 1 and 2 Clement, letters attributed to an early bishop of Rome, copies of which also appeared with the Didache in the discovered manuscript. There were parallels between the Didache and parts of the Epistle of Barnabas as well. These texts, along with others from the large body of literature known as the apocryphal New Testament, such as the Epistula Apostolorum (Letter from the Apostles), document the importance of apostolic instructions for the early church. The Didache seems to be the earliest text of this type, probably written early in the second century, and so it can be used to explain the emergence of the genre.

The Didache is now included in a small modern collection of early Christian texts that scholars call the Apostolic Fathers. This is literature thought to have been written by those who knew the apostles personally. Since the Didache does not have a signature, allowing the reader to think that it was written by the twelve apostles, it does not fit the rubric of "apostolic father." However, that lack of fit is the very feature that makes the Didache so important for our project. In distinction from the letters of 1 Clement and Ignatius which circulated under their own names (to be discussed in the next section), the Didache was probably compiled anonymously. It was a manual of instruction for a network of congregations, and the instructions were obviously taken from the teachings, views, and practices of those congregations. Naturally, the manual was composed with more than a little help from their overseers. It is therefore a very important document, for it lets us in on the kind of instructional literature written by overseers and eventually attributed to the apostles. It thus fills a niche in the early history of the emerging apostolic myth, a period during which acts of the apostles and letters from the apostles were being written but before it was thought necessary to spell out their instructions. It was written during a period of transition, when the question of authority to offer instruction to the churches was not yet critical. There is no mention of the apostles within the work and no internal evidence that the author thought it necessary to appeal to "the twelve apostles" as the source for his own authority. Thus the title must have been appended at a later time.

The Didache is a brief compendium of instructions, about the size of Q, the Gospel of Thomas, or the book of James. It begins with ethical instructions about the "two ways, one of life and one of death." The way of life is summed up in the commandments to love God and neighbor, elaborated in a series of "Thou shalts" and "Thou shalt nots" that cite some teachings of Jesus but go on to outline a rather extensive early Christian code of behavior. It touches upon matters such as giving and receiving alms, procuring abortion, the use of magic, pride, lust, obedience to one's masters and to the commandments of the lord, and so on. The way of death is described in a catalogue of vices and wicked practices. This takes up six of the sixteen chapters into which scholars have divided the text. Then follow succinct instructions on how to perform baptism, when and how to fast (on Wednesdays and Fridays, not on Mondays and Thursdays as "the hypocrites" do), when to say the "Our father" (three times a day), prayers for the meal of thanksgiving or eucharist, the treatment of itinerant prophets, the appointment of overseers and deacons to and by local congregations, and the command to ban with silence a member of the congregation who has "done a wrong to his neighbor" (Did. 15:3). The instructions end with a reminder of the coming judgment and a warning that one must "be found perfect at the last time" (Did. 16:2).

There are several interesting features of this manual of instruction. One is an overriding concern with the practice of alms, gift giving, and the support of dependents, itinerant teachers, and others who may ask for a handout. Generosity was obviously thought to be a prime Christian virtue, but in practice one had to be careful, for others could easily take advantage of the Christian. This was especially the case with "false" prophets who showed up and wanted the congregation to feed them. The instruction was not to "receive" any prophet who asked for food or money while speaking "in a spirit" (Did. 11:12), and not to allow any "true" prophet (who did not do that) to stay longer than two or three days unless he was willing to settle down, learn a craft, and "work for his bread" (Did. 12:2–5). It is obvious that the Didache was written with resident congregations in mind and that their overseers and deacons had grown weary of the hype and hoopla characteristic of an earlier period of itinerant, charismatic leadership. They no longer needed the showmanship of itinerant teachers and preachers. The pattern of congregational life over which they presided was sufficient. They had gotten together and agreed upon the practices, prayers, and rituals that defined the Christian way.

The prayers of thanksgiving (eucharist) for the community meal in chapters 9 and 10 are also significant. That is because they do not contain any reference to the death of Jesus. Accustomed as we are to the memorial supper of the Christ cult and the stories of the last supper in the synoptic gospels, it has been very difficult to imagine early Christians taking meals together for any reason other than to celebrate the death of Jesus according to the Christ myth. But here in the Didache a very formalistic set of prayers is assigned to the cup and the breaking of bread without the slightest association with the death and resurrection of Jesus. The prayers of thanksgiving are for the food and drink God created for all people and the special, "spiritual" food and drink that Christians have because of Jesus. Drinking the cup symbolizes the knowledge these people have that they and Jesus are the "Holy Vine of David," which means that they "belong to Israel." Eating the bread symbolizes the knowledge these people have of the life and immortality they enjoy by belonging to the kingdom of God made known to them by Jesus, God's child. And it is serious business. No one is allowed to "eat or drink of your Eucharist except those who have been baptised in the Lord's name" (Did. 9:5). We thus have to imagine a highly self-conscious network of congregations that thought of themselves as Christians, had developed a full complement of rituals, had much in common with other Christian groups of centrist persuasions, but continued to cultivate their roots in a Jesus movement where enlightenment ethics made much more sense than the worship of Jesus as the crucified Christ and risen son of God. Is that possible?

The answer is yes. These people were Jewish Christians much like the community reflected in Matthew's gospel. It is not unthinkable that both the Didache and the Gospel of Matthew stem from the same or closely related communities, though at slightly different times in their histories. The two texts have much in common, and the Didache mentions "the gospel" several times. There is also an additional, telling consideration. The section on the two ways is very much like other Jewish texts of ethical instruction. It was Christianized at some point simply by adding some teachings of Jesus to make precise the meaning of the ten commandments. For example, the second commandment of the way of life is to love one's neighbor and not do to another what one would not have done to oneself. This is based on a common Jewish practice of dividing the ten commandments into the two chief commandments, love of God and love of neighbor, supported by an often-cited commandment to love one's neighbor as one's self found in Leviticus 19:18, and derived from a contemporary Jewish formulation of the so-called negative golden rule. "Now," the Didache goes on to explain, "the teaching of these words is this: 'Bless those that curse you, and pray for your enemies, and fast for those that persecute you'" (Did. 1:2–3). It is not difficult to see what had happened. Sayings of Jesus from Q, possibly taken from the Gospel of Matthew, were used to spell out the meaning of the second commandment. Both the ten commandments and the teachings of Jesus win. The commandments win by becoming concrete and doable; the teachings of Jesus win by being treated on a par with the divine authority of the law of Moses. And both lose, of course, the ten commandments by being derailed into specifically Christian application, and the teachings of Jesus by becoming "mere" interpretation of the old, divine revelation. This is very much like the attempt to align the teachings of Jesus from Q with the law of Moses in the Gospel of Matthew. The major difference in this case is that, whereas Matthew emphasized the difference that Jesus' interpretations of the Torah made, the Didache does not. As a matter of fact, the Didache does not make a point of "the teaching" coming from Jesus at all. So something else happened to the teachings of Jesus between the time of Matthew and the time of the Didache.

What else happened can be seen in the formulation of the injunctions to "bless, . . . pray, . . . and fast. . . ." These amount to practical rituals that have been formalized. They are ways to respond to difficult circumstances and untoward people. Matthew's strategy was to reduce the import of the teachings of Jesus to attitudes and motivations, then claim that these were what the law of Moses intended. The Didache is interested in behavior, not mood. Throughout the instruction, the Christian ethic is described in terms of things you do and things you don't do. And Christian piety is spelled out in terms of a small list of daily and weekly rituals. This is very Jewish. It tells us that the community had succeeded in defining a workable pattern of distinctive behavior sufficient to support its claim to prepare for the kingdom of God. It did not need to make extravagant claims about Jesus, or about enabling personal transformation, or about links to special charismatic leadership. It distinguished itself readily from other Jewish groups simply by changing the days on which Jesus people were to fast. And, come to think of it, it may have distinguished itself consciously from other Christian groups simply by crafting its own prayers to God.

Thus the Didache is a significant text, documenting a confident Jewish Christianity from the early second century. This was a time when many Christian groups were experiencing a transition from fixation on the question of Jesus' authority and role as founder of a new religious movement to interest in and codification of the rules for community life. The author of the Didache was content to write anonymously, letting the instructions ride on the self-evident authority of the traditions in play. These included the Mosaic Torah, the teachings of Jesus, and the gospel story of Jesus. But they also included the ethical standards, ritual practices, and formal prayers that had become traditional within these congregations. The voice is that of a wise teacher who has been observant and knows what is best for this group. The author also speaks with authority: "My child, flee from every evil man" (Did. 3:1); "My child, regard not omens, for this leads to idolatry" (Did. 3:4); "Thou shalt not forsake the commandments of the Lord" (Did. 4:13); "Concerning the thanksgiving, give thanks as follows . . ." (Did. 9:1); "Let everyone who 'comes in the name of the Lord' be received" (Did. 12:1); and so forth. All these instructions are given in the same voice, with the same declarative sense of authority. It is the voice of one who knows what "the Lord" requires and, though the author sometimes refers to the commandments of the lord or the gospel of our lord as the source for an injunction, it is ultimately his own voice that is heard throughout the document. We do not know who this author was or exactly where to place him. But it would be easy to imagine a social location in some district of southern Syria or northern Palestine where a small group of congregations had formed. It would take a crisis of confidence to wrest this manual from these hands and pretend to hear the voices of the twelve apostles saying these things. In the meantime, other leaders of other congregations were not so bashful. They combined the genre of the letter with that of instructional literature and dared to sign their names. As we shall see, however, they could do that only because they claimed to stand in the apostolic tradition.

APOSTOLIC SUCCESSION

The term *apostolic fathers* is a seventeenth-century scholarly designation for a small group of writings believed to have been written by bishops and others who had known the apostles personally. The corpus consists of two letters attributed to Clement of Rome; seven letters of Ignatius, an early overseer of the congregation at Antioch; the Didache; a letter attributed to Barnabas, held to be Paul's companion; an apocalyptic vision written by a certain Hermas, about whom little else is known, revealed to him by an angel who appears as a shepherd and so named the Shepherd of Hermas; an account of the Martyrdom of Polycarp, an overseer at Smyrna thought to have known the "apostle" John; a letter of Polycarp; and the Epistle to Diognetus, an anonymous writing of uncertain date. The selection of these early Christian texts was meant to supply the necessary link in a literary history that ran from the writings of the apostles contained in the New Testament, through the apostolic fathers, to the later literature of the so-called patristic period in which the "fathers" of the church, beginning with Justin Martyr, Irenaeus, Clement of Alexandria, and Tertullian, developed their full-blown theological systems.

Critical scholars no longer think that any of these texts were written by authors who personally knew any of the disciples, or "apostles," of Jesus. And the assumed three-stage outline of early Christianity is now fully discredited. At each stage of this scheme there is not only a frustrating overlap in the chronology of the texts assigned to each, but a selection of texts that leaves out a great deal of literature that does not fit the pattern. The imagined pattern is that of a single-line development of orthodox Christianity in which each subsequent stage merely elaborates further a common core gospel. But even the small collection of texts known as the apostolic fathers, a collection meant to document the orthodox transmission of the gospel in contrast to all the other mistaken interpretations that threatened it, is a motley group of writings spanning the entire second century. It actually illustrates the diversity of early Christian thinking rather than its coherence. That scholars still refer to the literature of the apostolic fathers as a collection, and that publishers still publish it as a discrete corpus, merely demonstrates how deeply indebted the Christian imagination is to the apostolic view of history. It is, after all, the myth that supports the notion of apostolic succession, namely that there was a continuous line of teaching from Jesus, through the apostles, and on to the bishops who were thus able to guarantee the truth of the gospel and pass it on to their own successors.

In this and the last chapters we have watched the apostolic myth in the making. The emphasis has been upon the changing configurations of the apostles, the kind of literature attributed to them, and the various ways the emerging apostolic myth affected the authorship and authority of other early Christian literary production. Now the spotlight falls on the emerging office of the bishop and the way the authority of the bishop was construed. For this purpose, two sets of texts from the apostolic fathers are most helpful. These are the letters of Clement and Ignatius. Both men were in positions of leadership in their congregations writing about the importance of elders and overseers for the well-being of networks of Christian congregations. They wrote sometime around the first decade of the second century. In each case the occasion for the correspondence is fairly clear. Their responses share some common features despite some glaring differences in their conception of the Christian gospel. And, as we shall see, an early form of the apostolic myth was already involved in the authority each assumed for the oversight of both their own and other Christian congregations. The Greek term is still *episkopos*, which I have been translating as overseer. Now, however, with the role of the overseer under discussion as an essential ingredient in the very formation of Christianity as a social institution, it may be permissible on occasion to translate *episkopos* as bishop.

1 Clement

First Clement is a long letter of exhortation from the church at Rome to the church at Corinth. A report had been received that the elders in charge of oversight at Corinth had lost their position of authority, apparently as a result of ideological controversy. The congregation at Rome was disturbed by this news and wrote a letter to the Christians at Corinth reminding them of their importance as a leading congregation. The point of the protest was that their behavior threatened the unity, not only of their own congregation, but of the Christian churches as a whole, and gave dissident voices reason to slander the leadership of the Roman church. Clement is not referred to as the author in the earliest manuscript of this letter and was probably not *the* overseer at Rome at the time. But he may well have been an elder and the author of the letter, writing in the name of the church for its council of elders. Subsequent manuscripts do attach his name to the subscript at the end of the letter, and later legend remembers him as the second or third bishop at Rome, after Peter, who was said to have appointed him as his successor. The letter is, in any case, a very important document, the first bit of firsthand evidence we have from the Christian congregation at Rome. Scholars have usually dated the letter around 96 C.E. on the basis of a reference to "sudden and repeated misfortunes and calamities which have befallen us" (1 Clem. 1:1), taken to refer to an alleged persecution during the time of Domitian (81–96 C.E.) and with an eye on Eusebius' history of the church, written in the fourth century. A slightly later dating seems preferable, however, for the tenor of the teaching shares the concern of other early second-century writings with ordering Christian practice, piety, and oversight. A little more time would also help to account for the sense of importance that the Roman congregation obviously enjoyed.

Rome's response to the Corinthian situation focused on the scandal of upstarts failing to respect their council of elders. The issue of the views that divided the community was not addressed, only the fact of dissension and disharmony. Rome exhorted Corinth to renew the peace and harmony of the congregation by recognizing the elders as those who stood in the tradition of the apostles and the great exemplars of piety throughout all history. This is very curious. Piety was the standard for measuring Christian correctness, but the examples of piety were not limited to Jesus and the apostles. They were taken primarily from the epic of Israel and even included some honorable men from Greek tradition. The dissensions at Corinth could be resolved if only the dissenters would recognize the piety of these exemplars and submit in obedience to their example. They should do this, as Clement said, for the sake of regaining "faith, fear, peace, patience, long-suffering, self-control, purity, and sobriety" (1 Clement 64), a list of the virtues that defined Clement's understanding of Christian character. It is of course clear that Jesus, by virtue of the death he suffered for the sins of others, was the prime example of the humility and obedience Clement recommended (1 Clement 16) and that he regarded this gospel as the "glorious and venerable rule of our tradition" (1 Clem. 7:2). But Clement did not leave it there, urging his readers to "review" with him "all the generations, and let us learn that in generation after generation the Master [God] has given a place of repentance to those who will turn to him" (1 Clem. 7:5). Thus repentance is announced as the theme for the exhortation, with a not-so-thinly-veiled suggestion that what Clement wanted the dissenters at Corinth to do was repent.

The letter is lengthy, sixty-five chapters in comparison with the Didache's sixteen. It unfolds with a list of topics intended to address the situation at Corinth. Envy is the first topic, and it is obviously considered a very bad vice. This, by the way, agreed with an attitude about envy that was widespread during the Greco-Roman age. One might even say that envy, together with desire, was the cardinal sin or root vice in the popular philosophies of the time. To suggest that the dissenters at Corinth were motivated by envy would have been very strong censure. Humility, obedience, and piety, on the other hand, were very good virtues. Greek thought would not have contrasted envy with humbleness, instead choosing self-control as the antidote, but at Clement's stage of Christian thinking, obedience to the authorities was the issue. Repentance also was considered good, and Clement was at pains to show that repentance had always been met with forgiveness. The spin in this case was to leave unexplored the difference between repenting of having been disobedient to God, the case that could be illustrated with examples from the Israel epic, and repenting of having been disrespectful to the elders. Since, according to the underlying Jewish-Christian pattern, repentance and forgiveness lead back to a life of righteousness and virtue, the exhortation ended on the encomiastic note of praise for those who exemplified these virtues and a glorious description of the congregation whose peace and harmony was grounded in the piety of humility, Christian love, and obedient Christian service. As each topic is introduced, a roster of illustrious examples is presented, some mentioned in passing, some storied at length, and the implication is simply that one could and should imitate them. The strategy is obvious, and although the dissenters can hardly have been persuaded to repent on the spot, the argument for Christian piety may have sounded right to some. A later overseer at Corinth, Dionysius, reported in 170 C.E. that the letter was still being read in the Corinthian congregation.

Paul's letter to the Romans in the late 50s is the only other hard evidence we have that a Christian congregation formed in Rome during the first century. And it is clear that Clement knew about Paul and the Christ myth. But to move from Paul to Clement is to step into another world. The gospel according to Clement was not a proclamation of the "power of God" effecting human transformation. The content of the gospel for Clement was the image of Christ as the superlative example of a Christian piety. That's all. The rest of his program was an amalgam of a Jewish ethic of righteousness, a Greek theory of virtue by imitation, and a touch of Roman practicality, all in the interest of a congregational concept that sounds suspiciously like a combination of the Jewish diaspora synagogue and the Greek club. At this juncture in the history of the Roman congregation, what it meant to be a Christian was a relatively simple matter, what it meant to be a congregation of Christians under the authority of a council of elders was also a relatively simple matter, and what it meant to be a congregation of Christians at Rome, a congregation in the position of counseling other congregations in matters of conduct, was simply taken for granted. Is this an indication of what the Christian church would become? Yes, but only an indication. Clement avoided the real issues of ideology, practice, and relations with other groups, such as gnostic Christians, Jewish synagogues, and the Roman Empire, that were brewing at the time and which must have been the occasion for the letter. These issues were serious, would have to be addressed by later Christian thinkers, and would make a difference in the way Christianity defined itself. Clement's naïveté about the illustrious examples of piety in every generation would be put to the test. What a Christian *thought* about God, Jews, Romans, Greeks, and the Jewish scriptures would become important. And the council of elders would give way to a monarchical episcopate with a single bishop in charge of the major congregation in a district. Rome would have to compete for the supremacy it eventually won and work out its definition of the Christian faith in debate with strong intellectual leaders of differing opinions, both in Rome and in other centers of Christianity throughout the Mediterranean.

It is this curious combination of authority and naïveté that makes 1 Clement such an interesting document. If we dare ask how such a combination could be managed, we can gain another perspective on the emerging apostolic myth. Clement was not as concerned, as Luke soon would be, to develop the concept of the apostles into a golden age, to make sure that Paul and Peter had preached the same gospel, and to account for the spread of the gospel from Jerusalem to Rome. He simply took it for granted that Peter and Paul were "noble examples" and "pillars of the church" (1 Clement 5) and that what he called "the rule of our tradition" (1 Clem. 7:2), "the rule of obedience" (1 Clem. 1:3), "the words of Christ" (1 Clem. 2:1; 13:1), or simply "the gospel," came from the apostles. As he put it, "The apostles received the gospel for us from the Lord Jesus Christ, Jesus the Christ was sent from God. The Christ therefore is from God and the apostles from the Christ." He then mentions their superior status in the "order of God's will," their confidence in the resurrection, and their obedience to their commission as apostles. Then he says, "They preached from district to district, and from city to city, and they appointed their first converts . . . to be overseers and deacons of the future believers" (1 Clement 42). This is the earliest expression we have of the apostolic myth. It is not developed; it does not mention texts; it does not say that the written gospels were memoirs of the apostles. In fact, Clement may still have been using sayings collections instead of narrative gospels as his source for the teachings of Jesus (Cameron 1984, 91–124). But with such an apostolic notion gaining ground, it is not too difficult to see why the literary production of the first century would eventually have to be attributed to the apostles. It is the myth that gave Clement and the congregation at Rome the authority to write the exhortation. Why should one listen to them? How did they know what the true "rule of our tradition" was? They knew because they had it from the apostles.

The Letters of Ignatius

Reading the letters of Ignatius is not a pleasant experience. His letters are addressed to the churches at Smyrna, Ephesus, Magnesia, Tralles, Philadelphia, and Rome. In the citations that follow, I will abbreviate the full titles ("Ignatius to the Romans") by reference to the addressees (e.g., Romans). Compared with other early Christian writings there is no room in these letters for the reader to spar with the author. Instead of listening in on Jesus addressing his disciples or watching Paul rank his arguments against opponents and straw men or considering the instructions from the apostles for future Christians from a distance, when reading Ignatius one encounters Ignatius. And he is a true believer. He does not invite his readers into a world larger than his own desire to "attain" God (Romans 4:1). He does not ask them to think about the reasons for being a Christian or its costs and consequences. He does not even give any instructions for the Christian life. But he does make two appeals. One should honor one's overseer, he said, and one should pray for Ignatius and get ready to celebrate his martyrdom. As he said, "Christianity is not a matter of persuasion, but of greatness" (Romans 3:3). And there is only one moment of greatness. It is the moment when the martyr (*martyr*) makes the great confession (*martyria*). "I seek Him who died for our sake." "Suffer me to follow the example of the passion of my God." "I long for the beasts that are prepared for me"(Romans 5:2; 6:1, 3). Unfortunately, nothing in his letters indicates that he really did not mean it. He writes naively about his faith, and he expresses his mimetic desire without embarrassment. It is frightening to read him at length. It is a shock to think that the Christ myth had lost its social logic so completely within the span of half a century and that it was now available for such a personal internalization. Ignatius had taken Paul seriously, and he wanted nothing more than to imitate Christ's death, to be "ground by the teeth of wild beasts that I may be found pure bread of Christ" (Romans 4:1).

The story is that Ignatius, the bishop at Antioch, was on his way to Rome under Roman guard, having been arrested and put in chains. There is no reference anywhere in his letters to the reasons for his arrest and no evidence elsewhere of the circumstances of his arrest or the fact of his being executed. What we learn from the letters is that Ignatius stopped over at Smyrna, where he was received by the bishop of the local Christian congregation, Polycarp. The stay was apparently long enough for delegations to arrive from Ephesus, Tralles, and Magnesia, led by their leaders whom Ignatius recognized as overseers and deacons. While still at Smyrna, apparently, he wrote letters to these congregations to be taken back by their delegations. Later, from Troas, he wrote letters to Smyrna and Polycarp as well as one to the congregation at Philadelphia, all to be delivered by companions who had accompanied him from Smyrna. At some point, he also wrote a letter to the Romans in anticipation of his arrival there.

The content of each letter is similar. Ignatius compliments the congregation on their bishop, thanks them for their concern on his behalf, and exhorts them to be subject to their bishop, to honor their elders, and to recognize the Christian service of their deacons. Here and there he also asks them to pray for him in his trial and for the church at Antioch, which is now without an overseer. Interwoven is his own confessional understanding of following the Christian way, his concern for the unity and peace of the Christian churches, and his view that, since the bishops represent both Christ and God to their congregations, the proper regard for them ultimately is obedience. Allusions along the way indicate that bishops were presiding over the congregational meetings and meals, that they were charged with the welfare of every member of the congregation, and that individual Christians were expected to consult with them about their most personal questions and needs. This picture of the organization of Christian congregations in Asia Minor is startling, given the stormy histories assumed from the letters of Paul. And the self-assured authority of Ignatius, not only as a bishop of a local congregation, but as one who thought he had the right to counsel other congregations about subjection to their bishops, is completely unexpected. No wonder the letters of Ignatius are famous as proof for the episcopal form of the early Christian church.

These letters are usually dated between 108 and 117 C.E., the last half of Trajan's rule, slightly later than the letter of 1 Clement and about the time of Luke's Acts of the Apostles. The apostolic myth is in place, but in distinction from Clement's and Luke's interest in history as the best way to imagine the link between the apostles and the overseers, Ignatius is content to construct a hierarchical pattern of governance for the church on the model of a Platonic universe. In this model the apostles have their place under the authority of Christ, just as Christ is under the authority of God. This model is thoroughly Greek in its conception as an interlocking series of archetypes and copies. It functioned for Ignatius as the revelation to Christians of God's pleasure, will, and rule. It was a pattern to be copied in the organization of the Christian congregation. Copying it as a pattern also reflects a thoroughly Greek mentality, where the similarity between a pattern and its copy meant that they shared a common essence and where the imitation of a model resulted in substantive identity. Ignatius refers to this model over and over again to remind Christians of the divine authority of their bishops and elders and to impress upon them the importance of obedience to them. There is a bit of slippage in the application of the model owing to the fact that, if the hierarchy of bishop, elder, and deacon is set in analogy to the hierarchy of God, Christ, and apostles, the bishop would stand in the place of God and his own subjection to Christ and the apostles would not be clear. Ignatius does sometimes equate the authority of the bishop with that of God, but he prefers to make the comparison with Christ. As for the elders, they are sometimes compared with Christ and sometimes with the apostles as those to whom the congregation should give heed. So the correspondence is not perfect, but the point is clear. Imitating the model is the principal way to incorporate the truth of the gospel in the life of the congregation and the life of the individual Christian. As Ignatius puts it in one place, "Be zealous to do all things in harmony with God, with the bishop presiding in the place of God, and the elders in the place of the council of the apostles, and the deacons. . . . Be united with the bishop and with those who preside over you as an example and lesson of immortality" (Magnesians 6). Note, however, that the model itself consists of a series of models and copies linked internally by the notion of *mimesis* (imitation). Precisely what did it mean to "follow God," to "imitate the Lord," to regard the apostles as "examples," to "heed" the bishop, to "be subject to the elders," and to "honor" the deacons?

The model integrates two different but easily related values. One is the honor due to superiors, a virtue basic to the hierarchical model of families, societies, and governments in antiquity. The other is the honor due the martyrs for their integrity and endurance when called upon to suffer the noble death. Putting together these two types of honor as the lens through which to view the significance of the Christ myth, Christ's obedience unto death becomes the way he honored God's sovereignty and so became the model of obedience to be imitated. The system is not without its conceptual flaws, for by dying the noble death for the sake of becoming the model for others, Christ was also regarded as moving up a notch in the hierarchy to obtain divinity and become the Christians' lord. But Ignatius was not an intellectual and may not have been capable of seeing the flaws in his conception of the Christian faith. He was, by his own admission, a simple Christian in the tradition of Paul's gospel, "a follower of the blessed Paul" (Ephesians 12:2), using language reminiscent of Paul's letters throughout, and wanting very much to "fight with the beasts" from Syria to Rome, just as Paul had done, all in the interest of imitating Paul, imitating the martyrdom of Christ, and "imitating God" (Ephesians 12:2; Romans 4:1; and elsewhere) in order to "attain" or "encounter God."

Ignatius' sense of authority is directly related to his own mimetic desire to "follow the example of the passion of my God" (Romans 6:3) and so "to be someone" (Romans 9:2) for whom the Romans will sing a hymn of praise to God after his death and ascension into heaven (Roman 2:2). We do not know whether that happened. But we do know that later legend told the story of his martyrdom, that letters continued to be written under his pseudonym, and that his letters were copied and read over and over again throughout the history of the church. His conception of the ultimate confession of the Christian faith and his own attitude of meekness when confronted with this "opportunity" (Romans 2:1) were apparently found to be fitting expressions of Christian piety. He was given a prominent place among the bishops and others who exemplified the model in the martyrological literature of the second and third centuries. And his letters are still referred to as the Epistles of Saint Ignatius.

His importance for the historian is that, after Paul and John (the author of Revelation), Ignatius is the first Christian personality from whom we have a signed statement. He thus announces the sense of presence and authority that bishops and others will have from this point on. The apostolic myth is a critical factor in the change that took place. Jesus becomes an example. But so do the apostles. And so do the bishops. And the example is one of long suffering in the face of conflict and persecution. That was the way that led to eternal life. In the literature and iconography of the second and third centuries, Jesus is regularly depicted as the good shepherd, the one who can lead the believer into heaven. Thus the piety of Ignatius, though startling in its sudden appearance and naïveté, is very close to what the Christian ideal will become. This ideal is distinctive in its combination of this-worldly and otherworldly interests. An encounter with the forces that wield real power in the public and social arenas of this world is involved. But so is an audacious dismissal of interest in or desire for full participation in the life of this social arena. As Ignatius said, "The ends of the earth and the kingdoms of this world shall profit me nothing. It is better for me to die in Christ Jesus than to be king over the ends of the earth" (Romans 6:1). This strange attitude toward the public arena, and its concomitant view of life after death, differs from the attitudes of gnostic, docetic, Jewish, philosophical, civil, and other religious mentalities of the time. It was to turn centrist Christians into fearless fighters for the recognition of a this-worldly church that disdained the world in the interest of an otherworldly kingdom.

10

CLAIMING ISRAEL'S EPIC

The easy confidence of the early bishops in their watered-down gospel was soon to be shattered. They had disregarded the conceptual contradictions in the Christian myth and overlooked the social reasons for dissension and controversy in their own congregations. They had conveniently dismissed the differing views and practices of other Christian groups in locations throughout the empire such as Eastern Syria, Palestine, Alexandria, and North Africa. Their call for peace and unity within a congregation and for respectability in view of the Romans was well intentioned and apparently somewhat successful. But it was anchored in a vague and vaporous sense of divine pleasure in loyalty and in the threat of an eventual judgment as the ultimate hurdle on the way to eternal life. This may have been enough for many parishioners whom the bishops helped in the practical matters of living and getting along with one's neighbors. But for thoughtful persons, concerned about the logic of the bishops' myth, the simple, apostolic gospel was not enough to take pride in the novel religion that was taking its public place in the Greco-Roman world. It was time for scholarly debate among the various Christian traditions and for Christian intellectuals to give an account of the new religion that Greeks, Romans, and others might be able to understand.

The next generation of Christians produced such intellectuals. Marcion of Sinope (in Pontus, northern Asia Minor), Valentinus of Alexandria, and Justin of Samaria converged on Rome around 140–150 C.E. to battle for extremely different views of what Christianity should be. Slightly later, several more joined the fray with voluminous literary output to argue for other conceptions of the new religion: Irenaeus, born in Asia Minor and writing from Lyons, but with thoroughly Roman loyalties; Clement of Alexandria, originally from Athens, who laid the foundation for "Christian philosophy" as head of the catechetical school in Egypt; and Tertullian of Carthage in North Africa, who defended the faith against everything Greek, pagan, gnostic, and immoral. The apostolic myth would survive, but only as part of a much larger, more complex understanding of history and the world than the early bishops could have imagined. The mythic history of the church would eventually have to include a tortured reading of the epic of Israel in order to make it end with the Christ, as well as an odd conception of humankind in order to give Christians their start at the very creation of the world. A peculiar understanding of God would need to be rationalized, and the ambiguous role of the church in the Roman Empire would have to be explained.

The bright young intellectuals that arose in the second Christian century asked the bishops to step aside, brushed off the wobbly foundation upon which the bishops had been standing, and discovered that the stones were not well set. They found that the mythic foundation of the church was much in need of repair, if not reconstruction. First they chipped away at the foundation stones and found it possible to rearrange some. But then they set to work constructing some new and very complex systems of thought in order to place God and his Christ at the center of a comprehensive view of cosmos and history, and to trace the hidden paths for people in quest of eternal salvation. With them we enter the era of the "fathers," the so-called patristic age when mythmaking took the form of constructing theologies. They certainly had their work cut out for them, trying to make sense of the Christian gospel in the middle of the second century. Having been to school, they were eager to keep the whole world in view, and they felt as if the whole world was watching them. All were well prepared for the challenge, thoroughly at home in the culture of Greek logic, thought, and literature. They were also well read in the Jewish scriptures and thoroughly acquainted with the many traditions of Christian thought. And they took to the field with banners flying. If there was any sense to be made of the new religion, these intellectuals would have to make it.

A theology that supported centrist interests finally won, though it took two hundred years or more to work it out in competition with other views. The remarkable thing about this Christian view of the world is that its complex system of thought was created to support a single claim. The claim was that Christians were the legitimate heirs of the epic of Israel, that the Jews had never understood the intentions of their God, and that the story of Israel, if one read it rightly, was "really" about the coming of Christ. It may seem strange that such a far-fetched claim would determine the Christian conceptions of God, the world, and human history. But that is what happened, and there were some reasons why it had to be, given the way Christianity had emerged. These reasons, and the arguments for the systems that these first theologians came up with, are the subject of this chapter. We are at the point where the beginnings of Christian theology and the construction of the Christian epic were the same enterprise. A Christian theology of centrist persuasion was impossible without laying claim to the legacy of the history of Israel, but making that claim meant that a new centrist theology would have to be invented and defended. As we shall see, the centrist "fathers" won, the Jewish scriptures became the Christian Old Testament, and Western Christianity as we know it today finally had its myth and ritual act together.

MARCION

Marcion of Sinope triggered the explosion. He was the rich son of a bishop in Pontus, reared on Paul's version of the Christ myth, and extremely well read in early Christian literature and the Jewish scriptures. As he looked around at his fellow Christians, some things did not make sense. Christians were still trying to be loyal to the Jewish God even after they learned that they did not have to keep his law. But the God who gave the Jews their law could not be the same as the God who sent his son to proclaim mercy. Marcion thought the Jewish God was obviously overly concerned with justice and that his role in the story of the people he chose to govern was one of judgment, wrath, and violence in the interest of ethnic purity and exclusive control. The wise, kind God whom Jesus made known, a God previously unknown, a God of mercy and compassion for all humankind, was much different. And after Paul, according to Marcion, something had gone wrong in the church as well. It must have been the other apostles who were soft on Judaism. It must have been the Judaizers who wrote most of the gospels and worked over the epistles of Paul. The church was in danger of losing its orientation to the incomparable gospel of Christ, the first revelation of the alien God, the only God who was good and desired that all human souls receive eternal life. The first line of Marcion's famous *Antitheses* was: "O wonder beyond wonders, rapture, power, and amazement is it, that one can say nothing at all about the gospel, nor even conceive of it, nor compare it with anything" (cited in Harnack 1990, 66). So Marcion set out to save the day for the new and unique religion.

According to Marcion, the Jewish God, the creator of this hostile world, was not worthy of worship. And the Jewish scriptures with their laws and stories of punishment and sacrifice should be discarded. In their place Christians needed only their own records of the appearance of Christ and his announcement of the God who was good. But what to do about the writings of the wrongheaded apostles and the tampering they must have done to the epistles of Paul? The answer was obvious: Reject all the early Christian writings that were written by apostles who did not grasp the novelty of the Christian revelation, and excise the additions to the letters of Paul made by later Judaizers. And so the first New Testament canon of literature was born. It contained ten (excised) letters of Paul and one abbreviated Gospel of Luke. Polycarp called Marcion "the first-born of Satan," and Justin and Tertullian would write at length against his views. That is because Marcion had rejected the apostolic myth and put his finger on some embarrassing, unresolved contradictions in the bishops' view of the gospel. As for his own views, he did find a hearing at Pontus, Ephesus, and Rome. Congregations formed, a school started, and a Marcionite church spread throughout the empire and toward the east. Entire villages became Marcionite Christians, and the Marcionites challenged centrist theologians for several hundred years.

Marcion's theology was simplistic and rife with internal contradictions of its own. But it was understandable, and people could actually do what was required. He

started with Paul's contrast between the law and the gospel in his letter to the Galatians. He then used Paul's concept of the "flesh" to negate the material world created by the Jewish God and discount his laws which, according to Marcion, were all
obsessed with physical conditions and concerns with the "flesh." Christ, on the
other hand, revealed the love of God and introduced the holy spirit, the divine and
cosmic principle set in opposition to the flesh. Thus Christian spirituality consisted
in living a disciplined life, designed to minimize interest in and control by the
"flesh," as the proper worship of the true but alien spiritual God of love. The average Christian may not have jumped at the chance to live such a disciplined life, but
the codes were clear and the system simple. People were attracted to the anti-Jewish
interpretation of the new Christian religion; centrist bishops and other intellectuals
were horrified. And consternation reigned among the intellectuals, for there were
no ready answers to the questions Marcion raised about Christians paying homage
to the Jewish God. As Trypho put the question to Justin, compounding the embarrassment of a Marcion by the fact that Trypho was a Jew, "You expect to receive
favors from God, yet you disregard his commandments" (Justin, *Dialogue* 10).
With Marcion, a basic contradiction in the logic of the bishops' myth came to the
surface, and the old, unresolved question about the function of the Mosaic law
turned into a new and troubling question about the nature of God.

VALENTINUS

To make matters worse, Valentinus appeared in Rome about this time from Alexandria. He also understood himself to be a fully convinced and committed Christian,
working out a theological system with practical consequences for the average congregation. According to Valentinus, Christ had made it possible for Christians, not
only to know *about* God, but to know him by "acquaintance," as Bentley Layton
translates *gnosis* (1987). If Christians had this kind of *gnosis*, they would realize they
were God's offspring. If Valentinus had left it there, no one would have disagreed,
for what Christian would have wanted to say that Christians were not "acquainted"
with God? But Valentinus was a gnostic Christian, and his idea of acquaintance referred to a special kind of knowledge that only a revealer from the realm of cosmic
light could make known. So with both Marcion and Valentinus converging on
Rome, the very center of centrist Christianity would have to be the place where the
battle for Christian orthodoxy would ensue. To set the scene, we need to know what
was going on in Alexandria, the city where Valentinus had studied and worked out
his system of Christian gnostic theology before coming to Rome.

Alexandria was the world's center for books, learning, and philosophical speculation. All the traditional schools of Greek philosophy and science were represented,
and the mood of the time was to find a way to fit them all together in some grand
scheme that might account for everything in the vast universe of information that
was coming into view. The larger the horizon, the more abstract the concepts. And

so the time was ripe for a resurgence of Platonic philosophy, which we now call middle Platonism. Plato distinguished between a physical world perceived by the senses and its mental pattern lodged in the mind of being. The idea of transcendent being, Plato's "god," was generally attractive, and a revival of interest in Plato's myth of creation as told in the Timaeus pervaded the academic scene. In this myth, Plato started with the standard distinction between an archetype and its image, a ranked pair of pattern and copy commonly used to describe the relationship between such things as a seal and its impression, a model and its imitation, or a plan and the object made from it. Plato used the metaphor to imagine a god thinking up the plan for the great world city, which he kept in his mind. Then a *demiurgos* or craftsman entered the story and kept his eye on the pattern while shaping matter (*hyle*) into the material world. Plato's story became the rage in Alexandria. It made it possible to hang on to some lofty ideas about the core of reality being ultimately constructive, unified, and perfect even while living in the midst of a world where cultural fragmentation and social chaos reigned. It also made it possible to retain a positive connotation for craftsmanship (*techne*, skill, technique), a basic metaphor and concept for theories of discourse (rhetoric), social construction, and cosmic design. Sophists and philosophical charlatans had given *techne* a negative connotation because of the way they manipulated or (mis)used language. And as we shall see, the Platonic notion of the world as a construct could also easily backfire, supposing one had reason to think that the craftsman had made a mistake. But it was very difficult to imagine any constructive project that did not involve a creative use of technology, and Plato's myth blessed *techne* by making it fundamental to the way in which the world was created.

As for the Jews who lived in Alexandria, two hundred years of allegorical interpretation of the books of Moses had been conveniently summed up in the works of Philo of Alexandria (30 B.C.E.–45 C.E.). At the literal level, the books of Moses were history. But at the deeper level of meaning, Moses had encoded every term and story as a symbol of the perfect world that God, whom Philo called the One Who Is, had in mind. And there in Moses' account of the genesis of Adam and the world (Genesis 1 and 2), a two-layer creation was obvious: first the perfect pattern, then its copy in the material world. Philo concluded, as did other Jewish exegetes, that Plato must have learned about the creation of the two-layer world from Moses. At first these Jewish exegetes thought that Plato's reading of Moses was slightly confused. That was because Plato seemed to distinguish between the highest god, or being itself, in whose mind the pattern was conceived, and the *demiurgos*, a kind of second god, who created the material universe as a copy of the mental pattern. To start with two gods did not sound right. But Jewish thinkers of Philo's ilk had already dared to imagine the *logos* (reason) as the divine son and *sophia* (wisdom) as the divine consort of God and call them second-level divine beings through whom God had created the world. They had also noticed the difference between two names for God in the books of Moses and concluded that *Lord* was the name of a divine power that administered justice, while *God* was the name of a divine being concerned with the protection and care of his children. Reading Philo, one can see that the Jewish intellectuals of Alexandria had prepared the way for later Christian thinkers. They had already made three great conceptual leaps that Christian theologians would follow. They had found a way to (1) merge the Jewish notion of God as a personal agent in history with the Greek notion of the divine as a cosmic being, (2) distribute the attributes and manifestations of a solitary, transcendent god to second-level divinities and cosmic powers, and (3) read the Jewish scriptures as an allegory of the divine activity of God in cosmos and creation without destroying its literal significance as the history of Israel.

A third major development of the intellectual climate in Alexandria was the emergence of gnostic thought with its orientation to myths of creation and redemption. We cannot be sure of the exact time or circumstance when gnostic myths were first entertained, whether during the first or second centuries and whether impelled by Greco-Egyptian, Jewish, or Christian concerns and speculations. According to gnostic thought as developed in the classical treatises of the second and third centuries, the world was a hostile environment in which to live. Gnostics felt lost and disoriented. They had no place to call their home. They were sensitive to the question of personal identity and worried about not knowing where one came from, where one belonged, and whither one might be going. Human destiny seemed to be fated, and the forces of fate were blind. For the most part, according to gnostics, humans lived in a stupor, acting out childish desires and playing into the hands of fate and the "rulers of the world." But some (the gnostics) had been awakened by an emissary from the realms of light to the knowledge that they were the children of God. They had, moreover, always been the children of God, though they had "forgotten" their true ancestry because of the material darkness in which they found themselves. Their ancestry, they discovered, was in an elect people. They belonged to a strain of the human race whose genealogy stretched back to the foundation of the world when humans were first created. They had come from God and carried in them still the "spark" of divine life that defined their true selves and determined their ultimate destiny. That destiny was to return home to God, the divine parent, the original source of their light and life, and the place of eternal belonging. And so their *gnosis* was a knowledge, not only of God, but of the self as well.

Gnostics explained their situation in the world by means of elaborate accounts of creation and a complex myth of redemption. Bentley Layton (1987) has helped us understand the structure of this gnostic mythology. Four scenes unfolded in evolutionary sequence. In the first scene, spheres of power called emissions or emanations were generated by the highest god, pure spirit. These formed a spiritual universe called the entirety, both enveloping and being enveloped by the highest god, a sort of aura of self-reflection that expanded in concentric spheres of ever greater distance from their divine generator. In the second scene, the material universe was created as an imperfect copy of the divine universe by means of some error, accident, or deceit. This tragedy was an indispensable moment in all variants of the gnostic myth of creation, though it was variously described. Somehow, usually at the lower reaches of the spiritual universe, something went wrong. A female emanation generated a false desire or gave birth to a monster or fell out of the entirety into the formless matter below. Some myths say that she tried to imitate the creation of the highest god but could not do so because she acted alone. Others say that her offspring, Ialdabaoth, a malformed, blind, and envious power, was the one who created the material world in order to rule over it in imitation of the highest god. In a third scene, humans were created and the divine spark was implanted in the ancestral gnostic. In one prominent version of the myth, Ialdabaoth was tricked into letting this happen by one of the more beneficent powers from the world above, and the protognostics were identified as the generation of Seth, the third son of Adam and Eve. Ialdabaoth's response was to encase the gnostics in bodies and drug the human race into forgetting its divine origin. In the fourth scene, a revealer appeared from the realm of light to rekindle the spark of *gnosis* and show the gnostics the way back home.

At first it might appear that such a myth was an appropriate response to the times. According to this view, gnostics had internalized the anxiety of personal disorientation typical for many in the soulless, Roman world. On second thought, however, gnostics had taken their lack of social location far more seriously than other peoples, and they had drawn a radically pessimistic conclusion about the very nature of the entire universe in which they lived. This radically negative view of the created world surfaced so suddenly, and strikes the historian as so novel and inexplicable, that scholars have been at a loss to account for it. Something terrible must have happened to precipitate such despair, but the attempt to trace its origin to a single event or moment of mythmaking has not been successful. Part of the problem is that the large corpus of gnostic texts from the second and third centuries, including but not limited to the Coptic-Gnostic library from Nag Hammadi, contains features derived from both Christian and Jewish mythologies. Another is that neither the Christian nor the Jewish antecedent mythologies provide enough clues to explain the switch to the inverse, negative, gnostic view of the world.

In the Christian-gnostic myth of redemption, for instance, Jesus figures as the revealer through whom the knowledge of divine life and destiny was made known. Language and themes from the Christ myth and the gospels frequently occur, and the cosmic destiny of Jesus seems to provide the major pattern for the *gnosis* that brings salvation to the gnostic individual. This reveals a Christian investment in the process of gnostic mythmaking, but it hardly explains why Christians would have needed to paint the world so darkly in order to lay claim to such a salvation. Given what we know about the obstacles faced in the early history of Christian thought and congregation, such a negative view of the world is surely an overreaction.

In the gnostic myth of creation, the myth that accounts for the negative view of the world and for the divine origin of the gnostics as an elect race, the Genesis account of creation and its long tradition of Platonic interpretation in the Jewish circles represented by Philo hover in the background. The difference between Philo and the gnostics is that the lower-level creation of the material universe is good according to Philo, and for gnostics it is bad, the result of a tragic error or dark design. Some scholars have suggested that this reversal of attitude may have been a result of Jewish trauma in response to the loss of their temple, land, and government at the hands of the Romans in 70 C.E., exacerbated perhaps by the disastrous consequences of Bar Kochba's failed revolt in 135 C.E. Jewish trauma does seem to permeate many gnostic writings, but it alone does not seem to be enough to account for the complete denigration of the creator-god of Genesis or the attraction to the myth of redemption that solved the gnostics' problem. So we must proceed with caution in our attempt to understand Valentinus.

Valentinus happens to be our first witness to Alexandrian Christianity and, judging from his own theological system, Alexandrian Christians had been heavily influenced by the intellectual climate just described. Platonic philosophy, Philonic interpretation of Moses, and some form of gnostic thought are all strongly represented. As for the particular kind of Christian persuasion that spread to Egypt in the first place, it must have been closer to Thomas Christianity and the Johannine circle than a Pauline or Matthean form of Christianity. But its origins are, unfortunately, exceedingly unclear. Valentinus himself, or perhaps it was one of his successors in the school he started, claimed apostolic tradition through Theudas, one of Paul's companions, and thus back to Paul. That would have been a serious pitch for being recognized as centrist, and it is true that Valentinus was well acquainted with both the Christ myth and the gospel story. But his system of interpretation tells against a centrist training. Enlightenment, not faith, was the benefit that Christ made available, according to Valentinus, and his roots in a Johannine or Thomas Christianity shine through in his writings. We have fragments from Irenaeus and Clement of Alexandria, a sermonlike treatise called the *Gospel of Truth*, literature produced by his followers, and descriptions of his system of thought from Irenaeus and other heresiologists. What we learn from these sources is that Valentinus, or the Alexandrian Christianity he represents, had taken some long steps on the way to a gnostic mythology.

According to Valentinus, the significance of Jesus' appearance as the Christ could only be understood as a divine manifestation in the midst of a world born in tragedy. It was the second major act in a two-fold cosmic drama, the first of which was the very creation of the world. According to Valentinus, "error" occurred at the outer reaches of a series of paired "aeons" (powerful concentrations of time and space emanating from the divine source). After eight, then ten, then twelve more aeons were generated, "error" lost contact with the highest power and tried to shape the matter that lay outside the "entirety." But she worked while "empty" and "in a fog." She became the "mother" who produced beings outside the spiritual universe, one of whom was a thieving "craftsman," who then molded the matter into a semblance of the perfect world. Somehow, the "human being," the "christ," and even the "church" also came into being at that time as prototypes that would play a role in the second major act.

In the second act of this cosmic drama, Jesus as the Christ became the revealer of the divine realm and the redeemer of those predestined to return to it. How the Christ was generated, and how Jesus became the incarnation of the divine Christ, is unclear in Valentinus' system. But the point is unmistakable. It was *gnosis* (acquaintance, or knowledge by insight) that Christ made possible. Nothing within the world created in error could clarify the human situation and let Christians know of their true identity as children of the highest god. Only a message sent from the highest god, the appearance of Jesus, his son, could make it clear that Christians were the elect children of God whose spiritual destiny was to "rest" in his presence in the realms of light and life above.

Marcion and Valentinus spelled big trouble for the centrist Christian leaders at Rome. Together they succeeded in challenging the logical foundations of the Christian gospel and the apostolic myth. Unexamined assumptions were exposed, latent contradictions censured, and older rationales shown to be inadequate. After Marcion, a Christian thinker could not merely assume that the god and father of Jesus Christ was the same as the god of Israel, that Christians should be indebted to the ethical norms and sensibilities of the Jewish epic while rejecting the Jewish law, or that the main significance of Jesus' appearance was to expand the notion of Israel to include the gentiles. After Valentinus, Christians could not just assume that faith in the gospel and obedience to the rule of tradition were enough to capture the enlightenment manifest in the Christ myth. Neither could they assume that the God revealed in Jesus Christ was the creator of the universe, interested in and concerned about all the things that happened to his children in this world. These were serious challenges. They made it clear that all the previous Christian mythologies in the centrist tradition were rooted in simplistic logics. These mythologies amounted to artless claims upon the legacy of Israel and presumptuous invitations to think of Israel's God as having arranged for the transfer of his pleasure from the Jews to the Christians.

The problem was that the bishops' gospel, as unsophisticated as its logic was, supported a self-definition of Christianity that was well worth preserving. Even if the bishops had not been great intellectuals, they had succeeded in forming congregations around a set of values that few would want to see destroyed: stable families, social well-being, high moral standards, illustrious heritage, thanksgiving and praise to the God of creation, and the knowledge that all would be well at the end if only they all learned to live together in harmony. It was that concept of Christianity that was seeking a place in the sun. Who would rise to defend it, and what kind of a defense might it be?

JUSTIN MARTYR

Justin Martyr was born in Flavia Neapolis near Shechem in Samaria, and he called himself a Samaritan. But his grandfather Bacchius and father Priscus had Latinized Greek and Roman names, and his family was suspiciously Roman and well-to-do. Justin studied all the major Greek philosophies and assimilated a high level of Hellenistic education before converting to Christianity. His conversion took place by the seashore while walking and talking with a peasant, or so the story goes. He then turned to the books of Moses and the prophets and discovered the source of the ancient wisdom to which the Greeks, it was said, were indebted. This, according to Justin, was the wisdom that finally was fully revealed in the gospel of Jesus Christ. He traveled to Ephesus and then to Rome as a Christian itinerant philosopher, and he never gave up the philosopher's cloak. But in Rome he ran into Marcion and the teachings of Valentinus, and Justin became a theologian. What a scene! With Justin taking the position of an apologist for centrist Christianity, the fireworks began in defense of the Christian gospel. Apologies and polemics were written in response to the challenge that created the genres of Christian theology and literature for the next two hundred years.

The next period of Christian thinking would feature men like Justin, highly educated intellectuals, constructing systems of theological thought against the heresies within, and in debate with the "pagan" intellectuals without. Their horizons would include the Romans, the Greeks, and the Jews, as well as opposing schools of Christian thought. Marcionites, Valentinians, gnostics, Montanists, and Manichaeans would create confusion and draw down wrath as "heresies," only to give way in the fourth and fifth centuries to conflict among the different theologies firmly ensconced in the various centers of episcopate Christianity and to the councils Constantine called to adjudicate their differences. Justin set the pace with a treatise Against Marcion, another *Against All Heresies*, two *Apologies* addressed to the Roman emperor Antoninus Pius (137–161 C.E.), and a *Dialogue with Trypho*, a Jewish intellectual. The makings of yet another genre are also found lurking within his apologies. It was the *Exhortation to the Greeks*, a form of argument for which we have an excellent early example from Clement of Alexandria who wrote toward the end of the second century. This was literature of debate. Argumentation and the organization of treatises followed the rules of classical rhetoric. Theses and countertheses, charges and countercharges, arguments in favor and arguments against shaped the apologies, exhortations, and censures that controlled the process of redefining Christianity as a religion of reason. After Justin came Tatian in Syria, Athenagoras of Athens, Theophilus of Antioch, Melito of Sardis, Dionysius of Corinth, Irenaeus, Hippolytus, Tertullian, Clement of Alexandria, Origen, and others filling the pages of the next one hundred years. The genres stayed the same and the arguments as well. Thus the guns were blazing against all fronts, and the modern historian must sometimes wade through line after line of misfire before discovering the issue at stake and the reasons that really counted.

The claim that was made again and again consisted of the following two propositions: (1) that the Christian God was the creator of the world and the God of Israel's history, and (2) that the Christian way of life was exactly what God had had in mind for all humankind all along. This was exactly what the centrists had to propose to counter the challenges of Marcion and Valentinus. And as one might expect, the theologians of the church found arguments galore to buttress their claims. They found so many, in fact, that they were able to win simply by overwhelming their opponents with words. That at least is the impression one has as a modern reader of this apologetic literature. Their opponents must have conceded from sheer exhaustion, supposing that the opponents they addressed actually read them. Thus, if we take this literature at face value, the apologists were simply trying to save the day for the traditional notion of the Christian God by putting down the heresies and helping the faithful get their theology right. That they went on at such length would then be merely a sign of their eagerness in defense of the gospel.

As we read more closely, however, it is clear that the apologists were having trouble making their case. They were not content just to answer a Marcion or a Valentinus, as if the issue were merely a family matter. It was not just that Marcion and Valentinus had gotten the family history wrong and needed to be set right. They had introduced philosophical considerations about the gospel into Christian discourse. These considerations were like windows and mirrors surrounding the stage on which Christians were now performing. They forced Christians to take note of the way they looked to the rest of the intelligent world. Ouch. The Romans were now in earshot and the Greeks were in plain view, or so the apologists imagined. And so the luster of desire for honor and respect in the eyes of the Greeks and the Romans shimmers on every page. That sensibility marks a new twist in the history of Christian discourse. A new motivation for trying to think clearly began to control the arguments. It was as if a new set of faces was looking over their shoulders as the apologists put their pens to the paper. Their desire to be accepted on the world's own terms should not be considered strange, given the shift in cultural climate that had occurred and given the fact that the church's bright young thinkers had all been to school. For the apologists, the teachings of Marcion and Valentinus were not only wrong because they challenged the centrists' gospel, they were downright embarrassing when compared with respectable views of history and the world.

One of the more important features of the gospel that both Marcion and Valentinus had emphasized was the fact that it offered a *new* way to think about god, human beings, and the world. Until now, novelty had been celebrated as a claim to fresh vision, and as a means of distinguishing Christian congregations from other ways of achieving social identity. Suddenly it became clear that the very notion of Christians being a *novel* "race," children of a brand new god, made known in recent times by means of a messenger from *another* world, flew in the face of every cultural sensibility and philosophical persuasion in the Greco-Roman world. Novelty was not a sign of wisdom in the Greco-Roman world. What people wanted was a wisdom rooted in antiquity and worthy of the illustrious history of their own people and culture.

Another embarrassing feature of the Marcionite and Valentinian definitions of Christianity was the way they contrasted the god revealed in Jesus Christ with the God of the Old Testament. The image of a blind and jealous god as the craftsman who created the world was very unnerving, given the Greek penchant for integrating all their bodies of knowledge into a single system, a universe that hung together and had a place for everything. And the suggestion that Christians were above the law because law was something the jealous god had created, something from which the Christians' god had rescued them, did nothing to help relations with the Romans.

Thus the centrist theologians had to do more than put the heretics down. They had to come up with a system that might be considered a philosophy. In order to be seen as a legitimate philosophy, their theology would have to integrate concepts of god, creation, the universe, humanity, law, and their own cultural and political histories in some respectable conceptual system. That was a big order, and here the challenges of a Marcion and a Valentinus touched the nerve of serious conceptual contradictions at the core of the centrist gospel traditions. That is because the Christian god was not really the God of Israel's story, and Israel's story belonged to the Jews, not the Christians. How could Christians reasonably claim that the God of the story had really had Christians in mind all along? The Christ myth had dared such thoughts, and the subsequent Christian mythologies such as those of the synoptic gospels, Luke's Acts of the Apostles, 1 Clement, Ignatius, and the Didache had simply assumed that the myth's own logic was enough. But now a reasoned account was required, and the myth's assumptions would have to be argued on the basis of philosophical considerations. It would have to be argued that a non-Jewish people had Jewish roots, and that the Jewish scriptures told the story of the Christians' God. It was a very great challenge for a novel religion to claim antiquity and anchor its Christ myth in a philosophical system of creation, law, and illustrious epic.

The works of Justin Martyr can be used to illustrate and assess the centrists' response. His message to the Romans was that Christians as a people and Christianity as a religion were good for the society and its governance. The Romans were wrong to think that Christians were disloyal, atheists, or a new aberrant secret society practicing obscene rituals. When anyone brought a charge against a Christian, he advised, the Romans should ask for evidence that the Christian had actually broken some law. If so, let judicial proceedings begin. But just being a Christian was not a crime. And as for the charge of disloyalty, Christians did give allegiance to another lord and live by the laws of another "kingdom." But the Christians' kingdom was not of this world. It was the kingdom of God, the God who required of his subjects morals higher than any of the other gods demanded, and these morals were better for the Roman order than the ethics of any other peoples of the empire. Christians working for peace and creating good citizens were the best helpers the Romans had. Christians could instill fear in the hearts of ungodly people by convincing them of the final judgment of a righteous God. And the Romans could test that out if they would by comparing the teachings of Christ with the ethical instructions of any other teacher, philosopher, or god. They could compare what Christians said about the virtues of the Christ with the myths of all the other gods and heroes. And not to worry about the fact that the Christian religion was new, for the texts of the prophets of Israel, visionaries inspired by the spirit of God, and predating the poets and philosophers of the Greeks, had predicted everything about the Christ. These oracles and predictions should not surprise you, he said, for you also have your Sibyl. And the prophets of Israel even predicted what Rome would do when the Jews rejected the Christ: destroy Jerusalem and occupy the land. Thus you are in our picture. Would that you could see that our God is on your side. We'd be surprisingly good for you.

The line of argument for Greek ears ran a bit differently. The imagined threat from the Greeks was ridicule, not unfair trial and persecution. How foolish the talk of Christians must have sounded when compared with the classical schools of philosophy. One problem was that the teachings of Jesus were meager and, to tell the truth, disorganized and quite unclear. Another was that what Christians said about him was difficult to classify. Was he a teacher, a hero, or a god? And if a new god, or the son of a new god, how was he recognized and why did he take so long to appear? Surely these Christians could not be serious about a martyred god, a bodily resurrection, a new world order, and the generation of a new human race that belonged to another world. But of course the Christians were quite serious, and the apologists went to work to prove to the Greeks that it all made sense even on the Greeks' own terms.

The first volley was mainly strategic. Look at us and our high moral standards, Justin Martyr said, and look at your own orgies and drunken festivals. Something must be wrong with your own gods and goddesses. Look at them: proud, envious, licentious, and deceitful. Surely your philosophers did not learn about virtue from them. Do you know where your own philosophers got their wisdom? From Moses, that's where. It was while reading Moses that they discovered the wisdom (*sophia*) and reason (*logos*) of God that created the world and continue to empower and hold it together. And one of them, Socrates, was even willing to die for that truth. But what Greek was ever willing to die for Socrates? Now think of Jesus. He not only knew the thinking (*logos*) of God as philosophers know it, he knew it as God's son or personal self-expression (*logos*). And he revealed his Father's wisdom and thinking by the way he lived, as the very incarnation of the Father's message (*logos*) to us. And see how many Christians there are who are ready and willing to die for him. Now *that* is wisdom fit for both a philosopher and a theologian.

The apologists had found their touchstone, a philosophic concept capable of turning the Christian myth into a rational account of the world. It was the concept of the *logos*, a term that meant thought, reason, logic, and speech (in the sense of making a meaningful statement). The traditional English translation is "word," but that is hardly adequate. *Logos* did not refer to *a* word; for that the Greeks had another term (*rhema*). *Logos* referred to the thought that gave words their meaning by coming to expression in sentences, speeches, stories, myths, and histories. And just as had happened with other basic concepts of human and divine attribution, such as wisdom (*sophia*), spirit (*pneuma*), virtue (*arete*), power (*dynamis*), fate (*heimarmene*), and justice (*dike*), *logos* had already been personified and storied by intellectuals in other traditions. They had done that in the process of turning their own myths into coded allegories of philosophical wisdom. Cornutus, for instance, a first-century C.E. Stoic philosopher and teacher at Rome, submitted Greek mythology to alle-, gorical interpretation and explained that Hermes, the Greek messenger god, was a mythological metaphor for *logos*. That gave a bit of philosophical respectability to the myths about Hermes, but it also meant that the myths of Hermes now belonged to the *logos* as well. They would come to mind, that is, whenever *logos* was mentioned. Thus the *logos*, now both a concept and a mythological figure, could be storied as the messenger of the gods racing through the universe or popping up at the crossroads of the human quest for wisdom as a guide sent by the gods.

Philo of Alexandria actually preferred the figure of the *logos* and its mythology to that of wisdom in his allegorical commentaries on the five books of Moses. Using the figure of the *logos*, he was able to turn the stories of creation, the lives of the patriarchs, Moses and the law, and the high priest's robes and liturgy in the temple into allegories of the divine reason and power inherent in the grand cosmic process of bringing humans to the knowledge of God (Mack 1973). According to Philo, the *logos* was God's son, a second god, through whom the world was created as a rational and ordered universe. Born of mother wisdom and appearing in the world, the *logos* was the agent through whom the great leaders of Israel learned what God expected of them. It would not be wrong, according to Philo, to think of Moses, as well as the high priest and all the oracles and epiphanies of the divine recorded in the five books of Moses, as incarnations of the *logos* of God. Thus the figure of the *logos* was available when Christian thinkers had to construct a theology, challenged as they were to say how any thinking person could possibly believe in their myths. The concept of the *logos* was loaded in just the right ways. It never lost its basic meaning as the thought that turned words into reasonable speech, but in the course of philosophical and allegorical speculation it had taken on two additional connotations. *Logos* could now be used as one of the terms, along with spirit (*pneuma*) and mind (*nous*), for the glue, the spiritual "substance" that permeated the universe and held it together as a single system. It could also be imagined as the presence of the divine within the universe, a second god who "expressed" the thinking of the creator god and so was charged with the "instruction" of the human race. What a concept. Divine reason could now take the form of a cosmic god who appeared to humans in order to instruct them in the way in which they should think about the creator god.

Before Justin, the author of the Gospel of John had already used the figure of the *logos* to advantage in his opening poem. The divine *logos* had been seeking recognition since the creation of the world and finally "became flesh" in Jesus, God's son. Valentinus also had used the concept of the *logos* to imagine Jesus as the manifestation of a divine and cosmic entity, but just as one among many other personifications, such as God's "name," "emission," "anointing," or "repose." Whether Justin learned to apply the concept of the *logos* to the Christian myth from John's gospel, Valentinus, or some other school tradition is not clear. But Justin did make the critical move. He retrieved the *logos* from the realm of gnostic imagination where psychological symbols, such as "desire," kept mating with other psychological symbols, such as "error," to produce yet other psychological symbols, such as "blind ignorance," in the great family romance of the powers of God in the transcendent world of pure Platonic thought. Instead, Justin used the *logos* as a tracer for the rhyme and reason of the created universe and the rational capacity given to all human creatures to perceive it. Naturally for Justin, the *logos* had "spoken" most clearly in the divine instructions to the Israelites and had finally been revealed to Christians in the person of Jesus, God's son. But others, such as Socrates, who had come to the knowledge of the truth about God because of the *logos*, were also "Christians" even if they had not heard about Jesus. As Justin said, "[Christ] is the *logos* of whom every race of men were partakers, and those who live with *logos* are Christians, even though they have been thought atheists, as, among the Greeks, Socrates and Heraclitus, and men like them" (*Apology* 1:46; italics mine). Some *logos*! We need to hear more about it. As Justin wrote in his second *Apology*:

> When I learned of the evil camouflage which the wicked demons had thrown around the divine doctrines of the Christians to deter others from following them, I had to laugh at the authors of these lies, at the camouflage itself, and at the popular reaction. I am proud to say that I strove with all my might to be known as a Christian, not because the teachings of Plato are different from those of Christ, but because they are not in every way similar; neither are those of other writers, the Stoics, the poets, and the historians. For each one of them, seeing, through his participation of the seminal Divine Word [*logos*], what was related to it, spoke very well. But, they who contradict themselves in important matters evidently did not acquire the unseen wisdom and the indisputable knowledge. The truths which men in all lands have rightly spoken belong to us Christians. For we worship and love, after God the Father, the Word [*logos*] who is from the Unbegotten and Ineffable God, since He even became Man for us, so that by sharing in our sufferings He also might heal us. Indeed, all writers, by means of the engrafted seed of the Word [*logos*] which was implanted in them, had a dim glimpse of the truth. For the seed of something and its imitation, given in proportion to one's capacity, is one thing, but the thing itself, which is shared and imitated according to His grace, is quite another. (*Apology* 2:13)

Justin was the first, as far as we can tell, to coin the term *logos spermatikos*, "seed-like, spermlike reasoning." This was an extremely clever move, combining as it did the gnostic metaphor of divine "emissions" with the Hellenistic metaphor of "sowing seeds," both forms of production commonly used to refer to education (*paideia*, meaning both instruction and enculturation). In the Hellenistic tradition of education, *sowing seed* was understood as a metaphor taken from agriculture. In the tradition of gnostic thought, however, *sowing seed* was a metaphor implying sexual union and conception. Valentinus and the gnostics were fascinated with this metaphor, preferring *generation* over *craft* when imagining the creation of the world, and thinking of salvation as personal insight (*gnosis*) rather than in terms of forgiveness, vindication, social placement in the kingdom of God, or other ways of relating to God, such as honoring, imitating, or trusting. And generation did seem more appropriate than craftsmanship or manipulation as a metaphor for God the "father," preparing the way as it did for personal "acquaintance" (*gnosis*) with him as the primary term for salvation. But *craft* could still be used in relation to texts, social history, and discourse without negative connotation. *Craft* was the preferred term for rhetorical education and skill or "working with words," as the scholars said. What Justin achieved by coining the term *seedlike reason* was therefore a masterful tour de force. That was because the term *sperma* was commonly used for both kinds of seed. He was therefore able to cool the gnostic passion for sexual metaphors without entirely giving up the connotation of generation, even while taking the *logos* back as the rational principle of both the created order and the human mind.

This conceptual achievement made possible the next round of Christian intellectual activity. Clement of Alexandria and Origen would soon produce comprehensive systems of theology rooted in the concept of the *logos*. The *logos* was God's self-expression before the creation, at the creation, within the creation, in human beings as created in the image of God, in human history as the divine instructor inviting humans to the knowledge of God, in the oracles of God recorded in the Jewish scriptures, and especially in Christ, the fully human manifestation of God's message to humans. And even though the *logos* theology of the Alexandrian school would have to compete with other, more prosaic attempts to articulate the Christian faith, such as those of Tertullian the Roman lawyer and a later school of "literal" exegetes centered in Antioch, it is difficult to imagine the subsequent history of Christian thought, both in its Western and in its Eastern mutations, apart from its indebtedness to *logos* theology. The concept of the *logos* stayed in place as the philosophical foundation for Christian thinkers for the next several centuries. It was basic to the debates about the two natures of Christ, the doctrine of the triune God, and the way the Jewish scriptures became the "word" of God. It was the concept of the *logos* that made it possible to merge the notions of being, person, power, and text in a singular configuration and so account for both creation and redemption in a unified system of thought. The concept of the *logos* made it possible to position Jesus at the point where two great traditions of thought met and merged to form the religion we call Christianity.

Justin's apologies addressed to the Romans are quite conciliatory. His address to the Greeks is marked by reasoning and debate, with just a touch of censure. When we turn to his *Dialogue with Trypho*, however, the volume goes up and the rhetorical tone becomes disparaging. It is the same with all the other literature addressed to the Jews by other apologists, such as Tertullian's treatise entitled *Adversus Iudaios* ("Against the Jews"). This type of literature is obviously not authentic address. No

Jew worth his intellectual salt would have listened long to the "reasoning" these writings contain. Justin's *Dialogue with Trypho* barely keeps faith with the Greek genre it mimics. Trypho the Jew is an implausible fictional character serving as a straight man for Justin's preachments, chastisements, and tirades against the Jews. This treatise may be what Justin would have liked to say to "the Jews," had they stood still long enough, but he was actually talking to himself, and only other Christians overheard what he said. The soliloquy flows on and on without stopping long enough for Trypho to say more than an occasional, "I see, please go on." Why the heightened tone of censure and contention? It points to a cultural issue that had not been resolved. It reveals the consternation created by Marcion's challenge. It tells us that Christians were having difficulty coming to terms with their Jewish heritage. So the weaker the argument, the louder the voice. We will have to take a look at these arguments "against the Jews," boring and disgusting as most of them are, for unless we hear them we will not be able to understand the last chapter in our story about the Bible's formation. It may help just a bit to remember that the dialogue Justin was having with the imaginary Trypho and the arguments Tertullian was bringing against "the Jews" were really the terms of a heated and vociferous debate going on within themselves.

The embarrassment for centrist thinkers who had heard Marcion's challenge was that the Christian God was also the God of the Jews. He had chosen their patriarchs, rescued Israel from Egyptian bondage, raised up Moses to lead the people back to their land, revealed to them his law, chosen their kings, sent them prophets, chastised them in Babylon, anointed Cyrus to send them back, commissioned the temple in Jerusalem, and established the priestly liturgy so the Jews could celebrate his presence in the "house" where he would dwell. If the Christians no longer had anything to do with the Jews, their synagogues, or their laws, what did Christians have to do with their God, their history, and their scriptures? Had God changed his mind about the law? About his people? About the world he created for them? The need to settle such questions finally came to focus on the Jewish scriptures. The scriptures were documentation of that history, and Christians already had them in their possession. The argument would be that the Jewish scriptures could be read in support of the Christians' claim that they were being faithful to the God of Israel's story.

Thus Justin's *Dialogue with Trypho* is packed with "proofs" from scripture. There are lengthy citations, detailed arguments for this or that interpretation, as well as constant references to "what the scriptures say" in the midst of discussions on any and every topic. At first it seems that arguing about the meaning of the Jewish scriptures is called for just because Justin is in debate with a Jew. But the interpretation of the Jewish scriptures is where Justin's arguments come to rest in his treatises addressed to the Romans as well. And then one notices that the debates with the Greeks and the heretics also turn on the "proofs" from and about scripture. As a matter of fact, taking a second look at the apologetic literature of this period as a whole, one finds that an obsession with the Jewish scriptures marks all of them. The

Jewish scriptures are not being taken for granted as in earlier Christian writings where they were accepted as simply given, the property of Jews and Christians alike, open for debate perhaps, but not up for grabs. The apologists, in contrast, pored over the books of Moses in desperation and studied the prophets, the Psalms, and other writings in panic, not delight. They were looking for clues to some design other than the obvious. And like a dragon guarding a treasure, the same embarrassing question constantly rumbles just beneath the surface no matter what the topic for discussion might be. It was the question of how the history of Israel could possibly be read as the story of the Christians' God and thus count as the Christian epic, not the epic of Israel that obviously pointed toward the establishment of a Jewish theocracy in Jerusalem. This was a disturbing question because it required the absolute appropriation of a story that was not really theirs.

The "proofs" from scripture or, as Irenaeus would put it, *Proofs of the Apostolic Preaching*, fell into four classes or four ways of reading the scriptures in support of the Christian claim. There was (1) the proof from prophecy, (2) the *logos* allegory, (3) a theodicy, or vindication of the character of God, and (4) a revision of Jewish history. Each was important. All were necessary. Together they laid the foundation for the only reason Christians have ever had for including the Jewish scriptures in their Bible.

The apologists started with the proof from prophecy. The main argument had its roots deep within the gospel story, for prophetic prediction was fundamental to the logic of Mark's story and consciously elaborated as a theme in the Gospel of Matthew. The argument was that the prophets had predicted the coming of the messiah and that what happened when Jesus appeared "fulfilled" what the prophets had predicted. As Matthew put it, "This event happened to fulfill what the prophets said." The point of this kind of argument was simple and obvious. It supported the Christian claim that Jesus really was God's anointed, the one who had been "predicted" by the prophets to restore justice for God's people. As we have seen, several "messiah" mythologies were devised along this line during the earlier period of Christian mythmaking, although they were certainly not the only mythologies Christians constructed in order to understand themselves as people who belonged to God's kingdom. The apologists picked up the prophecy argument, not because they still needed to make a case for Jesus, but because that was the one argument embedded in the gospel that had its anchor firmly in the scriptures. The case for Jesus had been settled long ago, and far more important roles for Jesus than the messiah were now abuzz. He was, for instance, the son of God, a gnostic savior, *logos* of God, and so forth. What interested the apologists about the argument from prophecy was not so much what it said about Jesus as what it said about the prophets. How much did the prophets know, they wondered, how could they have known it, and why did the prophets write a prediction about Jesus into their preachments against the Jews?

Further research showed that *everything* about Jesus had been prophesied by the prophets, down to the smallest details: his birth, hometown, miracles, preaching, entry into Jerusalem, including the donkey on which he rode, rejection by the Jews, crucifixion by the Romans, resurrection, his offering salvation by "the blood of the grape" (*Apology* 1:32; Gen. 49:10), ascension into heaven, and acceptance by the gentiles. The prophets had not just predicted the coming of "a" messiah, or even of "the" messiah; they predicted Jesus! How could that be? The modern scholar's answer is that, if one is interested in making a comparison, the human imagination is capable of building a huge inventory of complex allegories on the basis of the smallest suggestion of similarity. Justin's answer was that only God could have known such details, and that it was "the spirit of prophecy" from God who had inspired all the predictions. It was the spirit of prophecy, not necessarily the prophets, who knew exactly all the things that would take place "as if they had already taken place" (*Apology* 1:42). And, since he had found some prophecies in the Psalms and in the books of Moses as well as in the books of the prophets, he concluded that the spirit of prophecy had spoken through Moses and David as well as the prophets. The happy result was that the Jewish scriptures as a whole could now be read as an allegory of the gospel story, encoded in advance by inspiration of the spirit of God.

To turn the argument from prophecy into a redefinition of the Jewish scriptures, now to be understood as an allegory of the gospel in advance of the gospel, something like the concept of the "spirit of prophecy" was needed. That is because the clues to the "hidden meaning" of the text were scattered, fragmentary, and enigmatic. There was no single story or story line in the Jewish scriptures that one could follow and decode as an allegory of the real story (of Jesus) behind the story (of Israel). The predictions were hiding here and there amidst a voluminous literature. The Christian exegete had to find them, match them up to details of the gospel story, and argue for reading them as a prediction of Jesus instead of belonging to the stories of Israel. And since they were predictions, their hidden "meanings" were references to a story not yet told, a story that only the "spirit of prophecy" could possibly have known about. Thus the predictions had lain dormant (in the scriptures!) until Jesus came along and his followers discovered that the predictions had been made. Like Alice in Wonderland, the modern reader will find this line of reasoning curiouser and curiouser, for the prediction finally does not predict at all. But Justin was caught in a vicious hermeneutical circle, and he could find no way to spin out. That is because the prophet-fulfillment link was the only "proof" he had.

Not to be stymied, Justin forged ahead instead of beating a retreat. His "spirit of prophecy" was only the point of departure for an even more fantastic search. This time he would look for the real speaker behind the purported speakers in all the places where a phrase rang gospel bells and an oracle might be suspected. Justin found the speaker in the concept of the *logos*, the "word" of God that took on many manifestations on the way to full incarnation in the person of Jesus. As he said:

> But when you hear the utterances of the prophets spoken as it were person-
> ally, you must not suppose that they are spoken by the inspired [prophets]
> themselves, but by the divine Word [*logos*] who moves them. For sometimes

he declares things that are to come to pass, in the manner of one who foretells the future; sometimes he speaks as from the person of God the Lord and Father of all; sometimes as from the person of Christ; sometimes as from the person of the people answering the Lord or his Father. . . . And this the Jews who possessed the books of the prophets did not understand, and therefore did not recognize Christ even when he came, but even hate us who say that he has come, and who prove that, as was predicted, he was crucified by them. (*Apology* 1:36)

With such a *logos* allegory in place, there was no end to the "proof" that the Jewish scriptures were *really* about the Christian gospel. To take but one example from among the myriad citations adduced by Justin, he argued at length that the voice from the burning bush to Moses, saying, "I am that I am, the God of Abraham, the God of Isaac, the God of Jacob, the God of thy fathers. Go down into Egypt, and bring forth my people," was in reality the voice of the son of God, the "first begotten *logos* of God" (*Apology* 1:63). He knew, of course, that the Jews took this saying to have been spoken by God himself, so he countered with a verse from Isaiah: "Israel does not know me, my people have not understood me" (Isaiah 1:3). This, Justin argued, showed that the Jews did not know their own God and thus could not read their own scriptures. This, he thought, confirmed the claim he had made that it was the *logos* who had spoken in the bush.

We can now add another application to the multifaceted concept of the *logos* that worked in Justin's favor. It is that the concept could be applied, not only to the Christian understandings of God, creation, and the Christ, but to the Jewish scriptures as well. The words of the scriptures could now be read as the words of God's *logos*, the encoded message or "Word of God" to his people. And since Christians were the only ones who had cracked the code, the Jewish scriptures were turned into the Christians' Word of God.

Marcion's challenge could now be answered: God did not change his mind. He had always spoken to the Jews, had tried to instruct them, and had sent forth his *logos* to them, but they had refused to listen. So God was not the problem; the people were the problem. They had forced God's hand to legislate the law, bring chastisements upon them, and finally to destroy their religion in order to redeem them. Unfortunately, they were too intransigent even for God. This refrain courses through all of the apologetic literature, not just the writings addressed to the Jews. The Jews were a disobedient people, hard of heart and stiff-necked. From a late twentieth-century point of view, it is a nauseating refrain that is best overlooked when reading the apologists. But the refrain was absolutely critical as an argument in the Christians' quest to vindicate the God of Israel from Marcion's slander. They were saying that God was not fickle, not unjust, not merely interested in slavish obedience. He was not a God of wrath who delighted only in judgment. It was, instead, the people who were wrong, so wrong that God had to treat them as they deserved, on a level they could understand. He gave them the law, for instance, to keep their sins in check. Thus the law was a temporary measure on God's part, not intended for all time. It was, as the apologists said, a "dispensation" meant only for the Jews. The law was a "covenant" that was meant to pass as soon as the Jews came to their senses and recognized the *logos*. As one might expect, the apologists turned again and again to the prophets for support, finding there the critique of the people demanded by their argument. The verse from Isaiah 1:3, just quoted in a previous paragraph, to the effect that "my people do not know me," Justin explained in another place as a word spoken personally by God "through Isaiah the prophet." He then cited more of the verse. It continues: "Woe, sinful nation, a people full of sins, a wicked seed, children that are transgressors, you have forsaken the Lord" (*Apology* 1:37). Critical oracles were easily found as well "from the person of Christ," such as "I have spread out my hands to a disobedient and gainsaying people, to those who walk in a way that is not good" (Isa. 45:2; *Apology* 1:38). The Christians had found their theodicy, an argument against Marcion and for the Christian claim that the God who revealed himself in Jesus Christ was the same as the God of creation and of the history of Israel. This vindication of the Christian character of Israel's God was achieved at the expense of the Jews (Efroymson 1979).

The fourth "proof of the apostolic preaching" could now be rendered. It was that the history of Israel did not and could not have ended with the Jews; but only with the Christians as its rightful heirs. The argument builds on the proofs from prophecy that predict the rejection of Christ by the Jews, their role in the crucifixion of Jesus by the Romans, the destruction of the temple, the desolation of the land, the foreign (Roman) occupation, and the expulsion of the Jews from Jerusalem by the Romans after the Bar Kochba revolt in 135 C.E. One might well wonder at this. The range of "historical" details thought to have been predicted by the prophets shows that the logic of Mark's gospel had been understood and the history of divine recompense had been extended past the destruction of the temple and into Justin's own time. One would have thought that a rehearsal of the temple's destruction would have been enough to free the epic of Israel from the end of Jewish history and let it feed into the Christian church. Not so. The point had to be made repeatedly that the Jews contemporary with the Christian apologists had been rejected by their God. Only so would the separation of the church from the synagogue be complete and the scriptures safely in the hands of the Christians. Thus, not content to leave the argument at the level of prophecy, a self-destructive and self-fulfilling principle discovered within the scriptures themselves, the apologists went on to describe the sorry state of contemporary Jews as further evidence of divine displeasure. Had not Christ himself castigated them? Were not the calamities that had befallen them deserved? Were they not now homeless wanderers, despised by the gentiles? As Justin explained to Trypho:

> Circumcision according to the flesh, which is from Abraham, was given for a
> sign; that you may be separated from other nations, and from us; and that you
> alone may suffer that which you now justly suffer; and that your land may be

desolate, and your cities burned with fire; and that strangers may eat your fruit in your presence, and not one of you may go up to Jerusalem. For you are not recognised among the rest of man by any other mark than your fleshly circumcision. For none of you, I suppose, will venture to say that God neither did nor does foresee the events which are future, nor foreordained his deserts for each one. Accordingly, these things have happened to you in fairness and justice, for you have slain the Just One, and his prophets before him; and now you reject those who hope in him and in him who sent him—God the Almighty and Maker of all things—cursing in your synagogues those that believe on Christ. (*Dialogue* 16)

But enough. What about finding clues in the epic to trace the Christian people as a "race" back to the beginnings of God's creation? Did not God have Christians in mind all along? Justin apparently had not thought it necessary to address this question. It was easier to rehearse the negative history of the Jews since the advent of Christ than it was to project the Christian church back into the history prior to Christ. But others would ask the question, and the gnostic approach was to suggest that the *idea* of the church had been structured into the order of creation since the beginning. The "church," for instance, was one of the "powers" generated in the spiritual "entirety," according to Valentinus. The gnostic approach was too far-fetched for centrist Christians, but what were they to think? Clear answers were not forthcoming, but a remarkable passage from Clement of Alexandria illustrates the desire to try. Clement had the benefit of Justin's *logos* theology and wanted to mediate between a gnostic and a centrist view of Christianity. In his *Exhortation to the Greeks*, Clement begins by telling them that the "new song" sung by the Christians, his metaphor for the gospel as a poetic philosophy, was not really new. It was as old as creation. It was the song of the *logos* of God. Then, stretching the notion of the *logos* to include Christians as the singers of the "new song," Christians become a sort of *logos* themselves, God's messengers to the Greco-Roman world. He dares the following image:

But we were before the foundation of the world, we who, because we were destined to be in him, were begotten beforehand by God. We are the rational images formed by God's *logos*, or reason, and we date from the beginning on account of our connection with him, because 'the *logos* was in the beginning' [John 1:1]. Well, because the *logos* was from the first, He was and is the divine beginning of all things; but because he lately took a name, —the name consecrated of old and worthy of power, the Christ,—I have called him a new song. (*Exhortation* 1)

Clement's "new song" rises above the hard-hitting, polemical rhetoric of a Justin or a Tertullian, two theologians who had to work very hard to argue for the Jewish scriptures and the epic of Israel as the rightful property of the Christians. With that battle won, a more constructive approach could be taken, even if a more fanciful one. To stick with Clement's metaphor, the gentler approach to the Jewish scriptures was one of tracing the new song and its singers from the beginning to the end of the story. As Clement put it, rehearsing the story of the exodus, "He exhorted the hard-hearted; but afterwards, through all-wise Moses and truth-loving Isaiah and the whole company of the prophets, He converts to the *logos* by more rational means those who have ears to hear" (*Exhortation* 1). So there always had been a remnant who heard the *logos* song, the most gracious reading of the Israel epic since the first letter of Clement of Rome. This new reading countered the constant search for prophetic oracles and later allowed Origen to find the song on every page of the Jewish scriptures. And yet, we should not be overly impressed by the graciousness of a Clement or an Origen. The song of the *logos* was, after all, a Christ hymn, not a Jewish psalm of praise. We are thus very close to the end of our story, for the song of the *logos* was the only foundation ever laid for justifying the treatment of the Jewish scriptures as Christian epic. We need only to explain how the "New Testament" collection of writings was joined to the "Old Testament" scriptures to form the Christian Bible.

11

CREATING THE
CHRISTIAN BIBLE

The Christian myth is an unfinished epic. The story begins at the creation of the world, spans human history, and ends in an apocalyptic destruction of the world. History pivots when Christ appears as the revealer of God's plan for humans, the world, and the kingdom that God has destined to replace the kingdoms of the world. Those who live according to the plan are promised eternal life, the survival of the cataclysm at the end of the world. Those who do not accept the plan will be destroyed. The myth is based on the Christian Bible, a collection of texts that begins with Genesis and ends with the Apocalypse to John. The texts that recount the history before the appearance of Christ are known as the Old Testament. Those that tell of the coming of the Christ are known as the New Testament. The Old Testament is composed of archaic Jewish scriptures in a certain arrangement. The New Testament consists mainly of first- and second-century apostolic gospels and letters, but it also includes the Acts of the Apostles, a first chapter of Christian history, and the Apocalypse to John, a vision of the grand finale. Between the apostolic acts and the apocalyptic ending, there is room for adding other chapters to the history of Christendom and/or the church.

Filling in the chapters of Christian history subsequent to the Acts of the Apostles has been done, not by adding written accounts to the Bible, but by keeping track of the heroes of the faith in other ways: marking the succession of the bishops and popes, memorializing the lives of saints, princes, and protectors of Christendom, and writing the histories of the missions of the church. Symmetry is achieved by balancing scenes from the Old Testament with scenes from the New Testament and the subsequent history of Christianity. Thus one finds on the portals of the medieval cathedrals the even balance of the Old Testament precursors on one side of the Christ and on the other the apostles, popes, and princes of subsequent Christian history. The Christ is pictured in the archway at the top both as an *axis mundi* and as the hinge of history. It is the Christian myth in pictures. It is the Christian epic brought up to date but without ending the story. Whether as apocalypse, purgatory, or the parting of the ways to heaven or hell, the ending of the Christian epic is always outstanding. Thus other chapters of the church in the world can be added. And even as the spread of Christianity elongates and complicates the monolinear thrust of the epic, balance is achieved by compressing the memory of Christian history to balance the new with the old. A newly Christianized people keep alive the memories of their missionaries and a bit of their own subsequent history, and then leapfrog over the long reaches of the two-thousand-year history of the church in order to hook up with the New Testament and take their guidance from the Bible.

All Christian communities make a place for the Bible. The Bible may, in fact, be the only feature of the Christian religion that all Christians have in common. Without the Bible the Christian myth would evaporate. A Christian community would not know how to orient itself to the world, and the thrust of the Christian imagination toward that grand finale would lose its energy and sense of direction. Without the epic framework provided by the Bible, all the other myths, rituals, and notions of salvation that have become traditional to the Christian religions would disintegrate or mutate into different cults or cultures.

While all Christians recognize the importance of the Bible, few speak of its significance as epic. It is thought to be inspired, called the Word of God, regularly read in the course of Christian ritual, appealed to for grounding the doctrines of salvation, and consulted as a guide to Christian faith and life. Beneath all of these ways in which the Bible is regarded, however, lies the fundamental reason for the Bible's importance. It is the story of God's purposes for humankind. The Bible is where the Christian notions of God and history are intertwined, the paradigms of salvation are set, the thrust toward the future is generated, and the charter for Christianity to expand throughout the world is given. No wonder the Bible is viewed as a sacred text by Christians. The Bible is the Christian myth. The Christian myth is the Bible. No wonder theologians refer to the Bible as the canon (from the Greek *kanon*, "measuring rod"), a complete and closed book of sacred scripture, a book to be consulted, but not to be explained. The fact that the Bible is the Christian myth has made it difficult to be critical and analytical about its composition. The fact that it is thought of as the Christian canon has made research about its formation extremely difficult to pursue.

Even theologians know that the Bible did not fall from heaven, of course, and that the history of its production spans more than one thousand years. That knowledge has made it necessary for scholars to give an account of its formation, and one would think that the notion of the Bible as canon would pop up at the end of this history. Oddly, however, the usual scholarly approach to the study of the formation of the Christian Bible *starts* with the concept of canon and tries to account for the history on its terms. Canon means "norm" or "standard," as in canon law or the canons of musical composition. Applied to the Bible, canon refers to the precise collection of texts found in the Bible as the only ones regarded by the Christian church

as "sacred," "normative," or authoritative for Christian ritual, reading, and instruction. Canon means "closed," "exclusive," "inspired," and "revealed" as "Word of
God." Because this concept has been so deeply etched in the Christian imagination,
Christian scholars have gone about their research on the formation of the Bible as if
it were a process of coming to see which books *belonged* to the canon. They have assumed that authors, intellectuals, and in fact all Jews and Christians of the Greco-
Roman period had in mind the concept of a biblical canon before there was a Bible.
That being the case, the task for scholars has been to trace the history of the "recognition" of the canon, those moments when Jews or Christians realized which books
were "in" the canon and which books were to be "excluded" from the canon. Naturally, as one reads the large literary production of about one thousand years, one can
find many references to "the writings"; to sets of writings, such as the five books of
Moses; to classifications of writings, such as "the law and the prophets"; to lists of
"their writings" or "our writings"; to certain writings as "holy"; to translations as
"inspired," such as an early Greek translation of the five books of Moses; to "disputed" writings, such as those attributed to apostolic authorship that were judged to
be pseudonymous. What one does not find is a concept of canon or any reference to
a closed canon of sacred scripture. Not to be stymied, biblical scholars sort through
the references just mentioned looking for the dates when this or that part of the
scriptural canon was set, "recognized," or "closed." It is as if the idea of the Bible
were in everyone's mind as a number of blank spaces that needed to be filled in with
the books of the Bible. A blank space would be filled in whenever someone recognized that a writing was "inspired" and so "belonged" in the Bible.

The creation of the Christian Bible is much more interesting and messier than
that. It is the story of fiercely fought cultural conquest. Age-old patterns of practice
and thought were twisted out of shape by an upstart religion within the space of
about two hundred years. Some cultural remnants were consigned to the archaic
past, others to oblivion, and others to the devil as the residue of pagan religions that
continued to haunt the new world order. The story of cultural conquest starts around
the middle of the second century. By the end of the fourth it was all over. Books had
been banned and burned, temples destroyed, martyrs killed, and pagan festivals exposed as licentious. The Roman imperium and system of governance were ex-
hausted. Greek learning and culture had been usurped by Christian theologians as a
mere "preparation for the gospel" (Eusebius). An enormous outpouring of intellectual energy had been invested in coming to terms with diverse cultural traditions and
in fighting over programs, philosophies, theologies, and practices in the interest of
this or that conception of God's big plans for the world. Scholars in all traditions, not
just Christian, but Jewish, Greek, Roman, Egyptian, and all the cultures that found
themselves in the cauldron of the Greco-Roman age, had devoted entire lives to the
conservation and accommodation of cultures. They had been thoroughly engaged in
learning foreign languages, translating texts, comparing cultures, creating concepts,
and arguing over the proprietary rights of huge, fantastic, imaginary worlds. And the

epic of Israel, the only epic from the ancient Near East that survived the pummeling of the earlier triumph of Hellenism, an epic tenaciously contested during the Roman period by every group with roots in Jewish culture, had been manipulated by Christians to their advantage and thoroughly revised by the Jews for theirs. Constantine had seen the light. Councils of bishops had been convened. Creeds, calendars, and rituals had been regularized. And the building of Christian basilicas had begun. The last tragic irony in the Christian appropriation of the Jewish heritage was the construction of the Church of the Holy Sepulchre in Jerusalem and the dawn of Christian pilgrimage to the Holy Land. It was then that the Latin translation of two collections of texts, the "Old" and the "New Testaments," established the book that would shape the mythic imagination of Christendom for the next one thousand years. Only then can we speak of "The (Christian) Bible."

The Jewish scriptures available to early Christians consisted of "the law," "the prophets," and "other writings that followed them," which is the way Ben Sira's grandson referred to Jewish literature as a whole about 130 B.C.E. (Sirach, Prologue). These writings did not constitute a closed canon of sacred literature, even though everyone knew that "the law" referred to the five books of Moses and that "the prophets" referred to a class of oracular writings in various collections from the history of Israel before and after the exile. As for "the other writings," it did not refer to a particular kind or class of writings, much less a closed collection. It was a term that referred to "our literature," including such books as Psalms and Proverbs, and the stories of Ruth and Esther. This literature had its place in the life of the Jewish community, serving as handbooks for prayers, lessons for instruction, and stories for festival occasions. Some of this literature was considered ancestral, as in the case of the Psalms of David, but that did not mean that psalms were no longer being written and added to the collection. The evidence from Qumran and the various translations of the Psalms into Greek tell us that they were. And Ben Sira's book of wisdom was written, dated, and signed without embarrassment as an addition to instructional literature on a par with "the other books of our ancestors." So what was the importance of the Jewish scriptures that excited early Christians and created such raging debates between Christians and Jews?

The common core of the Jewish scriptures was the five books of Moses. These books told the story of how Israel came to be. They also contained the charters, laws, and preachments for the kind of society that God expected of Israel. This combination of epic history and legal constitution governed the composition and logic of this literature from its earliest formation during the kingdoms of David and Solomon, and persisted through at least two subsequent revisions. The earliest form of the story is still debated by scholars, but the suspicion has been that, before the additions of the books of Deuteronomy and Leviticus and the major revisions of the patriarchal history that accompanied those additions, the story continued unbroken through the taking of the land to end with the court histories of David. This history was saved in the books of Joshua, Judges, Samuel, and Kings. If one adds them to the five books of Moses, one can certainly imagine an epic that served as an etiology for the Davidic monarchy and celebrated its glory.

From the time of the Davidic monarchy until the end of the second temple, this epic of Israel was revised again and again without changing its essential objective: the establishment of a temple-state in Jerusalem. Of course revisions were necessary in order to account for the changes in Jerusalem that history introduced: destructions, exiles, restorations, failures, shifts in party politics, and so forth. At first the revisions called for were achieved by rewriting the text, once by the deuteronomistic historian, later by the scribes of a priestly school. The deuteronomistic historian added the book of Deuteronomy and broke the link between the wilderness journey and the entrance into the land (Sanders 1972). The priestly scribes added the book of Leviticus and reworked the stories of sacrifice to mirror the plans for the second temple in the patriarchal covenants. When the Hellenistic age dawned at the turn of the third century B.C.E., ways were found to revise the epic without actually changing the text. The author of the book of Chronicles wrote a parallel account; Ben Sira composed an epic poem; the community of Qumran developed a form of commentary; Alexandrian Jews turned the epic into an allegory of the soul; and Jewish historians rewrote the antiquities as a separate text in the style of Greek historiography. And these were not the only ways in which the epic of Israel stimulated thought during the Hellenistic period. All of the enormous literary production by Jewish intellectuals during these three hundred years appealed to the epic as the source for precedent and authority to support their positions taken with respect to the state of the second temple in Jerusalem. All Jewish intellectuals assumed that the epic of Israel was an etiology for the temple-state in Jerusalem.

When the Romans left a smoldering desolation in the Jerusalem hills, creation crashed and the epic ended in tragedy, not triumph. What were Jews to do? Josephus tried to explain it as an unfortunate turn of events caused by inept Jewish leaders who would not cooperate with the Romans. But his arguments sound hollow and devoid of personal conviction. As he brought his history of the war to an end, he could not bring himself to settle for a purely political account. He lingered over the disaster as if, once told, there would be no more history to write. And he filled the last days with reports of cosmic portents and the voices of those who wandered through the streets crying out woes. It is telling that he ended this history with an account of Eleazar's speech to the remnants of the Jewish resistance at Masada. It was an exhortation to self-inflicted martyrdom as the only freedom left for those who wished to be loyal to the God of Israel.

A more pensive and poetic response was written about the same time, toward the end of the first century C.E. in the apocalyptic text called 4 Ezra. In it the history and promise of Israel are rehearsed in succinct, credolike laments that end with unanswerable questions, "O Adam, what have you done?"; "O Lord, what of the promises?"; "O God, how could you let it happen?"; "O Israel, where now is your salvation?" There was one final show of political resistance, a move of desperation by Bar Kochba in 135 C.E. who tried to drive the Romans out with messianic fervor. When the Romans said "Enough," colonized Jerusalem, renamed it Aelia Capitolina, and denied Jews access to their own city, all Jews everywhere knew that the temple-state in Jerusalem was now only a memory. The epic of the grand traditions of Israel would once more have to be revised.

The future lay with a creative confluence of the Pharisaic schools in Palestine, where the law of Moses underwent revision, with the diaspora synagogue as the "house" where Jews would meet to say their prayers. After the war, the legacy of the Pharisees and the institution of the diaspora synagogue were the only forms of Jewish life capable of converging to form what we now call rabbinic Judaism (from *rabbi*, my master, my teacher). The process of merging the two was slow, and the history is sparse. There is a legend about the Pharisees and leaders of the Jerusalem schools moving to Jamnia in the late first century, then some hard evidence that the schools were moved to Tiberius in Galilee during the second century. By the end of the second century C.E., the new codification of the law of Moses had produced the Mishnah ("to repeat and study"), a collection of sixty-three tractates on the laws that governed the "purity" of such things as foods, tithes, marriage, daily life, prayers, fasting, times, and places. By the end of the fourth century, diaspora synagogues had learned to acknowledge the authority of the academy where rabbis were trained to study and interpret the laws that governed diaspora Judaism.

Jacob Neusner, in many books, and Jonathan Z. Smith (1987) have helped us understand that the Mishnah was a translation of the temple system of sacrifice into a family system of rituals. The common values in the two systems that made possible the translation were (1) the notion of purity (things and people in their proper places), (2) the rules for cleansing things that had become unclean (rituals of rectification), and (3) the logic by which the system worked and could be applied to novel or accidental situations. The intellectual effort invested in this translation, and the aha! moments that must have spurred and accompanied the creativity, have not always been understood and appreciated by (Christian) historians. Moving from the narrative prescriptions in Leviticus to the temple rituals of sacrifice, to the reduced list of Pharisaic codes, to the abstraction of the concept of purity, to the realization of the intelligible system at the heart of the temple arrangement of sacrifices, to the perception of logic in the rules for rectifying wrongs, and to the patterns of behavior (*halakah*, law) that guaranteed the sanctity of the Jewish way of life in the diaspora (*halakah*, way) must have been quite an intellectual adventure! When it was over, one piece of a new mythology was firmly in place. Living by the purity codes would substitute nicely for the erstwhile temple services. That took care of the question about the social shape of Israel after the ruin of the temple. Israel would dwell in diaspora and congregate in synagogues where prayers would be said, teachers would read, and the people would learn to live by the law of Moses. That would count the same as having priests perform sacrifices in the temple at Jerusalem. Jews would not need a king, a high priest, or a temple-state in Jerusalem in order to be Jews. But social change also calls for the revision of a people's myth.

The first step in the creation of a new mythology consumed a major investment of time and intellectual energy. The struggle was to retain the essential logic of the old social order while switching social models from temple to synagogue. What about the thrust of the epic, from Moses through the kings and prophets, with its mandate to build a house for God in Jerusalem? How could the rabbis claim that the Mishnaic purity laws were really Mosaic, when Moses himself, all the kings and prophets, and all the other scriptures pointed toward Jerusalem? How could the rabbis claim that they were still in the tradition and school of Moses?

A second step was taken to answer this question. It resulted in the concept of the oral law, the myth that imagined Moses legislating the law in two forms, oral and written, the oral Torah inaugurating the schools of rabbinic *halakah* (to walk, to follow). We are not yet able to trace and date all the stages through which this myth must have passed. We can only speculate that some playful rabbi in Tiberius tried it out with his students: "Why not think of *halakah* starting with Moses?" They liked it. So there, tucked away in the Mishnah, in the tractate called The Fathers (*aboth*), they recorded the myth of the Torah from Moses. It begins:

> Moses received the law from Sinai and committed it to Joshua, and Joshua to the elders, and the elders to the prophets, and the prophets committed it to the men of the great synagogue. They said three things: Be deliberate in judgment, raise up many disciples, and make a fence around the law. Simeon the Just was of the remnants of the great synagogue. He used to say: By three things is the world sustained: by the law, by the [temple-] service, and by deeds of loving-kindness. Antigonus of Soko received [the law] from Simeon the Just. He used to say . . . [and so on].

A straight line runs from Moses through the judges and the prophets to the rabbis. Kings are not mentioned. And the "great synagogue," a reference to Ezra and company who brought the Torah from Babylon during the restoration, is now the link to the early history of Israel, not to the building of the second temple. Note also that Simeon the Just, a high priest of glorious memory from the third century B.C.E., and perhaps the Simeon eulogized by Ben Sira (Sirach 50), is not praised as a temple priest but appropriated as a link in the chain of rabbis. As the tractate unfolds, the chain effect continues through sixty teachers of the law from Simeon the Just to Judah the Patriarch, the last of the line, for he was the one who edited the Mishnah. Thus the rabbis solved the problem of the inappropriate second-temple epic by inventing a whole new history. The new history started with Moses, but skirted the history of the kings and the etiologies for the temple, and ended up with the academy of rabbis. It described a parallel history, in effect, and was a very clever revision of the temple epic because it was so simple. As we know, that myth would undergird rabbinic Judaism from that time until the present. To my knowledge, it has not yet been demythologized by scholars of Judaica.

That leaves the question of the Jewish scriptures. What about the literary legacy of Israel and second-temple times? Having worked out their arrangements for sanctifying life in the diaspora synagogues by means of *halakah*, what were the rabbis to do with the scriptures? Would they have to say that the scriptures were wrong? The large amount of literature written at the end of the second-temple period had interpreted the history of Israel in ways that were no longer helpful for Jewish life in the diaspora synagogues. As recently as the Bar Kochba resistance, Rabbi Akiba had been drawn into a messianic incitement and supported a war that resulted in disaster. The books of the prophets still had the Qumran tinge. Apocalyptic literature, with its visions of a dramatic restoration of theocracy in Jerusalem, was dangerous. And much of the other, earlier literature based upon the scriptures, such as the Wisdom of Solomon, was laced with cosmic mystique and Platonic dualism, hardly appropriate for a practical approach to piety. As the second century unfolded, moreover, the Jews' own scriptures were being read as judgments against them by both gnostics and Christians. The teachers of the law in Tiberius and the leaders of synagogues in the diaspora certainly had a problem on their hands.

The rabbis' response seems to have been a calculated move to protect their literary heritage in its classical form. Only texts written in Hebrew would be kept as part of the legacy. The appropriate use of these texts, moreover, would be debated. And the interpretation of these texts would focus, not on their social history, whether as archaic, epic, or apocalyptic, but on their value for ethical, moral, and meditational guidance. When the rabbis turned their backs on the Jewish scriptures in Greek translation, they left behind a large body of Jewish literature produced during the Hellenistic period. A Greek translation of the five books of Moses had been made as early as the third century B.C.E. in Alexandria. The prophets were translated into Greek sometime during the second century, and many other writings, such as Psalms, Proverbs, Job, Sirach, Tobit, Baruch, Jubilees, Testaments of the Twelve Patriarchs, the Psalms of Solomon, 2 Esdras (a Greek translation of Ezra-Nehemiah), and the apocalypse called 4 Ezra, continued to be written in Hebrew or Aramaic and translated into Greek during the first centuries B.C.E.-C.E. Other books, such as Judith, Wisdom of Solomon, the Maccabean literature, Aristeas, Additions to Esther and Daniel, Joseph and Asenath, the apocalypse called 2 Baruch, and 1 Esdras, were composed in Greek and still considered Jewish scriptures. These are only some examples from the large body of Jewish literature thought to be unhelpful or dangerous by the early rabbis. This literature survived because Christians continued to read it. Some of these writings eventually took their places on lists that Christians made of Jewish scriptures considered helpful for public reading in the churches. When, toward the end of the fourth century C.E., manuscripts began to be produced on the order of these lists, the Christian "Old Testament" finally can be recognized. Even then, however, other Jewish scriptures continued to be read and used. The Psalms of Solomon, for instance, were still being listed with the books of the Old Testament in the ninth century *Stichometry* of Nicephorus, and 4 Ezra was not finally excluded from the Christian Bible until the Council of Trent in 1546. Christians thought of all these writings as their scriptures. The rabbis wanted to consign this literature to oblivion. By rejecting it, they bequeathed the legacy of Hellenistic Judaism to the Christians.

Early Christians knew that the five books of Moses were more important than other books, both because they were ancient and because they contained the covenants and laws basic to all forms of Jewish society. They knew that "the law" and "the prophets" went together and that this combination was more fundamental for rehearsing the history of Israel than subsequent paraphrases or interpretations of that history. They knew that the Five Scrolls (*megilloth:* Song of Songs, Ruth, Lamentations, Ecclesiastes, and Esther) were stories read at the yearly festivals of the Jews. And they treated the Psalms and Proverbs as handbooks of prayer and meditation just as the Jews did. But ranking of this kind, based as it was on practical and functional considerations, did not produce a canon that limited sacredness or revelation to these texts. Jewish writings were Jewish scriptures, the God of the Jews was the Father of Jesus Christ, and the Christ had introduced about as much light and fire as anyone needed. Christian interest in Jewish texts was, after all, a secondary consideration. Consulting Jewish scripture had always been occasioned by some circumstance that had arisen in the course of early Christian history. If that circumstance called for a Christian revision of the epic, that is what Christians did. If it called for arguments against the Pharisees from the books of Moses, they could be found. If it called for a little help from the prophets, citations could be garnered. If it called for a Christian meditation on the Psalms, Christ hymns could be written. And if some citations from Jewish literature, such as the Testament of the Twelve Patriarchs, the Wisdom of Solomon, or the Maccabean histories, might help to make a point, these references also counted. A quick count of the references to non-canonical Jewish literature in the writings of the New Testament adds up to about 400 entries (McDonald 1989, 172–77). This means that early Christians were not dealing in sacred literature. They were involved in a new religious movement that had to construct its mythology with borrowed ingredients. They combed through the Jewish scriptures this way and that, not because they thought these texts contained the word of God, but because they were the literature of a parent culture.

As we have seen, the first attempts to make a connection with the history of Israel were not driven by a great claim to fulfill the promise of that history. The appeals to the epic in the miracle story chains and in the wisdom mythology of Q were simple attempts to see some reflection of the early Jesus people in stories that were shared in the popular epic imagination. The Jesus people wanted to borrow a sense of importance from mythic precedents and create a sense of continuity with Israel's illustrious history for their social movements. That was all. They had no desire or design to supplant the fundamental rationale of the epic. Their use of the scriptures was playful, spotty, and naïve, not programmatic. That is because their commitments to the Jesus movement were not based upon a reformation of second-temple Judaism or a novel, exclusive claim upon the epic of Israel. The Jesus movements were generated and grounded in other commitments and convictions.

It was not long, however, before trysts with the Pharisees called for giving serious thought to the five books of Moses. That meant coming to terms with the text of prime importance for both the epic of Israel and the constitution of Judaism. The first attempts at reading Moses were, however, ad hoc, defensive and polemical, not constructive or systematic. It was as if the Jesus people were saying, "Look, even in the light of *your* own scriptures, *we* look pretty good." This was the approach at the second level of Q, in the pronouncement stories, and even in Paul. As we have seen, Paul grasped the seriousness of the issue for his own version of the gospel, and he wanted very much to argue for a revision of the epic in favor of Christian congregations. He made a concerted effort in his letter to the Galatians to claim the promise of the epic while discounting the five books of Moses as Torah or law. It was a pitiful attempt, and Paul must have known that it was, for he later tried another approach in his letter to the Romans. None of these revisions made before 70 C.E. were convincing because the Christian movement could not match the obvious logic of the epic as an etiology for second-temple Judaism.

The destruction of the temple in 70 C.E. created a new situation for both Jews and Christians. History had not matched the epic's promise. The first Jewish response would have been to see the event, not as an unfortunate disaster perpetrated by the Romans, but as a divine judgment upon themselves. What evil had they done to justify such devastation? Mark understood the significance of that question and dared to supply the answer. According to Mark, God destroyed the temple because the Jews had destroyed the Christ. This time it was not the books of Moses that were researched in order to find some link with the past, but the prophets. Mark saw that the destruction of the temple marked the end of an era, and that it gave the Christians a chance to justify their existence as a movement not grounded in second-temple Judaism. The prophets had already been used by the Qumran community as the basis for a charge of divine displeasure with the temple establishment. Mark turned that prophetic critique to Christian advantage with a little help from deuteronomistic thinking. The temple's destruction must have been a deserved, divine retribution for the failure of the Jews to accept the Jesus-Christ movements. But Mark could not say why and how the shift of God's pleasure from Jews to Christians had taken place. He had found a way to coordinate the crucifixion, the destruction of the temple, and the warnings of the prophets. But he had not found a way to work back from this apocalyptic interpretation of recent events to any promise in the history of Israel that Christians might claim as their own.

From the composition of Mark's gospel in the 70s of the first century to the debate between Marcion and Justin Martyr in the mid–second century, several attempts were made to imagine the Christian movement as the legitimate heir of Israel's promise. The book of Hebrews is the most comprehensive effort of which we still have record. It was nervy, sensing how important the sacrificial system was to Jewish identity, daring to read the five books of Moses as a literature in anticipation of the Christ, and brashly making the connection by claiming that the death of

Christ was a self-inflicted sacrifice for sins. According to Hebrews, the Levitical core of the Mosaic law was only a shadow in anticipation of the Christ. The rhetorical force of its clever comparisons and contrasts is strong, hardly giving the reader a chance to catch a breath, much less disagree. But it had a fatal flaw. It was much too intellectual, avant-garde, extravagant, and gross for most Christian sensibilities. And Christians did not need it. The gospels were enough, and most Christians were busy with the construction of their apostolic myths, getting their own little histories from Jesus to their own times straight. Those who did refer to the Jewish scriptures during this period, such as Matthew, John, Luke, and 1 Clement, did so as if continuity could be taken for granted. Each used a single theme to make the connection: law for Matthew, *logos* for John, spirit for Luke, and examples of virtues and vices for 1 Clement. None of them took notice of the contradictions in their logic, nor had any of these authors a premonition of the devastating intellectual crisis soon to surface. In retrospect, all these claims upon the history of Israel appear very naïve.

Naïveté was no longer possible after Marcion. Suddenly the issues were clear and the stakes were high. The Jewish scriptures could no longer be read only as Jewish history, with the Christ event merely tacked on. Now the scriptures had to be texts with a distinctly Christian ring from beginning to end. They had to redeem the Jewish God for Christians and say that the God of Israel had always had Christians in mind. Marcion's challenge brought to an end all the innocent myths of Christians as the new or true Israel of God. It forced the church's intellectuals to argue for their claim to the legacy of Israel. They now had to trace the origin of the Christian truth from the beginning of creation, and the only way to do that was to render an allegorical interpretation of the Jewish scriptures. On the literal level, the scriptures recorded the history of the Jews, but underneath the surface, at a deeper level of meaning, the scriptures recorded the plan of God that came to light only in the Christians' Christ. We have noticed the way the concept of the *logos* was developed and put to use for this purpose. From Justin Martyr on, reading the Jewish scriptures as an allegory in advance of the Christian gospel would be standard practice.

In order to revise the Israel epic into a history of anticipation for the Christ, it was absolutely necessary to work with written texts. The history of Israel had to be in textual form so one could "demonstrate" that the history of Israel was "in reality" the epic precedent for Christianity. Reading these texts as an allegory in advance of the Christian gospel was tricky business, an open invitation to violate the constraints of normal logic, but it did not sound nearly as absurd as it would if the same claims were made without texts. So the Jewish scriptures suddenly became very important documents for Christian intellectuals who wanted to argue for the archaic origins of the Christian religion and philosophy. Already at the turn of the third century, Irenaeus was writing a full elaboration of what he called the Christian "rule of faith" (or *credo*, creed) and proving its truth by referring to the Jewish scriptures. The scriptures offered proof that the Christian view of human existence, we would say anthropology, had been whispered into the world from the moment of its creation by the spirit or *logos* of God. Irenaeus' treatise came to be called *The Proof of the Apostolic Preaching*. It is an example of the importance of the allegorical interpretation of the Jewish scriptures to all forms of Christian discourse after Justin Martyr. Wherever you turn to take up a text from the third-century, to Clement of Alexandria, Tertullian, Hippolytus, Origen, Cyprian, or others, the same obsession with the Jewish scriptures is evident. Without the Jewish scriptures, the Christian myth in the centrist traditions would have languished.

From Origen on, one can detect an interest in bringing Jewish scriptures together in a single codex for Christian use. Origen is also famous for his *Hexapla*, a scholarly work that set in parallel columns the Hebrew text, a Greek transliteration of the Hebrew text, and four Greek translations of a select group of Jewish scriptures on their way to becoming the Christian Old Testament. Since collection means selection, one also finds lists of texts being made from this time on. These lists generally agree on the five books of Moses, the histories of the kingdoms, the prophets, Psalms, and a small selection from the writings, including Job, Proverbs, the Song of Songs, and Ecclesiastes. The lists do not agree on their selection of other writings, such as Esther, Baruch, Sirach, or the Maccabean histories. And they do not agree on the order in which the books are listed. From the late second and early third centuries we have lists from Melito of Sardis and Origen. With Melito we also encounter the concepts of the "old" and "new testaments" (Campenhausen 1977, 266–68, 293). From the fourth century we have lists from Cyril of Jerusalem, Hilary of Poitiers, Epiphanius of Cyprus, Athanasius of Alexandria, and Jerome. We also have evidence that Christians were producing copies of these Jewish texts in the form of a codex. That means that they had been selected for binding together in a single book. The codices called *Vaticanus*, *Sinaiticus*, and *Alexandrinus* are all from the middle of the fourth to the middle of the fifth centuries, and, while they do not exactly agree on the number and order of the books they contain, it is clear that Christians were almost ready to imagine the Jewish scriptures as the Old Testament, a collection of texts that, when combined with a selection of early Christian writings as the New Testament, would produce the Christian Bible.

As for the texts we now call the New Testament, the history of collection, making lists, and producing codices is similar to that of the Jewish scriptures. A growing collection of Paul's letters was in circulation by the end of the first century and seems to have become a model for keeping together literature attributed to other apostolic authors. Marcion's selection of a small set of "Pauline" writings as authentic, and his rejection of all other early Christian literature, impelled the collection and defense of apostolic writings, just as it had the collection and defense of Jewish literature. Justin countered by appealing to the apostles as the transmitters of the gospels which he referred to as their "memoirs." And Tatian produced a harmony of the four gospels in Syriac around 170 C.E. Slightly later, Irenaeus argued against the gnostic "heresies" by comparing them with the truth of the four gospels, noting that the founder-teachers of various gnostic schools, such as Valentinus, had not been apostles, and by claiming that the apostolic tradition was the only guarantee of the Christian truth. He also used the terms *old testament* and *new testament* to refer to the Jewish scriptures and the apostolic writings, making the point that they both witness to the same God, the same truth, and the same faith, as that which had been transmitted orally from the apostles through the succession of bishops in the Christian church.

This interest in "apostolic" writings became a common feature of early third-century scholars. Tertullian, for instance, referred to the four apostolic gospels, thirteen letters of Paul, the Acts of the Apostles, Revelation, and one letter each from John, Peter, and Jude. Clement of Alexandria referred to the four gospels, Acts, fourteen letters of Paul (including Hebrews), one letter each from Peter and Jude, two letters of John, and Revelation. Scholarly criticism of early texts also began about this time, such as a dispute about the authenticity of the Gospel of Peter, on the basis of which Serapion of Antioch discouraged its being read in the churches of Syria around 200 C.E. And Origen wrote learned commentaries on many of these early Christian writings, including his famous commentary on the Gospel of John. However, there is no evidence from this period of a closed canon. Clement and Tertullian, for example, cited such texts as the Shepherd of Hermas, the letter of Barnabas, 1 Clement, the Sibylline Oracles, and Montanist prophecies on a par with the writings which would later become the New Testament. And even when, from the fourth century on, lists began to be made of early Christian writings appropriate for reading in the churches, there was no agreement on which ones to include. That is because apostolic authorship might be questioned and different groups of churches might have different collections of writings with which they had become familiar and to which they were partial.

The event that triggered the creation of the Christian Bible was the conversion of Constantine and the sudden reversal of imperial status experienced by the Christian churches. Constantine's conversion is often dated at 313 C.E. He became the sole emperor of the Roman Empire in 324 C.E. and called the first council of Christian bishops to meet in Nicaea in 325 C.E. One might think that the Christian churches would hardly be ready for such a momentous change in circumstance. But within a few short years under Constantine's prodding, baptistries and basilicas dotted the landscape, the site of the empty tomb had been "discovered" and the Church of the Holy Sepulchre built upon it, Christian iconography announced to the world its themes, bishops gathered in councils to agree upon Christian doctrine, ritual was regularized, the calendar of festival events was established, piety took the form of pilgrimage, salvation took the form of eternal life in the heavenly world, and Christendom was launched.

Is it any wonder that the Jewish scriptures and the apostolic writings were also transformed at this time into the Christian Bible? The main events along the way include a little assignment that Constantine gave to Eusebius, bishop at Caesarea, sometime around 325–330 C.E.; a festal letter of Athanasius of Alexandria in preparation for Easter in 367 C.E.; and Jerome's translation of the scriptures into Latin in

382 C.E. Constantine asked Eusebius to have fifty copies of "the sacred scriptures" prepared by professional transcribers for the new churches he planned to build in Constantinople. Eusebius does not say, but scholars assume, that both the Jewish scriptures and early Christian writings were included. Elsewhere, Eusebius does list the writings of the "New Testament" (*Ecclesiastical History* 3, 25), distinguishing (1) those about which their apostolic authenticity was unquestioned from (2) those about which apostolic authorship was disputed or was clearly not genuine. According to Eusebius, there was agreement about the four gospels, Acts, the letters of Paul, 1 John, and 1 Peter. Those disputed included James, Jude, 2 Peter, and 2 and 3 John. Those clearly not genuine were the Acts of Paul, Shepherd of Hermas, the Apocalypse of Peter, the letter of Barnabas, and the Didache. Some said Revelation was authentic, others said it was not. This is a wonderful bit of information from the first years of empire Christianity. At this point there was apparently agreement on the criterion of apostolicity but not on which books were apostolic. And, one should underline, the issue behind the disputed books was not whether they were to be included or excluded from a closed canon, as conservative scholars have always assumed, but whether their attribution to an apostle was authentic. It was a question at the level of scholarly debate and criticism.

We do not know which books Eusebius had copied for Constantine, but we can see that the emperor's request presented something of a challenge to Eusebius and that Eusebius' response was a thoughtful compliance. His action suggests that it would only be a matter of time before the bishops came to agreements about their "inspired oracles," as Eusebius called them, and presented them to the Roman world as a common basis for Christian authority. The pressure was on because Constantine thought of Christianity as a monolithic religion and wanted the bishops to agree. Standards and regularizing procedures were the orders of the day. Eusebius was called upon as a prominent bishop, scholar, and historian from a powerful and prestigious center of Christian activity to help Constantine understand what we would call the basic Christian myth and ritual. In addition to having copies of the sacred oracles prepared for Constantinople, Constantine also asked Eusebius to enlighten him about Easter, which he saw as the Christian festival closest to the core of the new religion. With shrewd insight, Constantine's mother said that the mother church should be built in Jerusalem where Easter could most appropriately be celebrated. Constantine agreed, but he needed both the oracles and a description of the ritual in order to know where and how to build the church. He also needed the Council of Nicaea to agree upon the date for the festival. From Constantine's point of view, all of this maneuvering was a matter of practical necessity, once he had decided to make Christianity the official religion of empire. There were, however, profound consequences at the level of Christian mythic mentality. One of the truly amazing features of the transformation that Christianity experienced in Constantine's hands was the acceptance of the mythic rationale that underlay the selection of sites for Christian worship. Jonathan Z. Smith (1987) has helped us understand the significance of this shift for subsequent Christian myth, mentality, architecture, and pilgrimage. After Constantine, miraculous events and saintly relics would mark places as holy and worthy of pilgrimage and veneration. The Church of the Holy Sepulchre was the first to be built in the "holy land," but within a few years many churches were dotting the landscape in Palestine, and all of them were built on sacred sites in commemoration of events recorded in the scriptures. Pilgrimage began immediately and, as Smith comments on *The Pilgrimage of Egeria*, ". . . story and text, liturgical action, and a unique place are brought together in relations of equivalence" (1987, 89).

Eusebius must have made a list of the writings under consideration for inclusion in the Christian Bible, but he did not say which ones he had copied for Constantine, whether the Old Testament was included in the copies, or which books belonged to that set. The Festal Letter of Athanasius, on the other hand, listed both the writings Christians should consider as the Old Testament, and those to be included in the New Testament. Athanasius' list of New Testament writings is identical to that in the Christian Bible, with the exception of a different location for the "catholic" letters (James, Peter, John, and Jude) which he placed right after Acts and before the Pauline letters. The selection of texts for the Old Testament is also very close to the Protestant Christian Bible. And since Athanasius goes on to list the Wisdom of Solomon, Sirach, Esther, Judith, and Tobit as helpful books that Christians were using for preliminary instruction in the Christian religion, his expanded list comes close to the Catholic Christian Bible as well. Other lists would be produced from the fourth to the ninth century, showing that total agreement was never reached. That was because local traditions were strong and continued to determine practice. Churches were linked in various configurations to centers of power in Rome, Constantinople, Antioch, Caesarea, Jerusalem, Alexandria, and Carthage. For a time, these centers battled for control of ideology and political influence throughout the empire, but eventually each withdrew to form a national church, as the history of Christianity and its present divisions show. There was, however, general agreement about the shape of the Bible, and Athanasius marks the point at which the writings listed for inclusion in the Christian Bible first solidified.

With Jerome, the lists and manuscripts of various collections of scriptures became the Christian Bible. Jerome was born in Stridon, Dalmatia, and was educated in Rome in Latin literature and rhetoric. His conversion to Christianity inaugurated a quest that took him to Trier, Antioch, Chalcis, Constantinople, Rome again, and Egypt. At the end of his journeys he founded a religious community in Bethlehem, where he spent the remainder of his life devoted to study (389–420 C.E.). He was a scholar, historian, and monk whose education in Latin literature was noted by the Roman bishop, Damasus, who asked him to refine and standardize a number of older Latin translations of the gospels. It was this desire for a standard, popular translation of the scriptures into Latin that resulted in the Christian Bible. The story does have some missing episodes and a bit of intrigue. Part of the intrigue has to do with the list of writings to be included in the Old Testament. Jerome was impressed by Melito's list of the Hebrew scriptures, and presumably he would have limited the Old Testament to it had not Augustine intervened to argue for a more expanded list. Augustine's list is very close to that of Athanasius, and Augustine prevailed, although we cannot be completely sure why Jerome acquiesced. At any rate, the Latin translation he produced became the standard Bible for the Roman church and Western culture until the Protestant reformation in the sixteenth century. It is still available in Roman Catholic circles as the Vulgate, or "popular" (language) Bible, and as the Douai version, a translation of the Vulgate into English made in the sixteenth century. In both Roman Catholic and Protestant circles, modern translations of the Bible overlook Jerome's Latin translation and base their work on the Hebrew and Greek manuscript traditions. But if Jerome's Latin no longer plays a decisive role in the production of biblical texts and translations, his selection of the writings to be included, and the order in which he placed them, still determine the Bible's shape in many of its modern editions.

When the Jewish scriptures and the apostolic writings were combined in a single book, the church finally had its story straight. The Bible could be used to claim antiquity for the Christian religion and serve as the Christian epic. Texts, traditions, and history meant honor in the eyes of persons encultured in the Greco-Roman age and legitimacy in the eyes of Roman officialdom. That the history was incredible, that the Old Testament was barely understandable to any except Christian exegetes and theologians, did not seem to matter. It actually worked to the advantage of Christian leaders, because only they could say what it really meant. And besides, what more did one expect from oracular texts? Allegorizing ancient myths was standard practice, and decoding signs and wonders was considered a professional skill. What Christians found positively helpful about the Old Testament, moreover, now that the age of writing literature "against the Jews" was (temporarily) a thing of the past, now that they did not need to direct all their exegetical energies to finding predictions of the Christ and judgments against the Jews, were the exemplary figures of virtue and piety that now seemed to fill the horizons of both the Old and New Testaments. Virtue and piety were exactly what Christians had emphasized in their bid for recognition by the Romans. If the Old Testament now produced illustrious examples of Christian virtues and these could be traced as a theme or stream of piety from the very beginning to the end of the Old Testament, that is, from the very beginning of the world to the coming of the Christ, the battle for the Jewish scriptures had been won. The church could now turn to the many other matters needing attention as Christianity became the official religion of the empire.

At every turn in the formal transformation of the church into a religion of empire, having the Bible in place was more than fortunate. It was absolutely necessary. Without these texts in place, without both the Old and the New Testaments, the church would not have had an appropriate charter for being a legitimate religion in the view of the fourth century. With these texts in place, the church could claim a firm foundation for its system of myth and ritual. The Old Testament cast light on the antiquity of the church's theology and creed. The gospels rendered an account of the church's origin and mission in the light of the Old Testament. The gospels and the letters centered on the singular events of the last supper and the death of the Christ, thus providing the scripts for Christian myth and ritual. And the apostolic literature provided a mandate for the mission of the church in the world and for the succession of its bishops in charge of its social institutions. But that is not the whole story.

Christianity came to be driven by two strong desires. One was to continue the expansion of Christendom. The biblical mandate was found in the great commission of Christ and the charge to the apostles that they take the gospel to the nations, as well as in the narrative logic of a story that had not found its ending. The goal was to work for the ending of the biblical epic by converting the whole world to Christianity. The thrust was forward, outward, and global. The second desire was to "return," if only in the imagination, to the "holy land" where the events took place that were significant to the origin of the religion and important for Christian faith. This peculiarity of the Christian imagination, where a rehearsal of its myth became at the same time a recalling of "historical" events, combined with a Greco-Roman sensibility about shrines and cults of the dead in Constantine's program. The result was a powerful, if implicit, rationale for pilgrimage to Palestine which began in the fourth century. Later forms of Christian pilgrimage, some real, some surrogate, show how deeply this mythic sensibility defined Christian imagination. One need only call to mind the crusades in the ninth and tenth centuries, the liturgies of procession to a shrine for meditation typical of medieval and renaissance Christianity, and the attraction of the "holy land" for Christian pilgrims and tourists in our own time. The thrust in this case is backward, inward, and toward a specific location.

There is deep irony involved in the tension created by these two thrusts. The two thrusts resulted from the Constantinian revolution and the mystique created by combining the Old and New Testaments into the Christian Bible. The original claim upon the epic of Israel, argued throughout the second and third centuries, was based upon the desolation of Jerusalem and the lack of fit between the epic's promise and history's pronouncement. The desolation of Jerusalem showed that the epic was really not meant to end with the construction of a temple in Jerusalem. That is why the Christians could step in as heirs to what they saw as the epic's global promise. It was the desolation of Jerusalem that made it possible for Christians to wrench the epic free from Jewish hands and read it as a history of God's intention to expand the borders of his people to include the whole, wide Christian world. Why, pray tell, would Christians want to go back to Palestine and build the mother church of Christendom in Jerusalem? There was nothing in the logic of the Christian appropriation of the epic of Israel to suggest Christian pilgrimage to Palestine. There was nothing in Luke's Acts of the Apostles, or in the apostolic myth as the bishops construed it, to suggest either a pilgrimage to Jerusalem or the global mission of a continually expanding empire Christianity. It was Christendom taking place, the coming of age of a world religion, that did it. With its rituals in place to commemorate the origins of a social institution, rituals that were based on the myth of a crucified and resurrected Christ, it seemed only right that the Jewish temple lay in ruins while the Church of the Holy Sepulchre took its place. Both the myth and the ritual were recorded in the New Testament, where, since the New and the Old Testaments had been put together, it could be shown that the logic of God actually called for the Christian redemption of that desolate land. Thus the logics of the Jewish scriptures and the apostolic writings were once again revised in the production of the Bible. And the Bible, for its part, would now become the mythic template for subsequent Christian mentality. There would always be two thrusts in tension within the Christian imagination, and two driving forces guiding Christian history.

One can trace the influence of the Bible and both of its thrusts from the fourth century into the modern period. The displays of biblical imagery and influence appear in the locations and names of the churches constructed in Palestine in the fourth century, in the diaries of pilgrims from the fourth and fifth centuries, the iconography of the basilicas built in the fifth and sixth centuries, and the superimposition of Christian festivals upon the Julian calendar to create the gospel cycle called the church year. Biblical influence continued in the development of cruciform architecture, the Christian missions throughout Europe, the rationale for the crusades, the epic iconography of the medieval cathedrals, and the maps that Columbus used to chart his voyages of discovery. And the Bible has provided the pattern for the Protestant reformation, the Catholic liturgy of the stations of the cross, the Christian missions in the age of modern empires, the rhetoric of responsibility in American politics, and the modern art of a Marc Chagall.

And so the story of the Bible finally returns to our point of departure, the mystique of these sacred scriptures in our modern world. Having followed that story to the point of the Bible's formation, we can now bewonder that mystique, make some observations on the ways the Bible continues to influence our cultural and social undertakings, and ask some questions about the helpfulness of its mythology for a postmodern age.

THE FASCINATION
OF THE BIBLE

The Bible was created when Christianity became the religion of the Roman Empire. It was a profoundly scintillating arrangement. An earthly king joined forces with the priests of the heavenly kingdom of God, and together they claimed the legacy of God's great plan for humankind. The Bible was the record of that plan and its troubled history from the very foundation of the world. The plan and the history were all-encompassing. The vast cosmic scope, and the sweep of the story as an unbroken thread through all of human history, told of the quest for a just and sustainable kingdom to remedy the world's ills and bring the nations to the knowledge and service of the one true God. Toward the end of that history, at the crucial point of revelation, when the plan of God was seen to include the nations and was ready to be announced to the world at large, the charge was given to the Christian church, as it had been given to Israel, to represent the kingdom's quest and see that it come to pass. Thus, with Constantine converted, the age-old model of the temple-state could start to work again, and the history of Christendom began. The king and the priest had finally seen each other in the light of this new arrangement, and the foundations were laid for an age of tensive balance between the scepter and the staff, an age that lasted, without reformation, for the next one thousand years. The kingdom of God that the church had in mind did not exactly match the kingdoms of the kings. But the church has seldom thought that strange. Just think. The church was finally positioned at the apex of power. It had in its hands the very power of the gods to shape the minds of the peoples of the world from the kings on down. That was more than a match for the kings who only controlled labor and the power to execute in matters of life and death.

Catholic churches have always tended to represent the kingdom of God on earth in their own institutional structures, creating religious associations and enclaves within the kingdoms of the world as real reminders of the all-encompassing spiritual worlds of eternal heaven and hell. Protestant churches have always tended to represent the kingdom of God by being a critical voice within society, as well as by calling on people to prepare for a future life in heaven, often with the threat of an apocalyptic alternative. In both cases, the churches have taken their places matter-of-factly within their host societies, comfortable as institutions with religious privilege, while representing a "kingdom" that they need not fully actualize in their own associations. To represent the kingdom of God on earth gives the churches a strange kind of authority. They can call the society at large to task for not living up to God's standards while pointing to another time and place when the kingdom of God will finally be revealed. The church itself is strangely exempt from that social and cultural critique.

To claim its right to speak with authority the church must always keep the Bible in its hands. The Bible creates the aura of a universal plan, and it grants the church its charter and charge to represent that plan in the histories of the peoples of the world. Without the Bible, the church would look ridiculous. How would it verify what it says it knows? How would it point to what it represents? How would it have any authority to speak? Why would any working society put up with its scoldings? But with the Bible in hand, the church can represent much, much more than it ever need display. It can represent the human quest for the kingdom of God which, according to the Bible, has been part of the plan of God from the beginning of creation. And it can know how the story will end. What more could anyone ask?

The Bible has been carried along wherever the church has ventured. It is the only object of the Christian religion that all forms of Christianity have in common. And the power of its epic is never more clear than in the way the Bible works when the church confronts another culture with its message of salvation. Conversion is a complex process, especially when the people of another culture encounter Christian missionaries entering the picture along with the worldly forces of their kings. The Bible's role as epic may not be obvious, and the Bible itself may not be noticed as the document that will force a radical reorientation of a people's sense of history and identity. And yet, that is exactly what inevitably occurs. For almost two thousand years, the church has drawn people after people into alignment with the biblical epic and the history of Western civilization that flows from it. The illustrious traditions of a people's own culture have invariably been forced into the shadows, if not threatened by complete erasure from their collective memory. To accept the Christian religion, people have always had to adjust their thinking to the very unusual notion of belonging to a people and a history that were not really their own.

To be confronted with having two histories, the history of one's own people and the Christian epic from the Bible, requires astonishing mental gymnastics. Think of knowing the history of your own country, people, and ancestral traditions, only to be addressed as a child of Abraham, an heir to the history of Israel, instructed by Moses, judged by the prophets, redeemed by the Christ, and enlightened by the apostles. That is the history that one will need to accept and internalize if one converts and cares about eternity. It is the only history that will count when the final accountings are tallied. But how can a people have two histories? How can that history and one's own history both be true? And even if one knows that both can't be equally true, the biblical history must always prevail if one wants to remain, or must remain, a part of the march of Western Christian culture. Saying yes to that history has been the price one had to pay for access to Western civilization. Most people have paid that price in sterling. And the story continues.

Before Coca-Cola and the Bible washed ashore on a small island in Southeast Asia, the Xantu waited for the right moment to hunt for the shark, blew on the conch shell when one had been killed, beat on the drums to call the people together for the feast, and told stories about their age-old agreement with the "great shark" not to kill more than they needed for food. After the intrusion by Western Christian culture, they hunted sharks for money, spent it at the canteen, learned to thump the Bible in the pulpit, and warned the women and children sitting there in the chapel's rows, that if they did not believe in Jesus as their savior, they would go to hell and burn forever. I have tried to imagine their somersaults when they first encountered the Christian epic. I have pondered the incredulity of my own ancestors in Sweden when they had to convert, in their case, by the sword. What do you suppose they thought when they first learned about Adam and Abraham and the Christ, and then discovered that their own ancestors, heroes, and gods would now have to lurk in the shadows as demigods and forest spirits? I have marveled at the temerity of Native American Christians seeking to recover something of their own cultural traditions, knowing all the while that these traditions had been systematically destroyed by those who brought them the gospel. Perhaps that is why I was sobered when I heard the headman of the Xantus say, that when the Christian missionaries first came he did not know why they wanted to destroy his stories and his culture, and now that they had destroyed them, he still did not know why.

My Korean students at the School of Theology at Claremont tell me that they know from recent experience what it means to convert to Christianity and that the acrobatics required of the historical imagination are not difficult to perform. They know they are Koreans and they know the history of their culture. They also know they are the true children of Abraham, or the children of the God of Abraham, because they are Christians. They are, they say, Korean Christians. When I shake my head in bewilderment, they smile. They tell me that God had Koreans in mind all along, but that it took a long time for the message to reach them because the Jews and the Catholic Christians, and even the American Protestant churches who finally did send them missionaries, dragged their feet and did not fulfill their missions as they were supposed to. Now it is their turn, they say. They will be the ones to take the gospel message quickly to the world. And so the history that started in the garden of Eden, history as told in the Christian Bible, the story that flows into the history of the Christian churches and through the history of Western civilization, has now shaped the collective memory of the Korean Christian people as well. It is too soon to tell what they eventually will do with the artifacts from their own past.

After Christian conquest and the conversion of a people, the Christian epic settles into place and the biblical account is taken for granted as the way Christian truth entered the world. It is then that the Bible takes on other functions and be-comes a sacred text. Sacred scriptures can be read in many different ways, and the Bible is no exception. It serves as the myth and ritual script for Christian liturgy, as a rich reservoir of lessons for instruction in the Christian life of faith and piety, and as an oracle for daily devotions and personal access to the spiritual realm. An assump-tion also settles into place along with the shift from epic to sacred text. It is assumed that there is a message, teaching, or view on every matter of importance tucked away somewhere in that primeval charter. And since the Bible is chock-full of sto-ries, poems, laws, ancient oracles, instructions, prayers, hymns, ancient proverbs, speeches, arguments, visions, and lamentations, the sheer size and complexity of the biblical record create the impression of boundless information. What more does one need?

The fact that the stories in the Bible were cast in ancient and archaic languages, and still sound strange in modern translations, does no harm. Oracles are always enigmatic, and enigmas create their own mystique. That the message is hidden or difficult to discern belongs to the Bible's fascination. Somewhere among the many stories and words, it is thought, is truth about the meaning of life that applies to every age. Christians call this truth the Word of God and use the term as a designa-tion for the Bible itself as a sacred text. The Word of God is "contained" in the Bible, they say, and because the Bible is written in language that is difficult to under-stand, it must be read with care in order to extract its messages. That is why it seems so fitting that the Bible has to be studied.

However, whether one studies the Bible for oneself or waits for professionals to find that message, looking for the Bible's answer to a question is very hard work. Christian ministers are taught how to perform this labor in Protestant seminaries. First one has to do an *exegesis* (from *ek*, out of, and *hegeomai*, lead), which means to "bring out" the meaning of a text. This is understood as an exercise in historical-literary criticism, and one must consult commentaries, concordances, and other compendia of information to discover the text's "original" message. But that is not all. One must then learn to perform a *hermeneutic* (from *hermeneia*, interpretation), which means to discover the "message" of the text for today. And oh, the long list of exegetical methods that have to be learned (to keep one's scholarly conscience as a critical historian of ancient texts), and the long list of hermeneutical methods that have to be mastered (to bridge the centuries and be relevant as a modern Christian minister). And the labor! Such labor, poring over those ancient oracles in the quest for some divine direction to guide us in our times! Think of the investment our so-ciety makes in terms of lives and labor in the hope of discerning the present import of that ancient word of God. Is it not an odd preoccupation for such a postmodern time as ours? Why is it that no one ever questions this investment of our energies in the study of these texts from antiquity? Why is it that such enchantment with these ancient writings never draws a smile or two?

There are three reasons why we have not smiled. The first is that the Bible func-tions as epic for the American dream of creating "one nation under God, indivisible, with liberty and justice for all." Epics are always taken seriously. They create cultural foundations and are dangerous to dislodge. The second is that the Bible is the myth and ritual text for Christianity. Sacred texts of a dominant religion are always taboo and never to be questioned. And the third reason is that the Bible functions as an oracle in popular parlance and practice. Discrediting an oracle is like touching a tar baby. It is very tricky business. In light of our study about the Bible's formation, however, and in view of our world-scape at the end of the twentieth century, these reasons are wearing thin. Each deserves thorough scrutiny by means of calm, measured, critical conversation in the public forum. We might start with some observations about the way in which each of these biblical functions actually works. Explanation is always a helpful move when confronted with mystique. I will discuss these functions in reverse order: first the oracular, then the function of the Bible as the church's ritual text, and finally the way the Bible works as the epic for an American sense of presence in the world.

A TRANSPARENT ORACLE

Those who study the Bible in quest of an answer to some question say it works, that answers are forthcoming. By this they mean that the study of the Bible does produce insights and instructions that address human circumstances of our time. This impression can be explained. It is an accidental by-product of the way the Bible combines two different collections of writings, the Old and the New Testaments. The way these two collections are connected forms a kind of equation for solving theoretical problems and produces a kind of grammar for thinking about human situations. The uncanny aspect of this equation is that it automatically activates cognitive functions that are basic for any and all human thought. Ultimately, it is the way this equation stimulates thought that gives the Bible its fascination as a book of sacred oracles and teases the reader into thinking that it holds the secret to profound understanding.

The Bible works its magic at the level of cognitive grammar in the following way. The balance between the old and the new sets up an equation of comparison and contrast. Comparison and contrast are fundamental modes of classifying things and thinking about them (J. Z. Smith 1982, 19–35). Some would say they are *the* fundamental cognitive functions. The old and the new also make a ranked pair, with the new superior to the old. All binary oppositions, all pairs of comparative or contrastive terms in the arenas of human thought are ranked (J. Z. Smith 1987, 42–46). The ranking may be arbitrary in such pairs as light/dark, up/down, male/female, but it is never missing. That is surely one reason why the contrast between the old and the new in the Christian Bible has never been questioned. It has been taken in stride as natural.

The signs contained in the Old Testament, moreover, need to be read at two levels of signification in order to work in the Christian equation. Those who created the Bible in the second to fourth centuries knew that the Jewish scriptures had to be allegorized in order to become Christian scriptures. We can now see the result of that strategy. It charged the biblical equation of old and new signs with linguistic sophistication. Only by shifting the signs from the Old Testament into metaphor, symbolism, or figural abstraction does the equation of the old and the new produce meaning. One must discover the latent significance of Old Testament texts in order to mark their correlation with Christian meanings. Thus one of the powers of the Bible is to force ironic readings of Old Testament texts, in order to produce Christian meanings. At this point, students of Claude Lévi-Strauss may want to recall his dictum to the effect that "meaning" is the sense of significance we experience when we find it possible to correlate two different systems of signs (1966; 1969).

The signs contained in the New Testament also produce a sense of dual signification, but the significance of a New Testament text is not created by an ironic layering or doubling of meaning, as is the case with the Old Testament. In the Old Testament a word or event has to refer to two different orders of discourse synchronically, or at the same time. The paschal lamb is first the Jewish paschal lamb, but it "really" refers to Jesus Christ as God's eternal intention. The double meaning of the words and events in the New Testament, on the other hand, is found in their application to a then and a now. We might say that the doubling of significance in this case is diachronic, except that it is a matter of the same event taking place at two different times in Christian history. Every Christian knows, however, that the events recorded in the New Testament were "unique" and that they happened "once for all." Nevertheless, it is just these events that are reenacted regularly in Christian ritual and recalled vividly to the Christian imagination whenever the New Testament is read ("Were you there when they crucified my Lord?"). This reenactment is also understood as an "event "("O sometimes it causes me to tremble"). Recreating these New Testament events by reading, recall, and response is an operation of memory and imagination fundamental for Christian thought and mentality. That vital contact with the originary past is what the church must repeatedly make available to Christians in order to live up to its charter as the vehicle for human transformation. This means that the marvelous intermingling of the unique event and its replication (a contradiction in terms, to be sure), or the sense of the incomparable Christ event as paradigmatic of the "novel" and the "new" in every Christian's own experience, is also a product of the Bible's cognitive equation.

The Bible's intrigue as a heady cognitive grammar is hardly ever consciously recognized by those who read it as the Word of God. It is taken for granted that the two collections of texts are different because history actually went that way, and that each collection has to be read at two levels of signification in order to understand the significance of that history. One of these collections, the Old Testament, automatically invites layered meanings and must be allegorized in order to understand the need for Christianity. The other, the New Testament, requires an imaginary replication of events in order to produce Christian experience. It is not recognized that allegorizing the Old Testament is a setup for the significance with which the

New Testament is loaded. That is because the equation of the two sets of texts would not work if the setup were acknowledged. With such an equation of two such laden texts, however, the possibilities for using the Bible to analyze any human problem are endless. That is because the equation activates basic cognitive functions of comparison and contrast, offers a very rich reservoir of narrative imagery, and provides a lens for both the ironic and paradigmatic interpretation of all human events, both then and now, simultaneously. This makes it possible to classify any human event and/or situation for analysis and interpretation. It also makes it possible to reclassify any human event and/or situation, supposing a new perspective were desired. Think of the possibilities for putting a Christian construction on contemporary events! Any event can be judged in the light of the "old," pre-Christian, human condition, or imagined as transformed by "participating" in the "new" event of the eternal Christ. It is no wonder that Christians think they hear the Bible talking to them. One can ask any question he or she wants of the Bible, turn the handle 'round and 'round, and get some kind of answer.

If the first answer does not appear to be helpful, the handle can always be cranked again until the right answer appears. It is a trick that happens all the time, right before my eyes in the classrooms of the School of Theology at Claremont. At first the study of a text may not seem to support a traditional Christian conviction, or the answer one hopes to find in the Bible. But with a little ingenuity, one can set up the comparison again with other emphases and make the answer come out right. It is a trick that seems to come naturally when studying the Bible. Having to use this trick in order for a story from the Bible to come out right (illustrate contemporary theological convictions and pointedly apply to a current situation) never puts the Bible in question. The Bible's design actually invites that kind of manipulation. With such a book as one's resource, one can assess any relationship critically, see any truth clearly, or find some portentous words for any occasion somewhere in the mix.

If that is all there were to it, the role of the Bible in our culture might be considered harmless. After all, every culture has had its basket of feathers, sticks, and stones, or other means for doing divination. Divination does seem to be a bit out of place for thoughtful people at the end of the twentieth century, but historians of religion have helped us see that what the shaman does should not be put down as magic and should not be overly mystified. The shaman's skill focuses thought on some specific problem. The procedure enables a person to work through some conundrum. Divining is a way of addressing practical human problems, acknowledging desires, recognizing limitations, sharing distress, and coming to terms with the accidental and the inevitable in life. If that were the only way the Bible worked its magic, no harm would be done.

That, however, is not the whole story. The Bible's guidance is not limited to divination in the interest of private experience and personal well-being irrespective of social and cultural conditions. The biblical equation is loaded in its application to social classifications, and calls for a certain cultural stance on the part of its readers.

That is because the Bible projects a thoroughly Christian, all-encompassing frame of reference for viewing the world. The Bible is the myth and ritual text for Christian congregations. It is the product and property of a sub-cultural social institution. Its use as a book of oracles is dependent upon its function within the Christian church.

AN OTHERWORLDLY SCRIPT

The Bible would have no power apart from its function as the script for Christian worship, and Christian worship would not be possible apart from the Bible. This holds true across the entire spectrum of Christian liturgies and forms of worship, from the Catholic Mass at an altar to the free-church sermon from a pulpit. Two archaic patterns of ritual congregation merged as a matter of course in the early centuries of the church's practice. One was what scholars call a covenant renewal, a gathering for the purpose of sealing a treaty. This form of congregation was typical for the ancient Near East. The other was the Greek practice of gathering for a festival meal (or "sacrifice") at the tomb of ancestral heroes. Both were occasions for memorial, epic rehearsal, recognition of the powers that be, stipulation of agreements, reminders of the consequences should one fail to keep the agreements, and the presentation of oaths and tokens of loyalty to the social contract. In Christian worship, the readings from the Old Testament function as epic rehearsal and lessons from the past to remind the people of the Lord's power and will. The readings from the New Testament function as stipulation for the present arrangement of authorities and agreements, and as a call to covenant renewal. The appropriate response is to say yes to the agreements and present one's offerings. Only so can one "go in peace."

As for the Christian ritual of sacrifice (called Mass, Eucharist, or Lord's Supper), it also needs the Bible as a script. Without the New Testament to say what it means, the Christian ritual would appear obscene. Although he did not intend to do so, Mark created the myth that eventually was read as the script for this ritual reenactment. He did that when he combined the Pauline traditions of the Christ myth and supper in his narrative of the crucifixion. By using the supper as the occasion for Jesus to offer his final instructions to his disciples, and interpreting the supper as Jesus' anticipation of the crucifixion, Mark inadvertently portrayed Jesus as a savior who presided over his own symbolic enactment of his own forthcoming death. The symbols of the cross and the supper collapsed in that narrative and, when finally the early Christian meal of thanksgiving was turned into a formal ritual in memory of that meal, a priest took Jesus' place at the table and the table became an altar for the symbolic reenactment of the sacrifice.

The way in which Christian myth and ritual are related to each other seems to be distinctive among the religions of the world where myths usually do one thing and rituals quite another. As Jonathan Z. Smith has helped us see, ritual marks the distinction between two spacial arrangements. The ritual place becomes a "here" that

coexists but differs from the world out "there," while myth marks the difference between a "then" of the storied time and the "now" of its rehearsal. Smith goes on to
say, "A different set of dynamics appears to be at work in the case of the Christian
conjoining of myth to ritual with respect to a quite particular, indeed, a unique,
place" (1987, 109–14). Smith was referring to the significance of the "conjoining" of
myth and ritual in the construction of the Church of the Holy Sepulchre in the
fourth century, hence his reference to the notion of a "unique place." We now can
note, however, that the merger of myth and ritual in Christian practice was not limited to the Constantinian development. Dislodged from its application to the "holy
land" and Christian pilgrimage in the seventh century, the Christian myth became a
script for ritual reenactment in the medieval church, and the Christian ritual became a reenactment of the mythic script. Thus the "then" of the Christian myth is
made present in the "here" and "now" of ritual; and entering the "here" of ritual becomes the occasion for being transported into the imaginary world of the myth.
When the Protestant reformers left the elaborate spiritual world of the medieval
Catholic church for a breath of fresh Renaissance air, they did not leave the Bible
behind, and they could not read it apart from Christian worship. The rule prevailed
that the church was actual only where the Word was preached and the sacraments
performed. To have the authority to preside over the enactment of the Eucharist,
and to say what happens when it is performed, still determine both status and power
within Protestant as well as Catholic Christianities. This means that Christian worship is designed to (con)fuse the imagination of the biblical times and places with
their present reenactment in ritual in the interest of accentuating the sense of contrast between the mythic world that the church represents and the world as it is experienced in the host society.

As with all myths and worldviews, the way the story goes and the way the world
is viewed in the Bible have a profound effect upon the way Christians treat others in
the worlds in which they live. This shaping function of a people's myth results in
shared patterns of thinking. These patterns of thinking result in legislation, in
agreements on values, and in attitudes and assumptions about the way the world
works or should work. Attitudes that are based on mythic agreements take the place
of unexamined assumptions. That, of course, is what myths are for. Myths turn the
collective agreements of a people into truths held to be self-evident. Myths do that
by projecting these truths onto the creation of the world, by telling about the time
when the society came into being on the basis of those agreements, or by imagining
a future time when judgment will fall if the agreements are not kept.

The reason the Bible is not an innocent bundle of figures for doing personal divination is that each of the factors in the biblical equation has already been given its
Christian valence. The "old" is the sign under which those who are not Christian are
viewed. These "others" always appear tarnished and fundamentally in need of repair
or redemption. The "new" is the sign under which the possibility of transformation
to Christianity is viewed. The Christian potential is seen as bright and shiny because

it points toward perfection and is grounded in the miraculous. The people of the old are under judgment; the people of the new are under grace. And so the terms of comparison and contrast have multiplied: law and gospel, constraint and freedom, ignorance and enlightenment, exclusivity and inclusivity, and so forth. Every Christian is familiar with these categories of difference, keeps them constantly in dialectical tension, and uses them when making judgments about his or her contemporary social world. Only Christians enjoy alignment with the bright side of the ranked pairs: freedom, enlightenment, inclusivity, the gospel, and salvation.

The difference in valence between the Old Testament and the New Testament is actively cultivated in the Christian use of the Bible. The standard lectionaries, where readings are selected for each Sunday of the year, set up the pairs for contrast with just such logic in mind. For those unfamiliar with the lectionaries, here is an example. In 1996, on the third Sunday in Lent, the Old Testament lesson will be Exodus 17:3–7, where the children of Israel were without water in the wilderness and were murmuring against Moses. The Psalm will be 95, where that incident in the wilderness is cited and the murmuring deplored as a sign of putting God to the test, a very bad thing to do. It signaled Israel's "hardness of heart." The New Testament lesson will be John 4:5–25, the story of the Samaritan woman at the well learning about Jesus as the true water of life. And the reading from Paul's letter to the Romans (5:1–11) will make the point that, in contrast to the Israelites at Meribah, where the murmuring took place, Christians live by faith in Christ and so do not put God to the test. One does not need to have a very active imagination to find a few sermons there, ready for the preaching. In the context of Christian worship, this balancing act of contrasting pairs between the Old and New Testament "lessons" is so automatic it is hardly noticed. Christian sensibility seems to know that it should not be noticed lest the equation lose the magic of its doubled dialectic.

Unfortunately, Christians have always had a hard time keeping their myths, histories, and present circumstances distinguished from one another. Just as early Christians imagined "the Jews" of Old Testament times as disobedient to God, and condemned "the Jews" of Jesus' time for crucifying Christ, so throughout the course of Christian history Christians have charged "the Jews" with "hardness of heart" (or worse) for saying "no thank you" to the Christian invitation to convert. They have been treated as scapegoats and whipping boys because of their mythic role as the launching pad for Christianity. But the radical ranking of Christians above their significant others has never been limited to Jewish-Christian relations. As a lens through which to view the world, the old-new formula in the composition of the Bible has resulted in a distinctively Christian mentality that views *all* non-Christians as pre-Christian.

This mentality includes an implicit claim to know the truth about God, history, and the human situation that other people do not know. People outside the domain of Christian knowledge are invariably ranked lower and in need of enlightenment or transformation. A mission to change the world is called for, and the changes that count are imagined as conversions for the others' own good. Confrontation and conflict can be taken in stride, for the cause is right, the powers of darkness are wrong, and the battle is of eternal consequence. God is involved, so the stakes are high. Miracles, judgments, and manifestations of divine power belong to the mythic picture and predispose the Christians to disparage the routine and grant privilege to sensational events. An external savior and a drama of salvation by means of destructive violence color the lens through which Christians look for meaning in human events. A tendency to deny the history of atrocities against infidels, Jews, and pagans is buttressed by the conviction that, although mistakes have been made, the Christian mission is kindly at the core and high-minded in the long run. When the Bible is actually quoted, then, in support of some righteous cause, its function as a weapon is hardly ever noticed. Wars against the enemies without and condemnation of the "sinners" within have always been thought "justified."

AN UNASSUMING EPIC

But what about our so-called secular culture in America? Has the Christian myth influenced the ways in which we as Americans take our place in the world? Is our deference to Christians and their Bible due to a "secular" mythic mentality rooted in the "Judeo-Christian tradition"? And is that sense of Judeo-Christian tradition dependent upon the Bible? Scholars of American studies are increasingly saying yes to these questions. Tracing that influence is difficult, however, not only because cultural mentalities are never easy to document, but also because we Americans have prided ourselves on being independent and free spirited, unbeholden to tradition and cultural constraints. Until very recently, the word *culture* was used only in relation to the arts and pretentious lifestyles (as in references to "high culture"). Melting-pot mentality called for obliterating "old world" ways. America was the land of freedom and opportunity. The goal was to shed cultural accoutrements and become a "naturalized" American, a bootstrap, can-do, independent soul. And as for religion, Americans have believed in the separation of church and state. Religion was a private affair, a matter of personal preference that was not supposed to affect the way we did business with one another. Thus tolerance was called for in assessing another's personal opinions and beliefs. Taboos were set against the public discussion of religions, their differences, and the difference each might make if allowed to control social codes or legislation. Americans have never felt comfortable with the idea of being influenced by anything, whether religion, culture, the arts, or forms of popular entertainment. Thus persons have been treated as if their religion did not have any social effect. And yet, we do talk easily about distinguishing features that make America a land or country that is different from other countries and their cultures. We refer to American mentality, values, social practices, attitudes, foreign policies, entertainment, and popular novels. And we all know about the American dream. The important thing to notice is that scholars have been able to show how closely these expressions of a common American culture correspond to features of the Christian myth.

In the prologue I briefly mentioned some biblical clichés frequently used to describe America's role among the nations, such as a "city set on a hill" and a "light to the nations." We may now add the constant appeal by our politicians to something called "the Christian heritage on which our nation was founded." No one seems to mind such reference, especially when that heritage is cast as the "Judeo-Christian tradition." If asked what is meant by the Judeo-Christian tradition, it is not long before the Bible is mentioned. In his book *Virgin Land*, Henry Nash Smith (1950) documents the history of our attitude toward the land and shows how our treatment of it has resonated with the biblical mandate to subdue the wilderness and turn it into a paradise fit for the righteous nation. Eugene Genovese (1974) and Elizabeth Fox-Genovese (1988) have disclosed the biblical basis for many of the social arrangements and practices in the South, including the justification for slavery. And *The Captain America Complex* has easily been traced to its biblical paradigms by Robert Jewett (1973). These are but three examples of a burgeoning body of literature that documents the ways in which the Bible has patterned American thought, practice, and policy.

The Bible is not the sole source of America's mythology, to be sure. The social construction of American mentality has drawn from many other experiences, ideas, and motivations. Political philosophies from the Enlightenment, economic theories born of the industrial revolution, the war for independence, the wisdom of the Continental Congress, the experience of the Revolutionary War, immigrant histories, and the "westward ho" have all left their mark upon our collective memory. But the Bible may be the crucial factor for bringing them all together and grounding our sense of righteousness, mission, and manifest destiny.

One need not be a Christian to think of being an American in just such terms. One needs only to think of America as the flowering of Western civilization with its cultural roots in the epic history recounted in the Bible. One need not believe in the Bible and its stories in order for that epic to have its effect. As when we've watched a powerful movie on the big screen, the story line of the biblical epic hangs in the air and affects our thoughts and outlooks. Its memorable images pop up involuntarily to help explain or interpret current affairs. Winks can glance off symbols from the epic as shortcut signs of recognition. Statements can be made and attitudes disclosed on issues of profound and far-reaching moment with a simple, single sigh in the presence of some epic reminder. No. One need not be a Christian to live in the world of collective memory and imagination created by the biblical epic. We only need to see that our "secular" mythologies also draw their power from their uncanny similarity to features of the biblical epic's memorable moments. Think of the Lone Ranger with his silver bullet coming into a town unable to solve its problems. Now think of Mark's Jesus with the power to cast out demons coming into a world unable to solve its problems. There is not much difference, after all. So, supposing we Americans want to join the human race and admit that, like others, we have a culture complete with its mythology, is not that mythology rooted in the Bible? To quiet the voice within that wants to say no, one need only ask, "What other story is there that all of us have heard?"

Unfortunately for this heritage, the time has come when many are wondering whether we have lost our Judeo-Christian moorings and what will become of us if we have. Since Vietnam, our sense of innocence and righteousness as a people has been shaken. With the end of the Cold War our villains in league with the evil empire have vanished. Recent waves of immigrants have not melted down. Our multicultural cities are neither converting nor celebrating their diversity. The gap between the rich and the poor keeps growing. Violence is apparently the order of the day. Our leaders lack social vision. The concept of social democracy is not working in America. Words like *liberal, peace,* and *justice*, which once were used as banners for our sense of national pride, are now spoken with a sneer. And as for the call to return to our roots, the objectives of the Christian Coalition and their political action committees do not square either with traditional Christian values or the humanitarian goals associated with the Enlightenment. New age quests, personality cults, Eastern religions, ethnic ideologies, and liberation movements tell us that religion still makes a difference. But these are "new religions," and the differences they are making do not fit the traditional Christian vision. Many are explicitly being pursued as alternatives to Christianity and the so-called Judeo-Christian tradition. What now are we to think about ourselves?

This litany of changes taking place in our social and cultural landscape marks our welcome to the postmodern age (Anderson 1990). For Christians and conservatives, the age of modernity was bad enough. After the Enlightenment we could no longer appeal to external saviors, acts of God, or transcendent powers for salvation, nor could we blame our failures on the demonic forces of evil. Social construction was a human enterprise, not based on the divine right of kings or anyone else, so we had to take responsibility for the way we worked the world. Not everyone wanted to see this point, to be sure. Old gods hardly die, and myths hold their power long after their social circumstances change. But the Christian gods have survived mainly by blessing our "progress," adding a pinch of "family values" to make the industrial ethos seem ethical, and promising "personal religious experiences" to those who wished to be "born again." That definition of Christianity kept open the possibility of private religion and "personal systems of belief," and it merged nicely with our long-standing romance with the concept of the individual, but it can't support the Christian visions of the kingdom of God, the righteous nation, and a world converted to Christianity.

Now the world is too much with us. And it is multicultural. The many peoples of the world have found their voices, and many have taken up residence among us. Most are not enamored of the Christian mission, or impressed with the history of Western colonization, use of power, and forms of control. Although participation in the markets of a growing global economy appears to be irresistible, the drive to preserve ethnic identities and cultural traditions is resurgent and strong. Recognizing that the world is full of many differing cultures and ways of thinking is the signature of belonging to the postmodern age. The term *postmodern* was coined by scholars of intellectual history who noticed that whether in science, philosophy, cultural history, or the humanities we were producing multiple theories of explanation. To acknowledge that fact meant taking a big step away from the modern era with its notion of working toward a single, comprehensive system of universal explanation. When one sees that there have been many ways in which people have structured workable societies, developed complex languages, worked out comprehensive symbol systems, ranked ethical and practical values, and coded behavior appropriate to a sustainable society, the postmodern view of our multicultural world is difficult to reject. It is no longer possible to think that only one worldview must be right.

A QUESTIONABLE MYTH

Living in this world of multicultural awareness has put tremendous pressure on the Christian myth and vision. It is true that Christian thinkers are still capable of imagining a perfect world. It would be a society that wants to balance powers, limit freedoms, control predation, negotiate interests, celebrate difference, mourn loss, appreciate the everyday, and enjoy one another's foibles. Yes, and delight in the privilege of living in a beautiful and fragile world, so fragile in fact, that the marvels of the human enterprise might be measured, not only by our efforts not to destroy one another, but by our efforts not to destroy the ecology of the natural world that supports us. But how to get there is no longer part of the vision. Whether anyone has the right or the responsibility to make sure we get there is no longer clear. Whether the vision stems from the Christian concept of the kingdom of God or our recent experience with social democracies is also very difficult to answer. And whether the Christian gospel offers any instruction at all for assembling the bits and pieces that will be needed to build such a sane society has become increasingly questionable.

A multicultural world groping toward the construction of smaller social democracies, each connected to a land charged with ethnic histories, linked together only in the interest of a global economy and to balance world powers, is not how the Christian epic was supposed to end. The epic is predicated on a set of ideals that runs counter to the direction the world is actually moving. The biblical epic is based on a worldview that is universalist in scope, monolinear in historical imagination, a singular system in organic conception, hierarchical in the location of power, dualistic in anthropology, and which has to have miracles, breakthroughs, and other dramatic or divine moments of rectification to imagine the adjustments that humans have to make when life and social circumstances change or get out of hand. These features of the worldview assumed and projected by the biblical epic are no longer helpful as ideals in our multicultural world.

For one thing, the importance of cultural and national boundaries is now known to be great, and the issue of crossing borders at will critical for rethinking policy that fosters good relations. Where in the reservoir of Christian myths and paradigms is there any instruction to stop at the border and swap introductions? For another, what about negotiating compromises and solving conflicts where interests differ, inequities occur, and cultural values clash? Is either the example of a crucified king or the threat of an apocalyptic destruction an appropriate frame of reference for working out such differences? And then there are the problems of the misuse of power, the possession of arms, greed, predation, and all the rest. These social issues are not academic. They strike to the heart of our present sense of confusion about who we are and what we should be doing. And they constitute a list of very serious questions for all thoughtful persons concerned about the future of our lives together on planet earth.

Should we turn to the Bible for answers? Those saying yes, from Waco to Washington, including all the recent pronouncements to that effect by Protestant churches, cannot be right. The surreptitious function of the Bible as America's epic mythology is causing as many problems as it is solving. We cannot go on "destroying them in order to save them," for instance, as the infamous line from the Vietnam War expressed it, if we want to contribute to the quest for a just world order. We cannot keep saying that it does not matter how we exploit the natural order since God will soon destroy it anyway, as James Watt's shabby logic revealed, if we want to project a sustainable habitat. So the time has come for some critical reassessment of our mythic foundations.

It will not be easy. Americans in general are not accustomed to cultural introspection. And Christians in particular have never thought to be critical of Christianity. Christians know about being critical, of course. They render critique on society all the time, but always from the vantage point of the Christian vision, a protected sphere of ideals held to be inviolate, never to be questioned. To look for the Christian influence at the core of Western culture and its social manifestations, and to wonder what the Christian religion has contributed to its troubles as well as its blessings, does not come naturally. And as for the contemporary challenge to sort through the mass of Christian values, beliefs, and symbols in a critical quest for renewed self-definition, that is not a skill that Christians have ever learned. Criticism from the traditional Christian point of view is either "prophetic" or judgmental and always directed outward. It is seldom pursued in the interest of calm analysis, humanistic understanding, and the making of constructive proposals at the level of cultural critique. Cultural critique is not good news. And cultural critique that comes to focus on the influence of the Christian myth at the heart of our national epic has usually been thought subversive.

Perhaps our study of the Bible can help. We have followed the course of its formation from the first Jesus movements to the church of Constantine's empire. In every case of literary expression we have caught sight of Christians constructing their myths in the interest of social arrangements governed by new social visions. The literature they produced is passionate and dogmatic, but also replete with arguments and reasons for the views they projected. We have seen them at the task of justifying their social experiments, sorting through traditional myths and values, bridging gaps between ideals and the real, and inculcating commitment to their new worldviews. The writings in the New Testament were not written by eyewitnesses of an overpowering divine appearance in the midst of human history. That is the impression created by the final formation of the New Testament. Dismantled and given back to the people who produced them, the writings of the New Testament are the record of three hundred years of intellectual labor in the interest of a thoroughly human construction.

The effect of the studied selection and arrangement of these texts must therefore be seen as remarkable. Mythic rationalizations for very different social notions and community traditions were forged into a concerted testimony for the one true gospel and its single story line. Differences among the various traditions represented in this selection were erased. Mark could be read through the eyes of Paul, and Paul could be read as a witness to the gospel according to Matthew, and so on. When combined with the Jewish scriptures, moreover, for the reasons we have been able to identify, the Christian Bible turns out to be a masterpiece of invention. It is charged with the intellectual battles and resolutions of untold numbers of persons who invested in a grand project three centuries in the making. It finally reads as the epic they imagined to sustain them, the history of God's plan to establish his kingdom on earth. To be quite frank about it, the Bible is the product of very energetic and successful mythmaking on the part of those early Christians.

We are the heirs of that legacy, as we are of the mythmaking of myriad Christians from that time to this who worked with these texts to produce yet other cultural configurations. As if taking a jewel in hand to catch the light in yet another facet, Christians have manipulated the biblical myths and symbols time and again to see themselves reflected anew somewhere in its story. The image of the Christ has shifted with each new epoch of that history (Duling 1979), as has the shape of the basilicas and cathedrals built to rehearse the biblical story. God's universe also had to expand in order to encompass the vast horizons of the Bible's story of creation and redemption. And the music of those cosmic spheres has been captured in a glorious history of Western chants, masses, anthems, and symphonies. The emergence of the distinctively Christian sense of awe, called worship, was another inculcation of the biblical epic, as were the Books of Days for private devotion, the first flowering of Christian art, and the Western orientation to texts and publications.

These creations of Christian culture have shaped our Western souls, though some archaic features linger only as a haunting resonance. And we also know something of the struggle to be emancipated from the cosmic encasement of the biblical world in our medieval past. From Petrarch's "discovery" of beauty in the natural world, through the Copernican revolution, Galileo's science, Renaissance art, the Reformation's revision of history, the emergence of "secular" theater, the founding of universities, Enlightenment literature, the industrial revolution, and the modern history of political theory and the nation-state, the "birth" was from the biblical womb and the struggle to be free was repeatedly adolescent. No wonder the Bible is still among us. No wonder the effect of the biblical epic can still be discerned in our nation's myths, our leaders' policies, and the people's dreams and attitudes.

But the world is spinning faster now, and the times have changed our hopes and fears and circumstances as never before. We face a situation in America, and predicaments around the world, that call for serious reflection, honest conversation, and hard intellectual labor. Shooting from the political hip will no longer do. Harking back to the Judeo-Christian tradition without spelling out what one means does not help. Facile references to the Bible are sounding shrill. We are very close to entertaining a public discourse about our nation's Christian heritage that does not rise above the level of demagoguery.

Thus this book may help. There are, in fact, two ways in which it might help, both of them due to its description of the historical and intellectual process of the Bible's formation. One benefit would be to help us see early Christian history as a chapter in the larger history of human social formation and mythmaking. That alone would take the edge off the Bible's mystique and let us analyze its logic just as we do with that of all other myths, religions, and their cultures. We have learned, for instance, that the Bible was produced in the process of social change and that the process included the mythmaking that eventually produced the Bible. Our study also tells us that mythmaking is hard work, requires the best intelligence a society can muster, uses lots of time and energy, and is in the last analysis a collective enterprise linked to shared interests in (re)making a social construction. And one more thing. Looking at early Christianity this way tells us that mythmaking is born both of new ideas and of the *re*arranging of traditional images already at hand. Some early Christians (but not all!) did want to think that they were starting with a big bang, but even to imagine this they had to work with old myths and models. Mythmakers never start completely from scratch. But if that is so, if early Christianity was a human labor in the *bricolage* (handicraft) of creating something new from the bits and pieces of ideas at hand, some new, some old, don't we also have to be circumspect as we do our own rethinking of what we are about? Thus, a second benefit might be the sense of distance from the Christian myth that results from such a redescription of that early history. Seeing that the early Christians had their reasons for imagining the world the way they did should come as a relief to any thoughtful person who has wondered about the helpfulness of the gospel story when tackling the social issues of our time. Understanding those reasons lets us appreciate the mythmaking of those early Christians even as we recognize that their reasons for telling their stories are not good enough to be our reasons for continuing to tell the stories just as they told them.

My own fantasy is to enter a hall and find high ceilings, lovely chandeliers, walls lined with bookshelves, wines in the alcove, hors d'oeuvres by the windows, and a wide table down the middle of the room with the Bible sitting on it. And there we are, all of us, walking around, sitting at the table, and talking about what we should do with that book. Some rules are in order. Everyone has been invited. Christians have not been excluded, but they are not the ones in charge. All of us are there, and all of our knowledge and expertise is also on the table. There are historians of religion, cultural anthropologists, and political scientists but also politicians, CEOs, and those who work in foreign affairs. The ethnic communities of Los Angeles County are all well represented, as are women, the disenfranchised, the disabled, and all the voiceless who have recently come to speech. Merchants are there, and workers, and the airline pilots. Everyone is present, and everyone gets to talk and ask questions. No one has a corner on what the Bible says. We blow our whistles if anyone starts to pout or preach. What we are trying to figure out is why we thought the Bible so important, whether it is so important, how it has influenced our culture, what we think of the story, whether we should laugh or cry at the "ending," how it fits or does not fit our current situation, and whether the story should be revised in keeping with our vision of a just, sustainable, festive, and multicultural world. Wouldn't that be something?

The questions we now need to be asking ourselves are not whether religions have cultural and social effect. We have seen enough in our time, at home and around the world, to know that they do. The questions will have to be much more critical with respect to the kinds of effects different religions have had in the making of cultures. We are just about ready to admit that different cultures *are* different and that they do make a difference in the way people think, behave, and relate to others. If comparative cultural analysis is the order for the day, don't we as Americans have to include our own myths and religions? And why *not* learn how to evaluate cultures in the light of the social issues and global horizons that challenge our times? Why can't we learn to talk about religion and culture in public as we look for ways to imagine and create the sane societies we desperately need in our multicultural world? If we want to do that, and I think we must, the taboo on the Bible that is now in place will have to be broken. The Bible is not the private property of the Christian churches. The biblical epic belongs to us all in the form of the Judeo-Christian heritage that is supposed to have given our nation its values and ethical foundation. The taboo is the sign that we all are complicit in the unacknowledged agreement to let that story stand. It is time to find out whether we think that wise. The only way to do that is to learn to talk openly in public forum about religion, culture, and the Bible.

APPENDIX A: EARLY CHRISTIAN LITERATURE

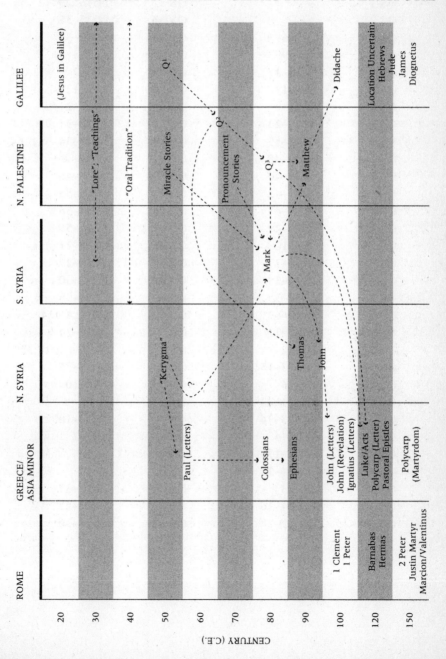

APPENDIX B: THE CONTENTS OF Q

Q SEGMENTS AS PRESENTED IN THE GOSPEL OF LUKE

Q	LUKE	Q	LUKE
QS 1	—	QS 32	11:16, 29–32
QS 2	—	QS 33	11:33–35
QS 3	3:1–6	QS 34	11:39–52
QS 4	3:7–9	QS 35	12:2–3
QS 5	3:16–17	QS 36	12:4–7
QS 6	4:1–13	QS 37	12:8–12
QS 7	6:20	QS 38	12:13–21
QS 8	6:20–23	QS 39	12:22–31
QS 9	6:27–35	QS 40	12:33–34
QS 10	6:36–38	QS 41	12:39–40
QS 11	6:39–40	QS 42	12:42–46
QS 12	6:41–42	QS 43	12:49–53
QS 13	6:43–45	QS 44	12:54–56
QS 14	6:46–49	QS 45	12:57–59
QS 15	7:1–10	QS 46	13:18–21
QS 16	7:18–23	QS 47	13:24–27
QS 17	7:24–28	QS 48	13:28–30
QS 18	7:31–35	QS 49	13:34–35
QS 19	9:57–62	QS 50	14:11; 18:14
QS 20	10:1–11	QS 51	14:16–24
QS 21	10:12	QS 52	14:26–27; 17:33
QS 22	10:13–15	QS 53	14:34–35
QS 23	10:16	QS 54	15:4–10
QS 24	10:21–22	QS 55	16:13
QS 25	10:23–24	QS 56	16:16–18
QS 26	11:1–4	QS 57	17:1–2
QS 27	11:9–13	QS 58	17:3–4
QS 28	11:14–23	QS 59	17:6
QS 29	11:23	QS 60	17:23–37
QS 30	11:24–26	QS 61	19:11–27
QS 31	11:27–28	QS 62	22:28–30

AN OUTLINE OF THE CONTENTS OF Q

The outline highlights two features of the design at the Q^2 level. One is the way in which Q^2 material frames units of interspersed Q^1 material. The other is a pattern of address that shifts back and forth between the community and it public:

Q^1 = Primary instructions addressed to the community.

Q^{2a} = Judgmental sayings that address "this generation."

Q^{2b} = Instructions to the community in the light of the judgmental sayings addressed to "this generation."

Q^1	Q^{2A}	Q^{2B}	
Introduction			(QS 1–2)
	John's Preaching		(QS 3–5)
Jesus' Teaching			(QS 7–14)
	What John and Jesus Thought		(QS 15–18)
Instructions for the Movement			(QS 19–20)
	Pronouncements Against Towns		(QS 21–22)
		Congratulations to Persons	(QS 23, 25)
Confidence in the Father's Care			(QS 26–27)
	Controversies with This Generation		(QS 28)
		Caution on Taking Sides	(QS 29–30)
	Judgment on This Generation		(QS 32)
		True Enlightenment	(QS 33)
	Pronouncements Against the Pharisees		(QS 34)
On Anxiety and Speaking Out			(QS 35–36)
		On Public Confessions	(QS 37)
On Personal Goods			(QS 38–40)
	The Coming Judgment		(QS 41–45)
Parables of the Kingdom			(QS 46)
	The Two Ways		(QS 47–48)
The True Followers of Jesus			(QS 50–53)
		Community Rules	(QS 54–55, 57–59)
	The Final Judgment		(QS 60–61)

APPENDIX C: THE PRONOUNCEMENT STORIES IN MARK

The following *chreiai* (anecdotes) can be found at the core of the pronouncement stories in Mark. All have been reconstructed by removing what ancient rhetoricians called the elaboration or the embellishments that turned *chreiai* into longer stories or speeches. The settings have been described to correspond with the issues addressed. All have been paraphrased in English translation to sharpen the point of the original repartee in Greek. The sign *C* means "challenge"; the sign *R* means "response." Those with a * identify issues that focus on purity codes.

MARK 1:35–38. DRAWING A CROWD

C: Everyone is looking for you!
R: Let's get out of here.

MARK 2:1–12. FORGIVING THE PARALYTIC*

C: That's blasphemy! Only God can forgive sins.
R: Which is easier, to forgive or to heal?

MARK 2:15–17. EATING WITH TAX COLLECTORS AND SINNERS*

C: Why do you do that? They're sick and dirty!
R: Those who are well don't need a doctor.

MARK 2:18–22. ON EATING AND FASTING*

C: Why don't you and your disciples fast?
R: Does anyone fast at a wedding?

MARK 2:23–28. PLUCKING GRAIN ON THE SABBATH*

C: Working on the sabbath violates the law!
R: Is it lawful to do good, or to do harm, on the sabbath?

MARK 3:22–30. CASTING OUT A DEMON*

C: You must get your power from a Syrian demon!
R: How can Satan cast out Satan?

MARK 3:31–35. A MOTHER'S CONCERN

C: Your mother is outside asking for you.
R: Who's my mother?

MARK 4:10–20. TEACHING WITH PARABLES

C: Why is your teaching only in parables?
R: So the others won't understand.

MARK 6:1-6. FAILING TO IMPRESS THE HOMETOWN FOLK

C: Showoff! We know your family.
R: A prophet is honored everywhere, except in his own hometown.

MARK 7:1-15. EATING WITH UNWASHED HANDS*

C: Disgusting! You and your disciples never bother to wash.
R: It's not what goes in that makes you dirty; it's what comes out.

MARK 7:24-30. A SYROPHOENICIAN WOMAN ASKS FOR AN EXORCISM*

C: (Jesus states the challenge) Let the children first be fed.
R: (The Woman responds) Even dogs get the crumbs.

MARK 8:11-12. PHARISEES ASKING FOR A "SIGN"

C: Give us a miracle, then we'll believe.
R: Would you? Why?

MARK 8:31-33. PREDICTING WHAT WILL HAPPEN IN JERUSALEM

C: Surely that will not happen to you.
R: Get behind me, Satan.

MARK 9:9-13. ASKING ABOUT THE COMING OF ELIJAH

C: Why do the scribes say Elijah comes first?
R: Because he does.

MARK 9:33-37. DISCUSSING GREATNESS

C: Who is the greatest?
R: The least.

MARK 9:38-40. ENCOUNTERING ANOTHER EXORCIST*

C: Why don't you stop him? He's not one of us.
R: If he's not our enemy, he must be our friend.

MARK 10:2-9. DISCUSSING DIVORCE*

C: What does the law say?
R: What does God say?

MARK 10:13-16. ENCOUNTERING CHILDREN

C: They're getting in the way while we talk about the kingdom.
R: They own the kingdom.

MARK 10:17-22. A MAN IS LOOKING FOR ETERNAL LIFE

C: Good teacher, what must I do ...?
R: Why do you call me good?

MARK 10:23–27. ON ENTERING THE KINGDOM OF GOD

C: Can the rich get in?
R: It's easier for a camel to go through the eye of a needle.

MARK 10:35–45. THE SONS OF ZEBEDEE

C: We'd like to be first in your kingdom.
R: The first will be the servants.

MARK 11:27–33. ON AUTHORITY

C: Where did you get your authority?
R: Where did John get his?

MARK 12:13–17. ON PAYING TAXES*

C: Should we pay taxes to Caesar?
R: Give to Caesar the things that are Caesar's.

MARK 12:18–27. ON IMAGINING LIFE IN HEAVEN WITH A WOMAN WHO HAD SEVEN HUSBANDS

C: Which one will God let her have?
R: Those who are alive.

MARK 12:28–34. ON THE GREATEST OF THE COMMANDMENTS

C: Teacher, you are right about the commandment.
R: You're getting close to the kingdom.

MARK 12:35–37. ON THE SON OF DAVID

C: The scribes say Christ is David's Son.
R: Then why does David call him his lord?

MARK 12:41–44. WATCHING A WIDOW BRING HER OFFERING TO THE TEMPLE

C: She only put in a penny!
R: That's more than the rich put in.

MARK 14:3–9. LETTING A WOMAN ANOINT HIM WITH PERFUME*

C: That's obscene!
R: It was lovely.

MODERN WORKS

Achtemeier, Paul J. "The Origin and Function of the Pre-Markan Miracle Catenae." *Journal of Biblical Literature* 91 (1972): 198–221.

Achtemeier, Paul J. "Toward the Isolation of Pre-Markan Miracle Catenae." *Journal of Biblical Literature* 89 (1970): 265–91.

Anderson, Walter Truett. *Reality Isn't What It Used to Be.* San Francisco: HarperSanFrancisco, 1990.

Boyarin, Daniel. *A Radical Jew: Paul and the Politics of Identity.* Berkeley and Los Angeles: Univ. of California Press, 1994.

Brown, Peter. "The Rise and Function of the Holy Man in Late Antiquity." *Journal of Roman Studies* 61 (1971): 80–101.

Burkert, Walter. *Ancient Mystery Cults.* Cambridge: Harvard Univ. Press, 1987.

Butts, James R, and Ron Cameron. "Sayings of Jesus: Classification by Source and Authenticity." *Foundations and Facets Forum* 3, no. 2 (1987): 96–116.

Cameron, Ron. "Alternate Beginnings—Different Ends: Eusebius, Thomas, and the Construction of Christian Origins." In *Religious Propaganda and Missionary Competition in the New Testament World: Essays Honoring Dieter Georgi,* edited by Lukas Bormann, Kelly Del Tredici, and Angela Standhartinger, 501–25. Novum Testamentum Supplements 74. Leiden: E. J. Brill, 1994.

———. *Sayings Traditions in the Apocryphon of James.* Harvard Theological Studies 34. Philadelphia: Fortress Press, 1984.

———. "'What Have You Come Out to See?' Characterizations of John and Jesus in the Gospels." In *Semeia 49: The Apocryphal Jesus and Christian Origins,* edited by R. Cameron, 35–69. Atlanta: Scholars Press, 1990.

Campenhausen, Hans von. *The Formation of the Christian Bible.* Philadelphia: Fortress Press, 1977.

Castelli, Elizabeth A. *Imitating Paul: A Discourse of Power.* Louisville, KY: Westminster/John Knox Press, 1992.

Collins, Adela Yarbro. *Crisis and Catharsis: The Power of the Apocalypse.* Philadelphia: Westminster Press, 1984.

Crossan, Dominic. *In Parables: The Challenge of the Historical Jesus.* New York: Harper and Row, 1973.

Detienne, Marcel, and Jean-Pierre Vernant. *Cunning Intelligence in Greek Culture and Society.* Translated by Janet Lloyd. Atlantic Highlands, NJ: Humanities Press, 1978.

Duling, Dennis C. *Jesus Christ Through History*. New York: Harcourt Brace Jovanovich, 1979.

————, and Norman Perrin. *The New Testament: Proclamation and Parenesis, Myth and History*. 3d ed. New York: Harcourt Brace, 1994.

Efroymson, David P. "The Patristic Connection." In *Antisemitism and the Foundations of Christianity*, edited by Alan T. Davies, 98–117. New York: Paulist Press, 1979.

Fox-Genovese, Elizabeth. *Within the Plantation Household: Black and White Women of the Old South*. Chapel Hill: Univ. of North Carolina Press, 1988.

Genovese, Eugene D. *Roll, Jordan, Roll: The World the Slaves Made*. New York: Pantheon Books, 1974.

Georgi, Dieter. *The Opponents of Paul in Second Corinthians*. Philadelphia: Fortress Press, 1986.

————. "Der vorpaulinische Hymnus Phil 2, 6–11." In *Zeit und Geschichte: Dankesgabe an Rudolf Bultmann zum 80. Geburtstag*, edited by Erich Dinkler, 263–93. Tübingen: J. C. B. Mohr (Paul Siebeck), 1964.

Goodenough, E. R. "The Political Philosophy of Hellenistic Kingship." *Yale Classical Studies* 1 (1928): 55–102.

Harnack, Adolf von. *Marcion: The Gospel of an Alien God*. Translated by John E. Steely and Lyle D. Bierma. Durham, NC: Labyrinth Press, 1990.

Jewett, Robert. *The Captain America Complex: The Dilemma of Zealous Nationalism*. Philadelphia: Westminster Press, 1973.

————, and John Shelton Lawrence. *The American Monomyth*. 2d ed. New York: Univ. Press of America, 1988.

Kee, Howard Clark. *Miracle in the Early Christian World*. New Haven: Yale Univ. Press, 1983.

Kelsey, David H. *The Uses of Scripture in Recent Theology*. Philadelphia: Fortress Press, 1975.

Kinneavy, James L. *Greek Rhetorical Origins of Christian Faith: An Inquiry*. New York: Oxford Univ. Press, 1987.

Kloppenborg, John S. *Q Parallels: Synopsis, Critical Notes, and Concordance*. Sonoma, CA: Polebridge Press, 1988.

Koester, Helmut. *Introduction to the New Testament*. Vol. 1, *History, Culture, and Religion of the Hellenistic Age*. Vol. 2, *History and Literature of Early Christianity*. Philadelphia: Fortress Press, 1982, second edition 1994–96.

Lévi-Strauss, Claude. *The Raw and the Cooked: Introduction to a Science of Mythology*. Vol. 1. Harper Colophon Books. New York: Harper and Row, 1975.

————, Claude. *The Savage Mind*. Chicago: The University of Chicago Press, 1966.

MacDonald, Dennis Ronald. *The Legend and the Apostle: The Battle for Paul in Story and Canon*. Philadelphia: Westminster Press, 1983.

McDonald, Lee Martin. *The Formation of the Christian Biblical Canon*. Nashville: Abingdon Press, 1989.

Mack, Burton L. *Logos und Sophia: Untersuchungen zur Weisheitstheologie im hellenistischen Judentum*. Studien zur Umwelt des Neuen Testaments 10. Göttingen: Vandenhoeck & Ruprecht, 1973.

————. *The Lost Gospel: The Book of Q and Christian Origins*. San Francisco: HarperSanFrancisco, 1993.

————. *A Myth of Innocence: Mark and Christian Origins*. Philadelphia: Fortress Press, 1988.

————. *Rhetoric and the New Testament*. Guides to Biblical Scholarship. Minneapolis: Fortress Press, 1990.

————. *Wisdom and the Hebrew Epic: Ben Sira's Hymn in Praise of the Fathers*. Chicago Studies in the History of Judaism. Chicago: Univ. of Chicago Press, 1985.

————, and Vernon K. Robbins. *Patterns of Persuasion in the Gospels*. Sonoma, CA: Polebridge Press, 1989.

McLean, Bradley. "On the Gospel of Thomas and Q." In *The Gospel Behind the Gospels: Current Studies on Q*, edited by Ronald A. Piper, 321–45. Supplements to Novum Testamentum 75. Leiden: E. J. Brill, 1995.

Meeks, Wayne A. "The Man from Heaven in Johannine Sectarianism." *Journal of Biblical Literature* 91 (1972): 44–72.

Miller, Merrill. "Beginning from Jerusalem ...: Reexamining Canon and Consensus." *Journal of Higher Criticism* 2 (forthcoming).

Miller, Robert J. "Prophecy and Persecution in Luke-Acts." Ph.D. diss., Claremont Graduate School, 1986.

Neusner, Jacob. *A History of the Mishnaic Law of Purities.* 20 vols. Leiden: Brill, 1974–77.

Neyrey, Jerome H. "The Idea of Purity in Mark's Gospel." *Semeia* 35: *Social-Scientific Criticism of the New Testament and its Social World* , edited by John H. Elliott, 91–128. Atlanta: Scholars Press, 1986.

Nickelsburg, George W. E. *Resurrection, Immortality and Eternal Life in Intertestamental Judaism.* Harvard Theological Studies 26. Cambridge: Harvard Univ. Press, 1972.

Ostling, Richard N. "A Step Closer to Jesus?" *Time* (January 23, 1995) 57.

Pearson, Birger A. "1 Thessalonians 2:13–16: A Deutero-Pauline Interpolation." *Harvard Theological Review* 64 (1971): 79–94.

The Revised Common Lectionary. Nashville: Abingdon Press, 1992.

Robbins, Vernon K. "By Land and by Sea: The We-Passages and Ancient Sea Voyages." In *Perspectives on Luke-Acts,* edited by Charles H. Talbert, 215–42. Perspectives in Religious Studies, Special Studies Series 5. Edinburgh: T. & T. Clark, 1978.

Sanders, James A. *Torah and Canon.* Philadelphia: Fortress Press, 1972.

Schmidt, Daryl. "The Syntactical Style of 2 Thessalonians: How Pauline is it?" In *The Thessalonian Correspondence,* edited by Raymond F. Collins, 383–93. Bibliotheca Ephemeridum Theologicarum Lovaniensium 87. Leuven: Leuven University Press, 1990.

Schoedel, William R. *Ignatius of Antioch: A Commentary on the Letters.* Hermeneia Commentaries. Philadelphia: Fortress Press, 1985.

Seeley, David. "The Background of the Philippians Hymn (2:6–11)." *Journal of Higher Criticism* 1 (1994): 49–72.

———. *Deconstructing the New Testament.* Biblical Interpretation Series 5. Leiden: E. J. Brill, 1994.

———. "Jesus' Death in Q." *New Testament Studies* 38 (1992): 222–34.

———. *The Noble Death: Paul's Concept of Salvation and Greco-Roman Martyrology.* JSNT Supplement Series 28. Sheffield, England: JSOT Press, 1990.

Smith, Dennis E. "Social Obligation in the Context of Communal Meals: A Study of the Christian Meal in I Corinthians in Comparison with Greco-Roman Communal Meals." Ph.D. diss., Harvard Univ., 1980.

Smith, Henry Nash. *Virgin Land: The American West as Symbol and Myth.* Cambridge: Harvard Univ. Press, 1950; reissued with new preface, 1970.

Smith, Jonathan Z. "Columbus and the Bible." Paper presented at Claremont Graduate School, Claremont, CA, 1986.

———. *Drudgery Divine: On the Comparison of Early Christianities and the Religions of Late Antiquity.* Chicago: Univ. of Chicago Press, 1990.

———. *Imagining Religion: From Babylon to Jonestown.* Chicago: Univ. of Chicago Press, 1982.

———. *Map Is Not Territory: Studies in the History of Religions.* 1978. Reprint, Chicago: Univ. of Chicago Press, 1993.

———. *To Take Place: Toward Theory in Ritual.* Chicago Studies in the History of Religions. Chicago: Univ. of Chicago Press, 1987.

Stowers, Stanley K. *The Diatribe and Paul's Letter to the Romans.* Chico, CA: Scholars Press, 1981.

———. "Greeks Who Sacrifice and Those Who Do Not: Toward an Anthropology of Greek Religion." In *The First Christians and their Social World: Studies in Honor of Wayne A. Meeks,* edited by L. M. White and O. L. Yarbrough, 295–335. Minneapolis: Fortress Press, 1995.

————. *A Rereading of Romans: Justice, Jews, and Gentiles*. New Haven: Yale Univ. Press, 1994.

Thiede, Carsten Peter. "Papyrus Magdalen Greek 17 (Gregory-Aland P⁴⁶). A Reappraisal," *Zeitschrift für Papyrologie und Epigraphik* 105 (1995) 13-20.

Williams, Sam K. *Jesus' Death as Saving Event: The Background and Origin of a Concept*. Harvard Dissertations in Religion 2. Missoula, MT: Scholars Press, 1975.

WORKS FROM ANTIQUITY

Ante-Nicene Fathers. 10 vols. 1870–72. Reprint, Grand Rapids: Eerdmans, 1951–78.

The Apostolic Fathers. Translated by Kirsopp Lake. 2 vols. Loeb Classical Library. Cambridge: Harvard Univ. Press, 1912–1960.

Bettenson, Henry. *Documents of the Christian Church*. 2d ed. 1963. Reprint, New York: Oxford Univ. Press, 1967.

Cameron, Ron, editor. *The Other Gospels: Non-Canonical Gospel Texts*. Philadelphia: The Westminster Press, 1982

Charlesworth, James H. *The Old Testament Pseudepigrapha*. 2 vols. Garden City, NY: Doubleday, 1985.

Diogenes Laertius. *Lives of Eminent Philosophers*. Translated by R. D. Hicks. Loeb Classical Library. Vol. 1. Cambridge: Harvard Univ. Press, 1925. Vol. 2, rev. ed. Cambridge: Harvard Univ. Press, 1938.

Elliott, J. K. *The Apocryphal New Testament: A Collection of Apocryphal Christian Literature in an English Translation based on M. R. James*. Oxford: Clarendon Press, 1993.

Epictetus. *The Discourses as Reported by Arrian*. Translated by W. A. Oldfather. 2 vols. Loeb Classical Library. Cambridge: Harvard Univ. Press, 1925–1928.

Eusebius. *Ecclesiastical History*. Translated by Kirsopp Lake and J. E. L. Oulton. 2 vols. Loeb Classical Library. Cambridge: Harvard Univ. Press, 1926–1932.

Grant, Frederick C. *Hellenistic Religions: The Age of Syncretism*. New York: Liberal Arts Press, 1953.

Josephus. *Antiquities*. 7 vols. Loeb Classical Library. Cambridge: Harvard Univ. Press, 1930–65.

Josephus. *The Jewish War*. 2 vols. Loeb Classical Library. Cambridge: Harvard Univ. Press, 1927–1928.

Jubilees. See Charlesworth, James H. *The Old Testament Pseudepigrapha*. 2:35–142. Garden City, NY: Doubleday, 1985.

Kloppenborg, John S., et al., editors, *Q-Thomas Reader*. Sonoma: Polebridge Press, 1990.

Layton, Bentley. *The Gnostic Scriptures: A New Translation with Annotations and Introductions*. Garden City, NY: Doubleday, 1987.

Lucian. 8 vols. Loeb Classical Library. Cambridge: Harvard Univ. Press, 1913–67.

Meyer, Marvin. *The Gospel of Thomas: The Hidden Sayings of Jesus*. San Francisco: HarperSanFrancisco, 1992.

Neusner, Jacob. *The Mishnah: A New Translation*. New Haven: Yale Univ. Press, 1986.

Odes of Solomon. See Charlesworth, James H. *The Old Testament Pseudepigrapha*. 2:725–71. Garden City, NY: Doubleday, 1985.

Philo. Translated by F. H. Colson and G. H. Whitaker, et al. 10 vols., 2 suppl vols. Loeb Classical Library. Cambridge Massachusetts: Harvard Univ. Press, 1929–62.

Plutarch. *Isis and Osiris*. Plutarch's Moralia V, 6–191. Loeb Classical Library. 1936. Reprint, Cambridge: Harvard Univ. Press, 1962.

Pritchard, James B., ed. *Ancient Near Eastern Texts Relating to the Old Testament*. Princeton: Princeton Univ. Press, 1955.

Robinson, James M. *The Nag Hammadi Library*. San Francisco: Harper & Row, 1977, third edition 1988.

XNBT

3/96

DATE DUE

V.B.